LEARNING TO USE

MICROCOMPUTER APPLICATIONS:

Paradox 4.5 for DOS

Gary B. Shelly
Thomas J. Cashman
Philip J. Pratt

SHELLY
CASHMAN
SERIES®

boyd & fraser publishing company

Special thanks go to the following reviewers of the Shelly Cashman Series Applications textbooks

Debbie Fansler, *Educational Consultant;* **Mike Feiler**, *Merritt College;* **Roy O. Foreman**, *Purdue University/Calumet;* **Suzanne Lambert**, *Broward Community College;* **Susan Sebok**, *South Suburban College; and* **Connie Willfahrt**, *Mid-State Technical College.*

Manufactured in the United States of America

ISBN 0-87709-292-3

SHELLY CASHMAN SERIES® and **Custom Edition**™ are trademarks of South-Western Publishing Company. Names of all other products mentioned herein are used for identification purposes only and may be trademarks of their respective owners. South-Western Publishing Company and boyd & fraser publishing company disclaim any affiliation, association, or connection with, or sponsorship or endorsement by such owners.

Library of Congress Cataloging-in-Publication Data

1 2 3 4 5 6 7 8 9 10 BC 8 7 6 5 4

CONTENTS

Introduction to Computers

Introduction to DOS 6

PROJECT 1 Working with Files on Disks

▼   **PROJECT 2 Managing and Organizing Files on Disks**

Paradox 4.5 for DOS

▼ **PROJECT 1 Creating a Database**

▼ **PROJECT 2 Querying a Database**

▼   ## PROJECT 3 Maintaining a Database

▼   **PROJECT 4 Presenting Data: Reports and Forms**

▼   **PROJECT 5 Graphing in Paradox**

Introduction to Computers

Objectives

After completing this chapter, you will be able to:

▶ Define the term computer and discuss the four basic computer operations: input, processing, output, and storage

▶ Define data and information

▶ Explain the principal components of the computer and their use

▶ Describe the use and handling of diskettes and hard disks

▶ Discuss computer software and explain the difference between system software and application software

▶ Describe several types of personal computer applications software

▶ Discuss computer communications channels and equipment and LAN and WAN computer networks

▶ Explain how to purchase, install, and maintain a personal computer system

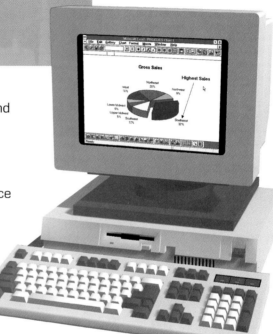

Every day, computers impact how individuals work and how they live. The use of small computers, called personal computers or microcomputers , continues to increase and has made computing available to almost anyone. In addition, advances in communication technology allow people to use personal computer systems to easily and quickly access and send information to other computers and computer users. At home, at work, and in the field, computers are helping people to do their work faster, more accurately, and in some cases, in ways that previously would not have been possible.

Why Study Computers and Application Software?

T oday, many people believe that knowing how to use a computer, especially a personal computer, is a basic skill necessary to succeed in business or to function effectively in society. As you can see in Figure 1, the use of computer technology is widespread in the world. It is important to understand that while computers are used in many different ways, there are certain types of common applications computer users need to know. It is this type of software that you will learn as you use this book. Given the widespread use and availability of computer systems, knowing how to use common application software on a computer system is an essential skill for practically everyone.

FIGURE 1
Computers in use in a wide variety of applications and professions. New applications are being developed every day.

Before you learn about application software, however, it will help if you understand what a computer is, the components of a computer, and the types of software used on computers. These topics are explained in this introduction. Also included is information that describes computer networks and a list of guidelines for purchasing, installing, and maintaining a personal computer.

What Is a Computer?

The most obvious question related to understanding computers is, "What is a computer?" A computer is an electronic device, operating under the control of instructions stored in its own memory unit, that can accept data (input), process data arithmetically and logically, produce output from the processing, and store the results for future use. Generally the term is used to describe a collection of devices that function together as a system. An example of the devices that make up a personal computer, or microcomputer, is shown in Figure 2.

FIGURE 2
Devices that comprise a personal computer.

What Does a Computer Do?

Whether small or large, computers can perform four general operations. These operations comprise the information processing cycle and are: input, process, output, and storage. Collectively, these operations describe the procedures a computer performs to process data into information and store it for future use.

All computer processing requires data. Data refers to the raw facts, including numbers, words, images, and sounds, given to a computer during the input operation. In the processing phase, the computer manipulates the data to create information. Information refers to data processed into a form that has meaning and is useful. During the output operation, the information that has been created is put into some form, such as a printed report, that people can use. The information can also be placed in computer storage for future use.

These operations occur through the use of electronic circuits contained on small silicon chips inside the computer (Figure 3). Because these electronic circuits rarely fail and the data flows along these circuits at close to the speed of light, processing can be accomplished in billionths of a second. Thus, the computer is a powerful tool because it can perform these four operations reliably and quickly.

The people who either use the computer directly or use the information it provides are called computer users, end users, or sometimes, just users.

FIGURE 3
Inside a computer are chips and other electronic components that process data in billionths of a second.

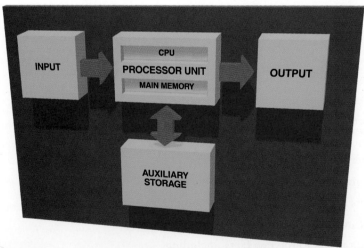

FIGURE 4
A computer is composed of input devices through which data is entered into the computer; the processor that processes data stored in main memory; output devices on which the results of the processing are made available; and auxiliary storage units that store data for future processing.

How Does a Computer Know What to Do?

For a computer to perform the operations in the information processing cycle, it must be given a detailed set of instructions that tell it exactly what to do. These instructions are called a computer program, or software. Before processing for a specific job begins, the computer program corresponding to that job is stored in the computer. Once the program is stored, the computer can begin to operate by executing the program's first instruction. The computer executes one program instruction after another until the job is complete.

What Are the Components of a Computer?

To understand how computers process data into information, you need to examine the primary components of the computer. The four primary components of a computer are: input devices, the processor unit, output devices, and auxiliary storage units (Figure 4).

Input Devices

Input devices enter data into main memory. Many input devices exist. The two most commonly used are the keyboard and the mouse.

The Keyboard   The most commonly used input device is the keyboard, on which data is entered by manually keying in or typing. The keyboard on most computers is laid out in much the same manner as the one shown in Figure 5. The alphabetic keys are arranged like those on a typewriter.

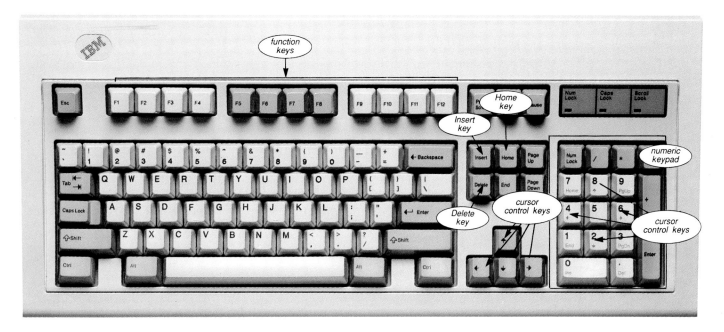

A **numeric keypad** is located on the right side of most keyboards. This arrangement of keys allows you to enter numeric data rapidly. To activate the numeric keypad you press and engage the NUMLOCK key located above the numeric keypad. The NUMLOCK key activates the numeric keypad so when the keys are pressed, numeric characters are entered into the computer memory and appear on the screen. A light turns on at the top right of the keyboard to indicate that the numeric keys are in use.

The **cursor** is a symbol, such as an underline character, which indicates where you are working on the screen. The **cursor control keys**, or **arrow keys**, allow you to move the cursor around the screen. Pressing the UP ARROW (↑) key causes the cursor to move upward on the screen. The DOWN ARROW (↓) key causes the cursor to move down; the LEFT ARROW (←) and RIGHT ARROW (→) keys cause the cursor to move left and right on the screen. On the keyboard in Figure 5, there are two sets of cursor control keys. One set is included as part of the numeric keypad. The second set of cursor control keys is located between the typewriter keys and the numeric keypad. To use the numeric keypad for cursor control, the NUMLOCK key must be disengaged. If the NUMLOCK key is engaged (indicated by the fact that as you press any numeric keypad key, a number appears on the screen), you can return to the cursor mode by pressing the NUMLOCK key. On most keyboards, a NUMLOCK light will indicate when the numeric keypad is in the numeric mode or the cursor mode.

FIGURE 5
This keyboard represents most desktop personal computer keyboards.

The other keys on the keypad—PAGE UP, PAGE DOWN, HOME, and END—have various functions depending on the software you use. Some programs make no use of these keys; others use the PAGE UP and PAGE DOWN keys, for example, to display previous or following pages of data on the screen. Some software uses the HOME key to move the cursor to the upper left corner of the screen. Likewise, the END key may be used to move the cursor to the end of a line of text or to the bottom of the screen, depending on the software.

Function keys on many keyboards can be programmed to accomplish specific tasks. For example, a function key might be used as a help key. Whenever that key is pressed, messages display that give instructions to help the user. The keyboard in Figure 5 has twelve function keys located across the top of the keyboard.

Other keys have special uses in some applications. The SHIFT keys have several functions. They work as they do on a typewriter, allowing you to type capital letters. The SHIFT key is always used to type the symbol on the upper portion of any key on the keyboard. Also, to temporarily use the cursor control keys on the numeric keypad as numeric entry keys, you can press the SHIFT key to switch into numeric mode. If you have instead pressed the NUMLOCK key to use the numeric keys, you can press the SHIFT key to shift temporarily back to the cursor mode.

The keyboard has a BACKSPACE key, a TAB key, an INSERT key and a DELETE key that perform the functions their names indicate.

The ESCAPE (ESC) key is generally used by computer software to cancel an instruction or exit from a situation. The use of the ESC key varies between software packages.

As with the ESC key, many keys are assigned special meaning by the computer software. Certain keys may be used more frequently than others by one piece of software but rarely used by another. It is this flexibility that allows you to use the computer in so many different applications.

The Mouse A mouse (Figure 6) is a pointing device you can use instead of the cursor control keys. You lay the palm of your hand over the mouse and move it across the surface of a pad that provides traction for a rolling ball on the bottom of the mouse. The mouse detects the direction of the ball movement and sends this information to the screen to move the cursor. You push buttons on top of the mouse to indicate your choices of actions from lists or icons displayed on the screen.

FIGURE 6
The mouse input device is used to move the cursor and choose selections on the computer screen.

The Processor Unit

The **processor unit** is composed of the central processing unit and main memory. The **central processing unit (CPU)** contains the electronic circuits that cause processing to occur. The CPU interprets instructions to the computer, performs the logical and arithmetic processing operations, and causes the input and output operations to occur. On personal computers, the CPU is designed into a chip called a **microprocessor** (Figure 7).

Main memory, also called **random access memory**, or **RAM**, consists of electronic components that store data including numbers, letters of the alphabet, graphics, and sound. Any data to be processed must be stored in main memory. The amount of main memory in computers is typically measured in kilobytes or megabytes. One **kilobyte (K or KB)** equals 1,024 memory locations and one **megabyte (M or MB)** equals approximately 1 million memory locations. A memory location, or **byte**, usually stores one character. Therefore, a computer with 4MB can store approximately 4 million characters. One megabyte of memory can hold approximately 500 pages of text information.

FIGURE 7
A Pentium microprocessor from Intel Corporation. The microprocessor circuits are located in the center. Small gold wires lead from the circuits to the pins that fit in the microprocessor socket on the main circuit board of the computer. The pins provide an electronic connection to different parts of the computer.

Output Devices

Output devices make the information resulting from processing available for use. The output from computers can be presented in many forms, such as a printed report or color graphics. When a computer is used for processing tasks, such as word processing, spreadsheets, or database management, the two output devices most commonly used are the printer and the television-like display device called a screen, monitor, or CRT (cathode ray tube).

Printers Printers used with computers can be either impact printers or nonimpact printers. An **impact printer** prints by striking an inked ribbon against the paper. One type of impact printer often used with personal computers is the dot matrix printer (Figure 8).

FIGURE 8
Dot matrix are the least expensive of the personal computer printers. Some can be purchased for less than $200. Advantages of dot matrix printers include the capability to handle wide paper and to print multipart forms.

FIGURE 9

On a dot matrix printer with a nine-pin print head, the letter E is formed with seven vertical and five horizontal dots. As the nine-pin print head moves from left to right, it fires one or more pins into the ribbon, making a dot on the paper. At the first print position, it fires pins 1 through 7. At print positions 2 through 4, it fires pins 1,4, and 7. At print position 5, it fires pins 1 and 7. Pins 8 and 9 are used for lowercase characters such as g, j, p, q, and y that extend below the line.

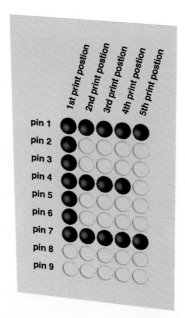

FIGURE 10 ▲

Two types of nonimpact printers are the laser printer (top) and the ink jet printer. Nonimpact printers are excellent for printing work that includes graphics.

FIGURE 11 ▶

Nonimpact printers do an excellent job of printing text in different typefaces, usually referred to as fonts. Technically, a font is a typeface in a particular size. It is common, however, to refer to the different typefaces as fonts. Dot matrix printers can print some fonts but usually at a slower rate and quality than nonimpact printers. The names of four different typefaces (fonts) are shown.

To print a character, a **dot matrix printer** generates a dot pattern representing a particular character. The printer then activates wires in a print head contained on the printer, so selected wires press against the ribbon and paper, creating a character. As you see in Figure 9, the character consists of a series of dots produced by the print head wires. In the actual size created by the printer, the characters are clear and easy to read.

Dot matrix printers vary in the speed with which they can print characters. These speeds range from 50 to more than 300 characters per second. Generally, the higher the speed, the higher the cost of the printer. Compared to other printers, dot matrix offer the lowest initial cost and the lowest per-page operating costs. Other advantages of dot matrix printers are that they can print on multipart forms and they can be purchased with wide carriages that can handle paper larger than 8 1/2 by 11 inches.

Nonimpact printers, such as ink jet printers and laser printers, form characters by means other than striking a ribbon against paper (Figure 10). Advantages of using a nonimpact printer are that it can print graphics and it can print in varying type sizes and styles called **fonts** (Figure 11). An **ink jet printer** forms a character by using a nozzle that sprays drops of ink onto the page. Ink jet printers produce relatively high-quality images and print between 30 and 150 characters per second in text mode and one to two pages per minute in graphics mode.

Laser printers work similar to a copying machine by converting data from the computer into a beam of light that is focused on a photoconductor drum, forming the images to be printed. The photoconductor attracts particles of toner that are fused by heat and pressure onto paper to produce an image. Laser printers produce high-quality output and are used for applications that combine text and graphics such as **desktop publishing** (Figure 12). Laser printers for personal computers can cost from $500 to more than $10,000. They can print four to sixteen pages of text and graphics per minute.

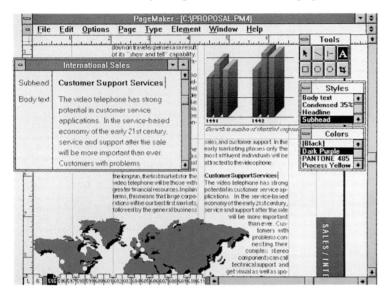

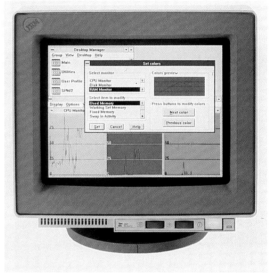

FIGURE 12
High-quality printed documents can be produced with laser printers and desktop publishing software.

Computer Screens Most full-size personal computers use a TV-like display device called a **screen, monitor,** or **CRT** (cathode ray tube) (Figure 13). Portable computers use a flat panel display that uses **liquid crystal display (LCD)** technology similar to a digital watch. The surface of the screen is made up of individual picture elements called **pixels**. Each pixel can be illuminated to form characters and graphic shapes (Figure 14). Color screens have three colored dots (red, green, and blue) for each pixel. These dots can be turned on to display different colors. Most color monitors today use super VGA (video graphics array) technology that can display 800 × 600 (width × height) pixels.

FIGURE 13
Many personal computer systems now come with color screens. Color can be used to enhance the information displayed so the user can understand it more quickly.

FIGURE 14
Pixel is an abreviation of the words picture element, one of thousands of spots on a computer screen that can be turned on and off to form text and graphics.

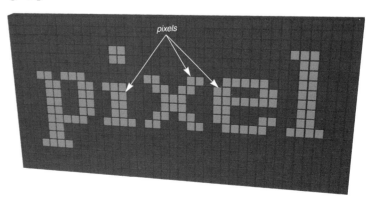

Auxiliary Storage

Auxiliary storage devices are used to store instructions and data when they are not being used in main memory. Two types of auxiliary storage most often used on personal computers are diskettes and hard disks. CD-ROM disk drives are also becoming common.

Diskettes   A diskette is a circular piece of oxide-coated plastic that stores data as magnetic spots. Diskettes are available in various sizes and storage capacities. Personal computers most commonly use diskettes that are 5 1/4 inches or 3 1/2 inches in diameter (Figure 15).

FIGURE 15
The most commonly used diskettes for personal computers are the 5 1/4-inch size on the left and the 3 1/2-inch size on the right. Although they are smaller in size, the 3 1/2-inch diskettes can store more data.

To read data stored on a diskette or to store data on a diskette, you insert the diskette in a disk drive (Figure 16). You can tell that the computer is reading data on the diskette or writing data on it because a light on the disk drive will come on while read/write operations are taking place. Do not try to insert or remove a diskette when the light is on as you could cause permanent damage to the data stored on it.

The storage capacities of disk drives and the related diskettes can vary widely (Figure 17). The number of characters that can be stored on a diskette by a disk drive depends on two factors: (1) the recording density of the bits on a track; and (2) the number of tracks on the diskette.

FIGURE 16
A user inserts a 3 1/2-inch diskette into the disk drive of a personal computer.

DIAMETER (INCHES)	DESCRIPTION	CAPACITY (BYTES)
5.25	Double-sided, double-density	360KB
5.25	Double-sided high-density	1.25MB
3.5	Double-sided double-density	720KB
3.5	Double-sided high-density	1.44MB

FIGURE 17
Storage capacities of different size and type diskettes.

Disk drives found on many personal computers are 5 1/4-inch, double-sided disk drives that can store from 360,000 bytes to 1.25 million bytes on the diskette. Another popular type is the 3 1/2-inch diskette, which, although physically smaller, stores from 720,000 bytes to 1.44 million bytes. An added benefit of the 3 1/2-inch diskette is its rigid plastic housing that protects the magnetic surface of the diskette.

The recording density is stated in bits per inch (bpi)—the number of magnetic spots that can be recorded on a diskette in a one-inch circumference of the innermost track on the diskette. Diskettes and disk drives used today are identified as being double-density or high-density. You need to be aware of the density of diskettes used by your system because data stored on high-density diskettes, for example, cannot be processed by a computer that has only double-density disk drives.

The second factor that influences the number of characters that can be stored on a diskette is the number of tracks on the diskette. A **track** is a very narrow recording band forming a full circle around the diskette (Figure 18).

FIGURE 18
Each track on a diskette is a narrow, circular band. On a diskette containing 80 tracks, the outside track is called track 0 and the inside track is called track 79. The disk surface is divided into sectors.

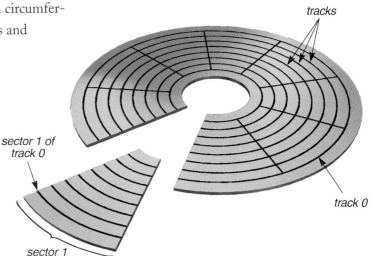

tracks

sector 1 of track 0

track 0

sector 1

The tracks are separated from each other by a very narrow blank gap. Each track on a diskette is divided into sectors. The term sector is used to refer to a pie-shaped section of the disk. It is also used to refer to a section of track. Sectors are the basic units for diskette storage. When data is read from a diskette, it reads a minimum of one full sector from a track. When data is stored on a diskette, it writes one full sector on a track at a time. The tracks and sectors on the diskette and the number of characters that can be stored in each sector are defined by a special formatting program that is used with the computer.

Data stored in sectors on a diskette must be retrieved and placed into main memory to be processed. The time required to access and retrieve data, called the **access time,** can be important in some applications. The access time for diskettes varies from about 175 milliseconds (one millisecond equals 1/1000 of a second) to approximately 300 milliseconds. On average, data stored in a single sector on a diskette can be retrieved in approximately 1/15 to 1/3 of a second.

Diskette care is important to preserve stored data. Properly handled, diskettes can store data indefinitely. However, the surface of the diskette can be damaged and the data stored can be lost if the diskette is handled improperly.

A diskette will give you very good service if you follow a few simple procedures:

1. Keep diskettes in their original box or in a special diskette storage box to protect them from dirt and dust and prevent them from being accidentally bent. Store 5 1/4-inch diskettes in their protective envelopes. Store the container away from heat and direct sunlight. Magnetic and electrical equipment, including telephones, radios, and televisions, can erase the data on a diskette, so do not place diskettes near such devices. Do not place heavy objects on a diskette, because the weight can pinch the covering, causing damage when the disk drive attempts to rotate.

2. To affix one of the self-adhesive labels supplied with most diskettes, it is best to write or type the information on the label before you place the label on the diskette. If the label is already on the diskette, use only a felt-tip pen to write on the label, and press lightly. Do not use ball point pens, pencils, or erasers on lables that are already on diskettes.

3. To use the diskette, grasp the diskette on the side away from the side to be inserted into the disk drive. Slide the diskette carefully into the slot on the disk drive. If the disk drive has a latch or door, close it. If it is difficult to close the disk drive door, do not force it—the diskette may not be inserted fully, and forcing the door closed may damage the diskette. Reinsert the diskette if necessary, and try again to close the door.

The diskette write-protect feature (Figure 19) prevents the accidental erasure of the data stored on a diskette by preventing the disk drive from writing new data or erasing existing data. On a 5 1/4-inch diskette, a write-protect notch is located on the side of the diskette. A special write-protect label is placed over this notch whenever you want to protect the data. On the 3 1/2-inch diskette, a small switch can slide to cover and uncover the write-protection window. On a 3 1/2-inch diskette, when the window is uncovered the data is protected.

FIGURE 19
Data cannot be written on the 3 1/2-inch diskette on the top left because the window in the corner of the diskette is open. A small piece of plastic covers the window of the 3 1/2-inch diskette on the top right, so data can be written on this diskette. The reverse situation is true for the 5 1/4-inch diskettes. The write-protect notch of the 5 1/4-inch diskette on the bottom left is covered and, therefore, data cannot be written to the diskette. The notch of the 5 1/4-inch diskette on the bottom right, however, is open. Data can be written to this diskette.

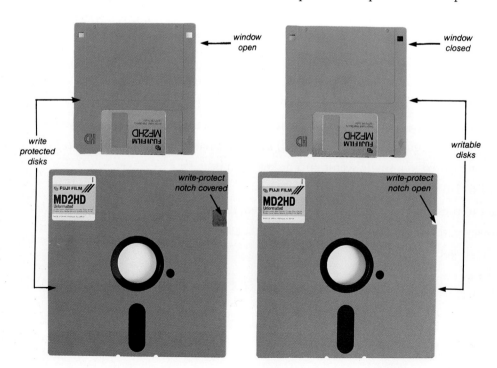

window open

window closed

write protected disks

writable disks

write-protect notch covered

write-protect notch open

Hard Disk   Another form of auxiliary storage is a hard disk. A hard disk consists of one or more rigid metal platters coated with a metal oxide material that allows data to be magnetically recorded on the surface of the platters (Figure 20). Although hard disks are available in removable cartridge form, most disks cannot be removed from the computer. As with diskettes, the data is recorded on hard disks on a series of tracks. The tracks are divided into sectors when the disk is formatted

The hard disk platters spin at a high rate of speed, typically 3,600 revolutions per minute. When reading data from the disk, the read head senses the magnetic spots that are recorded on the disk along the various tracks and transfers that data to main memory. When writing, the data is transferred from main memory and is stored as magnetic spots on the tracks on the recording surface of one or more of the disk platters. Unlike diskette drives, the read/write heads on a hard disk drive do not actually touch the surface of the disk.

The number of platters permanently mounted on the spindle of a hard disk varies. On most drives, each surface of the platter can be used to store data. Thus, if a hard disk drive uses one platter, two surfaces are available for data. If the drive uses two platters, four sets of read/write heads read and record data from the four surfaces. Storage capacities of internally mounted fixed disks for personal computers range from 80 million characters to more than 500 million characters. Larger capacity, stand-alone hard disk units are also available that can store more than one billion bytes of information. One billion bytes is called a gigabyte.

The amount of effective storage on both hard disks and diskettes can be increased by the use of compression programs. Compression programs use sophisticated formulas to replace spaces and repeated text and graphics patterns with codes that can later be used to recreate the compressed data. Text files can be compressed the most; as much as an eighth of their original volume. Graphics files can be compressed the least. Overall, a 2-to-1 compression ratio is average.

CD-ROM   Compact disk read-only memory (CD-ROM) disks are increasingly used to store large amounts of prerecorded information (Figure 21). Each CD-ROM disk can store more than 600 million bytes of data—the equivalent of 300,000 pages of text. Because of their large storage capacity, CD-ROM is often used for multimedia material. Multimedia combines text, graphics, video (pictures), and audio (sound) (Figure 22 on the next page).

FIGURE 20
The protective cover of this hard disk drive has been removed. A read/write head is at the end of the access arm that extends over the recording surface, called a platter.

FIGURE 21
CD-ROM disk drives allow the user to access tremendous amounts of prerecorded information — more than 600MB of data can be stored on one CD-ROM disk.

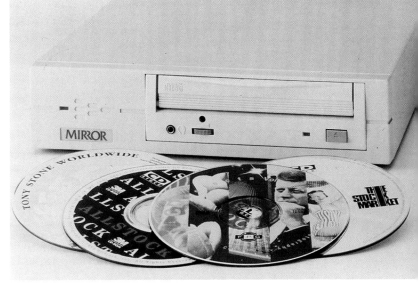

Computer Software

Computer software is the key to productive use of computers. With the correct software, a computer can become a valuable tool. Software can be categorized into two types: system software and application software.

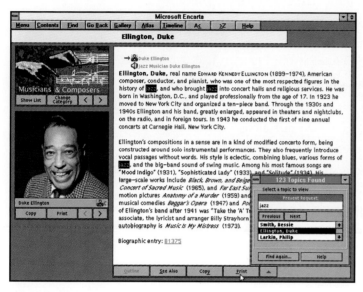

FIGURE 22
Microsoft Encarta is a multimedia encyclopedia available on a CDROM disk. Text, graphics, sound, and animation are all available. The photo-shaped icon at the top of the text indicates that a photograph is available for viewing. The speaker-shaped icon just below the camera indicates that a sound item is available. In this topic, if the user chooses the speaker icon with the mouse, a portion of Duke Ellington's music is played.

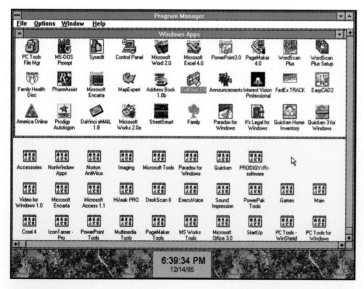

FIGURE 23
Microsoft Windows is a graphical user interface that works with the DOS operating system to make the computer easier to use. The small pictures or symbols on the main part of the screen are called icons. The icons represent different processing options, such as word processing or electronic spreadsheet applications, the user can choose.

System Software

System software consists of programs to control the operations of computer equipment. An important part of system software is a set of programs called the **operating system**. Instructions in the operating system tell the computer how to perform the functions of loading, storing, and executing an application and how to transfer data. For a computer to operate, an operating system must be stored in the computer's main memory. When a computer is started, the operating system is loaded into the computer and stored in main memory. This process is called **booting**. The most commonly used operating system on personal computers is **DOS (Disk Operating System)**.

Many computers use an **operating environment** that works with the operating system to make the computer system easier to use. Operating environments have a **graphical user interface (GUI)** displaying visual clues such as icon symbols to help the user. Each **icon** represents an application software package, such as word processing or a file or document where data is stored. **Microsoft Windows** (Figure 23) is a graphical user interface that works with DOS. Apple Macintosh computers also have a built in graphical user interface in the operating system.

Application Software

Application software consists of programs that tell a computer how to produce information. The different ways people use computers in their careers or in their personal lives, are examples of types of application software. Business, scientific, and educational programs are all examples of application software.

Personal Computer Application Software Packages

P ersonal computer users often use application software packages. Some of the most commonly used packages are: word processing, electronic spreadsheet, presentation graphics, database, communications, and electronic mail software.

Word processing software (Figure 24) is used to create and print documents. A key advantage of word processing software is its capability to make changes easily in documents, such as correcting spelling, changing margins, and adding, deleting, or relocating entire paragraphs. These changes would be difficult and time consuming to make using manual methods such as a typewriter. With a word processor, documents can be printed quickly and accurately and easily stored on a disk for future use. Word processing software is oriented toward working with text, but most word processing packages can also include numeric and graphic information.

Electronic spreadsheet software (Figure 25) allows the user to add, subtract, and perform user-defined calculations on rows and columns of numbers. These numbers can be changed and the spreadsheet quickly recalculates the new results. Electronic spreadsheet software eliminates the tedious recalculations required with manual methods. Spreadsheet information is frequently converted into a graphic form. Graphics capabilities are now included in most spreadsheet packages.

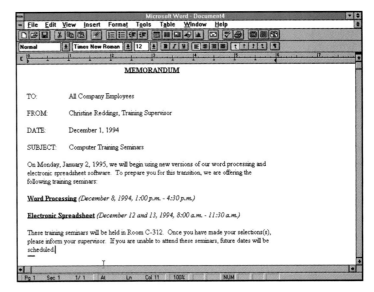

FIGURE 24
Word processing software is used to write letters, memos, and other documents. As the user types words and letters, they display on the screen. The user can easily add, delete, and change any text entered until the document looks exactly as desired. The user can then save the document on auxiliary storage and can also print it on a printer.

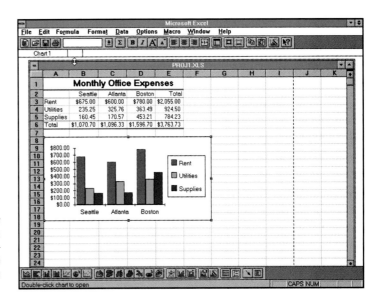

FIGURE 25
Electronic spreadsheet software is frequently used by people who work with numbers. The user enters the data and the formulas to be used on the data and calculates the results. Most spreadsheet programs have the capability to use numeric data to generate charts, such as the bar chart.

Database software (Figure 26) allows the user to enter, retrieve, and update data in an organized and efficient manner. These software packages have flexible inquiry and reporting capabilities that allow users to access the data in different ways and create custom reports that include some or all of the information in the database.

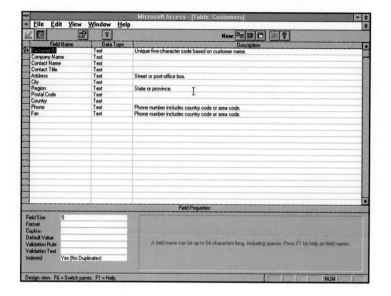

FIGURE 26
Database software allows the user to enter, retrieve, and update data in an organized and efficient manner. This database table illustrates how a business organized customer information. Once the table is defined, the user can add, delete, change, display, print, or reorganize the database records.

Presentation graphics software (Figure 27) allows the user to create documents called slides to be used in making presentations. Using special projection devices, the slides are projected directly from the computer. In addition, the slides can be printed and used as handouts, or converted into transparencies and displayed on overhead projectors. Presentation graphics software includes many special effects, color, and art that enhance information presented on a slide. Because slides frequently include numeric data, presentation graphics software includes the capability to convert the numeric data into many forms of charts.

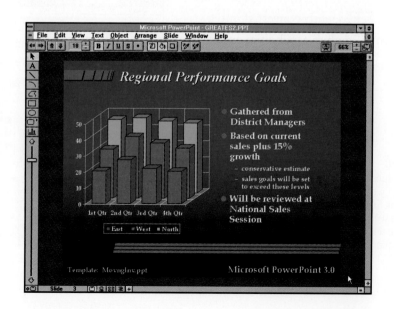

FIGURE 27
Presentation graphics software allows the user to create documents called slides for use in presentations. Using special projection devices, the slides display as they appear on the computer screen. The slides can also be printed and used as handouts or converted into transparencies to be used with overhead projectors.

Communications software (Figure 28) is used to transmit data and information from one computer to another. For the transfer to take place, each computer must have communications software. Organizations use communications software to transfer information from one location to another. Many individuals use communications software to access on-line databases that provide information on current events, airline schedules, finances, weather, and hundreds of other subjects.

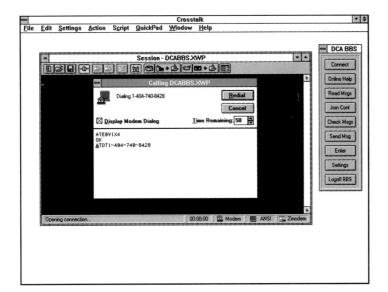

FIGURE 28
Communications software allows users to transmit data from one computer to another. This software enables the user to choose a previously entered phone number of another computer. Once the number is chosen, the communications software dials the number and establishes a communication link. The user can then transfer data or run programs on the remote computer.

Electronic mail software, also called **e-mail** (Figure 29), allows users to send messages to and receive messages from other computer users. The other users may be on the same computer network or on a separate computer system reached through the use of communications equipment and software.

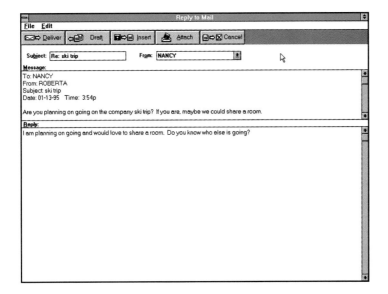

FIGURE 29
Electronic mail software allows users to send and receive messages with other computer users. Each user has an electronic mail box to which messages are sent. This software enables a user to add a reply to a received message and then send the reply back to the person who sent the original message.

What Is Communications?

*C*ommunications refers to the transmission of data and information over a communications channel, such as a standard telephone line, between one computer and another computer. Figure 30 shows the basic model for a communications system. This model consists of the following equipment:

1. A computer.
2. Communications equipment that sends (and can usually receive) data.
3. The communications channel over which the data is sent.
4. Communications equipment that receives (and can usually send) data.
5. Another computer.

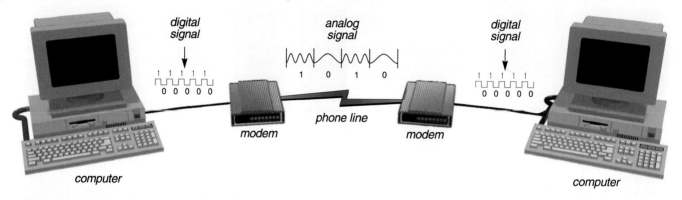

FIGURE 30
The basic model of a communications system. Individual electrical pulses of the digital signal from the computer are converted into analog (electrical wave) signals for transmission over voice telephone lines. At the main computer receiving end, another modem converts the analog signals back into digital signals that can be processed by the computer.

The basic model also includes communications software. When two computers are communicating with each other, compatible communications software is required on each system.

Communications is important to understand because of on-line services and the trend to network computers. With communications equipment and software, access is available to an increasing amount and variety of information and services. **On-line information services** such as Prodigy (Figure 31) and America On-Line offer the latest news, weather, sports, and financial information along with shopping, entertainment, and electronic mail.

International networks such as the Internet allow users to access information at thousands of Internet member organizations around the world. Electronic bulletin boards can be found in most cities with hundreds available in large metropolitan areas. An electronic **bulletin board system (BBS)** is a computer and at least one phone line that allows users to *chat* with the computer operator, called the **system operator (sys op)** or, if more than one phone line is available, with other BBS users. BBS users can also leave messages for other users. BBSs are often devoted to a specific subject area such as games, hobbies, or a specific type of computer or software. Many computer hardware and software companies operate BBSs so users of their products can share information.

Communications Channels

A **communications channel** is the path the data follows as it is transmitted from the sending equipment to the receiving equipment in a communications system. These channels are made up of one or more **transmission media**, including twisted pair wire, coaxial cable, fiber optics, microwave transmission, satellite transmission, and wireless transmission.

Communications Equipment

If a personal computer is within approximately 1,000 feet of another computer, the two devices can usually be directly connected by a cable. If the devices are more than 1,000 feet, however, the electrical signal weakens to the point that some type of special communications equipment is required to increase or change the signal to transmit it farther. A variety of communications equipment exists to perform this task, but the equipment most often used is a modem.

FIGURE 31
Prodigy is one of several on-line service providers offering information on a number of general-interest subjects. The topic areas display on the right. Users access Prodigy and other on-line services by using a modem and special communications software.

Computer equipment is designed to process data as **digital signals**, individual electrical pulses grouped together to represent characters. Telephone equipment was originally designed to carry only voice transmission, which is comprised of a continuous electrical wave called an **analog signal** (see Figure 30). Thus, a special piece of equipment called a modem converts between the digital signals and analog signals so telephone lines can carry data. A **modem** converts the digital signals of a computer to analog signals that are transmitted over a communications channel. A modem also converts analog signals it receives into digital signals used by a computer. The word modem comes from a combination of the words *mo*dulate, which means to change into a sound or analog signal, and *dem*odulate, which means to convert an analog signal into a digital signal. A modem is needed at both the sending and receiving ends of a communications channel. A modem may be an external stand-alone device that is connected to the computer and phone line or an internal circuit board that is installed inside the computer.

Modems can transmit data at rates from 300 to 38,400 bits per second (bps). Most personal computers use a 2,400 bps or higher modem. Business or heavier volume users would use faster and more expensive modems.

Communication Networks

A communication **network** is a collection of computers and other equipment using communications channels to share hardware, software, data, and information. Networks are classified as either local area networks or wide area networks.

Local Area Networks (LANs)

A **local area network**, or LAN, is a privately owned communications network and covers a limited geographic area, such as a school computer laboratory, an office, a building, or a group of buildings.

The LAN consists of a communications channel connecting a group of personal computers to one another. Very sophisticated LANs are capable of connecting a variety of office devices, such as word processing equipment, computer terminals, video equipment, and personal computers.

Three common applications of local area networks are hardware, software, and information resource sharing. **Hardware resource sharing** allows each personal computer in the network to access and use devices that would be too expensive to provide for each user or would not be justified for each user because of only occasional use. For example, when a number of personal computers are used on the network, each may need to use a laser printer. Using a LAN, the purchase of one laser printer serves the entire network. Whenever a personal computer user on the network needs the laser printer, it is accessed over the network. Figure 32 depicts a simple local area network consisting of four personal computers linked together by a cable. Three of the personal computers (computer 1 in the sales and marketing department, computer 2 in the accounting department, and computer 3 in the personnel department) are available for use at all times. Computer 4 is used as a **server**, which is dedicated to handling the communications needs of the other computers in the network. The users of this LAN have connected the laser printer to the server. Using the LAN, all computers and the server can use the printer.

FIGURE 32
A local area network (LAN) consists of multiple personal computers connected to one another. The LAN allows users to share softwre, hardware, and information.

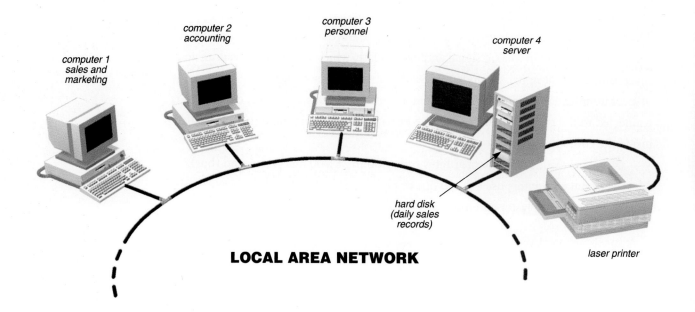

computer 1
sales and
marketing

computer 2
accounting

computer 3
personnel

computer 4
server

hard disk
(daily sales
records)

LOCAL AREA NETWORK

laser printer

Frequently used software is another type of resource sharing that often occurs on a local area network. For example, if all users need access to word processing software, the software can be stored on the hard disk of the server and accessed by all users as needed. This is more convenient and faster than having the software stored on a diskette and available at each computer.

Information resource sharing allows anyone using a personal computer on the local area network to access data stored on any other computer in the network. In actual practice, hardware resource sharing and information resource sharing are often combined. The capability to access and store data on common auxiliary storage is an important feature of many local area networks.

Information resource sharing is usually provided by using either the file-server or client-server method. Using the **file-server** method, the server sends an entire file at a time. The requesting computer then performs the processing. With the **client-server** method, processing tasks are divided between the server computer

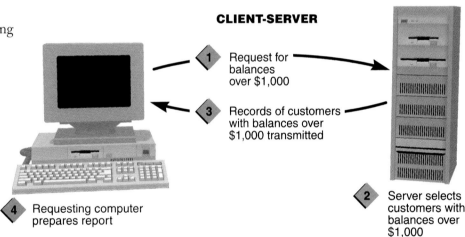

FILE SERVER

1 Request for customer file

3 Entire customer file transmitted

4 Requesting computer selects customers with balances over $1,000 and prepares report

2 Server locates and transmits entire customer file

CLIENT-SERVER

1 Request for balances over $1,000

3 Records of customers with balances over $1,000 transmitted

4 Requesting computer prepares report

2 Server selects customers with balances over $1,000

and the *client* computer requesting the information. Figure 33 illustrates how the two methods would process a request for information stored on the server system for customers with balances over $1,000. With the file-server method, all customer records would be transferred to the requesting computer. The requesting computer would then process the records to identify the customers with balances over $1,000. With the client-server method, the server system would review the customers' records and only transfer records of customers meeting the criteria. The client-server method greatly reduces the amount of data sent over a network but requires a more powerful server system.

FIGURE 33
A request for information about customers with balances over $1,000 would be processed differently by the file-server and client-server networks.

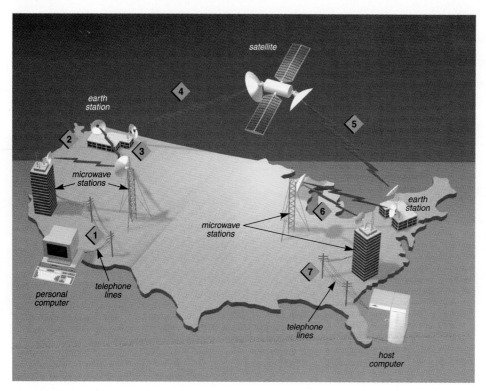

Wide Area Networks (WANs)

A wide area network, or WAN, is geographic in scope (as opposed to local) and uses telephone lines, microwaves, satellites, or a combination of communications channels (Figure 34). Public wide area network companies include common carriers such as the telephone companies. Telephone company deregulation has encouraged a number of companies to build their own wide area

FIGURE 34
A wide area network (WAN) may use a number of different communications channels such as telephone lines, microwaves, and satellites.

networks. Communications companies, such as MCI, have built WANs to compete with other communications companies.

How to Purchase a Computer System

T he desktop personal computer (PC) is the most widely purchased type of system. The following guidelines assume you are purchasing a desktop IBM-compatible PC, to be used for home or light business use. That is not meant to imply that Macintosh or other non DOS or Windows operating system computers are not worth considering. Software requirements and the need to be compatible with other systems you may work with should determine the type of system you purchase. A portable computer would be an appropriate choice if your situation requires that you have a computer with you when you travel.

1. Determine what applications you will use on your computer. This decision will guide you as to the type and size of computer.

2. Choose your software first. Some packages only run on Macintosh computers, others only on a PC. Some packages only run under the Windows operating system. In addition, some software requires more memory and disk space than other packages.

3. Be aware of hidden costs. Realize that there will be some additional costs associated with buying a computer. Such costs might include; an additional phone line or outlet to use the modem, computer furniture, consumable supplies such as diskettes and paper, diskette holders, reference manuals on specific software packages, and special training classes you may want to take. Depending on where you buy your computer, the seller may be willing to include some or all of these in the system purchase price.

4. **Buy equipment that meets the** *Energy Star* **power consumption guidelines.** These guidelines require that computer systems, monitors, and printers, reduce electrical consumption if they have not been used for some period of time, usually several minutes. Equipment meeting the guidelines can display the *Energy Star* logo.

5. **Use a spreadsheet like the one shown in Figure 35 to compare purchase alternatives.** Use a separate sheet of paper to take notes on each vendor's system and then summarize the information on the spreadsheet.

6. **Consider buying from local computer dealers and direct mail companies.** Each has certain advantages. The local dealer can more easily provide hands-on support, if necessary. With a mail order company, you are usually limited to speaking to someone over the phone. Mail order companies usually, but not always, offer the lowest prices. The important thing to do when shopping for a system is to make sure you are comparing identical or similar configurations.

System Cost Comparison Worksheet		Desired	#1	#2	#3	#4
Base System	Mfr	—	Delway			
	Model		4500X			
	Processor	486DX	486DX			
	Speed	50MHz	50			
	Pwr Supply	200watts	220			
	Exp Slots	5	5			
	Price		$995			
Memory	8MB Ram		incl			
Disk	Mfr		Conner			
	Size	>300MB	340			
	Price		incl			
Diskette	3 1/2					
	5 1/4					
	Combination		$50			
Monitor	Mfr		NEC			
	Model		5FG			
	Size	15in	15			
	Price		$300			
Sound	Mfr		Media Labs			
	Model		Pro			
	Price		$75			
CDROM	Mfr		NEC			
	Speed		450/200			
	Price		$100			
Mouse	Mfr		Logitech			
	Price		incl			
Modem	Mfr		Boca			
	Mod/fax Speeds	14.4/14.4	14.4/14.4			
	Price		$125			
Printer	Mfr		HP			
	Model		4Z			
	Type		laser			
	Speed	6ppm	8ppm			
	Price		$675			
Surge Protector	Mfr		Brooks			
	Price		$35			
Options	Tape Backup					
	UPS					
Other	Sales Tax		0			
	Shipping		$30			
	1 YR Warranty		incl			
	1 YR On-Site Svc		incl			
	3 YR On-Site Svc		$150			
Software	List free software		Windows			
			MS Works			
			diagnostics			
	TOTAL		**$2,535**			

FIGURE 35
A spreadsheet is an effective way to summarize and compare the prices and equipment offered by different system vendors.

7. **Consider more than just price.** Don't necessarily buy the lowest cost system. Consider intangibles such as how long the vendor has been in business, its reputation for quality, and reputation for support.

8. **Look for free software.** Many system vendors now include free software with their systems. Some even let you choose which software you want. Such software only has value, however, if you would have purchased it if it had not come with the computer.

9. **Buy a system compatible with the one you use elsewhere.** If you use a personal computer at work or at some other organization, make sure the computer you buy is compatible. That way, if you need or want to, you can work on projects at home.

10. **Consider purchasing an on-site service agreement.** If you use your system for business or otherwise can't afford to be without your computer, consider purchasing an on-site service agreement. Many of the mail order vendors offer such support through third-party companies. Such agreements usually state that a technician will be on-site within 24 hours. Some systems include on-site service for only the first year. It is usually less expensive to extend the service for two or three years when you buy the computer rather than waiting to buy the service agreement later.

11. **Use a credit card to purchase your system.** Many credit cards now have purchase protection benefits that cover you in case of loss or damage to purchased goods. Some also extend the warranty of any products purchased with the card. Paying by credit card also gives you time to install and use the system before you have to pay for it. Finally, if you're dissatisfied with the system and can't reach an agreement with the seller, paying by credit card gives you certain rights regarding withholding payment until the dispute is resolved. Check your credit card agreement for specific details.

12. **Buy a system that will last you for at least three years.** Studies show that many users become dissatisfied because they didn't buy a powerful enough system. Consider the following system configuration guidelines. Each of the components will be discussed separately:

Base System Components:	Optional Equipment:
486SX or 486DX processor, 33 megahertz	5 1/4" diskette drive
150 watt power supply	14.4K fax modem
160 to 300MB hard disk	laser printer
4 to 8MB RAM	sound card and speakers
3 to 5 expansion slots	CD-ROM drive
3 1/2" diskette drive	tape backup
14" or 15" color monitor	uninterruptable power supply (UPS)
mouse or other pointing device	
enhanced keyboard	
ink jet or bubble jet printer	
surge protector	

Processor: A 486SX or 486DX processor with a speed rating of at least 33 mega-hertz is needed for today's more sophisticated software, even word processing soft-ware. Buy a system that can be upgraded to the Pentium processor.

Power Supply: 150 watts. If the power supply is too small, it won't be able to support additional expansion cards that you might want to add in the future.

Hard Disk: 160 to 300 megabytes (MB). Each new release of software requires more hard disk space. Even with disk compression programs, disk space is used up fast. Start with more disk than you ever think you'll need.

Memory (RAM): 4 to 8 megabytes (MB). Like disk space, the new applications are demanding more memory. It's easier and less expensive to obtain the memory when you buy the system than if you wait until later.

Expansion Slots: 3 to 5 open slots on the base system. Expansion slots are needed for scanners, tape drives, video boards, and other equipment you may want to add in the future as your needs change and the price of this equipment becomes lower.

Diskette Drives: Most software is now distributed on 3 1/2-inch disks. Consider adding a 5 1/4-inch diskette to read data and programs that may have been stored on that format. The best way to achieve this is to buy a combination diskette drive which is only slightly more expensive than a single 3 1/2-inch diskette drive. The combination device has both 3 1/2- and 5 1/4-inch diskette drives in a single unit.

Color Monitor: 14 to 15 inch. This is one device where it pays to spend a little more money. A 15-inch super VGA monitor will display graphics better than a 14-inch model. For health reasons, make sure you pick a low radiation model.

Pointing Device: Most systems include a mouse as part of the base package.

Enhanced Keyboard: The keyboard is usually included with the system. Check to make sure the keyboard is the *enhanced* and not the older *standard* model. The enhanced keyboard is sometimes called the *101* keyboard because it has 101 keys.

Printer: The price of nonimpact printers has come within several hundred dollars of the lowest cost dot matrix printers. Unless you need the wide carriage or multi-part form capabilities of a dot matrix, purchase a nonimpact printer.

Surge Protector: A voltage spike can literally destroy your system. It is low-cost insurance to protect yourself with a surge protector. Don't merely buy a fused multi-plug outlet from the local hardware store. Buy a surge protector designed for com-puters with a separate protected jack for your phone (modem) line.

Fax Modem: Volumes of information are available via on-line databases. In addition, many software vendors provide assistance and free software upgrades via bulletin boards. For the speed they provide, 14.4K modems are worth the extra money. Facsimile (fax) capability only costs a few dollars more and gives you more communication options.

Sound Card and Speakers: More and more software and support materials are incorporating sound.

CD-ROM Drive: Multimedia is the wave of the future and it requires a CD-ROM drive. Get a double- or triple-speed model.

Tape Backup: Larger hard disks make backing up data on diskettes impractical. Internal or external tape backup systems are the most common solution. Some portable units, great if you have more than one system, are designed to connect to your printer port. The small cassette tapes can store the equivalent of hundreds of diskettes.

Uninterruptable Power Supply (UPS): A UPS uses batteries to start or keep your system running if the main electrical power is turned off. The length of time they provide depends on the size of the batteries and the electrical requirements of your system but is usually at least 10 minutes. The idea of a UPS is to give you enough time to save your work. Get a UPS that is rated for your size system.

Remember that the types of applications you want to use on your system will guide you as to the type and size of computer that is right for you. The ideal computer system you choose may differ from the general recommendation that is presented here. Determine your needs and buy the best system your budget will allow.

How to Install a Computer System

1. **Allow for adequate workspace around the computer.** A workspace of at least two feet by four feet is recommended.

2. **Install bookshelves.** Bookshelves above and/or to the side of the computer area are useful for keeping manuals and other reference materials handy.

3. **Install your computer in a well-designed work area.** The height of your chair, keyboard, monitor, and work surface is important and can affect your health. See Figure 36 for specific guidelines.

4. **Use a document holder.** To minimize neck and eye strain, obtain a document holder that holds documents at the same height and distance as your computer screen.

5. **Provide adequate lighting.**

6. **While working at your computer, be aware of health issues.** See Figure 37 for a list of computer user health guidelines.

7. **Install or move a phone near the computer.** Having a phone near the computer really helps if you need to call a vendor about a hardware or software problem. Oftentimes the vendor support person can talk you through the correction while you're on the phone. To avoid data loss, however, don't place diskettes on the phone or any other electrical or electronic equipment.

8. **Obtain a computer tool set.** Computer tool sets are available from computer dealers, office supply stores, and mail order companies. These sets will have the right-sized screwdrivers and other tools to work on your system. Get one that comes in a zippered carrying case to keep all the tools together.

9. **Save all the paperwork that comes with your system.** Keep it in an accessible place with the paperwork from your other computer-related purchases. To keep different-sized documents together, consider putting them in a plastic zip-lock bag.

10. **Record the serial numbers of all your equipment and software.** Write the serial numbers on the outside of the manuals that came with the equipment as well as in a single list that contains the serial numbers of all your equipment and software.

11. **Keep the shipping containers and packing materials for all your equipment.** This material will come in handy if you have to return your equipment for servicing or have to move it to another location.

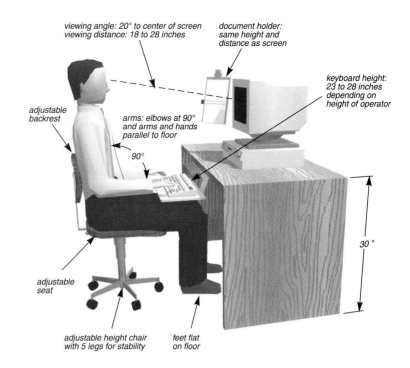

viewing angle: 20° to center of screen
viewing distance: 18 to 28 inches

document holder: same height and distance as screen

keyboard height: 23 to 28 inches depending on height of operator

adjustable backrest

arms: elbows at 90° and arms and hands parallel to floor

90°

adjustable seat

30 "

adjustable height chair with 5 legs for stability

feet flat on floor

FIGURE 36
More than anything else, a well-designed work area should be flexible to allow adjustment to the height and build of different individuals. Good lighting and air quality should also be considered.

COMPUTER USER HEALTH GUIDELINES
1. Work in a well-designed work area. Figure 36 illustrates the guidelines.
2. Alternate work activities to prevent physical and mental fatigue. If possible, change the order of your work to provide some variety.
3. Take frequent breaks. At least once per hour, get out of your chair and move around. Every two hours, take at least a 15 minute break.
4. Incorporate hand, arm, and body stretching exercises into your breaks. At lunch, try to get outside and walk.
5. Make sure your computer monitor is designed to minimize electromagnetic radiation
6. Try to eliminate or minimize surrounding noise. Noisy environments contribute to stress and tension.
7. If you frequently have to use the phone and the computer at the same time, consider using a telephone headset. Cradling the phone between your head and shoulder can cause muscle strain.
8. Be aware of symptoms of repetitive strain injuries; soreness, pain, numbness, or weakness in neck, shoulders, arms, wrists, and hands. Don't ignore early signs; seek medical advice.

FIGURE 37
All computer users should follow the Computer User Health Guidelines to maintain their health.

12. **Look at the inside of your computer.** Before you connect power to your system, remove the computer case cover and visually inspect the internal components. The user manual usually identifies what each component does. Look for any disconnected wires, loose screws or washers, or any other obvious signs of trouble. Be careful not to touch anything inside the case unless you are grounded. Static electricity can permanently damage the microprocessor chips on the circuit boards. Before you replace the cover, take several photographs of the computer showing the location of the circuit boards. These photos may save you from taking the cover off in the future if you or a vendor has a question about what equipment controller card is installed in what expansion slot.

13. **Identify device connectors.** At the back of your system there are a number of connectors for the printer, the monitor, the mouse, a phone line, etc. If they aren't already identified by the manufacturer, use a marking pen to write the purpose of each connector on the back of the computer case.

14. **Complete and send in your equipment and software registration cards right away.** If you're already entered in the vendors user database, it can save you time when you call in with a support question. Being a registered user also makes you eligible for special pricing on software upgrades.

15. **Install your system in an area where the temperature and humidity can be maintained.** Try to maintain a constant temperature between 60 and 80 degrees farenheight when the computer is operating. High temperatures and humidity can damage electronic components. Be careful when using space heaters; their hot, dry air has been known to cause disk problems.

16. **Keep your computer area clean.** Avoid eating and drinking around the computer. Smoking should be avoided also. Cigarette smoke can quickly cause damage to the diskette drives and diskette surfaces.

17. **Check your insurance.** Some policies have limits on the amount of computer equipment they cover. Other policies don't cover computer equipment at all if it is used for a business (a separate policy is required).

How to Maintain Your Computer System

1. **Learn to use system diagnostic programs.** If a set didn't come with your system, obtain one. These programs help you identify and possibly solve problems before you call for technical assistance. Some system manufacturers now include diagnostic programs with their systems and ask that you run the programs before you call for help.

2. **Start a notebook that includes information on your system.** This notebook should be a single source of information about your entire system, both hardware and software. Each time you make a change to your system, adding or removing hardware or software, or when you change system parameters, you should record the change in the notebook. Items to include in the notebook are the following:

✓ Serial numbers of all equipment and software.

✓ Vendor support phone numbers. These numbers are often buried in user manuals. Look up these numbers once and record all of them on a single sheet of paper at the front of your notebook.

✓ Date and vendor for each equipment and software purchase.

✓ File listings for key system files (e.g., autoexec.bat and config.sys).

✓ Notes on discussions with vendor support personnel.

✓ A chronological history of any equipment or software problems. This history can be helpful if the problem persists and you have to call several times.

3. **Periodically review disk directories and delete unneeded files.** Files have a way of building up and can quickly use up your disk space. If you think you may need a file in the future, back it up to a diskette.

4. **Any time you work inside your computer turn the power off and disconnect the equipment from the power source.** In addition, before you touch anything inside the computer, touch an unpainted metal surface such as the power supply. This will discharge any static electricity that could damage internal components.

5. **Reduce the need to clean the inside of your system by keeping the surrounding area dirt and dust free.** Diskette cleaners are available but should be used sparingly (some owners never use them unless they experience diskette problems). If dust builds up inside the computer it should be carefully removed with compressed air and a small vacuum. Don't touch the components with the vacuum.

6. **Back up key files and data.** At a minimum, you should have a diskette with your **command.com**, **autoexec.bat**, and **config.sys** files. If your system crashes, these files will help you get going again. In addition, backup any files with a file extension of **.sys**. For Windows systems, all files with a file extension of **.ini** and **.grp** should be backed up.

7. **Protect your system from computer viruses.** Computer viruses are programs designed to *infect* computer systems by copying themselves into other computer files (Figure 38). The virus program spreads when the infected files are used by or copied to another system.

FIGURE 38
How a virus program can be transmitted from one computer to another.

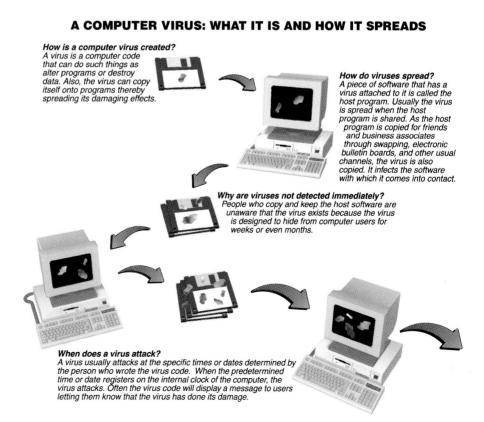

A COMPUTER VIRUS: WHAT IT IS AND HOW IT SPREADS

How is a computer virus created?
A virus is a computer code that can do such things as alter programs or destroy data. Also, the virus can copy itself onto programs thereby spreading its damaging effects.

How do viruses spread?
A piece of software that has a virus attached to it is called the host program. Usually the virus is spread when the host program is shared. As the host program is copied for friends and business associates through swapping, electronic bulletin boards, and other usual channels, the virus is also copied. It infects the software with which it comes into contact.

Why are viruses not detected immediately?
People who copy and keep the host software are unaware that the virus exists because the virus is designed to hide from computer users for weeks or even months.

When does a virus attack?
A virus usually attacks at the specific times or dates determined by the person who wrote the virus code. When the predetermined time or date registers on the internal clock of the computer, the virus attacks. Often the virus code will display a message to users letting them know that the virus has done its damage.

Virus programs are dangerous because they are often designed to damage the files of the infected system. Protect yourself from viruses by installing an anti-virus program on your computer.

Summary of Introduction to Computers

*A*s you learn to use the software taught in this book, you will also become familiar with the components and operation of your computer system. When you need help understanding how the components of your system function, refer to this introduction. You can also refer to this section for information on computer communications and for guidelines when you decide to purchase a computer system of your own.

Student Assignments

Student Assignment 1: True/False

Instructions: Circle T if the statement is true or F if the statement is false.

T F 1. A computer is an electronic device, operating under the control of instructions stored in its own memory unit, that can accept data (input), process data arithmetically and logically, produce output from the processing, and store the results for future use.

T F 2. Information refers to data processed into a form that has meaning and is useful.

T F 3. A computer program is a detailed set of instructions that tells a computer exactly what to do.

T F 4. A mouse is a communications device used to convert between digital and analog signals so telephone lines can carry data.

T F 5. The central processing unit contains the processor unit and main memory.

T F 6. A laser printer is an impact printer that provides high-quality output.

T F 7. Auxiliary storage is used to store instructions and data when they are not being used in main memory.

T F 8. A diskette is considered to be a form of main memory.

T F 9. CD-ROM is often used for multimedia material that combines text, graphics, video, and sound.

T F 10. The operating system tells the computer how to perform functions such as how to load, store, and execute an application program and how to transfer data between the input/output devices and main memory.

T F 11. Programs such as database management, spreadsheet, and word processing software are called system software.

T F 12. For data to be transferred from one computer to another over communications lines, communications software is required only on the sending computer.

T F 13. A communications network is a collection of computers and other equipment that use communications channels to share hardware, software, data, and information.

T   F   14. Determining what applications you will use on your computer will help you to purchase a computer that is the type and size that meets your needs.

T   F   15. The path the data follows as it is transmitted from the sending equipment to the receiving equipment in a communications system is called a modem.

T   F   16. Computer equipment that meets the power consumption guidelines can display the *Energy Star* logo.

T   F   17. An on-site maintenance agreement is important if you cannot be without the use of your computer.

T   F   18. An anit-virus program is used to protect your computer equipment and software.

T   F   19. When purchasing a computer, consider only the price because one computer is no different from another.

T   F   20. A LAN allows you to share software but not hardware.

Student Assignments 2: Multiple Choice

Instructions: Circle the correct response.

1. The four operations performed by a computer include _____ .
   a. input, control, output, and storage
   b. interface, processing, output, and memory
   c. input, output, processing, and storage
   d. input, logical/rational, arithmetic, and output

2. A hand-held input device that controls the cursor location is _____ .
   a. the cursor control keyboard
   b. a mouse
   c. a modem
   d. the CRT

3. A printer that forms images without striking the paper is _____ .
   a. an impact printer   b. a nonimpact printer   c. an ink jet printer   d. both b and c

4. The amount of storage provided by a diskette is a function of _____ .
   a. the thickness of the disk
   b. the recording density of bits on the track
   c. the number of recording tracks on the diskette
   d. both b and c

5. Portable computers use a flat panel screen called a _____ .
   a. a multichrome monitor
   b. a cathode ray tube
   c. a liquid crystal display
   d. a monochrome monitor

6. When not in use, diskettes should be _____ .
   a. stored away from magnetic fields
   b. stored away from heat and direct sunlight
   c. stored in a diskette box or cabinet
   d. all of the above

7. CD-ROM is a type of _____ .
   a. main memory
   b. auxiliary storage
   c. communications equipment
   d. system software

8. An operating system is considered part of _____ .
   a. word processing software
   b. database software
   c. system software
   d. spreadsheet software

9. The type of application software most commonly used to create and print documents is _____ .
   a. word processing   b. electronic spreadsheet   c. database   d. none of the above

10. The type of application software most commonly used to send messages to and receive messages from other computer users is _____ .
    a. electronic mail   b. database   c. presentation graphics   d. none of the above

Student Assignment 3: Comparing Personal Computer Advertisements

Instructions: Obtain a copy of a recent computer magazine and review the advertisements for desktop personal computer systems. Compare ads for the least and most expensive desktop systems you can find. Discuss the differences.

Student Assignment 4: Evaluating On-Line Information Services

Instructions: Prodigy and America On-Line both offer consumer oriented on-line information services. Contact each company and request each to send you information on the specific services it offers. Try to talk to someone who actually uses one or both of the services. Discuss how each service is priced and the differences between the two on-line services.

Student Assignment 5: Visiting Local Computer Retail Stores

Instructions: Visit local computer retail stores and compare the various types of computers and support equipment available. Ask about warranties, repair services, hardware setup, training, and related issues. Report on the knowledge of the sales staff assisting you and their willingness to answer your questions. Does the store have standard hardware packages, or are they willing to configure a system to your specific needs? Would you feel confident buying a computer from this store?

Index

Photo Credits

INTRODUCTION TO DOS

PROJECT
1

Working With Files on Disks

▼ OBJECTIVES

You will have mastered the material in this project when you can:

- Identify the purpose of DOS
- Boot your computer
- Establish the default disk drive
- Enter and correct DOS commands
- Clear the screen
- Format a disk

- View filenames on a disk
- Copy a file
- Rename a file
- Delete a file
- Recover a file
- Obtain help for DOS commands

▼ INTRODUCTION

Without an operating system, a computer is a useless piece of equipment. An **operating system** is a collection of programs that enables the user to communicate with the computer; it is the interface between you and the hardware (Figure 1-1). You make requests of the operating system, and the operating system, in turn, controls and manages the hardware. Thus, you issue instructions, and the operating system interprets and executes these instructions. For example, the instruction `cls` tells the operating system to clear the computer's screen.

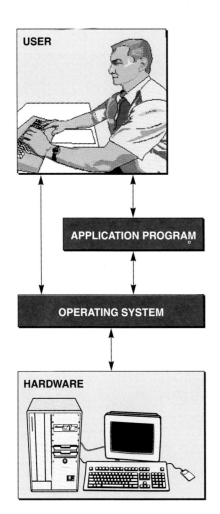

FIGURE I-I

When you use an application program, such as a word processor, electronic spreadsheet, or database management system, the application program interacts with the operating system. To use a computer to print a memo, for example, you first use the operating system to start the computer. You next instruct the operating system to begin the word processing program. At this point, you are interacting with the word processing program, which is interacting with the operating system, which is interacting with the hardware. When you instruct the word processing program to display

the memo on the screen, or *open* the file, the word processing program requests that the operating system find the memo file on disk, retrieve the file from the disk, and display its contents on the screen. The operating system provides essential services that the application software uses to perform its functions for you.

To use your computer effectively, you need to know when and how to interact with the operating system. IBM and IBM-compatible personal computers use the disk operating system called DOS. In Project 1, you will learn how to use DOS to work with your disk files.

PC Versus MS-DOS

Microsoft Corporation developed the operating system called **DOS** (pronounced doss), an acronym for **Disk Operating System**. DOS has been used since 1981 on IBM and IBM-compatible personal computers. Depending on the type of personal computer you are using, your operating system is called either PC-DOS or MS-DOS. **PC-DOS** is distributed by IBM for its Personal Computer (PC) and Personal System/2 lines of personal computers. All IBM-compatible personal computers use **MS-DOS**, distributed by Microsoft Corporation. PC-DOS and MS-DOS are essentially the same product. For purposes in this book, the term DOS is used to refer to both the PC-DOS and MS-DOS products.

DOS Versions

The numbers following a software product name, like DOS, indicate the specific version number and release number of the product. The version number is the number in front of the decimal point; the release number is the number following the decimal point. All software products have version and release numbers. Changes in a version number indicate a major improvement to the product, whereas changes in the release number indicate corrections or minor changes to a version of the product. Often, new releases of a version are prompted by a user(s) notifying the software manufacturer of a problem with the current release. For example DOS 1.1 corrected some minor problems with DOS 1.0; but DOS 2.0 made significant changes over DOS 1.1. New releases are also issued to accommodate minor hardware changes and upgrades. Table 1-1 lists the hardware changes and new features added with each new release, or version, of DOS.

TABLE I-I

DOS Version & Release	Major Features Supported	Year
6.2	New Data-Protection Technology, Disk Uncompression, Copy Overwrite Protection, Removal of DOS Shell—except for Step-Up program	1993
6.0	Disk Compression and Defragmenter, Memory Optimization, Improved Backup Utility, Anti-Virus Program	1993
5.0	Improved Memory Management, Recover Deleted Files and Formatted Disks, Online Help, Full-Screen Editor, 2.88 MB Disks	1992
4.0	Hard Disks Larger than 32MB, File Manager Shell (DOS Shell), Memory Supported Beyond 640KB	1988
3.3	IBM PS/2	1987
3.2	Token-Ring Networks, 3 1/2" Disks	1986
3.1	Networking	1985
3.0	IBM PC/AT, High Density 5 1/4" Disks	1984
2.1	PC Jr and Portables	1983
2.0	IBM PC/XT, Hard Disks	1983
1.1	Double-Sided Disks	1982
1.0	IBM PC, Single-Sided Disks	1981

Software developers try to maintain **upward compatibility** in their products. That is, all of the features in an earlier version and release remain supported by a later one. A word processing package that works when you use DOS 3.2, for example, should also work when you use DOS 6.2. Downward compatibility, however, is not common. Programs or equipment that require the features of DOS 6.2 will not function with DOS 5.0 or earlier versions.

Disk Configurations

You will probably use a computer with one of two common disk configurations. The first configuration has a hard drive and one or two diskette drives and operates as a stand-alone unit (Figures 1-2 and 1-3). Each drive has a **drive name**, which is a unique letter name preassigned to the drive. The hard drive name is C, and the diskette drive name is A.

FIGURE I-2

(a) Courtesy IBM Corporation

(b) Courtesy Compaq Computer

(a) Tower unit   **(b) Desktop unit**

FIGURE 1-3

(a) Courtesy Texas Instruments

(b) Courtesy IBM Corporation

(a) Notebook unit

(b) Desktop unit with a CD ROM drive

The second configuration connects your computer through a local area network with other computers (Figure 1-4). A **local area network**, or **LAN**, is a collection of connected computers that share data. One special computer on the LAN, called the **server**, has a high-capacity hard drive containing files that you can access from any connected computer. The server hard drive name is usually F. Each computer connected to the LAN may have either two diskette drives; one hard drive and one diskette drive; or one hard drive and two diskette drives. In a two diskette drive environment, the top or left drive name is A, and the bottom or right drive name is B.

LOCAL AREA NETWORK (LAN)

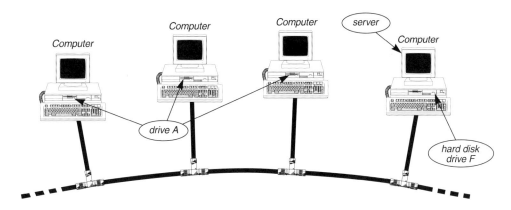

FIGURE 1-4

These DOS projects assume you have one hard drive and one diskette drive, unless otherwise stated. If you are using a computer with a different configuration, your instructor will inform you of the changes you need to make in the DOS projects.

▼ **STARTING THE COMPUTER**

DOS programs are originally purchased on diskettes, and then usually **installed**, or unpacked and copied, from the diskettes to a hard drive. To begin using DOS, it must be loaded from the hard drive into the memory of the computer, which is a process known as **booting** the computer. How you begin using the computer depends on your disk configuration and whether the computer has already been turned on.

LAN Environment

If you are using a computer on a LAN, the laboratory attendant will have already booted your computer. You do not need to perform any startup activities, unless your instructor gives you special instructions.

Stand-alone Mode

If your computer is not connected to a LAN, you are using it in **stand-alone mode**. You can boot stand-alone computers with a cold or warm boot. When cold or warm starting a computer, many computers require that the diskette drives be empty. If you boot many computers with a disk in the diskette drive, the message, Non-System disk or disk error Replace and press any key when ready, displays on the screen and the system halts. In this case, simply remove the disk from the drive and press any key to continue the boot process.

Cold Boot   Starting a computer by turning on the power switch is called a **cold start**, or **cold boot**. In a cold boot, the computer first runs some diagnostic tests on the circuitry and then loads DOS from the hard drive into memory. While DOS is booting, the hard drive status light flashes for a few seconds.

Because turning a computer off and then immediately on again can adversely affect its internal components, you should use a warm boot to restart a running computer.

Warm Boot   If the computer is already turned on, you can restart the computer without turning the power switch off and on. Restarting the computer in this way is called a **warm start**, **warm boot**, or **reset**. A warm start is much less stressful on a computer than a cold start. To begin a warm start, hold down the CTRL and ALT keys, press the DELETE key, and then release all three keys. As an alternative to pressing these three keys, some computers have a reset button you may press. In a warm boot, DOS is reloaded from the hard drive into memory, but the circuitry tests are not repeated. During the warm boot, the hard drive status light flashes for a few seconds.

▼   **UNDERSTANDING THE DOS ENVIRONMENT**

While the computer is booting, several messages tailored for your specific computer may appear on the screen. Eventually, the **DOS prompt** displays on the screen (Figures 1-5 and 1-6), indicating DOS is ready to receive your commands. (If your DOS prompt differs from the one in Figure 1-5 or 1-6, your instructor will explain the difference(s) to you.) The initial letter that appears in the DOS prompt indicates the drive that DOS was on when the computer was booted. Thus, the letter will vary depending on the disk configuration you are using. If DOS was loaded from the hard drive, the letter is a C (Figure 1-5); if DOS was loaded from a network server, the letter is usually an F (Figure 1-6).

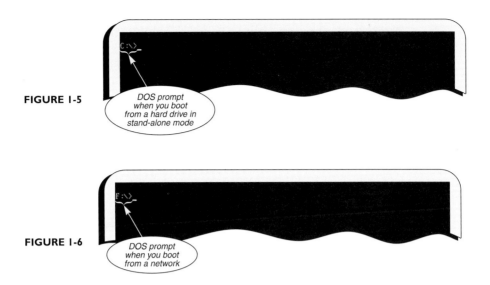

FIGURE 1-5

DOS prompt
when you boot
from a hard drive in
stand-alone mode

FIGURE 1-6

DOS prompt
when you boot
from a network

The Default Drive

The drive letter in the DOS prompt is also called the default drive. The **default drive** is the drive that DOS assumes contains programs and data to be used. Another term for the default drive is the **current drive**, because it is the drive in which DOS *currently* looks for files. At times you will need to change the default drive assignment. If you change the default drive assignment to a diskette drive, you must first place a disk in the drive. Follow these steps to change the default drive assignment from C to A.

TO CHANGE THE DEFAULT DRIVE ASSIGNMENT

STEP 1:   Insert the Student Diskette that accompanies this book into drive A.

A disk must be inserted into drive A before you change the default drive assignment.

STEP 2:   Type a : **and press the ENTER key.**

The default drive in the DOS prompt is now drive A (Figure 1-7). You could have entered the a in the a: in either uppercase or lowercase.

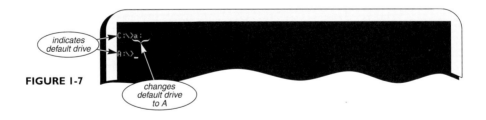

indicates
default drive

FIGURE 1-7

changes
default drive
to A

▼   ENTERING DOS COMMANDS

Now that you have booted the computer, you can enter DOS commands. **Commands** are instructions you type to tell DOS what you want to do. DOS includes a variety of commands to assist you in using the computer. Some commands might be status, or informative, commands because they instruct DOS to give you information. Other commands direct DOS to perform actions for you. You can enter commands, drive names, and other entries to DOS, in any combination of uppercase and lowercase letters. Following DOS commands, you press the ENTER key. When you press the ENTER key, DOS scans the most recently entered line for a valid command and then executes the command if it is found to be valid. If the command is not valid, you will receive a message telling you it is a bad command.

Displaying the Current DOS Version

As discussed earlier, many versions and releases of DOS exist today. To verify the version and release number loaded on your system, use the **ver command**.

TO DISPLAY THE LOADED DOS VERSION

STEP 1: Type ver **and press the ENTER key.**

DOS displays the version and release currently loaded into memory (Figure 1-8).

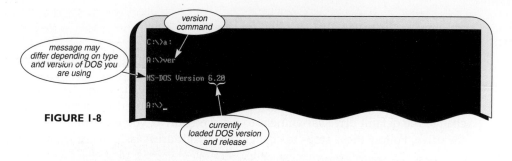

FIGURE 1-8

Clearing the Screen

Frequently, as you issue several commands or perform lengthy processes, the screen becomes cluttered. To clear the screen and place the DOS prompt on the first line of the screen, you use the **cls command**.

TO CLEAR THE SCREEN

STEP 1: Type cls **(Figure 1-9a) and press the ENTER key.**

The screen clears and the DOS prompt displays on the first line of the screen (Figure 1-9b).

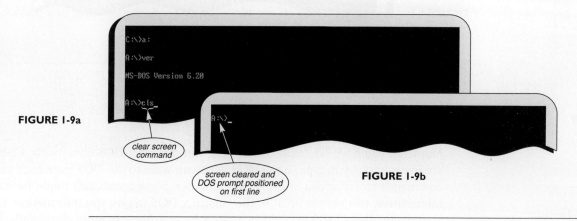

FIGURE 1-9a

FIGURE 1-9b

Whenever your screen becomes cluttered, you can enter the CLS command. As you proceed through this and the next project, you will notice we clear the screen frequently between DOS commands. Because the CLS command is used only to enhance readability, these two projects do not explicitly tell you to clear the screen.

Correcting DOS Commands

Even if you are an expert typist, you will sometimes make mistakes when you enter DOS commands. For this reason, DOS provides several keys that allow you to correct mistakes.

If you realize you have made a mistake and have *not yet* pressed the ENTER key, you can press the **BACKSPACE** key to erase the character(s) to the left of the cursor. For example, if you type vet to display the DOS version, you can press the BACK-SPACE key once and then type the letter r to complete the ver command. Then, press the ENTER key to display the DOS version.

If you type xls to clear the screen and have *not* yet pressed the ENTER key, you could press the BACKSPACE key three times to erase the three letters or you can press the ESC key and retype the entire command. When you press the **ESC key**, a backslash character (\) displays at the end of the typed line, and the cursor advances to the next line. You are now at the beginning of the next line and can begin over again (Figure 1-10). (If the backslash character does not display on your screen, your instructor will explain that the difference(s) is due to a program called doskey.)

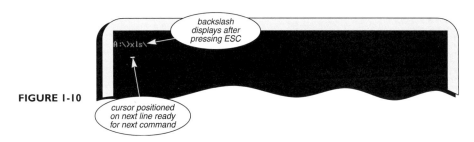

FIGURE 1-10

If you have already pressed the ENTER key after typing an erroneous command, DOS displays the error message, Bad command or file name, on the screen with a new DOS prompt below the error message. When this occurs, you either retype the entire command correctly and press the ENTER key, or press the **F3** function key to redisplay the command you just entered and modify it. The F3 key works well if the error you made occurred at the end of the command. For example, if you entered vet, you can press F3 to redisplay the entry vet (Figure 1-11), press the BACKSPACE key once to erase the letter t, type the letter r to correctly conclude the ver command, and press the ENTER key to display the DOS version.

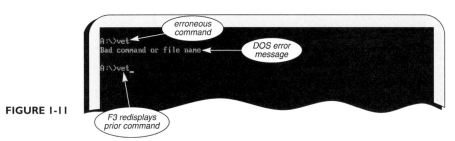

FIGURE 1-11

· ·

▼   **FORMATTING A DISKETTE**

Most diskettes you buy can be used immediately; that is, they have already been formatted. Because you can also buy *unformatted* diskettes, you need to know how to format a disk. **Formatting** is the process of preparing a disk so it can store data. DOS formats a disk by dividing it into **cylinders**, which are narrow recording bands forming a full circle around the disk, and **sectors**, which are sections of a cylinder.

Be careful with the disks you format because *formatting erases any existing files on the disk*. This is true for hard disks as well as diskettes. You must be extremely careful, therefore, with the disk drives you choose when you use the format command.

Diskettes are available in three sizes: 2 inch, 3 1/2 inch, and 5 1/4 inch. Diskettes are classified as double density, high density, and very high density. Very high density diskettes store more data than high-density diskettes; high-density diskettes store more data than double-density diskettes. Table 1-2 shows a comparison of these disks. To store data on a very high density diskette, you need a very high density drive on your PC. Likewise, you need a high density drive to store data on a high-density diskette.

TABLE 1-2

Disk Size	Density	Capacity in Bytes	Number of Double-Spaced Typewritten 8 1/2 by 11 Inch Pages
5 1/4"	Double	360K	125
5 1/4"	High	1.2M	375
3 1/2"	Double	720K	250
3 1/2"	High	1.44M	500
3 1/2"	Very High	2.88M	1000
2"	Double	360K	125

The read/write head in the disk unit comes into magnetic contact with the recording surface of all three disk sizes. With the 5 1/4-inch diskette, the read/write heads make contact through the slot hole in the diskette's protective jacket (Figure 1-12a). The 2- and 3 1/2-inch diskettes each have a shutter that automatically opens and exposes the recording surface when the diskette is placed in the disk drive (Figure 1-12b). Once inside the disk drive, the diskette spins inside its protective jacket.

5 1/4" DISKETTE

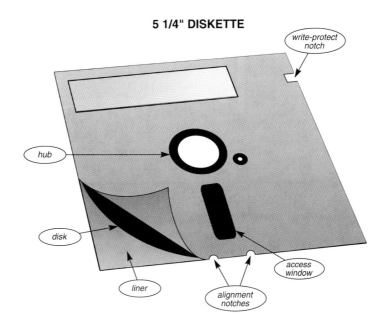

FIGURE 1-12a

3 1/2" DISKETTE

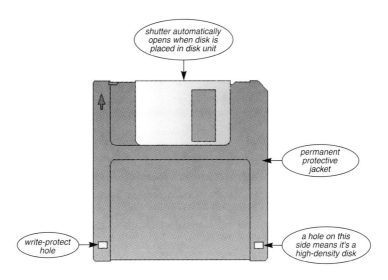

FIGURE 1-12b

Because disks vary by size and recording density, your **format command** may differ slightly from this book's description (see Table 1-3 on page DOS14). If it does, your instructor will inform you of necessary changes. Follow these steps to format a disk that is the same density as the drive in which you place it.

TO FORMAT A DISKETTE

STEP 1: **Remove the Student Diskette from drive A.**

STEP 2: **Type** `format a:`

DOS displays the format command followed by the drive to be formatted (Figure 1-13 on the next page). The disk you place in the A drive, indicated by the a:, will be formatted. To format a disk in a different drive, simply change the drive name before the colon.

FIGURE I-13

STEP 3: **Press the ENTER key.**

*DOS loads the format program to memory, begins to execute the format program, and displays the prompt, Insert new diskette for drive A: and press ENTER when ready... (Figure 1-14). A **prompt** is a message providing you with information or instructions regarding an entry you must make or an action you must take.*

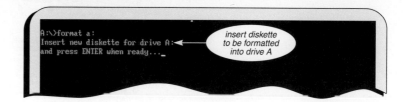

FIGURE I-14

STEP 4: **Insert the diskette you want to format into drive A. (Remember, when you format a diskette, any existing files are erased!)**

STEP 5: **Press the ENTER key.**

*DOS displays the disk capacity on the screen and the progress of the format process in terms of the percentage completed. When formatting is 100 percent complete (Figure 1-15), DOS asks you to enter a volume label with the prompt, Volume label (11 characters, ENTER for none)? You respond to this prompt by typing a volume label and pressing ENTER, or omitting the volume label by simply pressing ENTER. A **volume label** is an optional identifying name you give to a disk to help you distinguish one disk from another. A volume label consists of one to eleven characters. Although you can choose to not enter a volume label, it is recommended you use your last name as the volume label to identify your disk.*

FIGURE I-15

STEP 6: **(You should enter your last name as the volume label). Type the volume label (vermaat in the example), and press the ENTER key.**

DOS reports the total disk storage space; the number of bytes available for storage, which is the number of characters that may be saved; the size of each allocation unit, which equals one sector on a disk; the number of allocation units; and the assigned volume serial number (Figure 1-16). Beneath these informative messages, DOS asks you if you want to format another disk. You respond to this prompt by typing the letter Y for Yes or N for No.

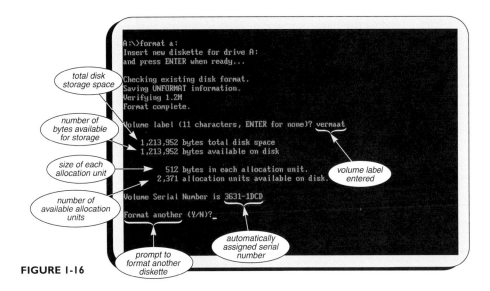

total disk
storage space

number of
bytes available
for storage

size of each
allocation unit

number of
available allocation
units

volume label
entered

automatically
assigned serial
number

prompt to
format another
diskette

FIGURE 1-16

STEP 7:   Type the letter n for No and press the ENTER key.

STEP 8:   Remove the disk from drive A. With a felt-tipped pen, write your first and last names and the words, Data Disk, on the external disk label supplied with the disk. Then, apply the disk label firmly on the disk. Reinsert the data disk into drive A.

The external label is used to identify one disk from another (Figure 1-17). The volume label you entered in Step 6 is an internal label and does not replace the need for an external label.

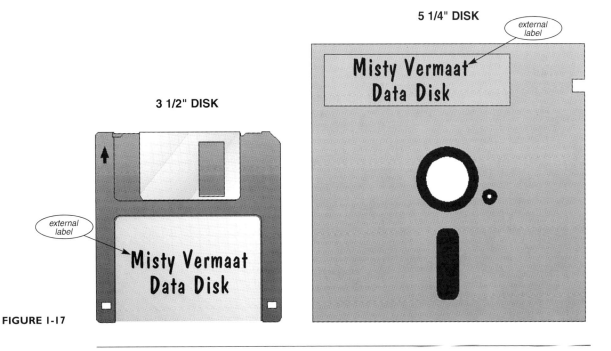

5 1/4" DISK

external
label

Misty Vermaat
Data Disk

3 1/2" DISK

external
label

Misty Vermaat
Data Disk

FIGURE 1-17

The format command shown in Step 2 on page DOS11 assumes the diskette and the drive are the same recording density. If you want to format a double-density diskette in a high-density drive, your method of formatting will differ slightly from this description. That is, you need to modify the parameters of the format command as shown in Table 1-3 on the next page. A **parameter** is the character or set of characters that follow the basic command. That is, format is the command and a: is the parameter. If, for example, you have a 5 1/4 inch double-density disk in a high-density drive, you need to enter format a: /f:360 as the command. Check with your instructor to see what, if any changes you need to make to Step 2 on page DOS11.

TABLE 1-3

Disk Size	Density	Capacity in Bytes	Format Command
5 1/4"	Double	360K	format a: /f:360
5 1/4"	High	1.2M	format a: /f:1.2
3 1/2"	Double	720K	format a: /f:720
3 1/2"	High	1.44M	format a: /f:1.44
3 1/2"	Very High	2.88M	format a: /f:2.88
2"	Double	360K	format a: /f:360

▼ SETTING UP YOUR DATA DISK

The Student Diskette that accompanies this book has several files you need for the remaining examples in this and the next project. A program has been written to copy the necessary files from the Student Diskette to your data disk. The program is on the Student Diskette that accompanies this book. Follow these steps to set up your data disk.

TO SET UP YOUR DATA DISK

STEP 1: **Remove your data disk from drive A. Insert the Student Diskette that accompanies this book into drive A. (Your system configuration may require you to insert the Student Diskette into drive B.)**

STEP 2: **Type** copydata **and press the ENTER key.**

STEP 3: **Follow the instructions given by the copydata program.**

STEP 4: **If it is not already in drive A, insert your data disk into drive A.**

▼ DISPLAYING FILENAMES ON A DISK

A disk is essentially an electronic filing cabinet. Just like you manage file folders in a filing cabinet, one of the functions of DOS is to store files containing programs and data on disks. To manage that file storage, DOS maintains a **directory**, or listing, of all of the files stored on a disk. To display the directory of a disk, you use the **dir command.**

TO DISPLAY FILENAMES ON A DISK

STEP 1: **Type** dir **and press the ENTER key.**

The directory, or listing, of files on the data disk in drive A displays on the screen (Figure 1-18). The directory listing itself consists of the filenames and extensions of the files on the disk, the number of bytes consumed by each file on the disk, the date and time the file was created or most recently modified. The message at the end of the directory listing indicates the number of files on the disk (in Figure 1-18 there are 11 files on the disk) and the remaining space available on the disk (1,173,504 unused bytes remain on the disk in Figure 1-18, but your number may differ if your data disk is a different size or has a different recording density). At the end of the directory listing, the DOS prompt redisplays on the screen, indicating that DOS is ready for your next command.

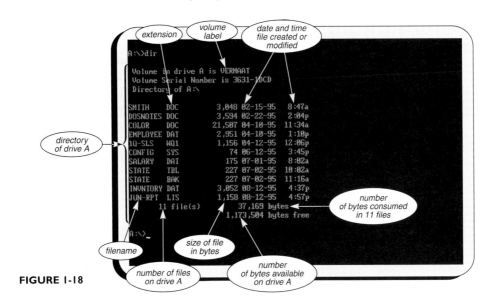

FIGURE 1-18

Filenames

In a filing cabinet, you place labels on the file folders to identify the contents of the folder. On a disk, a **filename** is a name that identifies the contents of the electronic file. Two basic types of files can appear on a disk: data files and program files. A **data file** is a collection of data created by an application program and used by the program. For example, the data can be numbers used to show sales revenue in a spreadsheet; names and addresses in a database file; or a word processing memo announcing the arrival of a new employee. A **program file** contains instructions that the computer follows to perform tasks. For example, a word processing software package contains a program(s) that enables you to create, modify, and print documents.

A filename consists of one to eight characters, which may include letters (A-Z), digits (0-9), or these special characters: underscore (_), caret (^), dollar sign ($), tilde (~), exclamation point (!), number sign (#), percent sign (%), ampersand (&), hyphen (-), braces ({ }), parentheses ( ), at sign (@), apostrophe ('), or the grave accent (').

Because you only have eight characters to represent the name of a file, you should create filenames that help to remind you what data is stored in the file. If your file contains employee data, for example, the filename EMPLOYEE is more meaningful than the filename FILE1, even though DOS will accept either filename.

Extensions

A filename can also have an optional extension, which identifies a file more specifically or describes its purpose. An **extension** consists of one to three characters and is separated from the filename by a period. The same characters permitted for a filename are permitted for an extension. Many application programs automatically assign special extensions to the files they create. For example, one version of Lotus automatically adds the extension WQ3. In this way, whenever you see the filename WQ3, you can identify the file as a Lotus file. If your application does not add an extension to a file, you may add an extension. If you create a word processing document file containing a letter to John Smith, for example, you could use the filename SMITH and the extension DOC to identify the file as a document file. The entire filename would be SMITH.DOC.

File Specifications

DOS identifies a file on a disk through a file specification. A **file specification** informs DOS where the file is located and gives its exact name. A DOS file specification can have up to four components: a drive, a path, a filename, and an extension. You cannot have any spaces in a file specification. Table 1-4 describes the contents of each of the four components in a DOS file specification.

TABLE 1-4

Name	Description
Drive	A drive consists of the one-letter drive name followed by a colon. The drive name specifies the drive containing the file you are requesting. For example, A. represents disk drive A. If you omit the drive, DOS assumes the default, or current, drive.
Path	A path is an optional reference to a subdirectory of files on the specified disk. A backslash (\) separates the drive from the path. (Paths are discussed in Project 2.)
Filename	A filename consists of one to eight characters.
Extension	An extension, if present, consists of one to three characters. A period separates a filename from an extension.

If you have a filename SMITH with an extension of DOC on the disk in drive A, the complete file specification would be A:SMITH.DOC. To see if this file exists on a disk, you would use the dir command as shown in the following steps. Remember, you do not put any spaces in the file specification.

TO USE A FILE SPECIFICATION IN THE DIR COMMAND

STEP 1:   **Type** `dir a:smith.doc` **and press the ENTER key.**

The directory entry for the file SMITH.DOC displays on the screen (Figure 1-19).

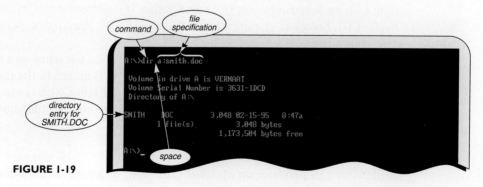

FIGURE 1-19

Internal Versus External Commands

When you boot a computer, several commands are placed into memory with DOS. These commands, called **internal commands**, may be entered at the DOS prompt at any time. Examples of internal commands used in this project are ver, cls, dir, copy, del, and rename.

An **external command** is one stored on the DOS disk as a program file. External commands must be read from the DOS disk into memory before they can be executed. For a hard disk or LAN configuration, the default drive contains these external commands, so no special steps are needed to use an external command. The format command is an example of an external command.

All DOS external commands have the special extensions COM, EXE, or BAT. To use external commands, simply type the filename (the extension is not required) with its required parameters and press the ENTER key.

▼ COPYING A FILE

Once you have formatted a disk, you can use it to store data or program files. When you store files on a disk, you may want to make duplicates of them. Using the **copy command**, you can copy a file to the same disk or to a different disk. It is *always* a good idea to copy the original files supplied with software you purchase to another disk, called a **working disk**, or **working copy**. Then, use the working copy for every-day work to protect the original disk from possible damage. A similar use of the copy command is to make a **backup copy** of a disk to guard against accidental loss of data. One frequently used technique is to make a backup copy of a file whenever you revise an existing file. For example, you might want to keep a disk backup copy of your personal financial statement in your safe-deposit box. Some application programs create a backup file automatically, using the extension BAK to indicate a backup file.

Copying a File from One Disk to Another Using the Same Name

Copying a file can be accomplished from any drive and to any drive. Follow these steps to copy the file DOSNOTES.DOC from drive A to drive C.

TO COPY A FILE FROM ONE DISK TO ANOTHER USING THE SAME NAME

STEP 1:   **Type** copy dosnotes.doc c: **and press the ENTER key. (If DOS asks Overwrite C:DOSNOTES.DOC (Yes/No/All)?, type the letter** y **and press the ENTER key.)**

DOS displays the message, **1 file(s) copied**, *indicating it made a duplicate of DOSNOTES.DOC on drive C (Figure 1-20 on the next page). Notice that after typing the command* copy, *you leave a space, then state the file specification of the file to be copied. In DOS terminology, this file is called the* **source file**. *Because you omitted the drive name from the source file, DOS looks on drive A, the default drive, for a source file with a filename of DOSNOTES and an extension of DOC. Following the source file, you leave a space and then type the* **target file**, *which is the file specification of the file once it is copied. The drive specifier c: in the target specification indicates that the file is to be copied to the hard drive. Because you omitted the filename and extension from the target specification, the target file will have the same filename and extension as the source file.*

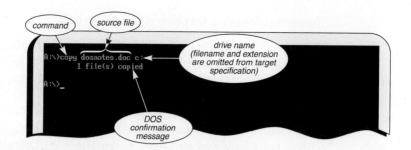

FIGURE 1-20

DOSNOTES.DOC is now on the disk in drive A and on drive C. To verify that DOSNOTES.DOC is on drive C, follow these steps.

TO VERIFY A FILE IS ON A DISK

STEP 1: **Type** `dir c:dosnotes.doc` **and press the ENTER key.**

The directory entry for the file DOSNOTES.DOC displays on the screen (Figure 1-21).

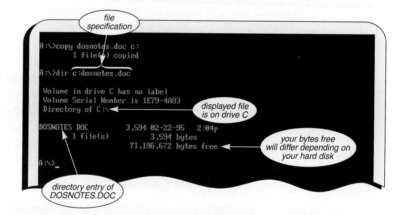

FIGURE 1-21

Copying a File from One Disk to Another Using a Different Name

When you copy a file from one disk to another, you can assign the target file a different name than the source file. For example, you might want to make a backup copy of the file DOSNOTES.DOC and then make draft changes to the original file. Follow these steps to copy the file DOSNOTES.DOC from drive C to drive A with the name DOSNOTES.BAK.

TO COPY A FILE FROM ONE DISK TO ANOTHER USING A DIFFERENT NAME AND VERIFY THE RESULTS

STEP 1: **Type** `copy c:dosnotes.doc a:dosnotes.bak` **and press the ENTER key.**

DOS copies the file DOSNOTES.DOC from drive C to drive A, giving it the name DOSNOTES.BAK on drive A. Notice the target filename and extension must be supplied when you want the target file to have a different name than the source.

STEP 2: **Type** `dir dosnotes.bak` **and press the ENTER key.**

The directory entry for the file DOSNOTES.BAK displays on the screen (Figure 1-22). Because you omitted the drive name from the file specification, DOS scans drive A, the default drive, for DOSNOTES.BAK.

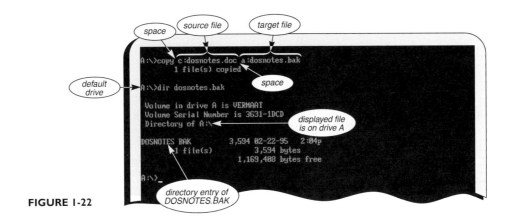

FIGURE 1-22

You have now verified that DOSNOTES.BAK is on drive A. It is an exact copy of DOSNOTES.DOC.

Copying a File to the Same Disk

In order to make a backup copy of a file on the same disk as the original file, the backup copy *must* have a different name than the source file. That is, you could not have a source file DOSNOTES.DOC and a target file DOSNOTES.DOC both on drive A. You could, however, have a source file DOSNOTES.DOC and a target file DOSFILE.TXT as illustrated in the following steps.

TO COPY A FILE TO THE SAME DISK AND VERIFY THE RESULTS

STEP 1: **Type** `copy dosnotes.doc dosfile.txt` **and press the ENTER key.**

DOS makes a duplicate of the file DOSNOTES.DOC on drive A, with the name DOSFILE.TXT. Recall that when you omit a drive from the file specification, DOS assumes the default drive. Thus, DOSFILE.TXT is being copied to drive A, the same drive as DOSNOTES.DOC.

STEP 2: **Type** `dir dosfile.txt` **and press the ENTER key.**

DOS displays the target file's directory entry (Figure 1-23).

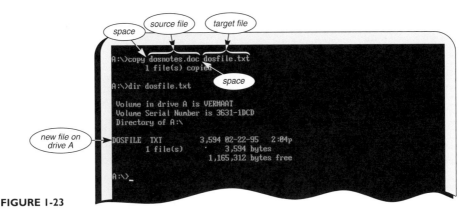

FIGURE 1-23

The file DOSNOTES.DOC now exists twice on the disk in drive A, once with the filename DOSNOTES.DOC and again under the name DOSFILE.TXT.

▼ **CHANGING THE NAME OF A FILE**

When you want to change the name of a file on a disk, you use the **rename command**. For example, some software packages require specific file extensions, and you might need to change one of your file's extensions to meet the package's requirements before you can use it with that software package. Follow the steps below to change the name DOSFILE.TXT to DOSFILE.DOC on drive A.

TO RENAME A FILE AND VERIFY THE RESULTS

STEP 1: **Type** `rename dosfile.txt dosfile.doc` **and press the ENTER key.**

DOS renames the file DOSFILE.TXT as DOSFILE.DOC. Notice DOS does not display a message confirming a successful renaming of the file. When using the rename command, you may abbreviate it with the characters ren.

STEP 2: **Type** `dir dosfile.doc` **and press the ENTER key.**

DOS displays the renamed file's directory entry (Figure 1-24).

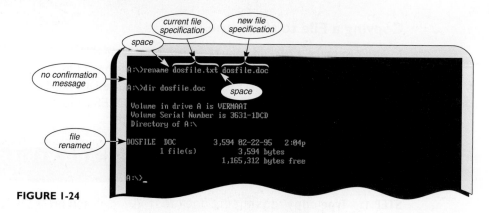

FIGURE I-24

You must be careful not to place a drive name on the file specification for the file's new name. Thus, you cannot rename a file and place the renamed file on a different drive. If you put a drive name on the new name, DOS displays the error message, `Invalid parameter`. If you attempt to change a file's name to a name already used by a file on the disk, DOS displays the error message, Duplicate file name or file not found, and does not change the name because each file on a disk must have a unique name.

▼ **REMOVING A FILE FROM A DISK**

Because a disk has a limited amount of space for storing files, you should periodically remove unneeded files from your disks to make room for new files. You use the **del command** or **erase command** to remove a file from a disk. Take care when using these commands because you do not want to mistakenly remove a file you mean to keep.

Follow these steps to remove the file DOSFILE.DOC from the disk in drive A.

TO DELETE A FILE AND VERIFY THE RESULTS

STEP 1:   Type `dir` **and press the ENTER key.**

DOS displays the list of files on the default drive (Figure 1-25).

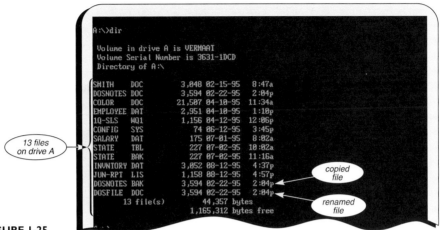

FIGURE 1-25

STEP 2:   Type `del dosfile.doc` **and press the ENTER key.**

DOS deletes the file DOSFILE.DOC from the disk in drive A. Notice DOS does not display a message confirming a successful deletion of the file.

STEP 3:   Type `dir` **and press the ENTER key.**

DOS displays the list of files on the default drive (Figure 1-26). Notice DOSFILE.DOC has been removed from the directory.

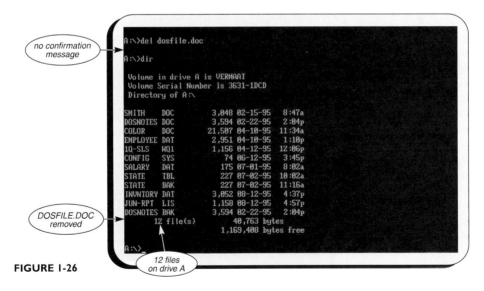

FIGURE 1-26

The file DOSFILE.DOC has been deleted. When you use the del command, DOS does not actually erase the file from the disk. Rather, it *flags* the file as deleted, which allows DOS to reuse the area of the disk occupied by the deleted file. Thus, you can recover, or *bring back,* a deleted file as long as DOS has not reused its space. To successfully recover a deleted file, you should use the **undelete command** as soon as you discover the file has been accidentally deleted. Follow the steps on the next page to recover the file DOSFILE.DOC from the disk in drive A.

TO RECOVER A DELETED FILE AND VERIFY THE RESULTS

STEP 1: **Type** `undelete` **and press the ENTER key.**

DOS scans the default disk drive for files that may be recovered and displays the directory entry of the file that may be recovered followed by the prompt, Undelete (Y/N)? (Figure 1-27). Notice the first letter of the filename has been replaced with a question mark (?). (Depending on the type of DOS you have, your screen may display slightly different messages for the undelete command.)

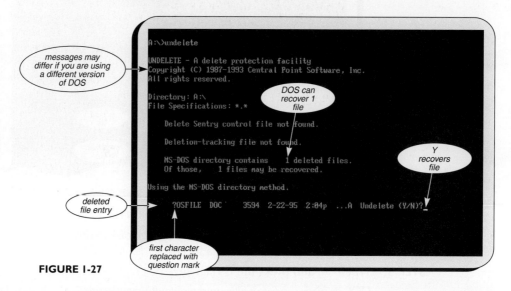

FIGURE I-27

STEP 2: **Type the letter** y.

DOS requests you to type the first character of the filename (Figure 1-28). Because the first character of the filename is replaced with a question mark when you use the delete command to erase a file, you need to supply a character for DOS to fill in as the first character of the filename.

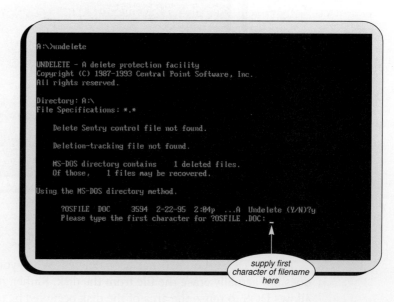

FIGURE I-28

STEP 3: **Type the letter** d.

DOS recovers the file DOSFILE.DOC and displays the message, File successfully undeleted.

STEP 4: Type dir **and press the ENTER key.**

DOS displays the list of files on the default drive (Figure 1-29). Notice DOSFILE.DOC has been recovered.

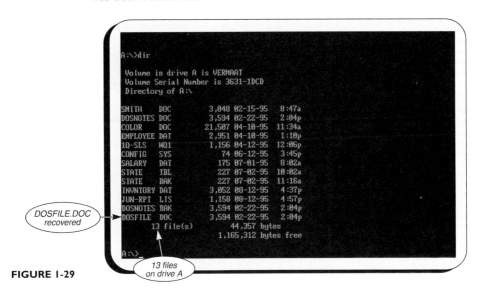

FIGURE 1-29

▼ OBTAINING HELP FOR DOS COMMANDS

Often, you are unsure of the purpose of a DOS command or how to correctly enter it. To assist you, DOS provides **online help** for all DOS commands. You can obtain help on a specific command from the DOS prompt. Follow these steps to obtain online help for the rename command.

TO OBTAIN HELP FOR THE RENAME COMMAND

STEP 1: Type ren **and press the SPACEBAR once. Type** /? **and press the ENTER key.**

DOS displays online help for the rename command (Figure 1-30).

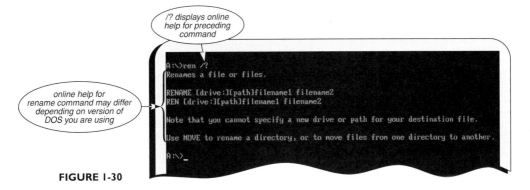

FIGURE 1-30

If you are unsure of which DOS command to use, you need to see a list of available commands by invoking the **Help window**, which displays all valid DOS commands.

TO INVOKE THE HELP WINDOW

STEP 1: Type help **(Figure 1-31).**

FIGURE 1-31

STEP 2: **Press the ENTER key.**

The Help window displays on the screen (Figure 1-32). All DOS commands display in the Help window. To obtain help on a particular command, use the arrow keys and/or TAB key to move the cursor to the command and then press the ENTER key. (Earlier versions of DOS have a different help system or no help at all.)

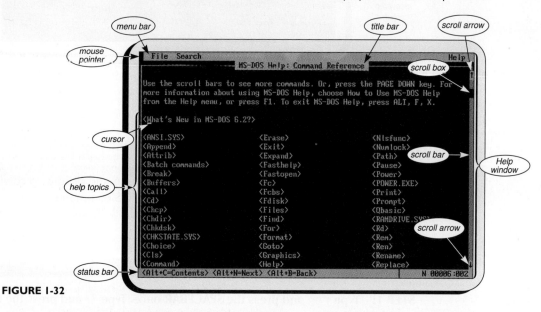

FIGURE 1-32

Help Window

A **window** is a rectangular portion of the screen used to display information. The Help window consists of a menu bar, title bar, scroll bar, status bar, and mouse pointer.

Menu Bar The first line at the top of the window is the menu bar. The **menu bar** lists the names of the available menus: File, Search, and Help. When you select a menu name from the menu bar, a list of commands displays.

Title Bar Just below the menu bar is the **title bar**, which displays the name of the current window. Initially, the title bar displays MS-DOS Help: Command Reference. (Your title bar may differ depending on the type of DOS you are using.)

Scroll Bar   Located along the right edge of the Help window, you use the **scroll bar** with a mouse to bring a portion of a document into view when the complete help discussion will not fit in the window. **Scroll arrows**, represented by upward and downward pointing arrows, are located at the top and bottom of the scroll bar. The **scroll box** is a solid, nonblinking box on the scroll bar, which moves as you move the cursor.

Status Bar   The line at the very bottom of the window is the **status bar**, which displays the special key combinations you use to move around the Help window and other informative messages.

Mouse Pointer   The **mouse pointer** is a character-sized, nonblinking rectangle that appears *only* if you have a mouse installed on your system.

Moving Around the Help Window

When you first start online help, the cursor is blinking below the first jump. A **jump** is a topic surrounded by angle brackets (< >). To display help information on a topic, you choose a jump. You can choose a jump with either the keyboard or the mouse.

Using the Keyboard   One method of moving the cursor from topic to topic is to use the following keys: TAB, HOME, END, PAGE UP, PAGE DOWN, and the four directional arrow keys. Table 1-5 illustrates how each of these keys moves the cursor in the Help window.

TABLE 1-5

Key	Action
TAB	Moves the cursor right to the next jump
SHIFT+TAB	Moves the cursor left to the previous jump
DOWN ARROW	Moves the cursor down one jump
UP ARROW	Moves the cursor up one jump
letter	Moves the cursor to the next jump beginning with the entered letter
SHIFT+letter	Moves the cursor to the previous jump beginning with the entered letter
PAGE DOWN	Moves the cursor down one screen
PAGE UP	Moves the cursor up one screen
HOME	Moves the cursor to the beginning of a line
END	Moves the cursor to the end of a line

Practice moving the cursor with the keyboard. Press the TAB key twice to move the cursor to the Erase topic. Next, type the letter u to move the cursor to the Undelete topic. Press the HOME key to move the cursor to the Dosshell topic, the first topic in the same line. Then, type the letter a to return the cursor to the DBLSPACE.SYS topic. Now, press the PAGE DOWN key to move the cursor down one screenful to the topic, and then press the PAGE UP key to return the cursor to the ANSI.SYS topic.

To display help on a topic, you first move the cursor to the topic and then press the ENTER key as shown in the steps on the next page.

TO DISPLAY HELP ON A TOPIC WITH THE KEYBOARD

STEP 1: **Press the TAB key twice.**

DOS positions the cursor in the Erase topic (Figure 1-33).

FIGURE 1-33

STEP 2: **Press the ENTER key.**

DOS displays help on the Erase command (Figure 1-34).

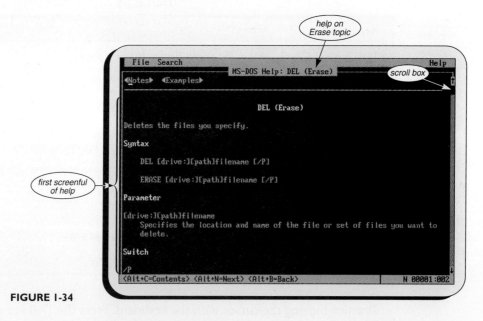

FIGURE 1-34

STEP 3: **Press the PAGE DOWN key.**

DOS displays the second screen of help on the Erase command (Figure 1-35).

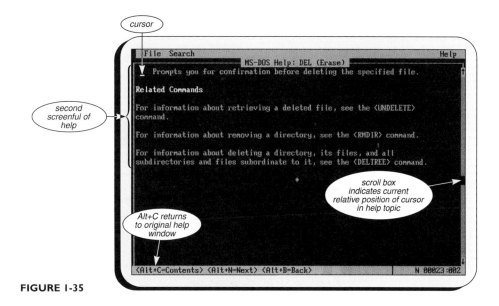

cursor

second
screenful of
help

scroll box
indicates current
relative position of cursor
in help topic

Alt+C returns
to original help
window

FIGURE 1-35

STEP 4: Press ALT+C; that is, while holding down the ALT key, press the letter C.

DOS returns you to the Command Reference Help window (see Figure 1-33 on the previous page).

Using a Mouse   If you do not have a mouse installed on your computer, you can move the cursor only by using the keyboard. When you have a mouse connected to your computer and the mouse driver software is loaded, you can use either the keyboard or the mouse to position the cursor on a help topic.

The mouse pointer is usually displayed on the screen as a highlighted rectangle. As you move the mouse on a flat surface, the mouse pointer moves on the screen. You can perform four basic operations with a mouse: point, click, double-click, and drag. Table 1-6 discusses each of these operations.

TABLE 1-6

Mouse Term	Action
Point	Move the mouse until the mouse pointer is in the desired location
Click	Press the left mouse button once and release it
Double-click	Press and release the left mouse button twice in rapid succession
Drag	Hold down the left mouse button; move the mouse pointer to the desired location; release the left mouse button

As described in Table 1-6, *point and click* means move the mouse pointer to a specified location and press the left mouse button.

TO DISPLAY HELP ON A TOPIC WITH THE MOUSE

STEP 1:   **Point to the Erase topic.**

The mouse pointer is positioned in the Erase topic (Figure 1-36).

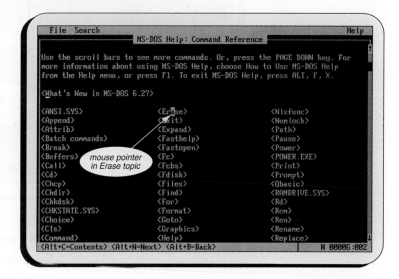

FIGURE 1-36

STEP 2:   **Click the left mouse button; that is, press the left mouse button once and release it.**

DOS displays help on the Erase command.

STEP 3:   **Point to the scroll bar beneath the scroll box (Figure 1-37).**

FIGURE 1-37

STEP 4:   **Click the left mouse button.**

DOS displays the second screenful of help on the Erase command (Figure 1-38). The scroll box moves downward on the scroll bar to indicate the current relative location of the cursor in the help topic.

FIGURE 1-38

STEP 5: Click the `Alt+C=Contents` **topic on the status bar; that is, point to the Alt+C and click the left mouse button.**

DOS returns you to the Command Reference Help window (see Figure 1-36 on the previous page).

The word click is often used when referring to the point and click operation. That is, point to the Erase topic and click is often stated simply as click the Erase topic.

The scroll bar is used with the mouse to scroll through a series of screens. You can drag the scroll box upward or downward to scroll up or down through the screens. To move up or down one screenful at a time, you can click anywhere above or below the scroll box on the scroll bar. To move the screen up or down one line at a time in the window, you can click the scroll arrow at the top or bottom of the scroll bar.

TO PRINT INFORMATION ON A HELP TOPIC

STEP 1: Press the TAB key twice and then press the ENTER key.

DOS displays help on the Erase command.

STEP 2: Press the ALT key.

*The word File is highlighted on the menu bar, which indicates the menu bar is activated (Figure 1-39 on the next page). The menu bar has three menu names: File, Search, and Help. To **pull-down** the commands in these menus, you type the highlighted letter in the menu name. That is, to pull-down the File menu, you type the letter f.*

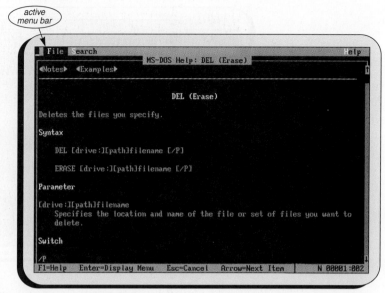

FIGURE I-39

STEP 3: **Type the letter** f.

The commands in the File menu display (Figure 1-40). Two commands are available in the File menu: Print and Exit. To execute a command, you type the highlighted letter in the command. That is, to print information displayed in the Help window, you type the letter p; to exit from the Help window, you type the letter x.

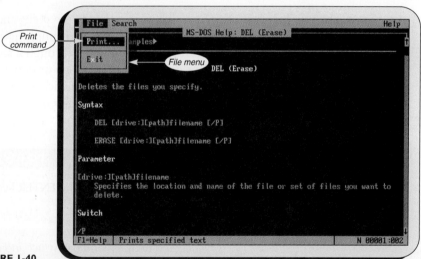

FIGURE I-40

STEP 4: **Type the letter** p.

*DOS displays the Print dialog box (Figure 1-41). A **dialog box** is a window requesting additional information from you. DOS asks if you want to send the help information to the printer or to a file. In the Print dialog box, the dot in parentheses (•) to the left of Printer on LPT1 is called a **bullet**. The bullet indicates the printer is selected. Thus, you press the ENTER key to send the help information to the printer.*

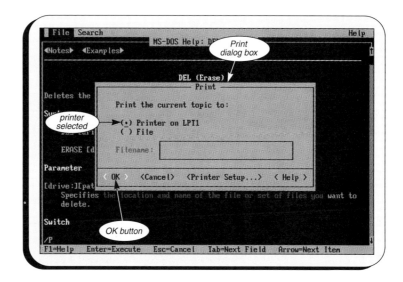

FIGURE 1-41

STEP 5:   Press the ENTER key. Remove the printout from the printer.

DOS prints the help information for the Erase command (Figure 1-42).

```
Notes►   Examples►
_____

                         DEL (Erase)
Deletes the files you specify.

Syntax

    DEL [drive:][path]filename [/P]

    ERASE [drive:][path]filename [/P]

Parameter

[drive:][path]filename
    Specifies the location and name of the file or set of files you want to
    delete.

Switch

/P
    Prompts you for confirmation before deleting the specified file.

Related Commands

For information about retrieving a deleted file, see the <UNDELETE>
command.

For information about removing a directory, see the <RMDIR> command.

For information about deleting a directory, its files, and all
subdirectories and files subordinate to it, see the <DELTREE> command.
```

FIGURE 1-42

STEP 6:   Press ALT+C.

DOS returns you to the Command Reference Help window (see Figure 1-36 on page DOS28).

Mouse Users: *Choose the Erase topic by clicking it. Click the File menu and choose the Print command by clicking it. Click the OK button in the Print dialog box. Click Alt+C= Contents on the status bar to return to the Command Reference Help window.*

TO EXIT THE HELP WINDOW

STEP 1:   **Press the ALT key to activate the menu bar. Type the letter** f.

DOS pulls down the File menu (Figure 1-43).

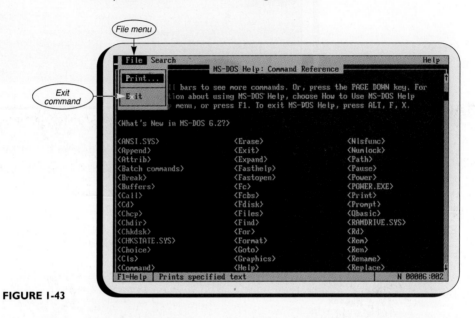

FIGURE 1-43

STEP 2:   **Type the letter** x.

The Help window disappears from the screen and the DOS prompt displays.

 Mouse Users: *Click the File menu and choose the Exit command by clicking it.*

....

▼   **PROJECT SUMMARY**

Project 1 illustrates how to boot DOS, format diskettes, name and display files, and access online help for DOS commands. In Project 1, you learned how to use these DOS commands to work with your files: ver, cls, copy, rename, delete, and undelete. All the activities you learned in this project are summarized in the Quick Reference.

▼   **KEY TERMS**

BACKSPACE *(DOS9)*
backup copy *(DOS17)*
booting *(DOS6)*
bullet *(DOS30)*
cls command *(DOS8)*
cold boot *(DOS6)*
cold start *(DOS6)*
commands *(DOS7)*
copy command *(DOS17)*
current drive *(DOS7)*
cylinders *(DOS10)*
data file *(DOS15)*
default drive *(DOS7)*
del command *(DOS20)*
dialog box *(DOS30)*
dir command *(DOS14)*
directory *(DOS14)*
Disk Operating System *(DOS3)*
DOS *(DOS3)*
DOS prompt *(DOS6)*
drive name *(DOS4)*
erase command *(DOS20)*
ESC key *(DOS9)*
extension *(DOS15)*

external command *(DOS17)*
F3 *(DOS9)*
file specification *(DOS16)*
filename *(DOS15)*
format command *(DOS11)*
formatting *(DOS10)*
help *(DOS23)*
Help window *(DOS23)*
installed *(DOS6)*
internal command *(DOS17)*
jump *(DOS25)*
LAN *(DOS5)*
local area network *(DOS5)*
menu bar *(DOS24)*
mouse pointer *(DOS25)*
MS-DOS *(DOS3)*
online help *(DOS23)*
operating system *(DOS2)*
parameter *(DOS13)*
PC-DOS *(DOS3)*
program file *(DOS15)*
prompt *(DOS12)*
pull-down menu *(DOS29)*
release number *(DOS3)*

rename command *(DOS20)*
reset *(DOS6)*
scroll arrows *(DOS25)*
scroll bar *(DOS25)*
scroll box *(DOS25)*
sector *(DOS10)*
server *(DOS5)*
source file *(DOS17)*
stand-alone mode *(DOS6)*
status bar *(DOS25)*
target file *(DOS17)*
title bar *(DOS24)*
undelete command *(DOS21)*
upward compatibility *(DOS4)*
ver command *(DOS8)*
version number *(DOS3)*
volume label *(DOS12)*
warm boot *(DOS6)*
warm start *(DOS6)*
window *(DOS24)*
working copy *(DOS17)*
working disk *(DOS17)*

▼   **QUICK REFERENCE**

The following table provides a quick reference to each task presented in the project.

Task	Command Syntax	Description
Change Default	drive name:	Changes the default or current drive
Clear Screen	cls	Clears the screen
Copy File	copy source target	Duplicates the source file specification to the target file specification
Directory	dir file-specification	Displays filenames on a disk
Erase File	del file-specification	Removes a file from a disk
Format Disk	format drive-name:	Prepares a new disk for use
Help	help	Invokes help window
Recover Deleted	undelete drive-name:	Attempts to bring back a deleted file
Rename File	ren currentname	Changes the name of the file
Version	ver	Displays DOS version loaded in memory

SHORT ANSWER ASSIGNMENTS

SHORT ANSWER ASSIGNMENT I
True/False

Instructions: Circle T if the statement is true or F if the statement is false.

T   F   1. DOS is an example of application software.

T   F   2. Microsoft developed DOS for use on IBM PCs.

T   F   3. The DOS version number identifies minor changes or corrections to a release.

T   F   4. The server hard disk on a LAN is usually drive C.

T   F   5. During a cold start, the computer first runs tests to diagnose its own circuitry.

T   F   6. To begin a warm boot, hold down the CTRL and ALT keys, press the ENTER key, and then release all three keys.

T   F   7. The dir command displays the contents of the files on a disk.

T   F   8. The format command is an example of a DOS prompt.

T   F   9. To change the default disk drive assignment to drive B, type b: and press the ENTER key.

T   F   10. You must enter all DOS commands in uppercase characters.

T   F   11. To access online help for DOS commands, type doshelp and press the ENTER key.

T   F   12. A:\> is an example of an extension.

T   F   13. A DOS file specification can contain a filename of one to eight characters and an extension of one to three characters.

T   F   14. A colon (:) separates a filename from an extension.

T   F   15. The format command is an external command.

T   F   16. You can format more than one diskette with one format command.

T   F   17. To make a duplicate of a file, use the copy command.

T   F   18. You can use the delete command to remove a file from a disk.

T   F   19. To bring back a deleted file, use the recover command.

T   F   20. To exit from online help, type Exit.

SHORT ANSWER ASSIGNMENT 2

Multiple Choice

Instructions: Circle the correct response.

1. DOS was developed by _____.
   a. Disk Operating Systems
   b. IBM
   c. LAN
   d. Microsoft

2. The 3 in DOS 3.2 refers to the _____.
   a. default
   b. release number
   c. version number
   d. prompt

3. The symbols C:\> _____.
   a. are collectively called the DOS prompt
   b. indicate the name of a program
   c. indicate the default disk drive
   d. both a and c

4. A file specification consists of all of the following except the _____.
   a. extension
   b. drive
   c. prompt
   d. filename

5. The _____ command divides a diskette into cylinders and sectors to prepare it to store data.
   a. delete
   b. rename
   c. copy
   d. format

6. To change the name of a file, use the _____ command.
   a. alter
   b. change
   c. rename
   d. assign

7. To remove a file from a disk, use the _____ command
   a. remove
   b. delete
   c. zap
   d. none of these

8. Listing the files on a disk is accomplished by typing _____ at the DOS prompt and pressing the ENTER key.
   a. list
   b. dir
   c. display
   d. files

9. To activate the menu bar in DOS online help, press the _____ key.
   a. F1
   b. ENTER
   c. CTRL
   d. ALT

10. To print a help topic in DOS online help, choose the _____ command from the _____ menu.
   a. Print, Print
   b. Print, Help
   c. Print, File
   d. File, Print

SHORT ANSWER ASSIGNMENT 3

Fill in the Blanks

1. _____ is a collection of programs that controls and manages the operation of the computer.

2. Microsoft Corporation developed the operating system known as _____.

3. _____ is a unique one-letter name preassigned to a disk drive.

4. The _____ on a LAN has a high-capacity hard disk containing files you can access from your computer.

5. To change the default drive, you type the letter of the new drive to be used, followed by a(n) _____.

6. In a file specification, C: is an example of a(n) _____.

7. In a file specification, the _____ is optional and consists of one to three characters.

8. The _____ command established cylinders and sectors on a disk in preparation for storing data.

9. Use the _____ command to change the name of a file on a disk.

10. Use the _____ command to recover a deleted file.

11. In DOS online help, the ALT key activates the _____ bar.

SHORT ANSWER ASSIGNMENT 4
Using DOS Commands

Instructions: Explain how to accomplish each of the following tasks using DOS.

Problem 1: Prepare a diskette using the format command and determine the amount of free space remaining on the disk.

Explanation: _____

_____

_____

Problem 2: List the files stored on the disk in drive A and determine the name of the most recently created or modified file.

Explanation: _____

_____

_____

Problem 3: Create a backup copy on drive A of the file DOSNOTES.DOC, using an extension of BAC and the same filename.

Explanation: _____

_____

_____

Problem 4: Change the name of the file DOSNOTES.BAC on drive A to THATFILE.DOC.

Explanation: _____

_____

_____

Problem 5: Remove the file THATFILE.DOC from the disk in drive A.

Explanation: _____

_____

_____

Problem 6: Recover the file THATFILE.DOC deleted from the disk in drive A.

Explanation: _____

_____

_____

SHORT ANSWER ASSIGNMENT 5
Understanding DOS Options

Instructions: Explain what happens after you perform each of the following DOS commands.

Problem 1: Type `format a:` at the C:\> prompt and press the ENTER key.

Explanation: _____

_____

_____

Problem 2: Type `dir b:` at the A:\> prompt and press the ENTER key.

Explanation: _____

_____

_____

Problem 3: Type `rename oldfile.abc newfile.abc` at the A:\> prompt and press the ENTER key.

Explanation: _____

_____

_____

Problem 4: Press the ALT key in the Help window.

Explanation: _____

_____

_____

Problem 5: Point and click a help topic in the Help window.

Explanation: _____

_____

_____

SHORT ANSWER ASSIGNMENT 6
Recovering from Problems

Instructions: In each of the following situations, a problem occurred. Explain the cause of the problem and how it can be corrected.

Problem 1: You attempt to boot the computer and the message, Non-System disk or disk error Replace and press any key when ready, displays on the screen.

Cause of Problem: _____

_____

Method of Correction: _____

_____

Problem 2: You are at the DOS prompt, and the default drive is A. You type C and press the ENTER key to change the default drive. DOS responds with the message, Bad command or file name.

Cause of Problem: _____

_____

Method of Correction: _____

_____

Problem 3: You are at the DOS prompt and the default drive is A. You type dir to display a list of files, but nothing happens.

Cause of Problem: _____

_____

Method of Correction: _____

_____

Problem 4: You type rename oldfile.bak b:newfile.new at the A:\> prompt and press the ENTER key. DOS responds with the message, Invalid parameter.

Cause of Problem: _____

_____

Method of Correction: _____

_____

SHORT ANSWER ASSIGNMENT 7
Understanding the Help Window

Instructions: In Figure SA1-7, arrows point to major components of the Help window. Identify the various parts of the screen in the space provided.

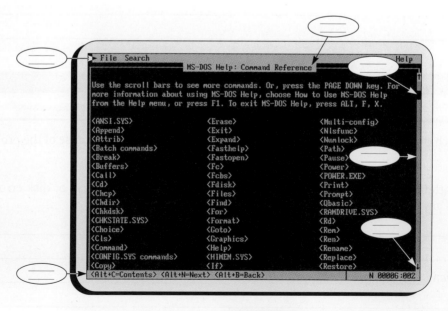

FIGURE SA1-7

HANDS-ON EXERCISES

HANDS-ON EXERCISE 1
Booting DOS and Formatting a Disk

Instructions: At the DOS prompt, perform the following tasks to boot your computer and format a new disk.

1. If the computer is not on a LAN:
   a. perform a cold boot.
   b. perform a warm boot.
2. If the computer is on a LAN:
   a. find out from your instructor if you are allowed to perform a cold boot. If so, perform a cold boot.
   b. find out from your instructor if you are allowed to perform a warm boot. If so, perform a warm boot.
3. Format a new disk using a volume label of seconddisk.
4. Do a directory of the newly formatted disk.
5. Print the directory by pressing the PRINT SCREEN key.

HANDS-ON EXERCISE 2
Working with DOS Commands

Instructions: At the DOS prompt, perform the following tasks to work with the files on your data disk. Each printout should be on a separate sheet of paper and labeled with the task number.

1. Insert your data disk into drive A.
2. List all of the files on the disk with the dir command.
3. Print the directory listing by pressing the PRINT SCREEN key.
4. Clear the screen.
5. List just the file called SMITH.DOC with the dir command.
6. Print the directory listing by pressing the PRINT SCREEN key.
7. Clear the screen.
8. Display the version of DOS you are using.
9. Print the version by pressing the PRINT SCREEN key.
10. Clear the screen.
11. Copy the file SMITH.DOC to a file called SMITH.TXT on the same disk in drive A.
12. Print the copy command by pressing the PRINT SCREEN key.
13. Rename the file SMITH.TXT to JONES.TXT.
14. Print the rename command by pressing the PRINT SCREEN key.

15. Delete the file JONES.TXT.

16. Print the delete command by pressing the PRINT SCREEN key.

17. Display all of the files on your data disk.

18. Print the directory listing by pressing the PRINT SCREEN key.

HANDS-ON EXERCISE 3
Working with DOS Help

Instructions: Invoke the Help window by typing `help` at the DOS prompt. Print Help on the following DOS commands. If Examples and/or Notes exist for any of the commands, print those as well. Each printout should be on a separate sheet of paper and properly labeled. Help on the cls command is shown in HOE1-3.

1. cls

2. ver

3. dir

4. format

5. copy

6. rename

7. del

8. undelete

```
                                          CLS

Clears the screen.

The cleared screen shows only the command prompt and cursor.

Syntax

      CLS
```

FIGURE HOE1-3

Managing and Organizing Files on Disks

▼ **OBJECTIVES**

You will have mastered the material in this project when you can:

- Create subdirectories
- List a subdirectory's files
- Change the current subdirectory
- Specify a path
- Use wildcard characters with DOS commands
- Copy groups of files from one disk or subdirectory to another

- Move files from one subdirectory to another
- Display and print large directory listings
- Remove subdirectories
- Check the status of a disk
- Copy an entire disk

▼ **INTRODUCTION**

Just as you organize the drawers in a filing cabinet, you must organize files on a disk. Disk files are usually organized by application. That is, word processing files are placed in a location separate from spreadsheet files. Because these locations often contain large numbers of files, you may copy, move, or delete a group of files, rather than just one file. In Project 2, you will learn how to organize and manage files on a disk.

Changing the Default Drive

Again in this project, it is assumed you are using a hard disk and one diskette drive with the drive names C and A, respectively. If you are using a different disk configuration, check with your instructor for the changes you should make in Project 2.

Continue to use the same data disk in this project that you used to complete Project 1. Follow these steps to change the default drive to A and to display the files on your data disk.

TO CHANGE THE DEFAULT DRIVE AND LIST A DIRECTORY

STEP 1: Insert your data disk from your completed Project 1 into drive A.

STEP 2: Type a: and press the ENTER key.

STEP 3: Type dir and press the ENTER key.

The default drive is changed to A (Figure 2-1). The list of files on the default drive, which is drive A in this case, displays on the screen. (Depending on your data disk's size and density, the bytes free at the bottom of your directory listing may differ from Figure 2-1.)

default drive changed to A

files from data disk used to complete Project 1

FIGURE 2-1

....

▼ **THE ROOT DIRECTORY AND SUBDIRECTORIES**

As you learned in Project 1, a disk is essentially an electronic filing cabinet. You organize the folders in a filing cabinet by placing them in appropriate drawers. On a disk, you organize the files by placing them into appropriate directories. Recall from Project 1 that a directory is a listing of files. Two types of directories exist on a disk: the root directory and subdirectories.

The Root Directory

Every disk has at least one directory, called the **root directory**. The root directory is automatically created when you format a disk. You have thirteen files in the root directory on your data disk in drive A (see Figure 2-1 above).

The root directory on a disk is limited in size. For example, a hard disk allows up to 512 entries, while a double-density diskette has room for 112 entries and a high density diskette holds 224 entries. If you reach the maximum number of entries, you cannot place another file on the disk even if you have space left on the disk.

If you had a few hundred file entries in the root directory, you would have difficulty managing these disk files. Imagine scanning through a list of several hundred files to find the names of files you created months ago. For this reason, you divide your files into smaller logical groups. For example, all word processing files can be placed in one location and spreadsheet files in a separate location.

Subdirectories

Subdirectories are logical divisions of a disk that *you* create. Because the number of entries in the root directory is limited, you can create subdirectories to place more files on a disk. Unlike the root directory, the number of files in a subdirectory is limited only by the amount of storage available on the disk. The main reason, though, to create subdirectories is for disk and file organization. The way you use a filing cabinet is similar to the way you use subdirectories; the filing cabinet (similar to a disk) is divided into separate drawers (similar to subdirectories) to store the file folders (similar to the disk files) in an organized and manageable way.

Subdirectories are often called directories. Technically speaking, though, all directories other than the root are subdirectories. Each subdirectory itself can contain one or more subdirectories. In these cases, the directory containing the subdirectory is called the **parent directory**, and the subdirectory in the parent directory is called the **child directory**.

You may, for example, create one subdirectory called WP to hold all your word processing files and another called SS for your spreadsheet files (Figure 2-2). The root directory then would contain fifteen entries: the thirteen files in the root directory and the WP and SS subdirectories.

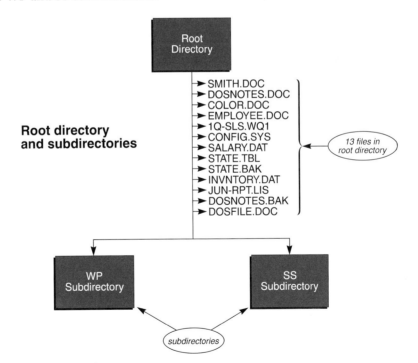

Root directory and subdirectories

FIGURE 2-2

You may want to further divide your WP subdirectory files into two groups, placing word processing program files in the WP subdirectory and word processing document files in a new subdirectory called WPDOCS. Because you can create a subdirectory under an existing subdirectory, you can create the WPDOCS subdirectory under the

WP subdirectory (Figure 2-3). In this case, WP would be the parent directory, and WPDOCS would be the child directory.

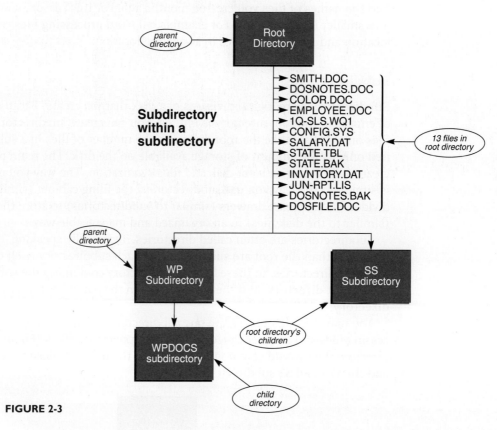

FIGURE 2-3

A subdirectory name, like a filename, can contain one to eight characters, followed optionally by a period and one to three characters for an extension. Subdirectory names, however, do not generally include extensions. The same characters permitted for a filename are permitted for a subdirectory name, which were discussed on page DOS15 in Project 1.

▼   MAKING SUBDIRECTORIES

To make a subdirectory, you use the **mkdir command**, usually abbreviated **md**. The first subdirectory you make on a disk is a child directory to the root directory. Follow these steps to make a subdirectory called WP.

TO MAKE A SUBDIRECTORY AND VERIFY THE RESULTS

STEP 1:   Type md **and press the SPACEBAR. Then, type** \wp **and press the ENTER key.**

DOS makes a subdirectory called WP. The root, indicated by the backslash character, is the parent directory, and WP is the child directory.

STEP 2:   Type dir **and press the ENTER key.**

DOS displays the files on drive A (Figure 2-4). The backslash following the A: in the Directory of A:\ message designates the root directory. Thus, A:\ indicates the files in the root directory on drive A are displayed. Notice the root directory now contains fourteen files. The new fourteenth file is actually the WP subdirectory entry and is identified as such by the <DIR> label in the directory listing.

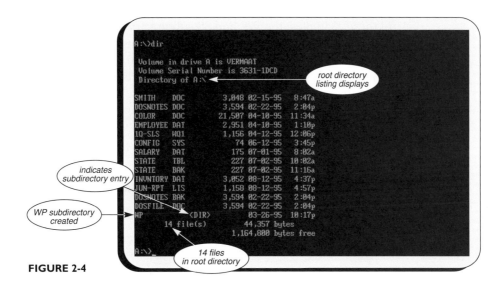

FIGURE 2-4

Follow these steps to make another subdirectory called SS.

TO MAKE ANOTHER SUBDIRECTORY AND VERIFY THE RESULTS

STEP 1:   **Type** md \ss **and press the ENTER key.**

DOS makes a subdirectory called SS. The root is the parent directory, and SS is the child directory.

STEP 2:   **Type** dir **and press the ENTER key.**

DOS displays the files on drive A (Figure 2-5). The root directory now contains fifteen files. The new fifteenth file is actually the SS *subdirectory entry and is identified as such by the* <DIR> *label in the directory listing.*

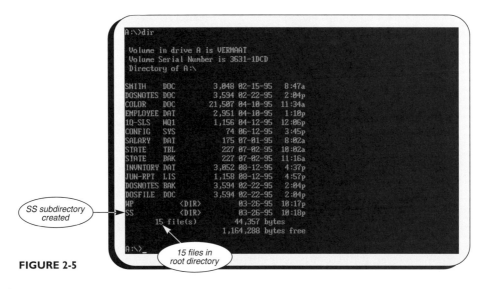

FIGURE 2-5

In these examples, the WP and SS subdirectories reside on the default drive (which is A) because you omitted the drive name from the subdirectory name when you created the subdirectories. If you specify a drive name with a subdirectory name, you must place a colon (:) after the drive name. For example, assume you wanted to make a subdirectory on drive C for your database files. To do this, you would enter md c:\db at the A prompt (A:\>).

Viewing the Contents of a Subdirectory

If you want to see the directory listing of the newly created WP or SS subdirectories, you need to specify the subdirectory's name in the dir command as shown in the following step.

TO DISPLAY A DIRECTORY LISTING OF A CHILD DIRECTORY

STEP 1:   **Type** dir \wp **and press the ENTER key.**

*DOS displays the message Directory of A:\WP, followed by the listing of files in the subdirectory (Figure 2-6). The \WP notation is called a **path** because its sequence indicates the path from the root to the list of files. The backslash character precedes the subdirectory name in the path, indicating the root directory is the parent and WP is the child directory.*

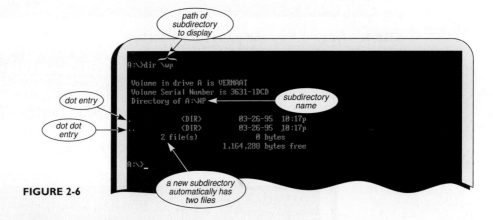

FIGURE 2-6

Because you have not yet placed any files in the WP subdirectory, you expect it to be empty; yet, its directory listing indicates 2 file(s), each with the <DIR> label. One has a filename of . (pronounced dot), and the other has a filename of .. (pronounced dot dot). The **dot entry** refers to the subdirectory WP, and the **dot dot entry** refers to the parent directory of WP, which in this case is the root directory on drive A.

When working with subdirectories, you can specify the entire path or, in some cases, just a partial path in the command. For example, the path \WP indicates the WP subdirectory is immediately below the root directory (represented by the backslash). To make the WP subdirectory, you just entered the command md \wp. However, if the root is your current directory, you could simply enter the command md wp, omitting the backslash. When you omit the parent directory(s) from a path, DOS assumes the subdirectory named in the command is a child to the current directory. For example, the command dir wp yields the same result shown in Figure 2-6 above because the root is the current directory and WP is a child to the root.

▼   **MAKING SUBDIRECTORIES WITHIN SUBDIRECTORIES**

As discussed earlier, you can make subdirectories within an existing subdirectory. You can, for example, make a subdirectory called WPDOCS beneath the WP subdirectory. You perform the same steps to make a subdirectory within a subdirectory as you did to make a subdirectory in the root directory. Follow these steps to create a subdirectory called WPDOCS under the WP subdirectory.

TO MAKE A SUBDIRECTORY WITHIN A SUBDIRECTORY AND VERIFY THE RESULTS

STEP 1:   Type md \wp\wpdocs **and press the ENTER key.**

DOS makes a subdirectory called WPDOCS under the WP subdirectory. WPDOCS is the child directory, and WP is the parent. The first backslash represents the root directory; the second backslash separates the parent directory from the child directory. Recall the series of characters \wp\wpdocs is referred to as a path.

STEP 2:   Type dir **and press the ENTER key.**

DOS displays the files on drive A (Figure 2-7). Notice the root directory still contains fifteen files, but the number of bytes free has changed from 1,164,288 (Figure 2-6 on the previous page) to 1,163,776 because you made a new subdirectory. Thus, this new empty subdirectory consumes 488 bytes of disk space (1,164,288 - 1,163,776).

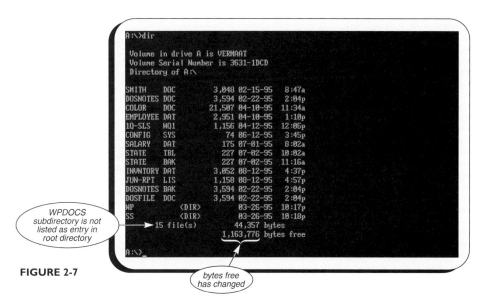

FIGURE 2-7

The child directory, WPDOCS, is not in the root directory listing because it is a subdirectory to WP. To see the directory entry for WPDOCS, you must display the directory listing for the WP subdirectory.

TO DISPLAY A DIRECTORY LISTING OF A CHILD DIRECTORY

STEP 1: Type `dir wp` **and press the ENTER key.**

DOS displays the directory for the WP subdirectory (Figure 2-8). Notice the sub-directory now contains three files: the dot entry, the dot dot entry, and the WPDOCS subdirectory entry. Because the root is the current directory and WP is a child to the root, the backslash is omitted from the path in this command.

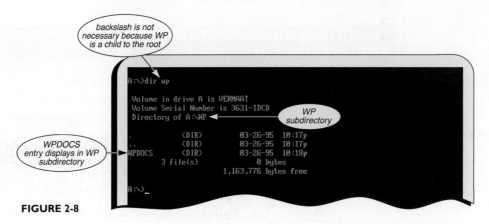

FIGURE 2-8

Instead of specifying the path to a child directory in the dir command, you can move into the child directory and issue the dir command directly from within the child directory. To do this, you must change directories.

▼ CHANGING DIRECTORIES

To change from one directory to another, you use the **chdir command**, usually abbreviated **cd**. With this command, you can change from a parent to a child directory, from one subdirectory to another subdirectory, or from a child directory to its parent.

Changing from the Root Directory to a Subdirectory

The root directory on the disk in drive A has two subdirectories as its children: WP and SS. Follow these steps to change from the root to the SS subdirectory.

TO CHANGE FROM THE ROOT TO A CHILD SUBDIRECTORY AND VIEW IT

STEP 1: Type `cd ss` **and press the ENTER key.**

The DOS prompt changes to reflect the current subdirectory name (Figure 2-9). This way, you always can tell what directory you are currently in simply by looking at the DOS prompt. Because the SS subdirectory is a child to the root, the back-slash may be omitted from the path. (If your prompt does not change, consult your instructor regarding the prompt command.)

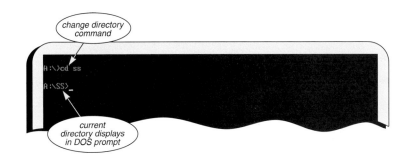

FIGURE 2-9

STEP 2: Type `dir` and press the **ENTER** key.

DOS displays the directory listing for the current directory, which is SS in this case (Figure 2-10).

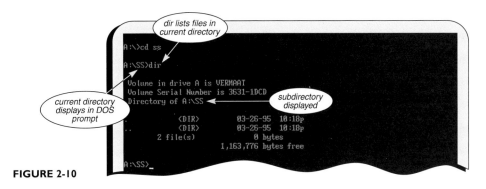

FIGURE 2-10

The Current Directory

Just as a default, or current, drive exists, each drive has a current directory. The **current directory** for a drive is the directory on which you are currently working; that is, DOS looks by default for files in the current directory of a drive. When you first access a disk, the root directory is the current directory. You can identify the current directory by looking at the DOS prompt or by entering the dir command as shown in Figure 2-10 above. You use the cd command to direct DOS to a subdirectory, which then becomes the current directory for that disk.

Changing from One Subdirectory to Another

On your data disk, WP and SS are two subdirectories, both children to the root. WPDOCS is a child to the WP subdirectory. Follow these steps to move from the SS subdirectory to the WP subdirectory.

TO CHANGE FROM ONE SUBDIRECTORY TO ANOTHER AND VIEW IT

STEP 1: Type `cd \wp` and press the **ENTER** key.

The DOS prompt changes to reflect the current subdirectory name. That is, the prompt is now A:\WP>, signifying you are in the WP subdirectory on drive A (see Figure 2-11 on the next page). Because WP is not a child to the SS directory, the complete path to the WP subdirectory is required in the cd command. That is, the backslash character is required.

STEP 2: **Type** dir **and press the ENTER key.**

DOS displays the directory listing for the current directory, which is the WP sub-directory (Figure 2-11).

FIGURE 2-11

When you change from one subdirectory to another, you must specify the complete path to the subdirectory from the root. That is, the first character in the path is the backslash followed by the subdirectory name. If you omit the leading backslash for the root, DOS assumes the directory name following the cd command is a child to the current directory. For example, if you entered cd wp (without the leading backslash), DOS displays the error message Invalid directory because the WP subdirectory is not a child to the SS subdirectory.

However, if you want to move from the WP subdirectory to the WPDOCS sub-directory, you do not need to specify the complete path of \wp\wpdocs because WPDOCS is a child to WP as shown in the following steps.

TO CHANGE FROM A PARENT TO A CHILD DIRECTORY AND VIEW IT

STEP 1: **Type** cd wpdocs **and press the ENTER key.**

The DOS prompt changes to reflect the current subdirectory name (Figure 2-12 below). That is, the prompt is now A:\WP\WPDOCS>, signifying you are in the WPDOCS subdirectory, which is a child to the WP subdirectory on drive A.

STEP 2: **Type** dir **and press the ENTER key.**

DOS displays the directory listing for the current directory, which is the WPDOCS subdirectory (Figure 2-12).

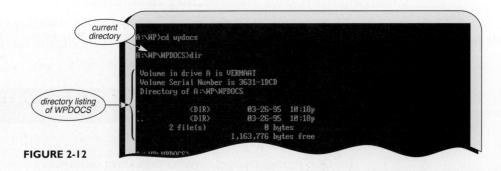

FIGURE 2-12

If you want to change from a child directory to its parent, you do not need to specify the path to the parent. Instead, you can specify the dot dot entry. Follow these steps to move from the WPDOCS subdirectory to the WP subdirectory.

TO CHANGE FROM A CHILD TO ITS PARENT AND VIEW IT

STEP 1: **Type** `cd ..` **and press the ENTER key.**

The DOS prompt changes to reflect the parent directory name. That is, the prompt is now A:\WP>, indicating you are in the WP subdirectory on drive A.

STEP 2: **Type** `dir` **and press the ENTER key.**

DOS displays the directory listing for the current directory, which is the WP subdirectory (Figure 2-13).

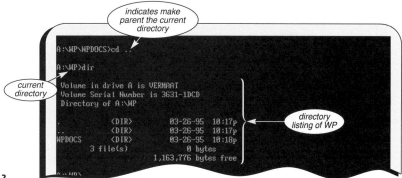

FIGURE 2-13

Changing Back to the Root Directory

The root directory is identified by a backslash. Thus, to change to the root directory, you enter a single backslash after the cd command as shown below.

TO CHANGE BACK TO THE ROOT DIRECTORY AND VIEW IT

STEP 1: **Type** `cd\` **and press the ENTER key.**

The DOS prompt changes to reflect the current directory name. That is, the prompt A:\> signifies you are in the root directory of drive A.

STEP 2: **Type** `dir` **and press the ENTER key.**

DOS displays the directory listing for the root directory, which is the current directory (Figure 2-14).

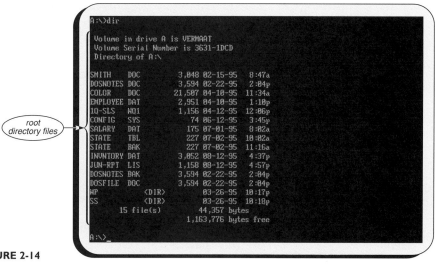

FIGURE 2-14

Summarizing Valid and Invalid Change Directory Command Entries

Because of the variety of ways you can change directories, Table 2-1 lists a variety of cd commands entered at the A:\> prompt. Some are valid; others are invalid. If valid, the table lists the result of the cd command; if invalid, the table lists the reason it is invalid.

TABLE 2-I

Assume you are at the A:\> prompt when you first enter the command.			
Command	**Valid/Invalid**	**Result/Reason**	**Display After Command Entered**
cd \wp\wpdocs	Valid	Makes WPDOCS the current directory	A:\WP\WPDOCS>
cd ..	Valid	Makes WP the current directory	A:\WP>
cd ss	Invalid	SS is not a child to the WP subdirectory	Invalid directory
cd \ss	Valid	Makes SS the current directory	A:\SS>
cd \	Valid	Makes the root directory the current directory	A:\>
cd ..	Invalid	Root does not have a parent directory	Invalid directory
cd wpdocs	Invalid	WPDOCS is not a child to the root	Invalid directory
cd wp	Valid	Makes WP the current directory	A:\WP>
cd wpdocs	Valid	Makes WPDOCS the current directory	A:\WP\WPDOCS>
cd \	Valid	Makes the root directory the current directory	A:\>

▼   ## INDICATING A PATH IN A FILE SPECIFICATION

Suppose you want to work on a spreadsheet you have already created and placed into a subdirectory. You would instruct DOS to find the file and display it on the screen. To do this, you must specify the path to the file. A complete path specifies the route DOS must take from the root directory through the subdirectories leading to the file. Recall from Project 1 that a file specification consists of up to four components: a drive, a path, a filename, and an extension. The path identifies the name of the directory and, if applicable, directories above it, each separated by a backslash (\). For example, the file specification A:\WP\DOSNOTES.DOC indicates the file DOSNOTES.DOC is located in the WP subdirectory on the A drive. The first backslash represents the root directory; the WP indicates the WP subdirectory; and the final backslash separates the subdirectory from the filename.

One way to specify a path is to include it in the command you are issuing. For example, you can indicate a path when copying a file. Follow these steps to copy the file DOSNOTES.DOC from the root directory to the WP subdirectory.

TO SPECIFY A PATH IN THE COPY COMMAND AND VERIFY THE RESULTS

STEP 1:   **Type** copy \dosnotes.doc \wp **and press the ENTER key.**

DOS copies the file DOSNOTES.DOC from the root directory to the WP subdirectory. In the copy command, the \dosnotes.doc is the source specification, *which indicates where the file is being copied from and its name. The \wp is the target specification, which indicates where the file is being copied to. The file DOSNOTES.DOC is now in both the root and WP directories.*

STEP 2: **Type** `dir wp` **and press the ENTER key.**

DOS displays the list of files in the WP subdirectory (Figure 2-15). The WP sub-directory now has four files, one of which is DOSNOTES.DOC.

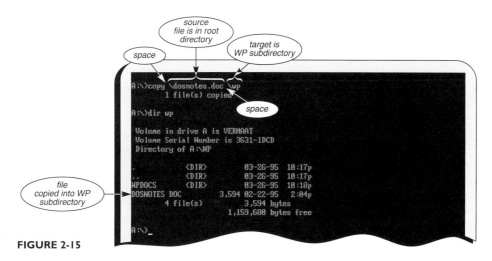

FIGURE 2-15

Because you omitted the filename and extension from the target in the copy command, the target file has the same name as the source file. You can have two files on a disk with the same name, as long as they reside in different directories. The complete path for the file in the WP subdirectory is A:\WP\DOSNOTES.DOC. The first back-slash indicates the root directory, and the second backslash separates the WP sub-directory from the filename.

▼ WILDCARD CHARACTERS

Using DOS commands such as copy, rename, and erase, you can access more than one file at a time. For example, you might want to copy all the files from one subdirectory to another subdirectory. To do this, you use a **wildcard character** in the file specification of a DOS command as a substitute for other characters. DOS recognizes two wildcard characters: the asterisk (*) and the question mark (?). The asterisk represents one or more characters, whereas the question mark represents a single character.

The Asterisk (*) Wildcard Character

To represent one or more characters in a file's name or extension, you use the **asterisk (*) wildcard character.** You can use the asterisk once in a filename and once in an extension. Wherever the asterisk appears, any character can occupy that position and all the remaining positions in the filename or the extension. To represent all file-names and all extensions, use the notation *.* — where the first * represents all file-names; the second * represents all extensions; and the period separates the filename portion from the extension portion. Follow the steps on the next page to copy all files from the root directory into the WP subdirectory using a single copy command.

TO COPY ALL FILES FROM ONE DIRECTORY TO ANOTHER AND VERIFY THE RESULTS

STEP 1: Type `copy *.* \wp` **and press the ENTER key.**

DOS begins copying files from the root directory to the WP subdirectory, but it encounters a duplicate (Figure 2-16a). That is, the file DOSNOTES.DOC is already in the WP subdirectory. To overwrite the existing DOSNOTES.DOC in the WP subdirectory with the new copy, type y.

STEP 2: Type `y` **and press the ENTER key.**

DOS copies all of the files in the root directory into the WP subdirectory, listing each source file name as it is being copied (Figure 2-16b). The *.* represents the source files, and the \wp represents the target subdirectory. Recall you put a space before the source and target specifications. The files now exist in both directories.

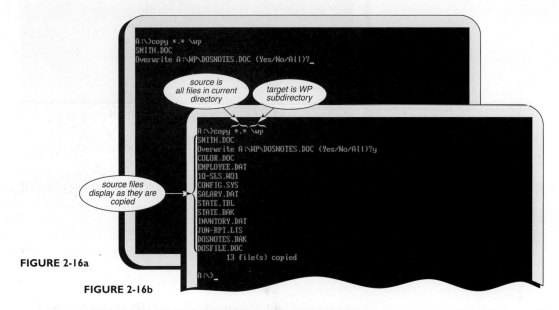

FIGURE 2-16a

FIGURE 2-16b

STEP 3: Type `dir wp` **and press the ENTER key.**

DOS displays the files in the WP subdirectory (Figure 2-17). The WP subdirectory now contains 16 files.

FIGURE 2-17

Instead of copying all files from one location to another, you can use the asterisk wildcard character to represent just the filename portion or just the extension portion of the file specification. In this way, you can copy a group of files in a directory. For example, you can copy all files with an extension of DOC from the WP subdirectory into the WPDOCS subdirectory. The root is your current directory. Because your source files are in a different directory than the current directory, you must specify the WP subdirectory path in the source specification. Use the following steps to copy a group of files.

TO COPY A GROUP OF FILES AND VERIFY THE RESULTS

STEP 1: **Type** `copy \wp\*.doc \wp\wpdocs` **and press the ENTER key.**

DOS copies all the files with an extension of DOC in the WP subdirectory into the WPDOCS subdirectory, listing each source file name as it is being copied (Figure 2-18). The *.doc represents the source files in the WP subdirectory, and the \wpdocs represents the target directory. The files with an extension of DOC now exist in both directories.

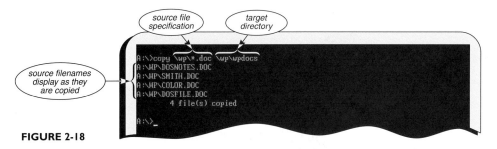

FIGURE 2-18

STEP 2: **Type** `dir \wp\wpdocs` **and press the ENTER key.**

DOS displays the files in the WPDOCS subdirectory (Figure 2-19). The WPDOCS subdirectory now contains six files.

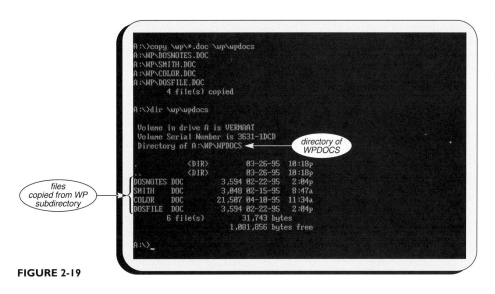

FIGURE 2-19

In addition to copying files from one directory to another subdirectory on the same disk, you can copy from a subdirectory on one disk to a subdirectory on a different disk. For example, to copy all the files from the WP subdirectory on the disk in drive

A to the WP subdirectory on drive C, you enter the command copy \wp*.* c:\wp at the A:\> prompt. In this case, \wp*.* is the source location of the files to be copied, and c:\wp is the target location.

If you have multiple subdirectories on a diskette and want to make a **backup copy**, or duplicate, of the entire diskette, you could use the *.* wildcard notation to copy all the files, one directory at a time. The problem is you have to reissue the copy command for each subdirectory on your diskette. A more efficient way to backup a diskette, with a single command, is discussed at the end of this project.

Wildcard characters can be used with any DOS command that uses file specifications. For example, you may want to erase all files in the WP subdirectory that begin with the letter s. First, you display these files; then you erase them as shown in the steps.

TO DISPLAY A GROUP OF FILES

STEP 1:   Type `dir \wp\s*.*` **and press the ENTER key.**

DOS displays the names of the files in the WP subdirectory that begin with the letter s (Figure 2-20). Four files display. The first s* refers to the filename portion of the file specification, and the second * refers to the extension portion. Thus, all filenames and extensions beginning with the letter s display.

files in WP
subdirectory that
begin with letter S

four files meet
criteria specified in
dir command

FIGURE 2-20

TO ERASE A GROUP OF FILES AND VERIFY THE RESULTS

STEP 1:   Type `del \wp\s*.*` **and press the ENTER key.**

DOS erases files in the WP subdirectory that begin with the letter s. DOS does not display a confirmation indicating the deletion was successful. Thus, you must view a directory listing to verify the results of the del command.

STEP 2:   Type `dir \wp\*.*` **and press the ENTER key.**

DOS displays the files in the WP subdirectory (Figure 2-21). The four files that began with the letter s were removed from the WP subdirectory. The other twelve files that do not begin with the letter s remain in the subdirectory.

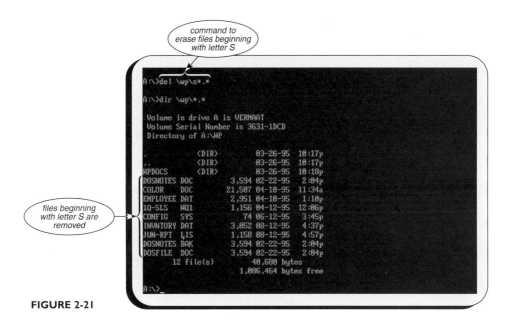

FIGURE 2-21

The Question Mark (?) Wildcard Character

To represent any character occupying one position in a filename or extension, you use the **question mark (?) wildcard character**. That is, the question mark wildcard character represents only a single character replacement, as opposed to the asterisk, which represents one or more characters. As with the asterisk wildcard character, you can use the question mark in any DOS command that uses file specifications. For example, you may know that a quarterly report is on your disk that you created with a spreadsheet package, but you do not remember the first two characters in its filename. In this case, you can use two question marks in the filename: one to represent the first position and one to represent the second position as shown below.

TO DISPLAY A DIRECTORY USING THE ? WILDCARD CHARACTER

STEP 1: Type `dir ??-sls.wq1` **and press the ENTER key.**

DOS displays the entry for the file 1Q-SLS.WQ1 (Figure 2-22). The ?? in the filename indicates that any character could exist in the first two positions of the filename, as long as the remaining characters are -sls and the extension is wq1. Recall that a file's extension indicates the type of file it is; thus 1Q-SLS is a worksheet file.

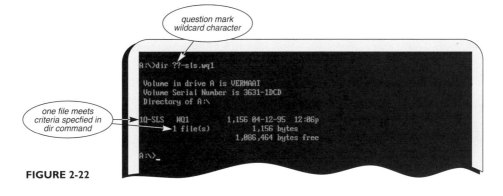

FIGURE 2-22

Summarizing the Wildcard Characters

Because you can use the wildcard characters in a number of DOS commands, Table 2-2 lists a variety of commands entered at the A:\> prompt using the wildcard characters. The results of the command are listed next to the command.

TABLE 2-2

Assume you are at the A:\> prompt when you first enter the command.	
Command	*Result*
dir state.*	Displays all files in the root directory with a filename of STATE.
copy state.* \ss	Copies files from the root directory that have a filename of STATE into the SS subdirectory.
dir \ss\state.*	Displays all files in the SS subdirectory with a filename of STATE.
del state.*	Erases all files in the root directory with a filename of STATE.
undelete state.*	Recovers all files in the root directory with a filename of STATE.
dir ?????.doc	Displays all files in the root directory that have five characters or less in their filename and an extension of DOC.
copy \wp*.* c:	Copies all files in the WP subdirectory on the current drive to the root directory on drive C.
copy \wp*.* c:\wp	Copies all files in the WP subdirectory on the current drive into the WP subdirectory on drive C.

▼ MOVING FILES

If you accidentally place files into the wrong directory, you can use the **move command** to transfer your files from one subdirectory to another subdirectory or from one drive to another drive. Moving files is different than copying files. When you copy files, they exist in both the source and target locations; when you move files, they are removed from the source location and exist only in the target location. Your disk, for example, has several files in the WPDOCS subdirectory. You can move all of the files in this subdirectory to the SS subdirectory as shown in the following steps. (In earlier versions of DOS, the move command is unavailable.)

TO MOVE ALL FILES FROM ONE DIRECTORY TO ANOTHER AND VERIFY THE RESULTS

STEP 1: **Type** dir \wp\wpdocs **and press the ENTER key. Type** dir ss **and press the ENTER key.**

DOS displays all files in the WPDOCS subdirectory and then all files in the SS subdirectory (Figure 2-23). WPDOCS contains six files and SS contains two files.

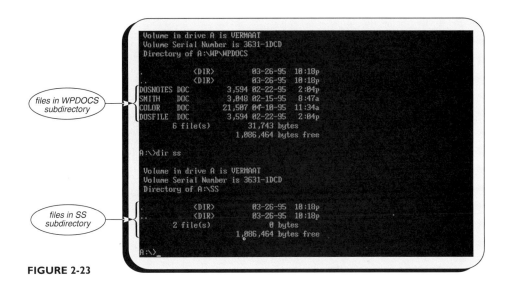

FIGURE 2-23

STEP 2: **Type** `move \wp\wpdocs\*.* \ss` **and press the ENTER key.**

DOS moves all of the files from the WPDOCS subdirectory into the SS subdirectory, listing each source file name as it is being moved (Figure 2-24). Notice, you must place a space before the source and target specifications. The files no longer exist in the WPDOCS subdirectory.

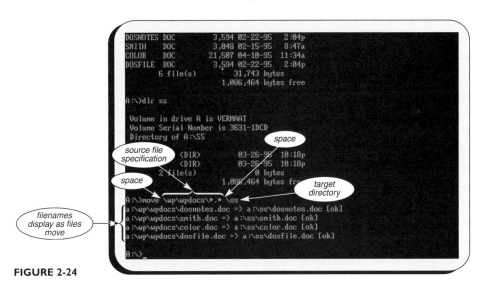

FIGURE 2-24

STEP 3: **Type** `dir \wp\wpdocs` **and press the ENTER key. Type** `dir ss` **and press the ENTER key.**

DOS displays all files in the WPDOCS subdirectory and then all files in the SS subdirectory (Figure 2-25 on the next page). Compare Figure 2-23 to Figure 2-25. Notice the files originally in the WPDOCS subdirectory are now in the SS subdirectory.

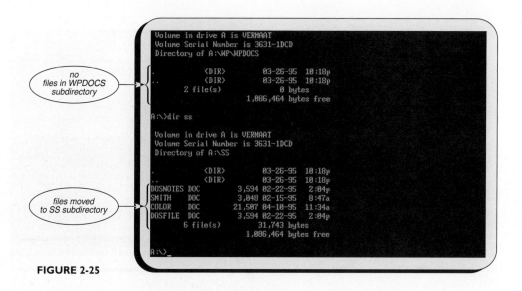

no files in WPDOCS subdirectory

files moved to SS subdirectory

FIGURE 2-25

▼ DISPLAYING AND PRINTING LARGE DIRECTORIES

In Project 1, you learned to use the dir command to list files on a disk. In this project, you have learned how to list all or a group of files in a specific directory. Additionally, you can specify a variety of other parameters for the dir command as shown on the following pages.

Using the Directory Command with a Large Number of Files

Many directories contain more files than can fit in one screen display with the standard dir command. To illustrate this limitation, you will make a copy of the files in the WP subdirectory into the root directory. You will give the backup files the same filename as the original files, but they will have an extension of DUP. Then, you will display the directory listing of the root directory.

TO DISPLAY A LONG DIRECTORY LIST

STEP 1:   **Type** copy \wp*.* *.dup **and press the ENTER key. When DOS asks if you want to overwrite A:\DOSNOTES.DUP, type** y **and press the ENTER key.**

DOS makes a duplicate copy of each file in the WP subdirectory, giving each target file the same filename with the extension of DUP and placing them in the root directory. Each source file lists as it is being copied (Figure 2-26).

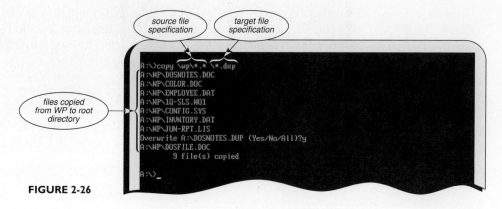

source file specification

target file specification

files copied from WP to root directory

FIGURE 2-26

STEP 2:   Type dir **and press the ENTER key.**

DOS displays the filenames in the root directory (Figure 2-27). The list is too long to fit on the screen. Thus, the first two files scroll off the top of the screen to make room for the bottom files, and you can view only the last screenful of files.

FIGURE 2-27

Because you may want to see the first screenful of files, DOS provides you with qualifiers for the dir command. A **qualifier**, which consists of a slash (/) followed by a single letter, changes the way a DOS command behaves. For example, you use the /p qualifier to pause your display as shown in the following steps.

TO PAUSE A DIRECTORY LISTING

STEP 1:   Type dir /p **and press the ENTER key.**

DOS displays the first screenful of files in the directory listing and pauses after displaying the message Press any key to continue . . . at the bottom of the screen (Figure 2-28). At this point, DOS waits for you to press a key on the keyboard, giving you a chance to read the first screenful of files in the directory listing.

FIGURE 2-28

STEP 2: **Press the ENTER key. (You could actually press any key.)**

DOS displays the next screenful of files in the directory listing (Figure 2-29). Because this screenful concludes the directory listing, the DOS prompt displays beneath the directory.

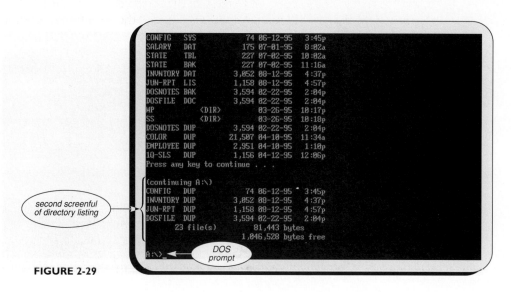

FIGURE 2-29

Another option of displaying a large directory listing is to use the /w qualifier to widen the display. The wide display allows more files to fit on the screen at a time as shown in the steps below.

TO WIDEN A DIRECTORY LISTING

STEP 1: **Type** dir /w **and press the ENTER key.**

DOS displays the root directory files in a wide format (Figure 2-30). Notice that only the filename and extension display in a wide directory listing. That is, the size of the files and time and date the files were created are not listed. Also, the filenames are separated from the extensions with a period, and subdirectory names are enclosed in brackets ([ ]).

FIGURE 2-30

Printing a Directory Listing

At times, you might like a hardcopy, or printout, of a directory listing. To obtain this printout, you must redirect the default output of the dir command. The default output is the screen. Thus, you want to redirect the screen output to the printer. The **redirect output symbol** is the greater than sign (>), and the code for the printer is PRN. Follow these steps to print a directory listing.

TO PRINT A DIRECTORY LISTING

STEP 1: **Ready your printer.**

STEP 2: **Type** `dir > prn` **and press the ENTER key.**

Because DOS is sending the directory to the printer, your screen does not display the directory listing (Figure 2-31).

directory listing does not display on screen

```
A:\>dir > prn

A:\>_
```

FIGURE 2-31

STEP 3: **Remove the hardcopy directory listing from the printer (Figure 2-32).**

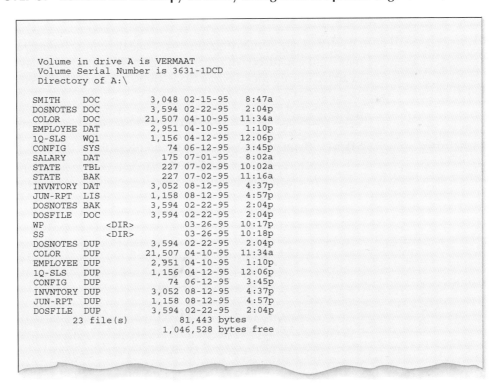

```
    Volume in drive A is VERMAAT
    Volume Serial Number is 3631-1DCD
    Directory of A:\

SMITH    DOC        3,048 02-15-95    8:47a
DOSNOTES DOC        3,594 02-22-95    2:04p
COLOR    DOC       21,507 04-10-95   11:34a
EMPLOYEE DAT        2,951 04-10-95    1:10p
1Q-SLS   WQ1        1,156 04-12-95   12:06p
CONFIG   SYS           74 06-12-95    3:45p
SALARY   DAT          175 07-01-95    8:02a
STATE    TBL          227 07-02-95   10:02a
STATE    BAK          227 07-02-95   11:16a
INVNTORY DAT        3,052 08-12-95    4:37p
JUN-RPT  LIS        1,158 08-12-95    4:57p
DOSNOTES BAK        3,594 02-22-95    2:04p
DOSFILE  DOC        3,594 02-22-95    2:04p
WP           <DIR>        03-26-95   10:17p
SS           <DIR>        03-26-95   10:18p
DOSNOTES DUP        3,594 02-22-95    2:04p
COLOR    DUP       21,507 04-10-95   11:34a
EMPLOYEE DUP        2,951 04-10-95    1:10p
1Q-SLS   DUP        1,156 04-12-95   12:06p
CONFIG   DUP           74 06-12-95    3:45p
INVNTORY DUP        3,052 08-12-95    4:37p
JUN-RPT  DUP        1,158 08-12-95    4:57p
DOSFILE  DUP        3,594 02-22-95    2:04p
       23 file(s)         81,443 bytes
                       1,046,528 bytes free
```

FIGURE 2-32

Other Qualifiers for the Directory Command

Several other qualifiers may be placed in the directory command to change the way it displays the directory listing. Table 2-3 lists several useful qualifiers available for the dir command.

TABLE 2-3

DIR Command with Parameter	Function
dir /p	Displays one screen of the listing at a time.
dir /w	Displays the listing in a wide format.
dir /a:d	Displays the listing of subdirectory names only.
dir /a:-d	Displays the listing of filenames only.
dir /o	Displays the listing in alphabetical order by name.
dir /o:e	Displays the listing in alphabetical order by extension.
dir /o:d	Displays the listing in alphabetical order by date and time.
dir /o:s	Displays the listing in alphabetical order by size, smallest first.
dir /o:-s	Displays the listing in alphabetical order by size, largest first.
dir /s	Displays the listing of the current directory and all of its subdirectories.

You can use as many qualifiers on one dir command as you like. For example, you may want a hardcopy directory listing of the root, as well as all of its subdirectories, in alphabetical order. Follow these steps to print this directory.

TO USE MULTIPLE QUALIFIERS WITH A COMMAND

STEP 1: **Type** dir /s/o > prn **and press the ENTER key.**

DOS prints the listing of the files in all subdirectories in the A drive in alphabetical order (Figure 2-33).

```
Volume in drive A is VERMAAT
Volume Serial Number is 3631-1DCD

Directory of A:\

SS            <DIR>         03-26-95   10:18p
WP            <DIR>         03-26-95   10:17p
1Q-SLS   DUP     1,156 04-12-95   12:06p
1Q-SLS   WQ1     1,156 04-12-95   12:06p
COLOR    DOC    21,507 04-10-95   11:34a
COLOR    DUP    21,507 04-10-95   11:34a
CONFIG   DUP        74 06-12-95    3:45p
CONFIG   SYS        74 06-12-95    3:45p
DOSFILE  DOC     3,594 02-22-95    2:04p
DOSFILE  DUP     3,594 02-22-95    2:04p
DOSNOTES BAK     3,594 02-22-95    2:04p
DOSNOTES DOC     3,594 02-22-95    2:04p
DOSNOTES DUP     3,594 02-22-95    2:04p
EMPLOYEE DAT     2,951 04-10-95    1:10p
EMPLOYEE DUP     2,951 04-10-95    1:10p
INVNTORY DAT     3,052 08-12-95    4:37p
INVNTORY DUP     3,052 08-12-95    4:37p
JUN-RPT  DUP     1,158 08-12-95    4:57p
JUN-RPT  LIS     1,158 08-12-95    4:57p
SALARY   DAT       175 07-01-95    8:02a
SMITH    DOC     3,048 02-15-95    8:47a
STATE    BAK       227 07-02-95   11:16a
STATE    TBL       227 07-02-95   10:02a
        23 file(s)        81,443 bytes

Directory of A:\SS

.            <DIR>         03-26-95   10:18p
..           <DIR>         03-26-95   10:18p
COLOR    DOC    21,507 04-10-95   11:34a
DOSFILE  DOC     3,594 02-22-95    2:04p
DOSNOTES DOC     3,594 02-22-95    2:04p
SMITH    DOC     3,048 02-15-95    8:47a
         6 file(s)        31,743 bytes

Directory of A:\WP

.            <DIR>         03-26-95   10:17p
..           <DIR>         03-26-95   10:17p
WPDOCS       <DIR>         03-26-95   10:18p
1Q-SLS   WQ1     1,156 04-12-95   12:06p
COLOR    DOC    21,507 04-10-95   11:34a
CONFIG   SYS        74 06-12-95    3:45p
DOSFILE  DOC     3,594 02-22-95    2:04p
DOSNOTES BAK     3,594 02-22-95    2:04p
DOSNOTES DOC     3,594 02-22-95    2:04p
EMPLOYEE DAT     2,951 04-10-95    1:10p
INVNTORY DAT     3,052 08-12-95    4:37p
JUN-RPT  LIS     1,158 08-12-95    4:57p
        12 file(s)        40,680 bytes

Directory of A:\WP\WPDOCS

.            <DIR>         03-26-95   10:18p
```

```
..           <DIR>         03-26-95   10:18p
         2 file(s)             0 bytes

Total files listed:
        43 file(s)       153,866 bytes
                       1,046,528 bytes free
```

FIGURE 2-33

Displaying the Directory Tree

Although you can use the /s qualifier on the dir command to list files in all subdirectories on a disk, you can display a neater representation of all subdirectories on a disk with the tree command. The **tree command** graphically lists the directory structure of a disk. With the tree command, you can list only directory names or both directory and filenames as shown in the steps on the next page.

TO GRAPHICALLY LIST THE DIRECTORY STRUCTURE OF A DISK

STEP 1: **Type** `tree` **and press the ENTER key.**

DOS displays the names of all of the directories on the default drive, beginning with the current directory (Figure 2-34). Because the current directory is the root, all subdirectories on the disk are displayed. Notice each child directory displays indented beneath its parent.

FIGURE 2-34

STEP 2: **Type** `tree /f /a > prn` **and press the ENTER key.**

DOS prints the files in all of the directories on the default drive beginning with the current directory (Figure 2-35). The /f qualifier instructs DOS to also list files with the directories. Because many printers cannot print the graphic lines, the /a qualifier instructs DOS to use text characters rather than the graphic characters in the tree output.

```
Directory PATH listing for Volume VERMAAT
Volume Serial Number is 3631-1DCD
A:.
|    SMITH.DOC
|    DOSNOTES.DOC
|    COLOR.DOC
|    EMPLOYEE.DAT
|    1Q-SLS.WQ1
|    CONFIG.SYS
|    SALARY.DAT
|    STATE.TBL
|    STATE.BAK
|    INVNTORY.DAT
|    JUN-RPT.LIS
|    DOSNOTES.BAK
|    DOSFILE.DOC
|    DOSNOTES.DUP
|    COLOR.DUP
|    EMPLOYEE.DUP
|    1Q-SLS.DUP
|    CONFIG.DUP
|    INVNTORY.DUP
|    JUN-RPT.DUP
|    DOSFILE.DUP
|
+---WP
|        DOSNOTES.DOC
|        COLOR.DOC
|        EMPLOYEE.DAT
|        1Q-SLS.WQ1
|        CONFIG.SYS
|        INVNTORY.DAT
|        JUN-RPT.LIS
|        DOSNOTES.BAK
|        DOSFILE.DOC
|
|   \---WPDOCS
\---SS
         DOSNOTES.DOC
         SMITH.DOC
         COLOR.DOC
         DOSFILE.DOC
```

FIGURE 2-35

To view the directory structure of a different disk, add the drive name followed by a colon as a parameter on the tree command. For example, the command tree c: /f displays the directory structure of drive C.

. . . .

▼   **REMOVING SUBDIRECTORIES**

When you no longer need a subdirectory, you can remove, or delete, it. You use the **rmdir command**, abbreviated **rd**, to remove a subdirectory from a disk. You must be in another directory before you can remove a subdirectory, and you must first move or remove all the files stored within it. DOS takes this precaution to prevent you from accidentally removing a subdirectory containing files you need to keep. Follow these steps to remove the SS subdirectory from the disk in drive A.

TO REMOVE A SUBDIRECTORY AND VERIFY THE RESULTS

STEP 1:   **Type** del ss **and press the ENTER key.**

DOS responds with the prompt, All files in directory will be deleted! Are you sure (Y/N)? (Figure 2-36). When you place a subdirectory name after the del command, you instruct DOS to erase all files in that subdirectory.

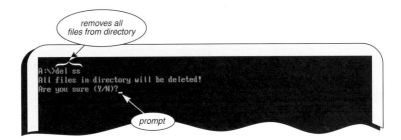

FIGURE 2-36

STEP 2:   **Type the letter** y **and press the ENTER key.**

DOS deletes all the files in the SS subdirectory.

STEP 3:   **Type** dir ss **and press the ENTER key.**

DOS displays the directory of SS (Figure 2-37). Notice it contains just two files: the dot and dot dot entries. A subdirectory with just these entries may be removed.

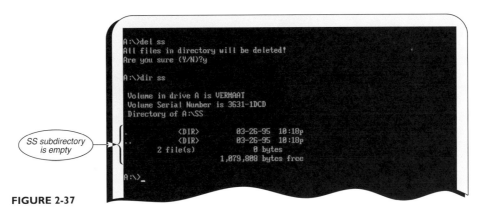

FIGURE 2-37

STEP 4:   **Type** cls **and press the ENTER key. Type** rd ss **and press the ENTER key.**

DOS removes the SS subdirectory from the disk in drive A.

STEP 5: Type tree **and press the ENTER key.**

DOS displays the directory structure of the disk in drive A (Figure 2-38). Notice the SS subdirectory is not in the list.

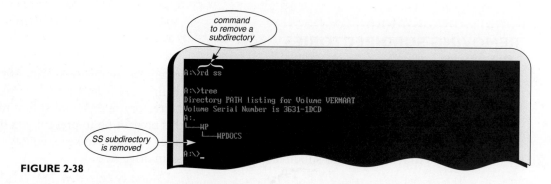

FIGURE 2-38

▼ CHECKING THE STATUS OF A DISK

You may want to know the number of directories and files you have on a disk. The **chkdsk command** checks the condition of your disk and reports disk statistics to you as shown in these steps.

TO CHECK THE STATUS OF A DISK

STEP 1: Type chkdsk **and press the ENTER key.**

DOS displays several lines of summary information (Figure 2-39). These lines indicate how many bytes (characters) can be stored on the disk; how much of this disk space is used by how many directories; how much of this disk space is used by how many files; and how much disk space is available for future storage. This command also reports allocation unit statistics and how much base memory you have on your computer and how much of the base memory is available for use.

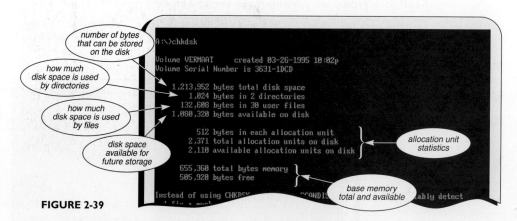

FIGURE 2-39

You should issue the chkdsk command periodically to determine if your disk has a problem. If the chkdsk command checks your disk and detects a problem(s), it displays diagnostic messages. If these messages display, ask your instructor for assistance.

▼   **COPYING AN ENTIRE DISKETTE**

With the copy command and wildcard characters, you can copy all of the files in a specific subdirectory to another subdirectory or disk. However, if you want to backup an entire disk (all subdirectories and all files), you should use the **diskcopy command**. The source and destination disks will be identical at the conclusion of the diskcopy; therefore, DOS destroys the existing contents of the destination disk as it copies the new information to it. Additionally, the source and target must be the same. That is, if the source is a 5 1/4 inch high-density disk, the target also must be a 5 1/4 inch high-density disk. Because most computer configurations today have drive A and B as different sizes or densities, you must specify the source and target drive as the same drive as shown in these steps.

TO COPY AN ENTIRE DISKETTE

STEP 1:   **Type** `diskcopy a: a:` **and press the ENTER key.**

DOS prompts you to insert the source diskette into drive A (Figure 2-40).

FIGURE 2-40

STEP 2:   **Insert the disk you want to copy from into drive A.**

STEP 3:   **Press the ENTER key (you can actually press any key).**

DOS begins reading the contents of the source disk into memory and then prompts you to insert the target diskette into drive A (Figure 2-41).

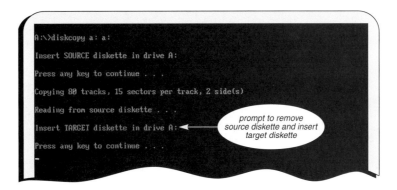

FIGURE 2-41

STEP 4:   **Remove the source disk from drive A. Insert the disk you want the files copied to into drive A. Remember, any existing files on the target diskette will be erased.**

STEP 5:   **Press the ENTER key (you can actually press any key).**

DOS begins writing the files from memory to the target diskette. Depending on the size and density of your disks and the DOS version you are using, DOS may prompt you to insert your source and target diskettes one or more times to swap data. After copying, DOS asks if you want to write another duplicate of this disk.

STEP 6: **Type the letter** n **for No.**

DOS assigns a volume serial number to the destination disk and asks if you want to copy another diskette (Figure 2-42).

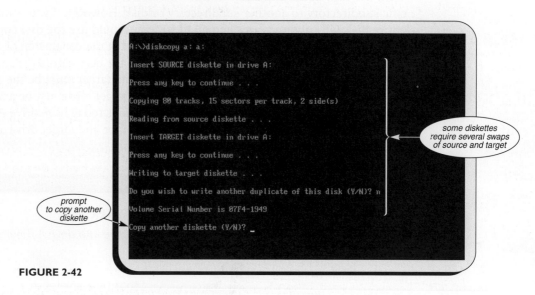

```
A:\>diskcopy a: a:

Insert SOURCE diskette in drive A:

Press any key to continue . . .

Copying 80 tracks, 15 sectors per track, 2 side(s)

Reading from source diskette . . .

Insert TARGET diskette in drive A:

Press any key to continue . . .

Writing to target diskette . . .

Do you wish to write another duplicate of this disk (Y/N)? n

Volume Serial Number is 07F4-1949

Copy another diskette (Y/N)? _
```

some diskettes require several swaps of source and target

prompt to copy another diskette

FIGURE 2-42

STEP 7: **Type the letter** n **for No.**

You return to the DOS prompt. Both the source and target diskettes are now duplicates of each other.

The diskcopy command only works with diskettes; therefore, you cannot use the diskcopy command to backup a hard disk.

▼ **PROJECT SUMMARY**

In Project 2, you learned how to make, change, and remove subdirectories; change the current directory and specify the path; use wildcard characters in commands; use qualifiers on the dir command; redirect output to the printer; and use the chkdsk and diskcopy commands. All the activities you learned in this project are summarized in the Quick Reference.

▼ **KEY TERMS**

asterisk (*) wildcard character *(DOS53)*

backup copy *(DOS56)*

chdir command (cd) *(DOS48)*

child directory *(DOS43)*

chkdsk command *(DOS68)*

current directory *(DOS49)*

diskcopy command *(DOS69)*

dot entry *(DOS46)*

dot dot entry *(DOS46)*

mkdir command (md) *(DOS44)*

move command *(DOS58)*

parent directory *(DOS43)*

path *(DOS46)*

qualifier *(DOS61)*

question mark (?) wildcard character *(DOS57)*

redirect output symbol (>) *(DOS63)*

rmdir command (rd) *(DOS67)*

root directory *(DOS42)*

subdirectories *(DOS43)*

tree command *(DOS65)*

wildcard characters *(DOS53)*

....

▼   QUICK REFERENCE

The following table provides a quick reference to each task presented in the project.

Task	Command Syntax	Description
Change Directory	cd directory-path	Changes the current directory on a disk
Check Disk Status	chkdsk	Verifies and reports a disk's condition
Make Subdirectory	md directory-name	Creates a new subdirectory
Move Files	move source target	Transfers the source file specification to the target file specification
Remove	rd directory-path	Removes a subdirectory from a disk
Tree	tree /f	Displays the directory structure of a disk

SHORT ANSWER ASSIGNMENTS

SHORT ANSWER ASSIGNMENT 1
True/False

Instructions: Circle T if the statement is true or F if the statement is false.

T   F   1. Every disk has at least two root directories.

T   F   2. A root directory has room to keep track of an unlimited number of files.

T   F   3. The root directory can also be a parent directory.

T   F   4. A subdirectory can have subdirectories.

T   F   5. A subdirectory name cannot have an extension.

T   F   6. The dir a: command always produces a directory listing of the files in the root directory of drive A.

T   F   7. To move from one subdirectory to another, use the move command.

T   F   8. The delete command can be used to remove a subdirectory and all of its files.

T   F   9. You can only use one wildcard question mark character in a command to identify a file's name.

T   F   10. Use the tree command to display the directory structure of a disk.

T   F   11. The chkdsk command displays the names of the subdirectories on a disk.

T   F   12. Both the source and target drive must be the same type when you use the diskcopy command.

T   F   13. Use the cd command to create a new subdirectory.

T   F   14. The redirect output symbol is an equal sign (=).

T F   15. The command dir /o prints a directory.

T F   16. A subdirectory can be both a parent and a child.

T F   17. The dot entry refers to the subdirectory, and the dot dot entry refers to its parent.

T F   18. The command cd.. always returns you to the root directory.

T F   19. The asterisk wildcard character is used to represent one or more characters in a file's name or extension.

T F   20. The command del wp removes the wp subdirectory from the default drive.

SHORT ANSWER ASSIGNMENT 2
Multiple Choice

Instructions: Circle the correct response.

1. To make a new subdirectory, use the _____ command.
   a. cd
   b. md
   c. rd
   d. td

2. The _____ is the first entry in a path.
   a. backslash
   b. filename
   c. subdirectory name
   d. drive name

3. Filenames are grouped on disks into _____.
   a. current directories
   b. source and target filename entries
   c. internally labeled entries
   d. directories and subdirectories

4. The _____ command is used to transfer files from one location to another.
   a. del
   b. move
   c. copy
   d. tree

5. The _____ qualifier tells the dir command to display one screenful of files at a time.
   a. /a
   b. /p
   c. /w
   d. /o

6. The _____ command is used to duplicate the contents of a disk.
   a. chkdsk
   b. rd
   c. tree
   d. diskcopy

7. Which wildcard character means match all characters that follow?
   a. asterisk (*)
   b. ampersand (&)
   c. percent sign (%)
   d. question mark (?)

8. Which command returns you to the parent directory?

   a. cd .
   b. cd ..
   c. cd >
   d. cd <

9. To print a directory listing, enter the _____ command.

   a. print dir
   b. print > dir
   c. dir < prn
   d. dir > prn

10. The _____ command is used to check the status of a disk.

   a. chkdsk
   b. status
   c. checkdisk
   d. diskcheck

SHORT ANSWER ASSIGNMENT 3
Fill in the Blanks

1. The special file directory created when a disk is formatted is called the _____ directory.

2. A _____ is a directory that you make on a disk.

3. Use the _____ command to make a subdirectory.

4. The _____ character is used to represent the root directory.

5. Use the _____ command to delete a subdirectory.

6. Use the _____ command to move files from one subdirectory to another.

7. The _____ command enables you to change from one subdirectory to another.

8. Use the _____ command to display the number of directories on a disk.

SHORT ANSWER ASSIGNMENT 4
Using DOS Commands

Instructions: Explain how to accomplish each of the following tasks using DOS.

Problem 1: Copy all of the files from the root directory on the disk in drive A to the root directory of the disk in drive A.

Explanation: _____

_____

_____

Problem 2: Make a subdirectory named SUB1 on your disk in drive A.

Explanation: _____

_____

_____

Problem 3: Transfer all files from the SUB1 subdirectory to the SUB2 subdirectory.

Explanation: _____

_____

_____

Problem 4: Erase the files in subdirectory SUB1 and remove subdirectory SUB1.

Explanation: _____

_____

_____

SHORT ANSWER ASSIGNMENT 5
Understanding DOS Commands

Instructions: Explain what will happen after you perform each of the following DOS commands.

Problem 1: Type copy g*.* c: at the A:\> prompt and press the ENTER key.

Explanation: _____

_____

_____

Problem 2: Type erase d?s.* at the C:\> prompt and press the ENTER key.

Explanation: _____

_____

_____

Problem 3: Type diskcopy a: a: at the A:\> prompt and press the ENTER key.

Explanation: _____

_____

_____

Problem 4: Type dir \dos at the C:\> prompt and press the ENTER key.

Explanation: _____

_____

_____

SHORT ANSWER ASSIGNMENT 6
Recovering from Problems

Instructions: In each of the following situations, a problem occurred. Explain the cause of the problem and how it can be corrected.

Problem 1:   You type cd .. and press the ENTER key. DOS responds with the message Invalid directory.

Cause of problem: _____

_____

Method of correction: _____

_____

Problem 2:   The current drive is A, and the current directory is DIRA. You attempt to delete subdirectory DIRA and DOS responds with the message, Invalid path, not directory, or directory not empty.

Cause of problem: _____

_____

Method of correction: _____

_____

Problem 3:   Your computer has a hard disk, and the root directory contains 512 files. Even though you know you have enough room for the file, when you attempt to store another file in the root directory, DOS prevents you from doing it.

Cause of problem: _____

_____

Method of correction: _____

_____

Problem 4:   You want to display a directory one screenful at a time, and type the command `dir p` and press the ENTER key. DOS displays the message, File not found.

Cause of problem: _____

_____

Method of correction: _____

_____

SHORT ANSWER ASSIGNMENT 7
Directories on a Hard Drive or LAN

Instructions: If you used a hard disk or LAN to complete Project 2, perform the following tasks on the computer you used to complete Project 2.

1. Determine which directories you have on drive C, if you are using a hard disk, or on drive F, if you are using a LAN.

2. Draw a diagram of this directory structure.

HANDS-ON
EXERCISES

HANDS-ON EXERCISE 1
Working with Directories

Instructions: At the DOS prompt, perform the following tasks to create the subdirectories specified below. Each printout should be on a separate page and properly labeled.

1. Place a newly formatted disk into drive A and make these subdirectories in the root directory: SPSHEET, WORDPROC, GAMES, HOUSE, and MODEM.

2. Make two subdirectories in the SPSHEET subdirectory: FINANCES and EXPENSES.

3. Make three subdirectories in the WORDPROC subdirectory: WORKMEMO, PERSONAL, and WORDLIST.

4. Use the tree command to print the directory structure.

5. Make the HOUSE subdirectory the current directory.

6. Copy two or more files into the HOUSE subdirectory. You can use the files from either your data diskette or Student Diskette.

7. Copy all the files in the HOUSE subdirectory to the FINANCES subdirectory.

8. Use the tree command to print the directory structure with files.

9. Move the files from the HOUSE subdirectory to the EXPENSES subdirectory.

10. Remove the GAMES subdirectory from your disk.

11. Remove the EXPENSES subdirectory from your disk.

12. Use the tree command to print the directory structure with files.

HANDS-ON EXERCISE 2
Working with Directories

Instructions: At the DOS prompt, perform the following tasks to print the directory listings specified below. Each printout should be on a separate page. Handwrite the task number on the printout.

1. Insert your data diskette into drive A.

2. Print the directory listing for the root directory.

3. Print the directory listing for the WP subdirectory.

4. Print a wide directory listing for the root directory.

5. Print an alphabetical directory listing of all directories on the disk.

6. Print a directory listing of files in the root that begin with the letter s.

7. Print a directory listing of files in the WP subdirectory that have an extension of DOC.

8. Print a directory listing of files in the root directory that have five characters or less in their filename.

9. Print a directory listing of just directory names on the disk.

HANDS-ON EXERCISE 3
Working with Disks

Instructions: At the DOS prompt, perform the following tasks to work with your disks.

1. Make a duplicate copy of your data diskette.

2. Verify that both disks are identical by doing a chkdsk on both disks. Print the output from each chkdsk.

3. Verify that both disks are identical by doing a tree command with files on both disks. Print the output from each tree command.

Introduction to Paradox 4.5

for DOS

Creating a Database

··········
▼   **OBJECTIVES**

You will have mastered the material in this project when you can:

- Describe databases and database management systems
- Start Paradox
- Describe the features of the Paradox screen
- Select commands from menus
- Create a table
- Define the fields in a table
- Exit Paradox

- Add records to a table
- Close a window
- Print the contents of a table
- Use Table view and Form view to view data
- Manipulate windows
- Use the Help System
- Understand how to design a database to eliminate redundancy

··········
▼   **WHAT IS A DATABASE?**

Creating, storing, sorting, and retrieving data are important tasks. In their personal lives, many people keep a variety of records such as names, addresses, and phone numbers of friends and business associates, records of investments, records of expenses for tax purposes, and so on. These records must be arranged for quick access. Businesses must also be able to store and access information quickly and easily. Personnel and inventory records, payroll information, customer records, order data, and accounts receivable information are all crucial and must be readily available.

The term **database** describes a collection of data organized in a manner that allows access, retrieval, and use of that data. A **database management system (DBMS)**, like Paradox, allows you to use a computer to create a database; add, change, and delete data in the database; sort the data in the database; retrieve data in the database; and create forms and reports using the data in the database.

In Paradox, a database consists of a collection of tables. Figure 1-1 shows a sample database for an organization. It consists of two tables. The Customer table contains information about the customers of the organization. The Sales Rep table contains information about the organization's sales representatives.

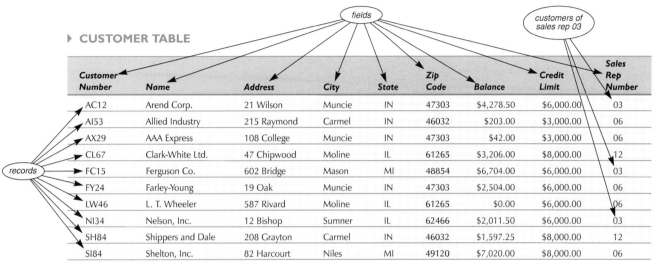

CUSTOMER TABLE

Customer Number	Name	Address	City	State	Zip Code	Balance	Credit Limit	Sales Rep Number
AC12	Arend Corp.	21 Wilson	Muncie	IN	47303	$4,278.50	$6,000.00	03
AI53	Allied Industry	215 Raymond	Carmel	IN	46032	$203.00	$3,000.00	06
AX29	AAA Express	108 College	Muncie	IN	47303	$42.00	$3,000.00	06
CL67	Clark-White Ltd.	47 Chipwood	Moline	IL	61265	$3,206.00	$8,000.00	12
FC15	Ferguson Co.	602 Bridge	Mason	MI	48854	$6,704.00	$6,000.00	03
FY24	Farley-Young	19 Oak	Muncie	IN	47303	$2,504.00	$6,000.00	06
LW46	L. T. Wheeler	587 Rivard	Moline	IL	61265	$0.00	$6,000.00	06
NI34	Nelson, Inc.	12 Bishop	Sumner	IL	62466	$2,011.50	$6,000.00	03
SH84	Shippers and Dale	208 Grayton	Carmel	IN	46032	$1,597.25	$8,000.00	12
SI84	Shelton, Inc.	82 Harcourt	Niles	MI	49120	$7,020.00	$8,000.00	06

SALES REP TABLE

Sales Rep Number	Last Name	First Name	Address	City	State	Zip Code	Sales	Commission Rate
03	Harrison	Monica	12 LaGrange	Parkton	MI	48154	$52,348.00	0.07
06	Thompson	Charles	1564 Birchview	Auburn	IN	46706	$78,202.00	0.05
12	Juarez	Mara	722 Davison	Chicago	IL	60614	$28,222.00	0.07

FIGURE 1-1

The rows in the tables are called records. A **record** contains information about a given person, product, or event. A row in the Customer table, for example, contains information about a specific customer.

The columns in the tables are called fields. A **field** contains a specific piece of information within a record. In the Customer table, for example, the fourth field, City, contains the city where the customer is located.

The first field in the Customer table is the Customer Number. This is a code assigned by the organization to each customer. Like many organizations, this organization calls it a *number* even though it actually contains letters. The customer numbers have a special format. They consist of two uppercase letters followed by a two-digit number.

These numbers are *unique*; that is, no two customers will be assigned the same number. Such a field can be used as a **unique identifier**. This means that a given customer number will appear in only a single record in the table. There is only one record, for example, in which the customer number is CL67. A unique identifier is also called a **primary key**. Thus, the Customer Number field is the primary key for the Customer table.

The next seven fields in the Customer table include the Name, Address, City, State, Zip Code, Balance, and Credit Limit. For example, customer AC12 is Arend Corp. It is located at 21 Wilson in Muncie, Indiana. The Zip Code is 47303. Its current balance (the amount it owes to the organization) is $4,278.50. Its credit limit (the amount its balance should not exceed) is $6,000.00.

The Sales Rep Number field in the Sales Rep table is a number assigned by the organization to each sales representative. These numbers are unique, so the Sales Rep Number is the primary key of the Sales Rep table.

The other fields in the Sales Rep table are Last Name, First Name, Address, City, State, Zip Code, Sales, and Commission Rate. For example, sales representative 03 is Monica Harrison. She lives at 12 LaGrange in Parkton, Michigan. Her Zip Code is 48154. So far this year, she has sold $52,348.00 worth of product. Her commission rate is 7% (0.07).

The last field in the Customer table, Sales Rep Number, serves a special purpose. It *relates* customers and sales representatives. Each customer has a single sales representative. The last field gives the number of the customer's sales representative.

Using the Sales Rep Number field, you see, for example, that the sales representative number for customer AC12 is 03. To find the name of this sales representative, look for the row in the Sales Rep table containing 03 in the Sales Rep Number field. Once you have found it, you will see the name of the sales representative is Monica Harrison. To find all the customers for whom Monica Harrison is the sales representative, look through the Customer table for all the customers containing 03 in the Sales Rep Number field. Her customers are AC12 (Arend Corp.), FC15 (Ferguson Co.), and NI34 (Nelson Inc.).

▼ WHAT IS PARADOX?

Paradox is a powerful database management system (DBMS) that allows you to create and process data in a database. To illustrate the use of Paradox, this book presents a series of projects. The projects use the database of customers and sales representatives. In Project 1, the two tables that comprise the database are created and the appropriate records are added to them. The project also uses a form to display the data in the tables and prints a report of data in the tables.

▼ USING A MOUSE WITH PARADOX

In Paradox, you can use a mouse to accomplish many of the tasks you can accomplish with the keyboard. The procedures for using a mouse are displayed with the special mouse icon. An instruction to *click* some portion of the screen means to move the mouse pointer to that portion of the screen, press the left mouse button, and then release it. An instruction to *drag* some item on the screen means to move the mouse pointer to the item, press and hold the left mouse button, move the item to the new location, and then release the mouse button.

▼   STARTING PARADOX

To start Paradox, use commands similar to those listed in the steps below. These commands assume that the database is on a disk that will be in drive A. If this is not the case, substitute the letter of the appropriate drive. Again, if this is not the case make the appropriate substitution. If you have any questions concerning the precise commands you will need, check with your instructor.

TO START PARADOX

STEP 1:   Type a: **and press the ENTER key.**

The drive containing the data disk is now the default drive.

STEP 2:   Type paradox **and press the ENTER key.**

For this command to work, the directory containing Paradox must be included in the DOS path. Often this will happen automatically when you boot the computer. If Paradox does not start when you execute this command, the Paradox directory is probably not included in the path. Check with your instructor to see what you should do in that case.

STEP 3:   When the Paradox logo displays on the screen, press the ESC key to remove it.

The Paradox main screen displays (Figure 1-2).

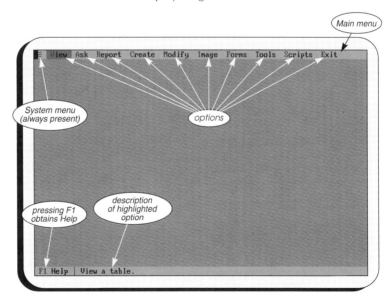

FIGURE 1-2

▼ WORKING WITH PARADOX

The Paradox Main Screen

The top line on the screen in Figure 1-2 on the previous page is the menu bar. It contains the **Main menu**. A **menu** is simply a list of options from which you can choose. The names on this line (View, Ask, Report, and so on) are the options on the menu. When working with Paradox, you will encounter situations where the list of options at the top of the screen is different, but the menu line always plays the same role — a collection of options.

The bottom line on the screen gives a description of the option on which the cursor is located. A **cursor** is a blinking underscore or a highlighted block indicating the location on the screen or pointing to an item you can select (for example, an option on a menu). The bottom line also indicates the effect of certain special keys. Currently, for example, it indicates that pressing F1 provides help.

In between the top line and the bottom line is the workspace. The **workspace** is where the work actually takes place.

When working with data from a table, Paradox refers to the copy of the data that is on the screen as an **image**, which is displayed in the workspace. It is possible to have more than one image in the workspace at the same time. Each image is displayed in a special type of box, called a **window.**

The ESC Key

The key labeled Esc is called the ESC (Escape) key. Sometimes you may accidentally choose the wrong option, or you may not want to proceed with some action you have started without being sure how to get out of it. When this happens, press the ESC key. In some cases, this immediately returns to the Main menu. In others, Paradox will provide specific instructions concerning the action necessary to escape from the task.

Using Menus

There are two ways to choose an option from the Main menu. The first is to use the LEFT ARROW or RIGHT ARROW key to move to the desired option and then press the ENTER key. The second is to type the highlighted letter.

Selecting a Menu Using the Arrow Keys When using the arrow keys to select a menu, press the RIGHT ARROW key until the cursor is on the menu option name and then press the ENTER key. After selecting this menu option, you will see the menu you selected. You would see the menu in Figure 1-3, for example, if you moved the cursor to the the Scripts menu name and then pressed the ENTER key.

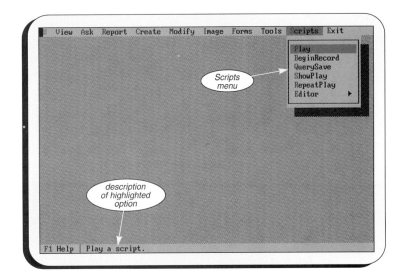

FIGURE 1-3

To choose a command from it, use the UP or DOWN ARROW key to move the cursor to the command and then press the ENTER key. If you don't want to proceed with this action at this time, press the ESC key to remove the menu from the screen.

Selecting a Menu by Typing the First Letter   In Paradox, you can also choose an option or command by typing the highlighted letter of the option or command. If you type the letter R (in either uppercase or lowercase), for example, the Report menu displays (Figure 1-4). From this menu, you can choose by typing the first letter of the command. To remove this menu from the screen, press the ESC key.

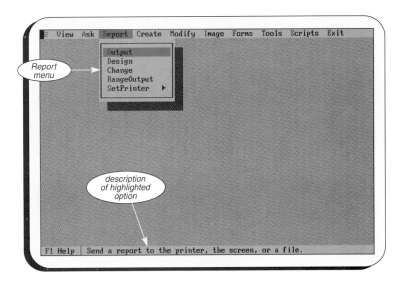

FIGURE 1-4

Producing a Cursor in the Menu   There are times when there is no cursor (highlighted block) on the menu line at the top of the screen. The menus are always available, however. Press F10 and a cursor will appear. Then make the selection by using either of the techniques previously discussed.

The following summarizes selecting an option from the Main menu or a command from a menu:

1. If there is no cursor (highlight) on the menu bar, press F10.
2. To move the cursor from one menu option to another, use the arrow keys or type the first letter of the option.
3. To choose the option or command on which the cursor is located, press the ENTER key.

Mouse Users: *To choose a command or menu option, click the command or menu option; that is, move the mouse pointer to the command or option and then click the left mouse button.*

Using DO-IT! or Cancel

The F2 key is called the **DO-IT!** key. Pressing F2 completes the task on which you are working and returns control to the Main menu. Some of the menus contain a DO-IT! command. Choosing this command from the menu does the same thing as pressing F2.

▶ **STRUCTURE OF CUSTOMER TABLE**

Field Name	Type	Size	Key
Customer Number	A	4	*
Name	A	20	
Address	A	15	
City	A	15	
State	A	2	
Zip Code	A	5	
Balance	$		
Credit Limit	$		
Sales Rep Number	A	2	

Most menus that contain a DO-IT! command also contain a **Cancel command**. Choosing the Cancel command causes Paradox to abandon the changes and return to the Main menu. In some cases, pressing the ESC key will also abandon changes and return to the Main menu. In many situations, however, the only way to cancel the changes is by using the Cancel command.

Mouse Users: *If the F2 key indicator appears on the bottom line of the screen, clicking the F2 key indicator has the same effect as pressing F2.*

▶ **DATA FOR CUSTOMER TABLE**

FIGURE I-5

Customer Number	Name	Address	City	State	Zip Code	Balance	Credit Limit	Sales Rep Number
AC12	Arend Corp.	21 Wilson	Muncie	IN	47303	$4,278.50	$6,000.00	03
AI53	Allied Industry	215 Raymond	Carmel	IN	46032	$203.00	$3,000.00	06
AX29	AAA Express	108 College	Muncie	IN	47303	$42.00	$3,000.00	06
CL67	Clark-White Ltd.	47 Chipwood	Moline	IL	61265	$3,206.00	$8,000.00	12
FC15	Ferguson Co.	602 Bridge	Mason	MI	48854	$6,704.00	$6,000.00	03
FY24	Farley-Young	19 Oak	Muncie	IN	47303	$2,504.00	$6,000.00	06
LW46	L. T. Wheeler	587 Rivard	Moline	IL	61265	$0.00	$6,000.00	06
NI34	Nelson, Inc.	12 Bishop	Sumner	IL	62466	$2,011.50	$6,000.00	03
SH84	Shippers and Dale	208 Grayton	Carmel	IN	46032	$1,597.25	$8,000.00	12
SI84	Shelton, Inc.	82 Harcourt	Niles	MI	49120	$7,020.00	$8,000.00	06

▼   **CREATING A TABLE**

A Paradox database consists of a collection of tables. In creating a database, you are to create each of the tables within it. Creating a table is a two-step process. First, you enter the structure, that is, the collection of field names and field characteristics that comprise the table (Figure 1-5). Second, you add the records to the table. In this project, for example, you must create both the Customer and Sales Rep tables shown in Figure 1-1 on page P3.

Beginning the Table Creation

To begin creating a table, use the Create menu option of the Main menu as shown in the following steps.

TO CREATE A TABLE

STEP 1:   **Choose the Create menu option from the Main menu.**

The dialog box shown in Figure 1-6 displays. You are to enter a name for the table at the cursor location.

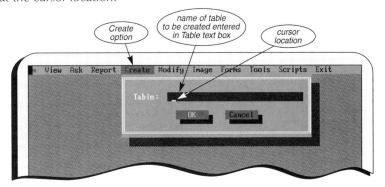

FIGURE 1-6

STEP 2:   **Type** Customer **as the name of the table and press the ENTER key.**

The Create: Customer window displays (Figure 1-7). You will define the structure by entering the names and types of all the fields in the table (top of Figure 1-5).

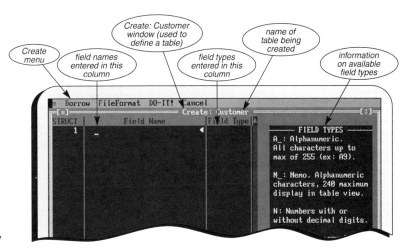

FIGURE 1-7

In the Create: Customer window, the FIELD TYPES list box describes the possible field types.

The rules for **field names** are:

1. They must be no more than 25 characters long.
2. The first character must not be a blank.
3. The remaining characters cannot be square brackets ([ ]), braces ({ }), parentheses (( )), double quotation marks ("), number signs (#), or the special combination consisting of a hyphen followed by a greater-than sign (->). In these projects, you will use only letters and numbers.
4. The same name cannot be used for two different fields in the same table.

Each field has a field type. A **field type** indicates the type of data that can be stored in the field. The possibilities are:

1. **Alphanumeric.**   The field can contain any characters.
2. **Memo.**   The field can contain large amounts of text.
3. **Numeric.**   The field can contain only numbers. The numbers can be either positive or negative. Fields of this type can be used in arithmetic operations.
4. **Currency.**   The field can contain only dollar amounts. The values will be displayed with dollar signs. Like numeric fields, currency fields can be used in arithmetic operations.
5. **Date.**   The field can contain only a legitimate date stored in one of the forms — mm/dd/yy, dd-mon-yy, or dd.mm.yy (for example, 11/05/95 or 05-Nov-95 or 05.11.95).

The field names, types, sizes, and key information for the Customer table are shown at the top of Figure 1-8. The following steps define these fields.

TO DEFINE THE FIELDS

STEP 1:   Type Customer Number **in the Field Name column and press the ENTER key.**

The screen shown in Figure 1-8 displays. The cursor is now in the column labeled Field Type.

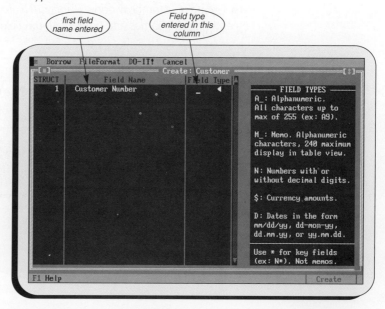

FIGURE 1-8

STEP 2: **Type** A4* **and press the ENTER key.**

The entries for the first field are complete. The field type for customer numbers is A, the **field size***, or width, is 4, and the field is a key field.* **Key field** *is the Paradox term for primary key (see page P3). The key field must be the first field in the table. To designate a field as a key field, follow the field type with an asterisk (Figure 1-9).*

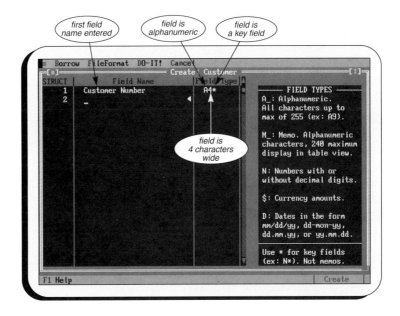

FIGURE I-9

STEP 3: **Enter the information for the remaining fields as shown in Figure 1-10. For currency fields, only type the dollar sign. You don't have to indicate a field size.**

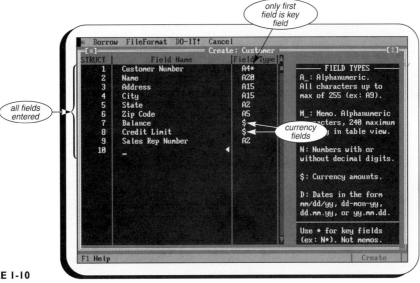

FIGURE I-10

STEP 4:   Press F2 (DO-IT!) to save the table to disk.

Paradox returns to the main screen (Figure 1-11). The Customer table is stored on the disk in drive A using the filename CUSTOMER.

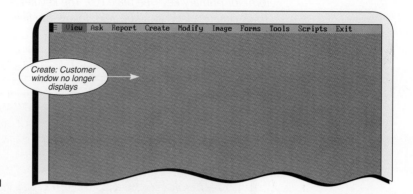

View Ask Report Create Modify Image Forms Tools Scripts Exit

Create: Customer window no longer displays

FIGURE 1-11

You can also achieve the same result by pressing F10 and choosing DO-IT! from the menu. If for some reason you do not want to save your work, press F10 and choose Cancel from the menu.

Changing the Structure

When creating a table, check the entries carefully to ensure they are correct before pressing F2. If you make a mistake and discover it before pressing the ENTER key, correct the error by pressing the BACKSPACE key until you have removed the incorrect characters. Then, type the correct characters. If you don't discover a mistake until after moving to another field in the structure, correct it by using the keys shown in Table 1-1.

TABLE 1-1

Key	Purpose
UP ARROW	Move the cursor up one row.
DOWN ARROW	Move the cursor down one row.
RIGHT ARROW	Moves the cursor one column to the right.
LEFT ARROW	Moves the cursor one column to the left.
HOME	Moves the cursor to the first field.
END	Moves the cursor to the last field.
INSERT	Inserts a field at the cursor position.
DELETE	Deletes the field at the cursor position.
BACKSPACE	Moves the cursor one position to the left and deletes the character in that position
ENTER	Completes the current entry and moves the cursor to the next column. If the cursor is in the last column in a row, moves it to the first column in the next row.
CTRL+END	Moves the cursor to the rightmost column

If you accidentally add an extra field to the structure, move the cursor to the field name and press the DELETE key. This action removes the field from the structure.

If you forget a field, move the cursor to the Field Name column on the row where the field should be inserted and press the INSERT key. The remaining fields move down one row, making room for the missing field. Make the entries for the field in the usual manner.

 Mouse Users: *To move to an entry to be changed, click the entry. Then make the appropriate change.*

As an alternative to modifying the structure, you may want to start over, especially if the changes are significant. To start over, press F10 and choose Cancel.

Changing the Structure of a Previously Saved Table

It is easiest to correct errors in the structure before you save the table (that is, before you press F2). If you don't discover the error until later, you can still fix it.

To make changes to the structure of a previously saved table, choose the Modify option from the Main menu, choose Restructure, and then select the table. Change the structure using the techniques of the previous section and then press F2.

▼   **EXITING PARADOX**

The first step in creating the Customer table (building the structure) is now complete. You can immediately begin adding records to the table. If you prefer not to do this all in one session, you can exit Paradox at this point by choosing Exit from the Main menu as illustrated in the following steps.

TO EXIT PARADOX

STEP 1:   Choose Exit.

The Exit menu displays (Figure 1-12).

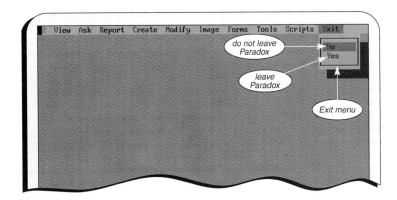

FIGURE 1-12

STEP 2:   Choose Yes.

Control returns to DOS. After you exit Paradox, remove your diskette from drive A.

To reenter Paradox, start it in the manner illustrated on page P5.

▼ ADDING RECORDS TO THE CUSTOMER TABLE

Adding Initial Records

In this section, you are to add customers into a special Entry table and then have Paradox add these records to the Customer table when you are done. This is called the **DataEntry mode** and is especially useful when adding several records at a time. The special keys for DataEntry mode are shown in Table 1-2.

TABLE 1-2

Key	Purpose
UP ARROW	Moves the cursor up one row.
DOWN ARROW	Moves the cursor down one row.
RIGHT ARROW	Moves the cursor one column to the right.
LEFT ARROW	Moves the cursor one column to the left.
HOME	Moves the cursor to the first record.
END	Moves the cursor to the last record.
CTRL+HOME	Moves the cursor to the leftmost column.
CTRL+END	Moves the cursor to the rightmost column.
CTRL+RIGHT ARROW	Moves right one screenful.
CTRL+LEFT ARROW	Moves left one screenful.
INSERT	Inserts a new record at the cursor position (only in one of the editing modes).
DELETE	Deletes the record at the cursor position (only in one of the editing modes).
BACKSPACE	Moves the cursor one position to the left and deletes the character in that position (only in one of the editing modes).
ENTER	Completes the current entry and moves the cursor to the next column. If the cursor is in the last column in a row, moves it to the first column in the next row.
PAGE DOWN	Moves down one screenful.
PAGE UP	Moves up one screenful.

To use DataEntry mode, choose the Modify menu option on the Main menu followed by the DataEntry command as shown in the following steps.

TO ADD RECORDS USING DATAENTRY MODE

STEP 1: Choose the Modify menu option from the Main menu and move the cursor to DataEntry (Figure 1-13).

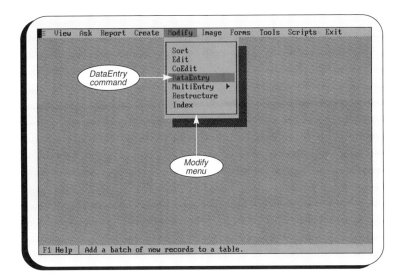

FIGURE 1-13

STEP 2: Press ENTER to choose DataEntry.

Paradox instructs you to enter the name of the table (Figure 1-14). Either type the name or press the ENTER key. If you press the ENTER key, Paradox displays a list of available tables. You can then choose from the list by moving the cursor to the desired table with the arrow keys and then pressing the ENTER key.

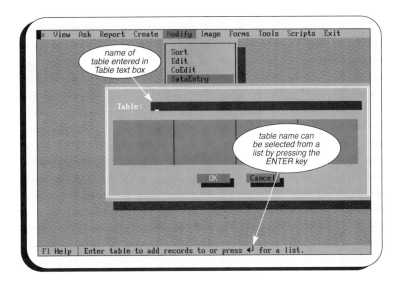

FIGURE 1-14

STEP 3: **Press the ENTER key.**

A list of available tables displays (Figure 1-15). Only one table (Customer) is currently listed.

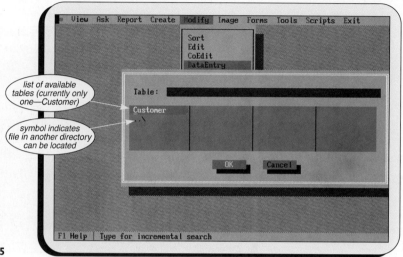

FIGURE 1-15

STEP 4: **Be sure the cursor is on Customer and press the ENTER key.**

The Data Entry: Customer window displays (Figure 1-16).

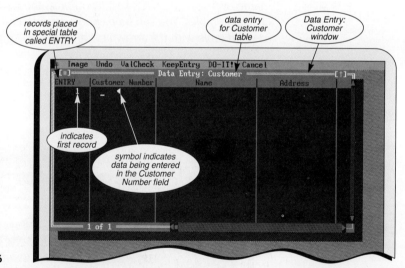

FIGURE 1-16

 Mouse Users: *To choose a table, click the name of the table you want and then click the OK button.*

Notice in the lower right-hand corner of the screen the word DataEntry indicating that Paradox is in DataEntry mode. When Paradox is in DataEntry mode, the special DataEntry menu instead of the Main menu is shown at the top of the screen. By choosing either DO-IT! or Cancel from this menu, Paradox will return to the Main menu. You are to enter data into the table named ENTRY. The window name indicates that it is DataEntry for the Customer table. Therefore, at the conclusion of data entry, the records will be added to the Customer table.

Space for a first record displays on the screen. The cursor is in the Customer Number field, indicating you should enter a customer number. The following steps add the first two records to the ENTRY table.

TO ADD RECORDS TO THE CUSTOMER TABLE

STEP 1: Type `AC12`, the first customer number (Figure 1-17). Be sure to type both the A and the C in uppercase. Press the TAB key to complete the entry and move the cursor to the Name field.

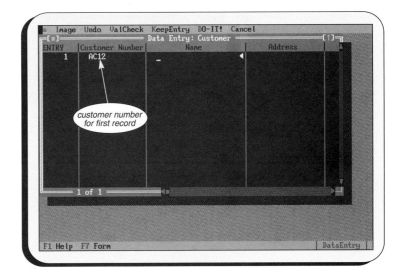

FIGURE 1-17

STEP 2: Type `Arend Corp.` and press the TAB key. Type the address, `21 Wilson`.

The Customer Number, Name, and Address fields are entered (Figure 1-18). Other fields are not currently visible.

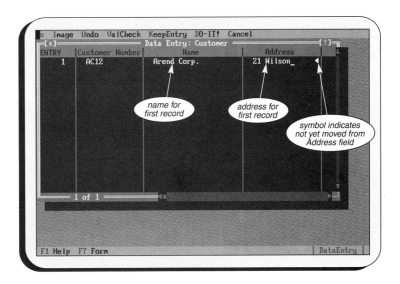

FIGURE 1-18

STEP 3:   **Press the TAB key.**

The fields shift to the left, making room for the City, State, and Zip Code fields (Figure 1-19).

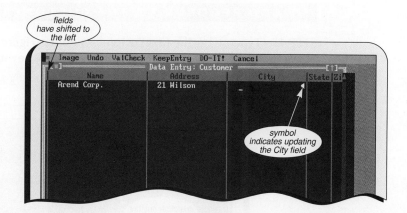

FIGURE 1-19

STEP 4:   **In the City field, type** `Muncie` **and press the TAB key. Type the state,** `IN`**. Type the zip code,** `47303`**. Type the balance,** `4278.50`**. Type the credit limit,** `6000`**. Press the TAB key after each entry. Type the Sales Rep Number,** `03`**.**

The data for the first record has been typed (Figure 1-20).

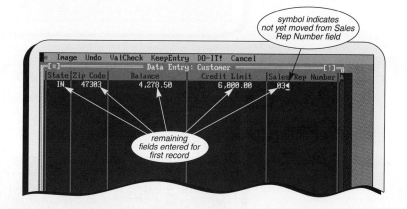

FIGURE 1-20

STEP 5:   **Press the TAB key.**

The fields shift back to the right, the first record is stored, and the cursor moves to the customer number on the next row (Figure 1-21). The first record has been entered and Paradox is ready for you to enter a second record.

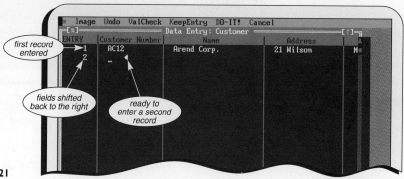

FIGURE 1-21

▶ CUSTOMER TABLE

Customer Number	Name	Address	City	State	Zip Code	Balance	Credit Limit	Sales Rep Number
AC12	Arend Corp.	21 Wilson	Muncie	IN	47303	$4,278.50	$6,000.00	03
AI53	Allied Industry	215 Raymond	Carmel	IN	46032	$203.00	$3,000.00	06
AX29	AAA Express	108 College	Muncie	IN	47303	$42.00	$3,000.00	06
CL67	Clark-White Ltd.	47 Chipwood	Moline	IL	61265	$3,206.00	$8,000.00	12
FC15	Ferguson Co.	602 Bridge	Mason	MI	48854	$6,704.00	$6,000.00	03
FY24	Farley-Young	19 Oak	Muncie	IN	47303	$2,504.00	$6,000.00	06
LW46	L. T. Wheeler	587 Rivard	Moline	IL	61265	$0.00	$6,000.00	06
NI34	Nelson, Inc.	12 Bishop	Sumner	IL	62466	$2,011.50	$6,000.00	03
SH84	Shippers and	208 Grayton	Carmel	IN	46032	$1,597.25	$8,000.00	12
SI84	Shelton, Inc.	82 Harcourt	Niles	MI	49120	$7,020.00	$8,000.00	06

FIGURE 1-22

STEP 6:   **Use the techniques in Steps 1 through 5 to add the data for the second record in Figure 1-22.**

The two records are added and the cursor is in the Customer Number field for a third record (Figure 1-23).

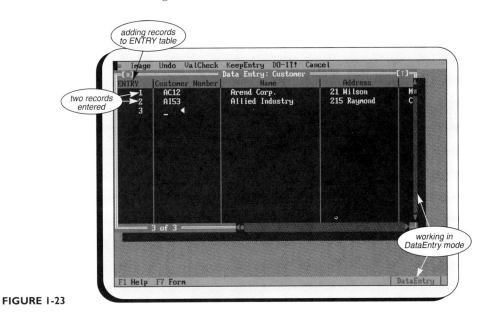

FIGURE 1-23

STEP 7:   Press F2 (DO-IT!).

The records are added to the Customer table and Paradox returns to Main mode (Figure 1-24). The Main menu is on the screen and the word Main appears in the lower right-hand corner. An image of the Customer table is on the screen and it contains the two records just entered.

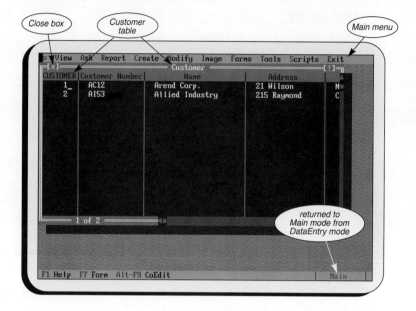

FIGURE 1-24

Closing the Window

When you have finished working with a table, close the table by closing the window containing the image of the table, and perform the following step.

TO CLOSE THE WINDOW

STEP 1:   Press F8.

The image of the Customer table is no longer displayed on the screen (Figure 1-25).

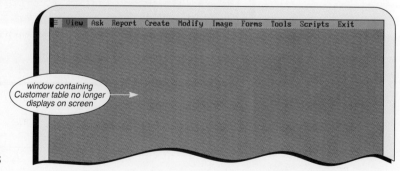

FIGURE 1-25

Mouse Users: *To close a window, click the Close box ([■]) in the upper left corner of the screen.*

▼   ADDING ADDITIONAL RECORDS

Records can be added to a table that already contains data using a process identical to the process of adding records to an empty table. The following steps illustrate how to add the remaining records to the Customer table.

In steps, when you are instructed to choose two or more menu options and commands in succession, the options will be separated by a vertical line. This is a common shorthand notation that shortens the wording from choose Modify, choose DataEntry to choose Modify|DataEntry.

TO ADD THE REMAINING RECORDS TO THE CUSTOMER TABLE

STEP 1:   **Choose Modify|DataEntry.**

STEP 2:   **Press the ENTER key.**

Paradox displays a list of the tables on disk.

STEP 3:   **With the cursor on Customer, press the ENTER key.**

STEP 4:   **Add the remaining eight records in Figure 1-22 (on page P19) using the same techniques used to add the first two records.**

The records display (Figure 1-26). The cursor is in position for another record.

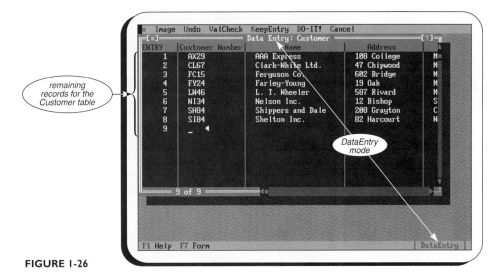

FIGURE 1-26

STEP 5:   **Press F2 to complete the data entry process.**

Paradox adds the records to the Customer table.

STEP 6:   **Press F8 to remove the image of the Customer table from the screen.**

Paradox maintains the data so it is always ordered by the primary key. Because Customer Number is the primary key of the Customer table, the data in the table will automatically be arranged so the customer numbers are in alphabetical order. The data just entered happened to be in the correct order. If you enter a record containing a customer number that is not in alphabetical order, however, Paradox will automatically place it in order once you have completely entered the record. For example, if you add a record with customer number PR29, Paradox will move the record so it appears between the record for customer NI34 and the one for customer SH84. In general, records are always ordered in ascending order by the key field.

Correcting Errors in the Data

Just as when you created the table, check the entries carefully to ensure they are correct. If you make a mistake and discover it before pressing the TAB key, correct it by pressing the BACKSPACE key until the incorrect characters are removed and then typing the correct characters.

If you discover an incorrect entry later, use the keys shown in Table 1-2 on page P14 to correct them. If the record to be corrected is not on the screen, use the UP ARROW or DOWN ARROW key to move the cursor to it. If the field to be corrected is not visible on the screen, use the LEFT ARROW or RIGHT ARROW key to shift all the fields until it displays. Then make the correction.

If you accidentally add an extra record, move to the record and press the DELETE key. This will remove the record from the table. If you forget a record, add it using the same procedure as for all the other records. Paradox will automatically place it in the correct location in the table.

Occasionally a record you thought you added is not in the table. In this case, you probably made a mistake entering the customer number. Suppose, for example, that when you typed the fifth record in Figure 1-22 (Ferguson Co.), you accidentally entered the customer number for the sixth record (FY24). When you later try to add the sixth record, Paradox rejects the addition, because a record with the same customer number (FY24) is already in the table. If this occurs, check the customer numbers carefully, make any necessary corrections, and then add the new record.

▼ PRINTING THE CONTENTS OF A TABLE

When working with a database, you will often need to obtain a printed copy of the contents of the table. Figure 1-27 shows a printed copy of the contents of the Customer table. Because the Customer table is substantially wider than will fit on the paper, a portion shows on one page (Figure 1-27a) and the rest shows on the second page (Figure 1-27b).

```
10/04/94                      Standard Report              Page  1


Customer Number  Name                  Address          City         State
---------------  --------------------  ---------------  -----------  -----
AC12             Arend Corp.           21 Wilson        Muncie       IN
AI53             Allied Industry       215 Raymond      Carmel       IN
AX29             AAA Express           108 College      Muncie       IN
CL67             Clark-White Ltd.      47 Chipwood      Moline       IL
FC15             Ferguson Co.          602 Bridge       Mason        MI
FY24             Farley-Young          19 Oak           Muncie       IN
LW46             L. T. Wheeler         587 Rivard       Moline       IL
NI34             Nelson Inc.           12 Bishop        Sumner       IL
SH84             Shippers and Dale     208 Grayton      Carmel       IN
SI84             Shelton Inc.          82 Harcourt      Niles        MI
```

FIGURE 1-27a

```
Zip Code  Balance           Credit Limit      Sales Rep Number
--------  ----------------  ----------------  ----------------
47303             4,278.50          6,000.00  03
46032               203.00          3,000.00  06
47303                42.00          3,000.00  06
61265             3,206.00          8,000.00  12
48854             6,704.00          6,000.00  03
47303             2,504.00          6,000.00  06
61265                 0.00          6,000.00  06
62466             2,011.50          6,000.00  03
46032             1,597.25          8,000.00  12
49120             7,020.00          8,000.00  06
```

FIGURE 1-27b

To print a report, use the **Output command** on the **Report menu**. After choosing
the Output command, you will enter the table name for the report. The process is
illustrated in the following steps.

TO PRINT A REPORT

STEP 1:   Choose Report|Output (Figure 1-28).

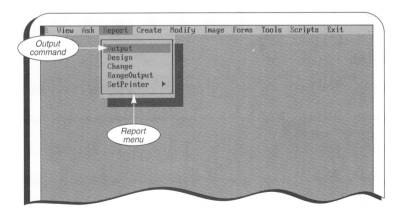

FIGURE 1-28

STEP 2: **In the Table text box, type** Customer **and press the ENTER key.**

The screen shown in Figure 1-29 displays. The lowest box lists all available reports. Currently the only report available is labeled R. This is the standard report and is created automatically by Paradox. Later, when you create your own reports, they will also appear on this list.

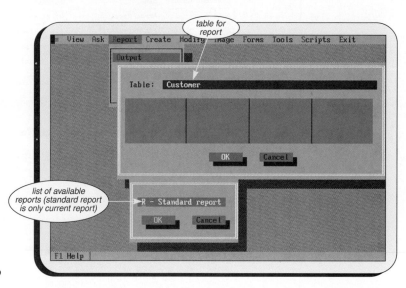

FIGURE 1-29

STEP 3: **Press the ENTER key to choose the standard report.**

The menu of output destinations displays (Figure 1-30). The commands send the report to the printer, the screen, or to a disk file.

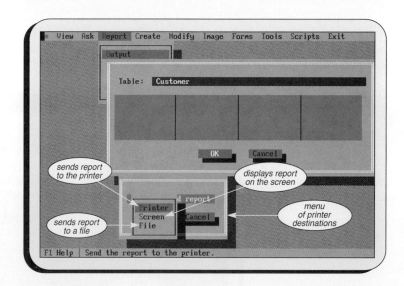

FIGURE 1-30

STEP 4: **Choose Printer.**

The report shown in Figures 1-27a and 1-27b on the previous page prints.

If you know you want the standard report sent to the printer and an image of the table for the report is on the screen, you can use this shortcut; simply press ALT+F7. If you want the report sent to the screen or a disk file, use the steps previously outlined.

▼ CREATING ADDITIONAL TABLES

A database typically consists of more than one table. The sample database contains two, the Customer table and the Sales Rep (Slsrep) table. Repeat the process of creating a table and adding records for each table in the database for the Slsrep table. The structure and data for the table are given in Figure 1-31. The steps to create the table follow.

▶ STRUCTURE OF SALES REP (SLSREP) TABLE

Field Name	Type	Size	Key
Sales Rep Number	A	2	*
Last Name	A	12	
First Name	A	8	
Address	A	15	
City	A	15	
State	A	2	
Zip Code	A	5	
Sales	$		
Commission Rate	N		

▶ DATA FOR SALES REP (SLSREP) TABLE

Sales Rep Number	Last Name	First Name	Address	City	State	Zip Code	Sales	Commission Rate
03	Harrison	Monica	12 LaGrange	Parkton	MI	48154	$52,348.00	0.07
06	Thompson	Charles	1564 Birchview	Auburn	IN	46706	$78,202.00	0.05
12	Juarez	Mara	722 Davison	Chicago	IL	60614	$28,222.00	0.07

FIGURE 1-31

TO CREATE THE SLSREP TABLE

STEP 1:   Choose the Create menu option from the Main menu.

STEP 2:   Type `Slsrep` (the name of the table) and press the ENTER key.

STEP 3:   Enter the field names and types shown in Figure 1-32.

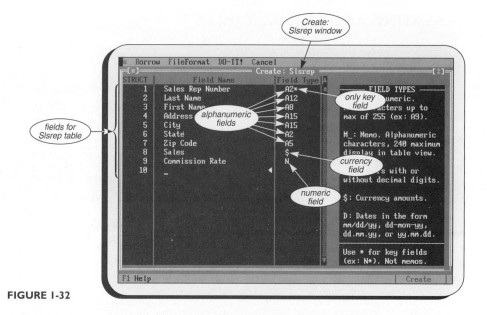

FIGURE I-32

STEP 4:   Press F2.

Paradox saves the Slsrep table to disk.

▼   ADDING RECORDS TO THE SLSREP TABLE

When adding records to the Slsrep table, use the following steps.

TO ADD RECORDS TO THE TABLE

STEP 1:   Choose Modify from the Main menu and move the cursor to DataEntry (Figure 1-33).

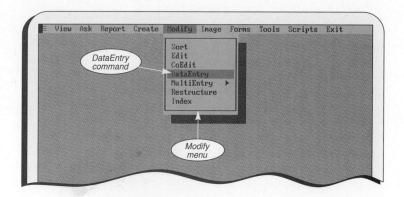

FIGURE I-33

STEP 2: Press the ENTER key to choose DataEntry.

STEP 3: Type `Slsrep` and press the ENTER key to select the Slsrep table.

STEP 4: Use the techniques illustrated on the previous page to add the three records shown in the lower part of Figure 1-31.

The three records display (Figure 1-34). The cursor advances to the position for a fourth record.

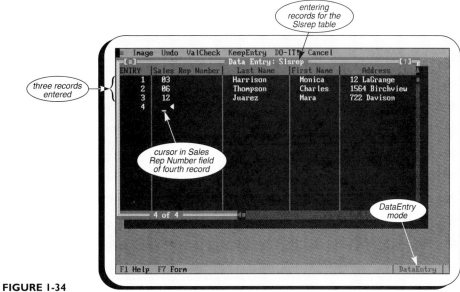

FIGURE 1-34

STEP 5: Press F2 to add the records to the Slsrep table.

STEP 6: Press F8 to remove the image of the Slsrep table from the screen and return to the main screen.

....

▼   VIEWING DATA

In creating tables, you have used **Table view**, that is, the data on the screen is displayed as a table. In Table view, use the keys described in Table 1-2 on page P14 to manipulate the records. You can also use Form view, in which you see a single record at a time.

The advantage in using Table view is that multiple records display at the same time. The disadvantage is that unless there are very few fields in the table, all the fields will not be able to display at the same time. With **Form view** only a single record displays, but all the fields display. Fortunately, it is easy to switch back and forth between views.

The following steps use Table view and then Form view to view a table.

TO VIEW A TABLE

STEP 1:   Choose the View menu option from the Main menu.

The dialog box shown in Figure 1-35 displays. At this point, you can type the name of the table and press the ENTER key. Alternatively, you can press the ENTER key and then select the table from a list of available tables.

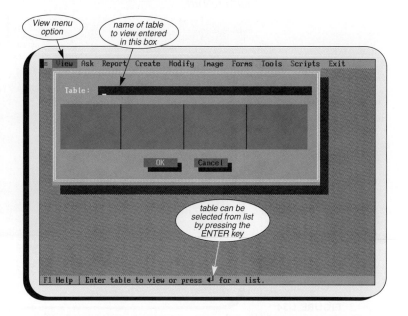

FIGURE I-35

STEP 2:   Select the Customer table by typing Customer **and pressing the ENTER key.**

The data in the Customer table is currently displayed in Table view (Figure 1-36).

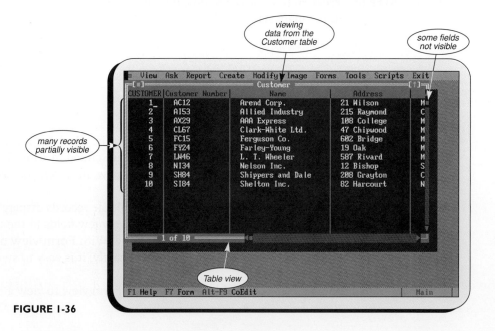

FIGURE I-36

STEP 3:   Press F7.

*The data is now displayed in Form view (Figure 1-37). The Standard Form heading at the top of the screen indicates that the form is a special form called the **standard form**. This is a built-in form automatically created by Paradox.*

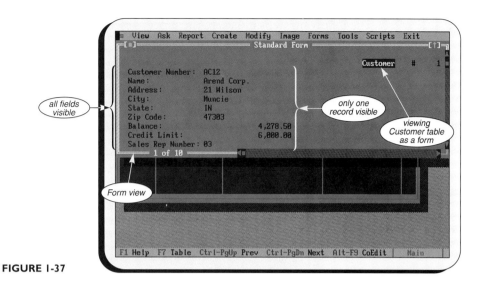

FIGURE 1-37

Pressing F7 transfers back and forth between Table view and Form view. Form view is used much like Table view. The keys shown in Table 1-3 are to be used with Form view. Other than some slight differences (for example, to move to the next record, press the PAGE DOWN key rather than the DOWN ARROW key), the operations are the same for Table view (Table 1-2).

TABLE 1-3

Key	Purpose
UP ARROW	Moves the cursor up one field.
DOWN ARROW	Moves the cursor down one field.
RIGHT ARROW	Moves the cursor to the next field.
LEFT ARROW	Moves the cursor to the previous field.
HOME	Moves the cursor to the first record.
END	Moves the cursor to the last record.
CTRL+HOME	Moves the cursor to the first field.
CTRL+END	Moves the cursor to the last field.
INSERT	Inserts a new record at the current position (only in one of the editing modes).
DELETE	Deletes the record at the current position (only in one of the editing modes).
BACKSPACE	Moves the cursor one position to the left and deletes the character in that position (only in one of the editing modes).
CTRL+BACKSPACE	Deletes the current field (only in one of the editing modes).
ENTER	Completes the current entry and moves the cursor to the next field. If the cursor is in the last field in a record, moves it to the first field in the next record.
PAGE DOWN	Moves to the next record.
PAGE UP	Moves to the previous record.
CTRL+PAGE DOWN	Moves to the same field of the next record.
CTRL+PAGE UP	Moves to the same field of the previous record.

The following steps illustrate the process by moving to a different record and a different field and then returning to Table View.

TO MOVE TO A DIFFERENT RECORD AND THEN RETURN TO TABLE VIEW

STEP 1: Press CTRL+PAGE DOWN three times to move to the fourth record.

STEP 2: Press the TAB key twice to move to the Address field.

The fourth record displays in the form (Figure 1-38). The cursor is in the Address field.

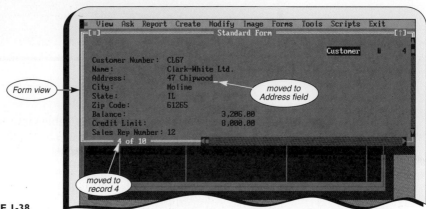

FIGURE 1-38

STEP 3: Press F7 to enter Table view.

The data displays in Table view (Figure 1-39). The cursor is in the fourth record and the Address field.

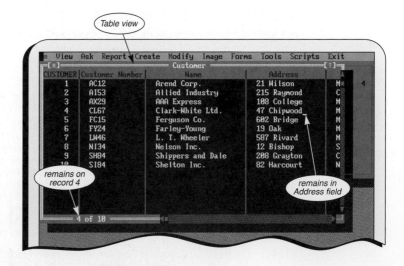

FIGURE 1-39

STEP 4: Press ALT+F8 to close both the window containing the table and the window containing the form.

Pressing ALT+F8 is a rapid alternative to repeatedly pressing F8. Pressing F8 only closes the active window. Pressing ALT+F8 closes all windows.

▼   WORKING WITH WINDOWS

Paradox allows you to display several windows simultaneously on the screen and move from one window to another with ease. A window can be maximized so it occupies the maximum possible portion of the screen and it can also be restored to its original size. It is easy to resize windows and move them around on the screen.

The following steps activate two windows, each containing a separate table.

TO ACTIVATE TWO WINDOWS SIMULTANEOUSLY

STEP 1:   **Choose View from the Main menu.**

STEP 2:   **Choose or enter the Customer table as the table to view.**

An image of the Customer table displays in a window on the screen (Figure 1-40).

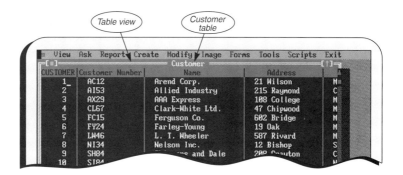

FIGURE 1-40

STEP 3:   **Press F10 to produce a cursor in the Main menu and then choose View.**

STEP 4:   **Choose or enter the Slsrep table as the table to view.**

An image of the Slsrep table also displays in a window (Figure 1-41). Notice that the Customer window is almost completely hidden by the Slsrep window.

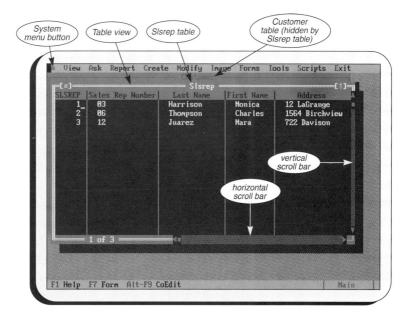

FIGURE 1-41

Only one of the two windows is active. The window with the double border is called the **active window**. This window contains the table you can manipulate.

Mouse Users: *In the upper right-hand corner of the active window is the Maximize| Restore icon (Õ). It currently contains an up arrow. Clicking this icon maximizes the window; that is, the window becomes as large as possible. Clicking this icon in a maximized window restores it to its original size.*

Mouse Users: *The bar down the right-hand side of the active window (Figure 1-41) is called the **vertical scroll bar**. Clicking the arrowhead at the top of the vertical scroll bar moves the cursor up one row. Clicking the arrowhead at the bottom moves the cursor down one row. Dragging the small rectangle in the scroll bar up or down in the bar moves the cursor up or down several rows at a time. Moving it all the way to the bottom moves the cursor to the last row. Moving it back to the top moves the cursor to the first row. Moving it to approximately the middle of the bar will move the cursor to approximately the middle row.*

Mouse Users: *The bar at the bottom of the active window (Figure 1-41) is called the **horizontal scroll bar**. It is similar to the vertical scroll bar except it moves the cursor to the left or right instead of up or down. Clicking the arrowhead at the right of the horizontal scroll bar moves the window to the right one column. Clicking the arrowhead at the left moves the window one column to the left. Dragging the small rectangle in the scroll bar left or right moves the window to the left or right several columns at a time.*

Using the System Menu

You don't need a mouse to work with windows. Use the arrow keys to move around within the active window. You can also use the **System menu** button (≡) in the upper left-hand corner of the screen to achieve other results.

The following steps select the System menu.

TO USE THE SYSTEM MENU

STEP 1:   **Press F10.**

A cursor appears in the Main menu. It is positioned on the View menu option.

STEP 2:   **Press the LEFT ARROW key to move the cursor to the System menu button (≡) and then press the ENTER key.**

The System menu displays (Figure 1-42).

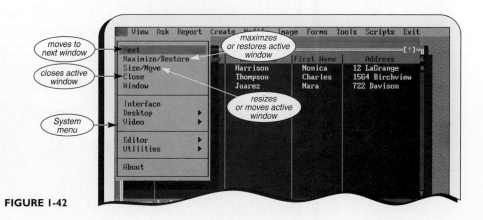

FIGURE 1-42

Mouse Users: *To choose the System menu, click the (≡) button.*

The System menu contains the following commonly used commands.

Next — Moves to the next window on the screen. The next window will become the active window. This is only relevant when there is more than one window on the screen.

Maximize/Restore — Maximizes the active window if it is not currently the maximum size. If it is maximized, restores it to its original size. Choosing this command has the same effect as clicking the Maximize/Restore icon.

Size/Move — Changes the size of the active window or moves the active window.

Close — Closes the active window. This has the same effect as clicking the Close box with the mouse or pressing F8.

Window — Produces a list of all the windows on the screen. Choosing a window from the list causes the chosen window to become the active window.

Desktop — Produces a list of commands that affect the arrangements of windows on the screen (desktop). The commands are Refresh (redraw the contents of the screen), Cascade (arrange the windows in a cascading pattern), Tile (arrange the windows in a tile pattern), and Empty (remove all windows from the screen). The normal arrangement is a cascading pattern. The windows overlap each other in the fashion illustrated in Figure 1-41. The tile pattern gives each window its own separate portion of the screen.

Maximizing a Window Using the Keyboard

To display the maximum possible portion of a table on the screen at the same time, you need to maximize the window containing the table. The following step maximizes a window.

TO MAXIMIZE A WINDOW

STEP 1: **Choose Maximize|Restore from the System menu.**

The active window expands to the maximum possible size (Figure 1-43).

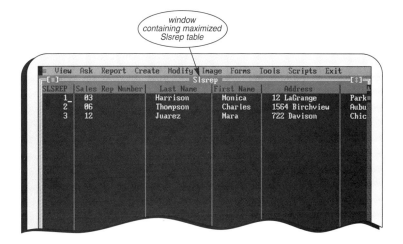

FIGURE 1-43

Restoring a Window to Its Original Size

Sometimes you will maximize a window for some specific task. After completing the task, you might want to restore the window to its original size. The following step restores the window to its original size.

TO RESTORE A WINDOW TO ITS ORIGINAL SIZE

STEP 1: Choose Maximize|Restore from the System menu.

The window resumes its original size.

Changing the Size of a Window and Moving a Window

In some cases, it may be convenient to change the size of a window. You may want to enlarge it to see more of the table or to shrink it to view a larger portion of other windows currently on the screen. You may also wish to move a window to a different position. The following steps change the size of a window.

TO CHANGE THE SIZE OF A WINDOW

STEP 1: Choose the System menu and then move the cursor to Size|Move (Figure 1-44).

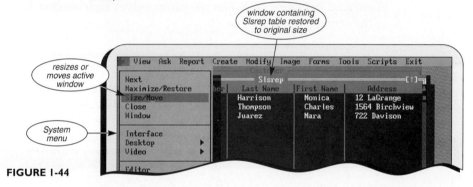

FIGURE I-44

STEP 2: Press the ENTER key to choose the Size|Move command. Hold down the SHIFT key and use the arrow keys to resize the window.

The window size changes to the size you indicated (Figure 1-45).

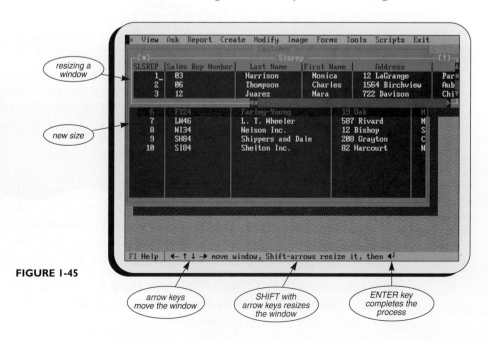

FIGURE I-45

STEP 3:   Press the ENTER key.

Moving a Window

To view the contents of windows behind the active window, Paradox allows you to move the active window to a new position on the screen. The following step moves a window.

TO MOVE A WINDOW

STEP 1:   Choose the System menu and then choose Size|Move. Use the arrow keys to move the window down to the bottom of the screen.

The window moves to the new position (Figure 1-46).

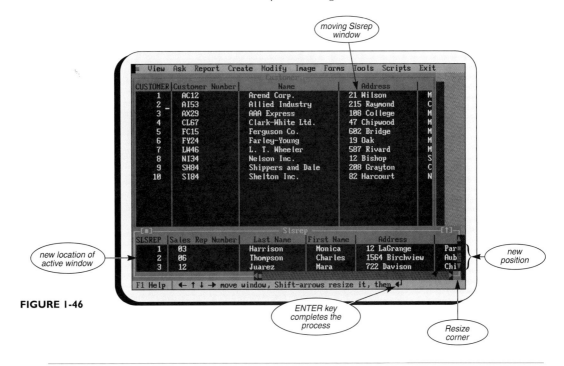

FIGURE 1-46

Mouse Users: *To change the size of a window, use the lower right-hand corner, called the Resize corner (⌐). Change the size by dragging the Resize corner to a new position. The size of the window changes as the corner is moved. To move a window, drag the top line of the window. The entire window moves as you move the line.*

Moving Between Windows

When there is more than one window on the screen, you frequently need to move back and forth between the windows. You can use the Next command on the System menu to do this, but pressing CTRL+F4 achieves the same result.

Function key equivalents for the other commands are also available. Pressing SHIFT+F5 is equivalent to choosing Maximize|Restore and pressing CTRL+F5 is equivalent to choosing Size|Move. Because you will not frequently use these other options, however, remembering these equivalent function keys is probably not worth the effort. You are often moving between windows, so it is helpful to remember CTRL+F4.

The following step illustrates how to move to a different window.

TO MOVE TO A DIFFERENT WINDOW

STEP 1: **Press CTRL+F4.**

The Customer window is now the active window and displays in front of the Slsrep window (Figure 1-47). Notice that it has the double border. Also notice that it is the window that now contains the Close box, the Maximize/Restore icon, and the scroll bars.

FIGURE 1-47

Mouse Users: *To move to a different window, click anywhere within the window.*

The following step closes all windows currently on the screen.

TO CLOSE ALL WINDOWS

STEP 1: **Press ALT+F8.**

Paradox closes all windows on the screen and returns to the blank Main menu screen.

▼ **USING THE HELP SYSTEM**

Paradox has an extensive Help System. To obtain help on a variety of topics, press F1. The following steps illustrate the process by obtaining help about the purpose of the various function keys.

TO OBTAIN HELP ON FUNCTION KEYS

STEP 1:   Press F1.

The screen shown in Figure 1-48 displays. This is the top-level Help screen. If you had been in the middle of a specific task, the help information would have applied to that task. The About the Paradox Help System box in Figure 1-48 contains information about special keys you can use while in the Help System. At the top of the Help screen, you will see a menu bar containing Paradox general help topics. Use these commands to move directly to specific topics. Choose the Paradox command to return to the activity on which you were working. As indicated in the bottom line of the screen in Figure 1-48, press F1 to see the Help Index of all the topics for which help is available.

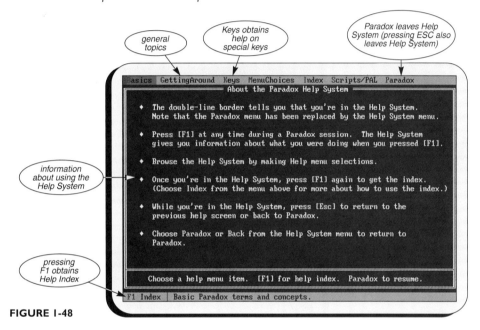

FIGURE 1-48

STEP 2:   Choose Keys.

The screen shown in Figure 1-49 displays. This screen presents general information on the use of function keys, control keys, and arrow keys. It does not provide specific information about function keys. You will use the FunctionKeys command to obtain specific information.

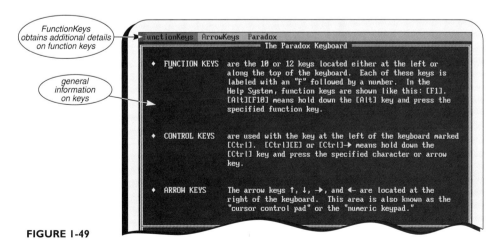

FIGURE 1-49

STEP 3: Choose FunctionKeys.

The screen shown in Figure 1-50 displays specific information on function keys. Choosing AltKeys produces the screen in Figure 1-51, which shows the purpose of the various ALT key and function key combinations.

When you have finished looking at the help information, use the Paradox command at the top of the screen to return to the activity on which you were working prior to seeking help.

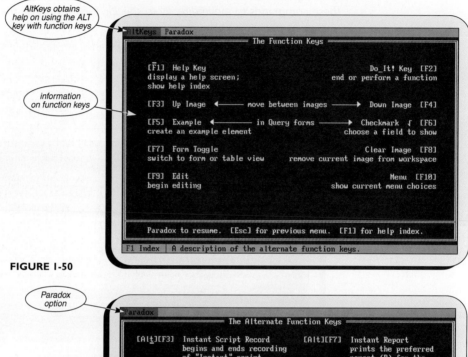

FIGURE I-50

FIGURE I-5I

STEP 4: Choose Paradox.

The help information no longer displays.

Mouse Users: *To display the Help System screen shown in Figure 1-48, click F1 or Help on the bottom line of the screen.*

Displaying the Help Index

To display the Help index, press F1 after entering the Help System. The screen shown in Figure 1-52 then displays. Use the UP ARROW or DOWN ARROW key to move the cursor through the list, or as a shortcut, press CTRL+Z to search. Then enter the word or topic you want. In either case, once the cursor is on the desired topic, press the ENTER key to see the appropriate help information. When finished, press the ESC key to return to the Help System menu and then choose Paradox to exit the Help System.

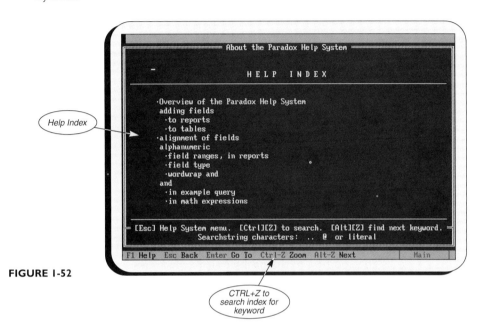

FIGURE 1-52

....

▼   ## DESIGNING A DATABASE

Database design refers to the arrangement of data into tables and fields. In the example in this project, the design is specified. In many cases, you will have to determine the design based on what you want the system to accomplish.

With large, complex databases the database design process can be extensive. Major sections of advanced database textbooks are devoted to this topic. Often, however, you should be able to design a database effectively by keeping one simple principle in mind: *Design to remove redundancy*. **Redundancy** means storing the same fact in more than one place.

To illustrate, you need to maintain the following information shown in Figure 1-53. In the figure, all the data is contained in a single table. Notice that the data for a given sales representative (number, name, address, and so on) occurs on more than one record. Storing this data on multiple records is an example of redundancy, which causes several problems:

1. Redundancy wastes space on the disk. The address of sales representative 03 (Monica Harrison), for example, should be stored only once. Storing this fact several times is wasteful.
2. Redundancy makes updating the database more difficult. If, for example, Monica Harrison moves, her address would need to be changed in several different places.

3. A possibility of inconsistent data exists. Suppose, for example, that you change the address of Monica Harrison on customer FC15's record to 146 Valley, but do not change it on customer AC12's record. In both cases, the sales representative number is 03, but the addresses are different. In other words, the data is *inconsistent*.

▶ **TABLE NAME**

Customer Number	Name	Address	City	State	Zip Code	Balance	Credit Limit	Sales Rep Number	Last Name	First Name	Address	City	State	Zip Code	Sales	Comm. Rate
AC12	Arend Corp.	21 Wilson	Muncie	IN	47303	4,278.5	6,000.0	03	Harrison	Monica	12 LaGrange	Parkton	MI	48154	$52,348.00	0.07
AI53	Allied Industry	215 Raymond	Carmel	IN	46032	203.00	3,000.0	06	Thompson	Charles	1564 Birchview	Auburn	IN	46706	$78,202.00	0.05
AX29	AAA Express	108 College	Muncie	IN	47303	42.00	3,000.0	06	Thompson	Charles	1564 Birchview	Auburn	IN	46706	$78,202.00	0.05
CL67	Clark-White Ltd.	47 Chipwood	Moline	IL	61265	3,206.0	8,000.0	12	Juarez	Mara	722 Davison	Chicago	IL	60614	$28,222.00	0.07
FC15	Ferguson Co.	602 Bridge	Mason	MI	48854	6,704.0	6,000.0	03	Harrison	Monica	12 LaGrange	Parkton	MI	48154	$52,348.00	0.07
FY24	Farley-Young	19 Oak	Muncie	IN	47303	2,504.0	6,000.0	06	Thompson	Charles	1564 Birchview	Auburn	IN	46706	$78,202.00	0.05
LW46	L. T. Wheeler	587 Rivard	Moline	IL	61265	0.00	6,000.0	06	Thompson	Charles	1564 Birchview	Auburn	IN	46706	$78,202.00	0.05
NI34	Nelson Inc.	12 Bishop	Sumner	IL	62466	2,011.5	6,000.0	03	Harrison	Monica	12 LaGrange	Parkton	MI	48154	$52,348.00	0.07
SH84	Shippers and Dale	208 Grayton	Carmel	IN	46032	1,597.2	8,000.0	12	Juarez	Mara	722 Davison	Chicago	IL	60614	$28,222.00	0.07
SI84	Shelton Inc.	82 Harcourt	Niles	MI	49120	7,020.0	8,000.0	06	Thompson	Charles	1564 Birchview	Auburn	IN	46706	$78,202.00	0.05

Duplicate sales rep names

FIGURE 1-53

The solution to the problem is to place the redundant data in a separate table, one in which the data will no longer be redundant. If you place the data for sales representatives in a separate table (Figure 1-54), the data for each sales rep will appear only once. Notice that you need to have the sales rep number in both tables. Without it, there would be no way to tell which sales rep was associated with which customer. All the other sales rep data, however, was removed from the Customer table and placed in the Slsrep table. This new arrangement corrects the problems:

1. Because the data for each sales representative is stored only once, space is not wasted.
2. Changing the address of a sales representative is easy. You have only to change one row in the Slsrep table.
3. Because the data for a sales representative is stored only once, inconsistent data cannot occur.

Sales rep data is in separate table

▸ **SLSREP TABLE**

Sales Rep Number	Last Name	First Name	Address	City	State	Zip Code	Sales	Commission Rate
03	Harrison	Monica	12 LaGrange	Parkton	MI	48154	$52,348.00	0.07
06	Thompson	Charles	1564 Birchview	Auburn	IN	46706	$78,202.00	0.05
12	Juarez	Mara	722 Davison	Chicago	IL	60614	$28,222.00	0.07

FIGURE 1-54a

▸ **CUSTOMER TABLE**

Customer Number	Name	Address	City	State	Zip Code	Balance	Credit Limit	Sales Rep Number
AC12	Arend Corp.	21 Wilson	Muncie	IN	47303	$4,278.50	$6,000.00	03
AI53	Allied Industry	215 Raymond	Carmel	IN	46032	$203.00	$3,000.00	06
AX29	AAA Express	108 College	Muncie	IN	47303	$42.00	$3,000.00	06
CL67	Clark-White Ltd.	47 Chipwood	Moline	IL	61265	$3,206.00	$8,000.00	12
FC15	Ferguson Co.	602 Bridge	Mason	MI	48854	$6,704.00	$6,000.00	03
FY24	Farley-Young	19 Oak	Muncie	IN	47303	$2,504.00	$6,000.00	06
LW46	L. T. Wheeler	587 Rivard	Moline	IL	61265	$0.00	$6,000.00	06
NI34	Nelson, Inc.	12 Bishop	Sumner	IL	62466	$2,011.50	$6,000.00	03
SH84	Shippers and Dale	208 Grayton	Carmel	IN	46032	$1,597.25	$8,000.00	12
SI84	Shelton, Inc.	82 Harcourt	Niles	MI	49120	$7,020.00	$8,000.00	06

FIGURE 1-54b

Designing to omit redundancy will help you to produce good and valid database designs.

▼ PROJECT SUMMARY

Project 1 introduced you to starting Paradox and creating a database. You learned how to create the tables in a database by defining the fields within the tables, and how to add records to the tables. Once you created the tables, you learned how to print the contents of the table as well as how to use a form to view the data in the table.

··

▼   **KEY TERMS**

active window *(P32)*   field *(P3)*   record *(P3)*
alphanumeric *(P10)*   field name *(P10)*   redundancy *(P39)*
Cancel command *(P8)*   field size *(P11)*   Report menu *(P23)*
Close command *(P33)*   field type *(P10)*   Size|Move command *(P34)*
Create menu *(P9)*   Form view *(P27)*   standard form *(P28)*
create a table *(P9)*   horizontal scroll bar *(P32)*   structure *(P8)*
currency *(P10)*   image *(P6)*   System menu *(P32)*
cursor *(P6)*   key field *(P11)*   Table view *(P27)*
database *(P2)*   Main Menu *(P6)*   unique identifier *(P3)*
database design *(P39)*   Maximize|Restore command *(P33)*   vertical scroll bar *(P32)*
database management system *(P2)*   memo *(P10)*   view menu *(P28)*
Data Entry mode *(P14)*   menu *(P6)*   window *(P6)*
date *(P10)*   Next command *(P33)*   workspace *(P6)*
DBMS *(P2)*   numeric *(P10)*
DO-IT! command or key *(P8)* Output command *(P23)*
Exit menu *(P13)*   primary key *(P3)*

··

▼   **QUICK REFERENCE**

In Paradox, you can accomplish a task in a number of different ways. The following table provides a quick reference to each task presented in Project 1 with its available options. The commands listed in the Menu column can be executed using either the keyboard or the mouse.

Task	Mouse	Menu	Keyboard Shortucts
Add Records in the ENTRY Table to the Actual Table	Click DO-IT! button	From Data Entry menu, choose DO-IT!	Press F2
Assign a Field Name			Type name, press TAB
Change Position in Form View			Use keys in Table 1-3 on
Change Position in Table View	Use scroll bars		Use keys in Table 1-2 on
Close a Window	Click Close box	From System menu, choose Close	Press F8
Close all Windows	Click all Close boxes		Press ALT+F8
Create a Table		From Main menu, choose Create	
Delete a Field			Press DELETE
Delete a Record			Press DELETE
Enter Data in a Field			Type Data
Escape from an Operation		From Exit menu, choose Cancel	Press ESC
Exit Paradox		From Exit menu, choose Yes	
Indicate a Field Size			Type the size after the field type

Task	Mouse	Menu	Keyboard Shortucts
Indicate a Field			Type appropriate letter
Indicate a Key Field			Type an asterisk
Maximize a Window	Click Maximize/Restore icon	From System menu, choose Maximize/Restore	Press SHIFT+F5
Move from Form View to Table			Press F7
Move from Table View to Form			Press F7
Move to a Different Window	Click window	From System menu, choose Next	Press F3 or F4
Print the Contents of a Table		From Output menu, choose Report	Press ALT+F7
Resize a Window	Drag Resize corner	From System menu, choose Size/Move	Press CTRL+F5
Restore a Window to Original Size	Click Maximize/Restore icon	From System menu, choose Maximize/Restore	Press SHIFT+F5
Save a Newly Defined	Click DO-IT! button	Choose DO-IT!	Press F2
View a Table		From Main menu, choose	

SHORT ANSWER ASSIGNMENT I
True/False

Instructions: Circle T if the statement is true or F if the statement is false.

T   F   1. The term database describes a collection of data organized in a manner that allows access, retrieval, and use of that data.

T   F   2. To produce a cursor within the menu options at the top of a Paradox screen, press F10.

T   F   3. To make any changes permanent, press F3, the DO-IT! key.

T   F   4. To begin creating a table, use the Create menu option on the Main menu.

T   F   5. Field names can be no more than 25 characters in length and cannot include numeric digits.

T   F   6. The only field type available for fields to be used in arithmetic operations is Numeric.

SHORT ANSWER ASSIGNMENT I (continued)

T F 7. Blanks can be included in a Paradox field name.

T F 8. To delete a field in a table structure, move the cursor to the field name, and press CTRL+D.

T F 9. To add a field, move the cursor to the Field Name column on the row where you would like to insert the field and press the INSERT key.

T F 10. After defining the field names, field types, and field widths, you name the table.

T F 11. Do not specify a field width for numeric and currency field types.

T F 12. To add records to a special ENTRY table, choose the Edit menu option from the Main menu and then choose the DataEntry command.

T F 13. To close a table, press F8.

T F 14. If you enter 10000 in a field that has been defined as a currency field type, the value will display as $10,000.00.

T F 15. Records are always ordered in the order in which they are entered.

T F 16. To delete a record from a table, move to the record and then press the DELETE key.

T F 17. To close all windows, press ALT+F7.

T F 18. To print a copy of a table's contents, choose the Output command from the Report menu.

T F 19. When you switch from Form view to Table view, the cursor is repositioned to the first field in the first record.

T F 20. To transfer back and forth between Table view and Form view, press F7.

SHORT ANSWER ASSIGNMENT 2
Multiple Choice

Instructions: Circle the correct response.

1. A database is _____.
   a. the same as a file
   b. a software product
   c. a collection of data organized in a manner that allows access, retrieval, and use of that data
   d. none of the above

2. Which of the following is not a benefit of controlling redundancy? _____.
   a. greater consistency is maintained
   b. less space is occupied
   c. update is easier
   d. all of the above are benefits

3. A field that uniquely identifies a particular record in a table is called a _____.
   a. foreign key
   b. secondary key
   c. primary key
   d. principal key

4. Paradox is a(n) _____.

   a. applications software package
   b. DBMS
   c. database
   d. both a and b

5. To make any changes permanent, press _____ which is the DO-IT! key.

   a. F1
   b. F2
   c. F3
   d. F8

6. A record in Paradox is composed of a _____.

   a. series of databases
   b. series of files
   c. series of records
   d. series of fields

7. To add records to a special ENTRY table, choose the _____ menu option from the Main menu and then choose the DataEntry option.

   a. Modify
   b. Append
   c. Data
   d. Edit

8. To remove a field from a table structure, press the _____ key(s).

   a. DELETE
   b. CTRL+D
   c. CTRL+DELETE
   d. CTRL+Y

9. To close a table, press _____.

   a. F2
   b. F4
   c. F8
   d. F10

10. To print a copy of a table's contents, choose the _____ command from the Report menu.

    a. Print
    b. Printer
    c. Output
    d. Standard Report

SHORT ANSWER ASSIGNMENT 3
Understanding the Paradox Main Screen

Instructions: Figure SA1-3 shows the Paradox main screen. Use this figure to answer the following questions.

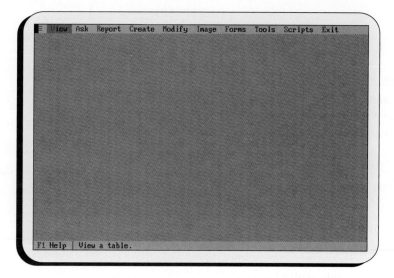

FIGURE SA1-3

1. Assume there is no cursor in the menu options at the top of the screen. How can you produce one?

   _____

   _____

2. How can you select a menu? List all alternatives.

   _____

   _____

3. Assume you have selected a menu and realize that you do want to proceed. How can you remove the menu from the screen?

   _____

   _____

4. What does the (º) symbol on the menu mean? When would you use it?

   _____

   _____

5. What information does the bottom line on the screen provide?

   _____

   _____

SHORT ANSWER ASSIGNMENT 4
Understanding the Create Table Screen

Instructions: Figure SA1-4 shows the left side of the Create: Customer screen. Use this figure to answer the following questions.

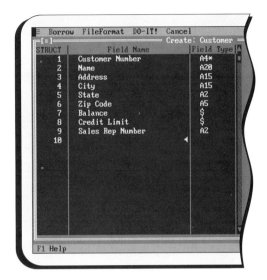

FIGURE SA1-4

1. Which fields can be used in mathematical operations?

   _____

   _____

2. What does the letter A indicate in the Field Type column, and the $ in the Field Type column?

   _____

   _____

3. What does the asterisk (*) indicate in the Field Type column?

   _____

   _____

4. Suppose you needed to insert a field for Customer Type immediately after the Zip Code field. The field is alphanumeric and is five characters in length. How would you accomplish this task?

   _____

   _____

5. Adding the Customer Type field was a mistake. The field needs to be deleted. How would you accomplish this task?

   _____

   _____

SHORT ANSWER ASSIGNMENT 5

Understanding Function Keys

Instructions: In Paradox, there are several function keys and key combinations that can be used as shortcuts to menu options. Describe the purpose of each function key or key combination listed below.

Key	Function

1. F8

_____

_____

2. ALT+F7

_____

_____

3. ALT+F8

_____

_____

4. F7

_____

_____

5. F4

_____

_____

SHORT ANSWER ASSIGNMENT 6

Understanding the Paradox Data Entry Screen

Instructions: The Data Entry screen for the Customer table is shown in Figure SA1-6. Use this figure to answer the following questions.

FIGURE SA1-6

1. Assume the cursor is in the Customer Number field of the first record. How can you move directly to the Sales Rep Number field?

   _____

   _____

2. You have just finished moving to the Sales Rep Number field and would like to change the customer name for customer AX29 from AAA Express to ABC Express. List the steps to accomplish this task.

   _____

   _____

3. You have just finished making the change in task 2 above and would like to change the amount in the Balance field for this record to $420.00. List the steps to accomplish this task.

   _____

   _____

4. You have just finished making the change in task 3 above and would like to delete the record for Customer Number NI34. List the steps to accomplish this task.

   _____

   _____

HANDS-ON
EXERCISES

HANDS-ON EXERCISE 1
Using the Help System

Instructions: Perform the following tasks using a computer.

1. Start Paradox.
2. Press F1.

HANDS-ON EXERCISE I (continued)

3. Press F1 again to see the Help Index (Figure HOE 1-1).

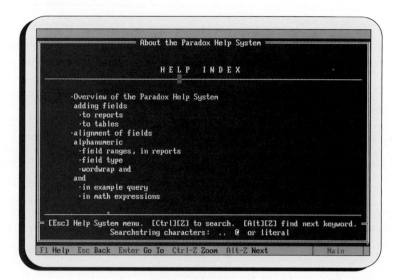

FIGURE HOE I-I

4. Press the DOWN ARROW key three times to move the cursor to the topic, Adding fields to tables, and then press the ENTER key.

5. Read the information and answer the following two questions.

   a. Can you place a non-key field before a key field?.

   _____

   _____

   b. How can you move a field?

   _____

   _____

6. Choose the Paradox menu option to exit the Help System.

7. Choose the Create menu option and then press F1.

8. Read the information and answer the following two questions.

   a. What characters can you use to name a Paradox table?

   _____

   _____

   b. What DOS extension does Paradox assign to a table name?

   _____

   _____

9. Choose the Paradox option to exit the Help System.

10. Press the ESC key to remove the Create menu from the screen.

11. Exit Paradox.

HANDS-ON EXERCISE 2
Viewing and Printing Data

Instructions: Start Paradox and open the Slsrep table from the Paradox subdirectory on the Student Diskette that accompanies this book. If you are not sure how to accomplish this, check with your instructor. The Slsrep table is shown in Figure HOE1-2. Perform the following tasks.

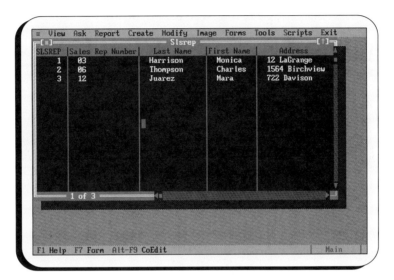

FIGURE HOE 1-2

1. Transfer to Form view. Explain the step(s) to accomplish this task.

_____

_____

2. Move to the Address field and then press the PAGE DOWN key.

3. Which record is currently on the screen, and where is the cursor?

_____

_____

4. Move to the City field and press CTRL+PAGE UP.

5. Which record is currently on the screen, and where is the cursor?

_____

_____

6. Transfer to Table view. Explain the step(s) to accomplish this task.

_____

_____

7. Close the Slsrep table. Explain the step(s) to accomplish this task.

_____

_____

HANDS-ON EXERCISE 2 (continued)

8. Print the Slsrep table.

9. Exit Paradox.

HANDS-ON EXERCISE 3
Working with Windows

Instructions: Start Paradox and open the Slsrep table from the Pdox45 subdirectory on the Student Diskette that accompanies this book. If you are not sure how to accomplish this, check with your instructor. Perform the following tasks.

1. Choose View and select the Customer table.

2. Resize the Customer window so there is no empty space at the bottom of the table. The bottom of the Slsrep table should show beneath the Customer table as shown in Figure HOE 1-3. Explain the steps to accomplish this task.

_____

_____

FIGURE HOE 1-3

3. Move the Customer table so it appears directly below the Slsrep table. Explain the steps to accomplish this task.

_____

_____

4. Close both tables. Explain the steps to accomplish this task.

_____

_____

5. Exit Paradox.

LABORATORY
ASSIGNMENTS

Each project ends with four Laboratory Assignments. In each project, Laboratory Assignment 1 involves a database of Parts, Laboratory Assignment 2 manages a database of Employees, Laboratory Assignment 3 deals with a database containing data about Movies, and Laboratory Assignment 4 uses a database containing information about the inventory of a bookstore.

The Laboratory Assignments are cumulative. That is, the assignment for Laboratory Assignment 1 in Project 2 builds on the assignment for Laboratory Assignment 1 from Project 1. Thus, be sure to work through the assignment completely before proceeding to the next project. If you do not do this, you will encounter difficulty later on.

LABORATORY ASSIGNMENT 1
Creating a Parts Database

Purpose: To provide practice in creating and updating a database.

Problem: A wholesale distribution company needs to maintain information on the parts they sell to local retail stores. The database they will use for this purpose consists of two tables. The Part table contains information on items that the distributor has in stock. The Item Class table contains information on the item class to which each part belongs. You are to create and update this database.

Instructions: The data and field charac-teristics for the Part table are shown in Figure LA1-1a. The data and field characteristics for the Item Class table are shown in Figure LA1-1b on the next page. You are to create both tables.

▶ **STRUCTURE OF PART TABLE**

Field Name	Type	Size	Key
Part Number	A	4	*
Part Description	A	10	
Units on Hand	S		
Item Class Code	A	2	
Warehouse Number	A	2	
Price	$		

▶ **DATA FOR PART TABLE**

Part Number	Part Description	Units on Hand	Item Class Code	Warehouse Number	Price
AX12	IRON	104	HW	3	24.95
AZ52	DARTBOARD	20	SG	2	12.95
BA74	BASKETBALL	0	SG	1	24.95
BH22	CORNPOPPER	95	HW	3	29.95
BT04	GAS GRILL	11	AP	2	149.99
BZ66	WASHER	52	AP	3	399.99
CA14	GRIDDLE	78	HW	3	39.99
CB03	BIKE	44	SG	1	299.99
CX11	BLENDER	112	HW	3	22.95
CZ81	TREADMILL	68	SG	2	349.95

FIGURE LA1-1a

LABORATORY ASSIGNMENT I (continued)

▶ **STRUCTURE OF ITEM CLASS TABLE**

Field Name	Type	Size	Key
Item Class Code	A	2	*
Item Class Description	A	15	

▶ **DATA FOR ITEM CLASS TABLE**

Item Class Code	Item Class Description
AP	Appliances
HW	Hardware
SG	Sporting Goods

FIGURE LA 1-1b

Perform the following tasks using Paradox.

1. Create the Part table using the field characteristics shown in Figure LA1-1a on the previous page. Use the name PART for the table.

2. Add the data shown in Figure LA1-1a to the Part table.

3. Print the table.

4. Create the Item Class table using the field characteristics shown in Figure LA1-1b. Use the name CLASS for the table.

5. Add the data shown in Figure LA1-1b to the Item Class table.

6. Print the table.

LABORATORY ASSIGNMENT 2
Creating an Employees Database

Purpose: To provide practice in creating and updating a database.

Problem: A small manufacturing company has a database of employees. The database consists of two tables. The Employee table contains informa-tion on the employees. The Department table contains information on the departments in which the employees work. You are to create and update this database.

Instructions: The data and field characteristics for the Employee table are shown in Figure LA1-2a. The data and field characteristics for the Department table are shown in Figure LA1-2b. You are to create both tables.

▸ **STRUCTURE FOR EMPLOYEE TABLE**

Field Name	Type	Size	Key
Employee Number	A	4	*
Employee Last Name	A	12	
Employee First Name	A	8	
Department Code	A	2	
Pay Rate	$		

▸ **DATA FOR EMPLOYEE TABLE**

Employee Number	Employee Last Name	Employee First Name	Department Code	Pay Rate
1011	Rapoza	Anthony	04	8.50
1013	McCormack	Nigel	04	8.25
1016	Ackerman	David	01	9.75
1017	Doi	Chan	03	6.00
1020	Castle	Mark	04	7.50
1022	Dunning	Lisa	02	9.10
1025	Chaney	Joseph	01	8.00
1026	Bender	Helen	03	6.75
1029	Anderson	Mariane	04	9.00
1030	Edwards	Kenneth	03	8.60
1037	Baxter	Charles	01	11.00
1041	Evans	John	02	6.00

FIGURE LA 1-2a

Perform the following tasks using Paradox.

1. Create the Employee table using the field characteristics shown in Figure LA1-2a. Use the name EMPLOYEE for the table.

2. Add the data shown in Figure LA1-2a to the Employee table.

3. Print the table.

4. Create the Department table using the field characteristics shown in Figure LA1-2b. Use the name DEPT for the table.

5. Add the data shown in Figure LA1-2b to the Department table.

6. Print the table.

7. Three new employees have just joined the company. Add the following three employees to the Employee table.

1056	Andrews	Robert	02	9.00
1057	Dugan	Mary	03	8.75
1066	Castleworth	Mary	03	8.75

8. Print the table.

▸ **STRUCTURE OF DEPARTMENT TABLE**

Field Name	Type	Size	Key
Department Code	A	2	*
Department Name	A	10	

▸ **DATA FOR DEPARTMENT TABLE**

Department Code	Department Name
01	Accounting
02	Marketing
03	Production
04	Shipping

FIGURE LA 1-2b

LABORATORY ASSIGNMENT 3
Creating a Movies Database

Purpose: To provide practice in creating and updating a database.

Problem: A family has a collection of video tapes. The family keeps handwritten information on the video tapes. This handwritten information consists of two tables. The Movie table contains information on the movies in the collection. The Director table contains information on the individuals who directed the movie. The family now wants to keep this information in a database. You are to create and update this database.

Instructions: The data and field characteristics for the Movie table are shown in Figure LA1-3a. The data and field characteristics for the Director table are shown in Figure LA1-3b. You are to create both tables.

▶ **STRUCTURE OF MOVIE TABLE**

Field Name	Type	Size	Key
Movie Number	A	3	*
Movie Title	A	18	
Year Made	N		
Movie Type	A	6	
Length	N	4	
Director Code	A	2	

▶ **DATA FOR MOVIE TABLE**

Movie Number	Movie Title	Year Made	Movie Type	Length	Director Code
001	Ann Thompson	1977	COMEDY	93	01
002	They Went Away	1964	COMEDY	93	04
003	A Crack in Time	1971	SCI FI	136	04
004	Too Late for Henry	1959	SUSPEN	136	03
005	The Dirty Car	1948	SUSPEN	80	03
006	They Know Too Much	1969	HORROR	109	03
007	The Old House	1978	DRAMA	95	01
008	The Dervish	1963	HORROR	119	03
011	Winston's Dog	1979	COMEDY	96	01
012	Escape from Zero	1958	SUSPEN	128	03
014	The Ninth Planet	1968	SCI FI	141	04
021	A Single Bullet	1939	WESTER	99	02
022	Rear Window	1954	SUSPEN	112	03
023	No Sheriff	1953	WESTER	116	02
024	Just Like Me	1940	DRAMA	128	02

FIGURE LA 1-3a

▶ **STRUCTURE OF DIRECTOR TABLE**

Field Name	Type	Size	Key
Director Code	A	2	*
Director Name	A	18	

▶ **DATA FOR DIRECTOR TABLE**

Director Code	Director Name
01	Allward, Stacy
02	Markle, Amy
03	Rodriguez, Juan
04	DeNoyer, K.Z.

FIGURE LA 1-3b

Perform the following tasks using Paradox.

1. Create the Movie table using the field characteristics shown in Figure LA1-3a. Use the name MOVIE for the table.

2. Add the data shown in Figure LA1-3a to the Movie table but do not press the DO-IT! (F2) key.

3. Make the following three changes to the data in the ENTRY table.
   a. Change the title for movie number 004 to No Time for Henry.
   b. The Year entry for The Dervish is incorrect. Change it to 1960.
   c. Delete the record for movie number 23.

4. Add the now correct data into the Movie table.

5. Print the table.

6. Create the Director table using the field characteristics shown in Figure LA1-3b. Use the name DIRECTOR for the table.

7. Add the data shown in Figure LA1-3b to the Director table.

8. Print the table.

LABORATORY ASSIGNMENT 4
Creating a Books Database

Purpose: To provide practice in designing, creating, and updating a database.

Problem: A small bookstore owner has a book inventory database. A report giving the data for this database is shown in Figure LA1-4 on the next page. The owner has asked you to design the database for the bookstore owner; that is, you must determine the tables, fields, primary keys, and field characteristics. When you have finished designing the database, you are to create the tables and then update the database.

LABORATORY ASSIGNMENT 4 (continued)

▸ **BOOK TABLE**

Book Code	Title	Author	Publisher's Name	Publisher Code	Book Type	Price	Units on Hand
0189	The Old Hat	Frank Adams	Planars Books	PB	FIC	$4.95	2
1351	The Box	Marybeth	Stoyers-Insen	SI	HOR	$5.95	1
138X	Death Becomes	Maria Comio	Bantam Books	BB	MYS	$3.50	3
2226	From the River	Joseph Loekse	Bantam Books	BB	SFI	$17.9	3
2295	It Struck Twice	Marybeth	Vanderlwand	VI	HOR	$22.9	0
2766	The Black Tiger	Frank Adams	Planars Books	PB	FIC	$4.95	2
3743	First and Last	Frank Adams	Planars Books	PB	FIC	$3.50	0
3906	Whirlwind	Pamela Perry	Bantam Books	BB	SUS	$4.95	1
6128	His Name Was Evil	Maria Comio	Planars Books	PB	MYS	$3.95	3
6171	One Last Chance	Pamela Perry	Samstra and Simons	SS	SUS	$21.9	4
6328	In Right Field	Pamela Perry	Bantam Books	BB	SUS	$4.95	2
7405	Night Madness	Pamela Perry	Bantam Books	BB	SUS	$4.95	0
7443	Ellen	Marybeth	Stoyers-Insen	SI	HOR	$5.95	1
9373	She Won't Shoot	Jodie Nichols	Samstra and Simons	SS	FIC	$21.9	2

FIGURE LA 1-4

Instructions: Create both the Book and the Publisher tables.

Perform the following tasks using Paradox.

1. Using the data shown in Figure LA1-4, determine the fields and field characteristics for the Book table. Determine the primary key. Once you have done so, create the table. Use the name BOOK for the table.

2. Add the data shown in Figure LA1-4 to the Book table.

3. Print the table.

4. Using the data shown in Figure LA1-4, determine the fields and field characteristics for the Publisher table. Determine the primary key. Once you have done so, create the table. Use the name PUBLISH for the table.

5. Add the data shown in Figure LA1-4 to the Publisher table.

6. Print the table.

Querying a Database

▼ OBJECTIVES

You will have mastered the material in this project when you can:

- Understand the purpose of queries
- Understand the purpose and characteristics of the Answer table
- Create a new query
- Use a query to display all records and all fields
- Run a query
- Print the answer to a query
- Close the Answer table
- Close a query
- Clear a query
- Use a query to display selected fields
- Use character data in conditions in a query
- Use wildcards in conditions

- Use LIKE in conditions
- Use numeric data in conditions
- Use comparison operators
- Use compound conditions involving AND
- Use compound conditions involving OR
- Sort the answer to a query
- Join tables in a query
- Restrict the records in a join
- Use computed fields in a query
- Calculate statistics in a query
- Use grouping with statistics
- Save a query
- Use a saved query

▼ WHAT ARE QUERIES?

The Paradox database management system offers many useful features, among them the capability to answer questions. At the top of Figure 2-1 on the following page, for example, there are several questions regarding the Customer table created in Project 1:

- What is the balance of customer CL67?
- Which customers' names begin with Sh?

• Which customer's name sounds like Sheldon?
• How much available credit do the customers currently have?
• In which states does Sales Rep 03 have customers?

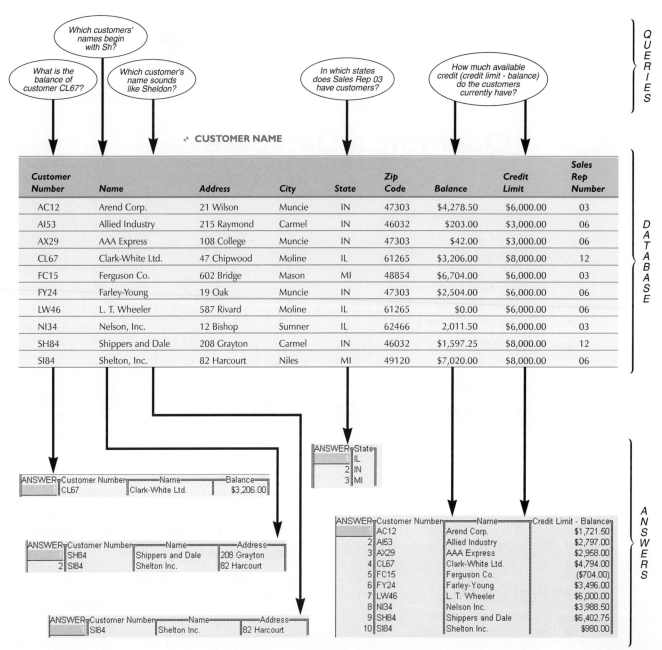

FIGURE 2-1

When posing a question to Paradox, or any other database management system, the question is called a **query**. A query is a question represented in a way that Paradox can understand.

Thus, to ask Paradox a question, first create a corresponding query using the techniques illustrated in this project. Then instruct Paradox to **run the query**, that is to perform the steps necessary to obtain the answer. When finished, Paradox displays the answer to the question in the format shown at the bottom of Figure 2-1.

▼   CREATING A QUERY

Create a query by making entries in a special form called a **Query form**. A Query form displays in a window called a **Query form window**. Before using Query forms, you should be familiar with a few special concepts.

Clearing the Workspace

It's important to keep the workspace from becoming too cluttered. To remove the current form (the one in which the cursor is located) from the workspace, press F8. To remove all forms from the workspace, press ALT+F8. In general, after finishing with a query, clear the workspace. The only exception would be if the next query is similar to the current one. In such a case, it may be simpler to modify the current query rather than to start from scratch.

The Answer Table

When Paradox runs a query, it places the results in a special table called Answer. A form of this table automatically displays in the workspace. After the workspace has been cleared, the Answer table continues to exist and can be used like any other table. The Answer table has two special characteristics:

1. When another query is run, the results will become the new Answer table. The new version of the Answer table will overwrite the old one.
2. When you exit Paradox, the Answer table will be deleted.

Printing the Results

To print the results of a query, print the contents of the Answer table. Use the same technique used to produce the standard report in Project 1. Choose Report, choose Output, choose the Answer table, choose the standard report, and then choose the destination (printer, screen, or file). If you know in advance the report should go to the printer and the Answer table is the active one, press ALT+F7.

Moving Between Forms

When working with Query forms, there will often be two or more forms on the screen and you will need to move between them. To move to the previous form on the screen, press F3. To move to the next form, press F4.

The first step in creating a query is to create a new Query form. Use the Ask menu option as illustrated in the following steps.

TO CREATE A NEW QUERY

STEP 1:   Press F10 and choose the Ask menu option (Figure 2-2).

The dialog box shown in Figure 2-3 displays, asking for the name of the table.

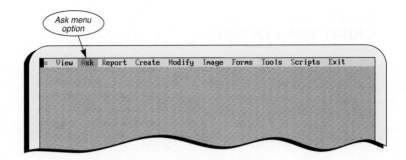

FIGURE 2-2

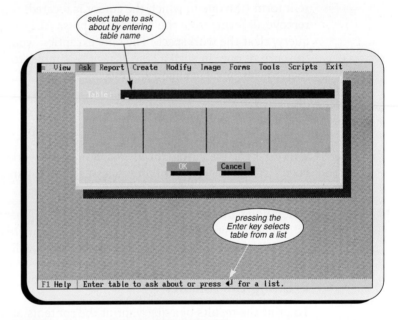

FIGURE 2-3

STEP 2:   Type Customer **and press the ENTER key.**

A Query form window displays on the screen (Figure 2-4). It contains a Query form for the Customer table.

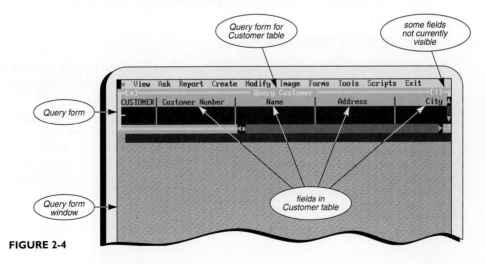

FIGURE 2-4

On the Query form, you tell Paradox which fields in the database table you want included in the answer. Also on the Query form, you enter conditions, such as the customer number must be CL67. When you use conditions, only the record or records on which the condition is true will be included in the answer. Special keys used with Query forms are shown in Table 2-1.

TABLE 2-1

Key	Purpose
UP ARROW	Moves the cursor up one row.
DOWN ARROW	Moves the cursor down one row.
RIGHT ARROW	Moves the cursor one column to the right.
LEFT ARROW	Moves the cursor one column to the left.
TAB	Moves the cursor one column to the right.
SHIFT+TAB	Moves the cursor one column to the left.
CTRL+HOME	Moves the cursor to the beginning of the line.
CTRL+END	Moves the cursor to the end of the line.
INSERT	Turns insert mode on and off.
DELETE	Deletes all entries from the current row of the Query form.
BACKSPACE	Moves the cursor one position to the left and deletes the character in that position.
ENTER	Completes the current entry and moves the cursor to the next column. If the cursor is in the last column in a row, moves it to the first column in the next row.
F1	Gets help.
F2	Executes a query. Places the results in the Answer table.
F3	Moves to the previous form on the screen.
F4	Moves to the next form on the screen.
F5	Creates an example.
F6	Adds a checkmark. Field will be included in results unless the checkmark is already there. If the checkmark is already present, removes the checkmark.
CTRL+F6	Adds a check-descending mark. Field will be included in the results but the display will be in descending order.
ALT+F6	Adds a check-plus mark. Field will be displayed. Unlike a checkmark, duplicates will be displayed.
F8	Clears the current form.
ALT+F8	Clears all forms and returns to the Main menu.
F10	Brings menus to the screen.

▼   **INCLUDING ALL FIELDS IN THE ANSWER TABLE**

To indicate that a field is to be included in the answer, place a **checkmark** (✓) in the field. To place a checkmark in a field, first move the cursor to the field by pressing the RIGHT ARROW key, which moves the cursor one field to the right, or the LEFT ARROW key, which moves it one field to the left. Once the cursor is in the correct field, press **F6 (Check)**.

Mouse Users: *To move the cursor to a field, click the field.*

The quickest way to include all the fields in a query is to move the cursor under the name of the table (CUSTOMER) and press F6. The following steps place checkmarks in all fields.

TO INCLUDE ALL FIELDS IN THE ANSWER TABLE

STEP 1: **Make sure the cursor is under CUSTOMER in the Query form.**

STEP 2: **Press F6.**

All fields now have checkmarks, indicating that all fields will be included in the answer (Figure 2-5).

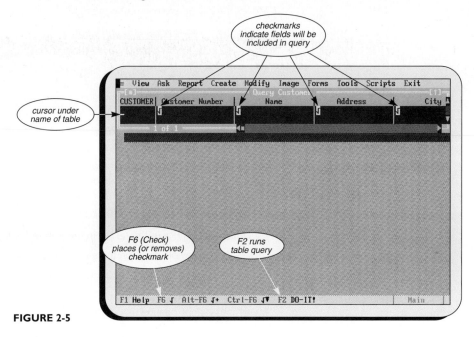

FIGURE 2-5

▼ RUNNING A QUERY TO CREATE THE ANSWER TABLE

After creating query, you need to run it. To run a query, press F2 (the DO-IT! key). Paradox performs the steps necessary to obtain the answer, which it places in the special table called Answer. It automatically displays the Answer table on the screen.

 Mouse Users: *To run a query, click the F2 that appears at the bottom of the screen.*

The following step runs the query.

TO RUN A QUERY TO CREATE THE ANSWER TABLE

STEP 1: **Press F2.**

Paradox executes the query. It places the answer in the Answer table, which displays in a window on the screen (Figure 2-6).

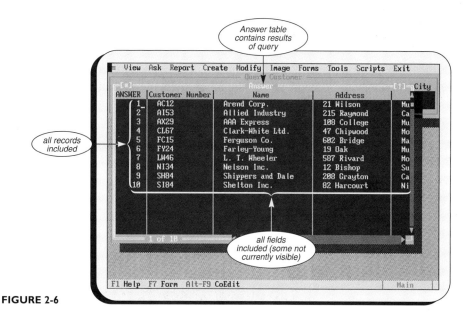

FIGURE 2-6

Because no conditions were included on the Query form (Figure 2-5), Paradox displays all the customer records in the Answer table.

▼ PRINTING THE ANSWER TO A QUERY

The answer to a query is contained in the Answer table. Thus, to print the information in the Answer table, use the same techniques as in Project 1. These steps are summarized below:

Step 1: Press F10 and choose Report|Output.
Step 2: Choose the Answer table.
Step 3: Choose the standard report.
Step 4: Choose the destination (Printer, Screen, or File) (Figure 2-7).

You can also press ALT+F7 to print the contents of the Answer table on the printer.

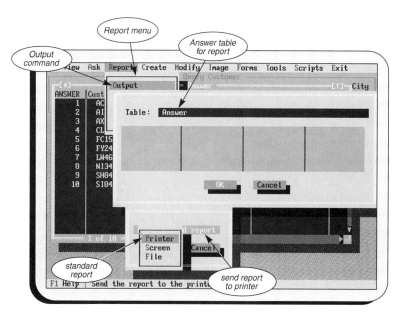

FIGURE 2-7

▼   **CLOSING THE ANSWER TABLE**

Once you have finished viewing or printing the Answer table, it is a good idea to remove it from the screen. Close the window containing the table by pressing F8 as shown in the following step.

TO CLOSE THE ANSWER TABLE

STEP 1:   Press F8.

The window containing the Answer table no longer displays on the screen (Figure 2-8). The Query form window remains on the screen.

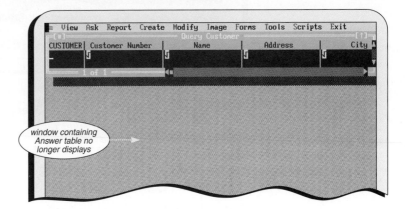

FIGURE 2-8

In the following examples in this project, be sure to close the Answer table after finishing with it.

▼   **CLOSING A QUERY**

To remove a Query form from the screen, close the Query form window by pressing F8. The following step closes the Query form window.

TO CLOSE A QUERY

STEP 1:   Press F8.

The Query form window no longer displays (Figure 2-9).

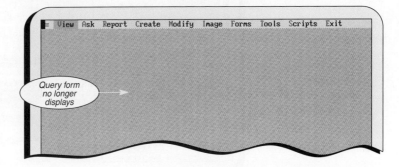

FIGURE 2-9

▼   CLEARING A QUERY FORM

If you make mistakes when creating a query, you can fix them individually. Alternatively, you may simply want to clear out all the checkmarks and conditions in the Query form and start over. One way to clear out the entries is to close the Query form window and then start a new query just as you did earlier. A simpler approach, however, is to press the DELETE key. Pressing the DELETE key clears all entries in the current row of the Query form.

▼   DISPLAYING SELECTED FIELDS IN THE ANSWER TABLE

Only the fields that contain checkmarks in the Query form window will be included in the Answer table. Thus, to display only certain fields, place checkmarks in those fields and no others. If you accidentally place a checkmark in the wrong field, press F6 a second time to remove the checkmark. Alternatively, press the DELETE key to clear the entire Query form and then start over.

The following steps create a query to show the customer number, name, and sales rep number for all customers by including checkmarks in only those fields.

TO INCLUDE SELECTED FIELDS IN THE ANSWER TABLE

STEP 1: **Press F10, choose Ask, type** `Customer`**, and press the ENTER key.**

Paradox opens a Query form window for the Customer table.

STEP 2: **Press the RIGHT ARROW key to move the cursor to the Customer Number field.**

STEP 3: **Press F6.**

A checkmark displays in the Customer Number field (Figure 2-10).

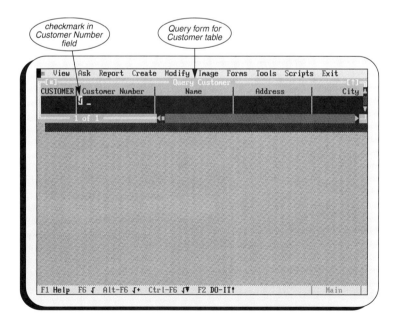

FIGURE 2-10

STEP 4:   **Press the RIGHT ARROW key to move the cursor to the Name field and then press F6.**

The Customer Number and Name fields both contain checkmarks (Figure 2-11). The Sales Rep Number field is not currently on the screen.

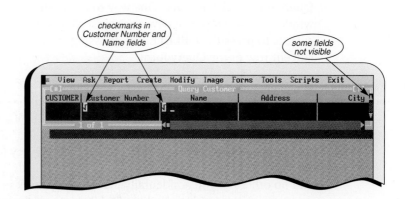

FIGURE 2-11

STEP 5:   **Press the RIGHT ARROW key until the cursor is in the Sales Rep Number field.**

The fields in the Query form shift to the left (Figure 2-12).

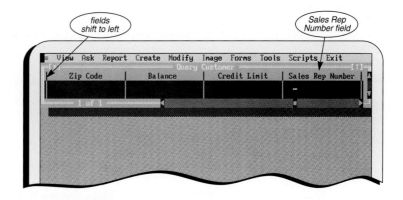

FIGURE 2-12

STEP 6:   **Press F6.**

A checkmark displays in the Sales Rep Number field (Figure 2-13).

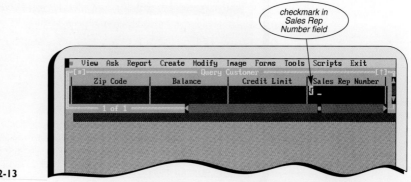

FIGURE 2-13

STEP 7:   Press F2 to run the query.

Paradox runs the query, producing the Answer table. The Answer table displays in a window on the screen (Figure 2-14). Only the Customer Number, Name, and Sales Rep Number fields are included in the Answer table.

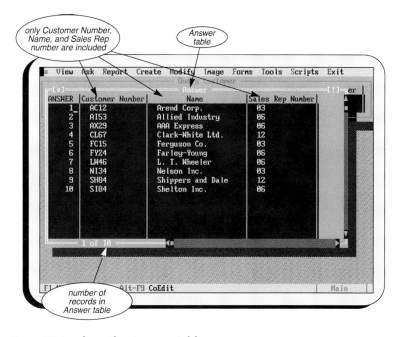

FIGURE 2-14

STEP 8:   Press F8 to close the Answer table.

▼   ENTERING CONDITIONS

When using queries, you usually are looking for those records that satisfy some condition. You might want the name of the customer whose number is CL67, for example, or the numbers, names, and addresses of those customers whose names start with Sh. To enter a condition, first move the cursor to the field in which you wish to place the condition.

Once the cursor is in the correct field, type the appropriate condition. If a condition is incorrect, correct it by repeatedly pressing the BACKSPACE key to remove the incorrect entry and then typing the correct condition. You can also press the DELETE key to clear the entire Query form and then start over.

The next examples illustrate the types of conditions available in Paradox.

▼   USING CHARACTER DATA IN CONDITIONS

Consider these two important rules for conditions in character fields (fields whose type is A) in a Query form. First, if there is any punctuation (like a comma) in the value, the value must be enclosed in quotation marks. Thus, if you were looking for a record in which the name is Smith, John, you would type

```
"Smith, John"
```

because the name contains a comma.

However, if the name is John Smith, you would only need to type

John Smith

because the name contains no special punctuation.

Second, with a few exceptions, conditions involving character fields are **case-sensitive**. This means that it is essential to use the right combination of uppercase and lowercase letters. If, for example, the name is stored in the database as Jones and you search for JONES, you will not find the record.

The following steps find the customer whose number is CL67. Because there is no punctuation, quotation marks are not necessary. However, you must enter both an uppercase C and an uppercase L because that is the way the entry appears in the database.

TO USE CHARACTER DATA IN A CONDITION

STEP 1: Be sure to have a clear Query form for the Customer table on the screen. (If you have a Query form for the Customer table on the screen, press the DELETE key. If not, choose Ask and then choose the Customer table.)

STEP 2: Press the RIGHT ARROW key to move the cursor to the Customer Number field, and then type CL67 (**Figure 2-15**).

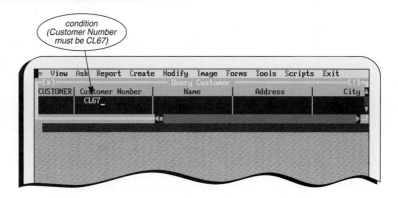

FIGURE 2-15

STEP 3: Use the arrow keys and the F6 key to place checkmarks in the Customer Number, Name, and Balance fields.

The Customer Number, Name, and Balance fields contain checkmarks although only the one in the Balance field is currently visible (Figure 2-16).

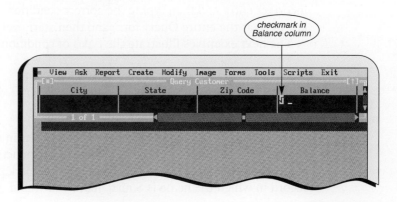

FIGURE 2-16

STEP 4:   Run the query by pressing F2.

The number, name, and balance of customer CL67 display in the Answer table (Figure 2-17).

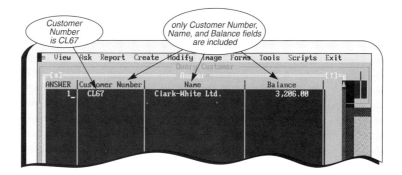

FIGURE 2-17

STEP 5:   Press F8 to close the Answer table.

▼   USING SPECIAL CHARACTER CONDITIONS

Two special types of conditions are available for character fields. The first involves the use of wildcards and the second involves the use of the LIKE operator. **Wildcards** are useful when you know that the value contains a certain pattern of characters. The **LIKE operator** allows you to find values that sound like a pattern of characters.

There are two special wildcard symbols. The first of the two wildcard symbols is the double period (..), which represents any collection of characters. Thus, Sh.. represents an uppercase S followed by a lowercase h followed by any collection of characters. The other wildcard symbol is the @ sign, which represents any individual character. Thus, T@m represents the letter T followed by any single character followed by the letter m.

The next example illustrates using a wildcard to find the number, name, and address of those customers whose names begin with Sh. For this example, because you don't know how many characters will follow the Sh, the double period wildcard is appropriate.

TO USE A WILDCARD

STEP 1:   Be sure to have a clear Query form for the Customer table on the screen.

STEP 2:   Place the cursor in the Name field and type Sh **followed by two periods** (Sh..)**. Use the arrow keys and the F6 key to place checkmarks in the Customer Number, Name, and Address fields.**

The Name field contains SH.., and checkmarks appear in the Customer Number, Name, and Address fields (Figure 2-18 on the next page).

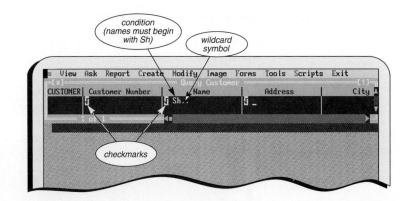

FIGURE 2-18

STEP 3:   Press F2.

The Answer table contains the two customers (Shippers and Dale and Shelton Inc) whose names begin with Sh (Figure 2-19).

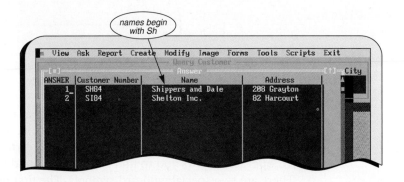

FIGURE 2-19

STEP 4:   Press F8 to close the Answer table.

Querying by Sound Using the Like Operator

Sometimes you might not know the exact spelling of a name for which you are searching. You might know only what the name sounds like. Paradox includes the special operator, LIKE, which indicates that the value must be *like*, that is, sound like, a particular pattern instead of matching it exactly. The following steps illustrate the use of the LIKE operator by finding all customers whose names sound like Sheldon Inc.

TO USE LIKE

STEP 1:   Be sure to have a clear Query form for the Customer table on the screen.

STEP 2:   Use the arrow keys and F6 key to place checkmarks in the Customer Number and Name fields.

STEP 3:   Type LIKE Sheldon Inc. **in the Name field.**

The entry appears in the Name field (Figure 2-20).

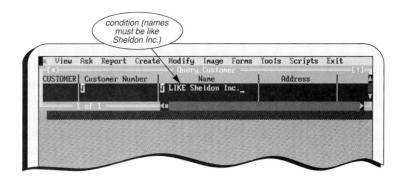

FIGURE 2-20

STEP 4: Press F2.

The Answer table contains the customer whose name is like Sheldon Inc. (Figure 2-21).

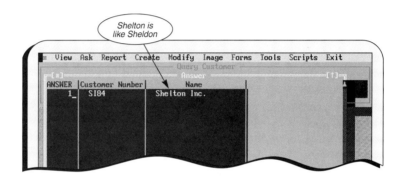

FIGURE 2-21

▼ USING NUMERIC DATA IN CONDITIONS

To use a number in a condition, do not use quotation marks. Type the number without any dollar signs or commas. The next example finds all customers whose credit limit is $6,000. To use numeric data in a condition, perform the following steps.

TO USE NUMERIC DATA IN A CONDITION

STEP 1: Be sure to have a clear Query form for the Customer table on the screen.

STEP 2: Use the arrow keys and F6 key to place checkmarks in the Customer Number and Name fields. Move the cursor to the Balance field (Figure 2-22).

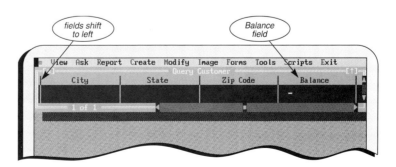

FIGURE 2-22

STEP 3: **Press F6 to place a checkmark in the Balance field and move the cursor to the Credit Limit field.**

The fields shift to the left. The cursor is in the Credit Limit field.

STEP 4: **Press F6 to place a checkmark in the Credit Limit field and type** 6000 **in the Credit Limit field (Figure 2-23).**

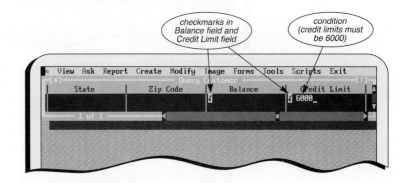

FIGURE 2-23

STEP 5: **Press F2 to run the query.**

The credit limits are not currently visible in the Answer table (Figure 2-24).

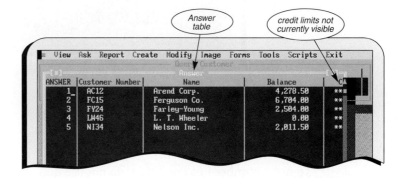

FIGURE 2-24

STEP 6: **Use the RIGHT ARROW key to move to the Credit Limit field.**

The credit limits are now visible. All credit limits in the Answer table are 6,000.00 (Figure 2-25).

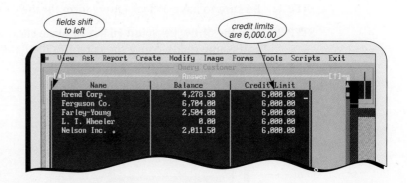

FIGURE 2-25

STEP 7: **Press F8 to close the Answer table.**

▼ USING COMPARISON OPERATORS

Unless otherwise specified, Paradox assumes that the conditions involve equality. The last query, for example, found those customers whose credit limit is *equal* to 6000. To use something other than equality, enter the appropriate comparison operator. The choices are: > (greater than), < (less than), >= (greater than or equal to), <= (less than or equal to), and NOT (not equal to).

The following steps use the > operator to find all customers whose balance is greater than $5,000.

TO USE A COMPARISON OPERATOR IN A CONDITION

STEP 1: Be sure to have a clear Query form for the Customer table on the screen.

STEP 2: Use the arrow keys and F6 key to place checkmarks in the Customer Number, Name, and Balance fields. Type >5000 in the Balance field. Place a checkmark in the Credit Limit field (Figure 2-26).

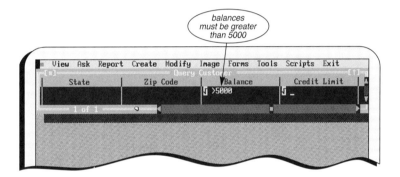

FIGURE 2-26

STEP 3: Press F2 to run the query.

The Answer table contains only those customers whose balance is more than 5,000.00 (Figure 2-27).

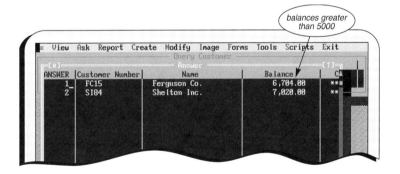

FIGURE 2-27

STEP 4: Press F8 to close the Answer table.

▼ USING COMPOUND CONDITIONS

Often there will be more than one condition the data must satisfy. This type of condition is called a **compound condition**. There are two types of compound conditions.

In **AND conditions**, both individual conditions must be true for the compound condition to be true. For example, an AND condition could be used to find those customers who have an $8,000 credit limit and are represented by sales rep 12.

OR conditions are true provided either individual condition is true. An OR condition could be used to find those customers who have an $8,000 credit limit or are represented by sales rep 12. In this case any customer whose credit limit is $8,000 would be included in the answer whether or not the customer was represented by sales rep 12. Likewise, any customer represented by sales rep 12 would be included whether or not the customer had an $8,000 credit limit.

AND Conditions

To combine conditions with AND, place the conditions on the same line. The following steps use an AND condition to display the number, name, balance, credit limit, and sales rep number for all customers whose credit limit is $8,000 AND who are represented by sales rep 12.

TO USE A COMPOUND CONDITION INVOLVING AND

STEP 1:   Be sure to have a clear Query form for the Customer table on the screen.

STEP 2:   Use the arrow keys and F6 key to place checkmarks in the Customer Number, Name, Balance, Credit Limit, and Sales Rep Number fields. Type 8000 in the Credit Limit field and 12 in the Sales Rep Number field (Figure 2-28).

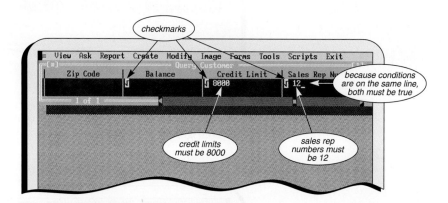

FIGURE 2-28

STEP 3:   Press F2 to run the query.

The credit limits and sales rep numbers are not currently visible (Figure 2-29). To see more of the table, maximize the window.

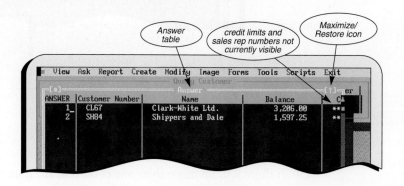

FIGURE 2-29

STEP 4:   **Press F10 to activate the menu bar. Press the LEFT ARROW key to highlight the System menu button. Press the ENTER key to pull down the System menu. Choose the Maximize/Restore command.**

The window is maximized (Figure 2-30). Credit limits and sales rep numbers are still not visible.

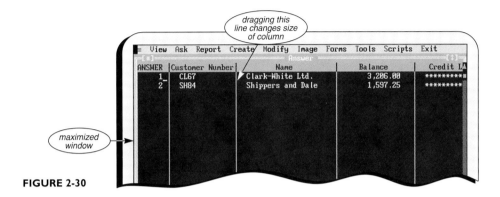

FIGURE 2-30

Mouse Users: *Click the Maximize/Restore icon to maximize the window.*

To fit more of a table on the screen, resize the columns in the table.

Resizing the Columns in the Answer Table

To resize a column in the Answer table, press F10, choose Image|ColumnSize, and then follow the directions on the screen.

TO RESIZE THE COLUMNS IN THE ANSWER TABLE

STEP 1:   **Resize the columns in the Answer table to those shown in Figure 2-31.**

All columns are now visible. The Answer contains only those customers who have an $8,000 credit limit AND who are represented by sales rep 12.

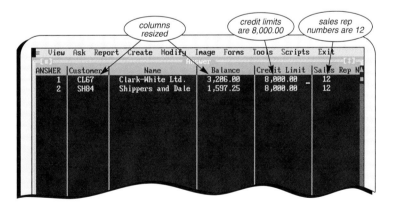

FIGURE 2-31

STEP 2:   **Press F8 to close the Answer table.**

Mouse Users: *To resize a column, drag the line to the right of the column.*

OR Conditions

To combine conditions with OR, the conditions must be put on separate lines. To add a second line to the Query form, press the DOWN ARROW key. (If you ever mistakenly add an extra line, remove it by pressing the DELETE key.) In addition to placing the conditions on separate lines, you must place the same set of checkmarks on both lines.

The next steps use an OR condition to display the name, balance, credit limit, and sales rep number for those customers who have an $8,000 credit limit OR who are represented by sales rep 06 (or both).

TO USE A COMPOUND CONDITION INVOLVING OR

STEP 1: Be sure to have a clear Query form for the Customer table on the screen.

STEP 2: Use the arrow keys and F6 key to place checkmarks in the Customer Number, Name, Balance, and Credit Limit fields. Type 8000 in the Credit Limit field. Place a checkmark in the Sales Rep Number field (Figure 2-32).

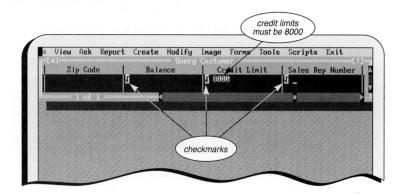

FIGURE 2-32

STEP 3: Press the DOWN ARROW key.

A second line appears in the Query form.

STEP 4: Use the arrow keys and F6 key to place checkmarks in the Customer Number, Name, Balance, Credit Limit, and Sales Rep Number fields in the second line of the Query form. Type 06 in the Sales Rep Number field (Figure 2-33).

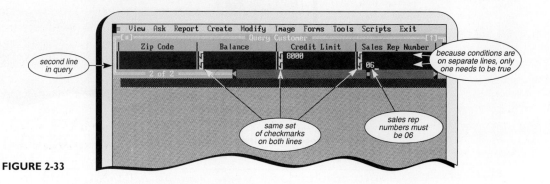

FIGURE 2-33

STEP 5: Press F2 to run the query.

STEP 6: Use the Maximize/Restore command to maximize the Answer table. Reduce the column sizes by using the Image|ColumnSize command so all the data is visible.

The answer contains those customers who have an $8,000 credit limit OR who are represented by sales rep 06 (Figure 2-34).

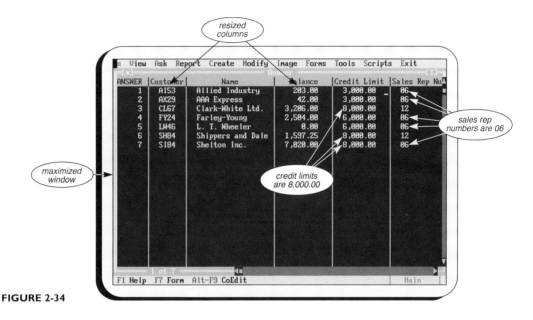

FIGURE 2-34

STEP 7: Press ALT+F8 to close the Answer table and Query Form window.

▼ SORTING DATA IN A QUERY

In some queries, the order in which the records in the answer are displayed really doesn't matter. All that is important is the particular records that display in the Answer table. It doesn't matter which one is first or which one is last.

In other queries, however, the order can be very important. You may want to see customers' balances and would like them arranged from the highest to the lowest. Perhaps the customers' addresses are to be listed by state. Further, within all the customers in a given state, they are to be listed by city.

To order the records in the answer to a query in a particular way, **sort** the records. The field or fields on which the records are sorted is called the **sort key**. If sorting on more than one field (such as sorting by city within state), the more important field (state) is called the **major key** and the less important field (city) is called the **minor key**.

Some sorting happens automatically. Paradox considers the first field with a checkmark the sort key. If there are two records with equal values in this first field, Paradox uses the second field with a checkmark (assuming there is one) to further order these records. In other words, the first field would be the major (or primary) key and the second would be the minor (or secondary) key. Another action Paradox takes automatically is to eliminate duplicates; that is, the Answer table will not contain two records that are identical.

The following example uses a checkmark to display the states where customers are located in the Answer table. The states are to be sorted and each state is to be listed only once. This is exactly the way the standard checkmark functions.

TO SORT DATA

STEP 1: **Be sure to have a clear Query form for the Customer table on the screen.**

STEP 2: **Use the arrow keys and F6 key to place a checkmark in the State field.**

The State field contains a checkmark (Figure 2-35).

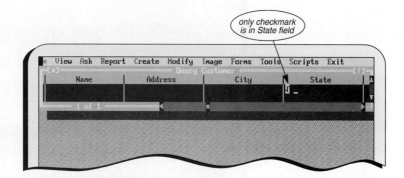

FIGURE 2-35

STEP 3: **Press F2.**

The Answer table contains the state names from the Customer table (Figure 2-36). The names display in alphabetical order. Duplicate state names do not display, so each state is listed only once.

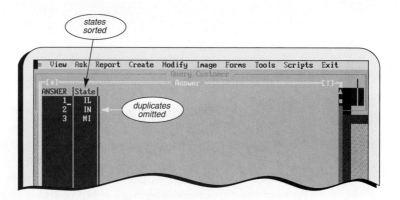

FIGURE 2-36

STEP 4: **Press F8 to close the Answer table.**

Including Duplicates in the Sorted Data

To list the states for all the customers, including duplicates, you cannot use the checkmark, because using checkmarks eliminates any duplicates. Instead of the regular checkmark, use **CheckPlus**. To use CheckPlus, press ALT+F6 instead of F6. The following steps include duplicates by using CheckPlus.

TO INCLUDE DUPLICATES

STEP 1: Be sure to have a clear Query form for the Customer table on the screen.

STEP 2: Move the cursor to the State field. Press ALT+F6 (CheckPlus).

The check-plus (✓+) mark displays in the State field (Figure 2-37).

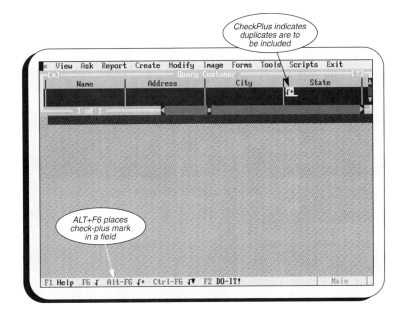

FIGURE 2-37

STEP 3: Press F2 to run the query.

The Answer table contains the state names from the database (Figure 2-38). They are not sorted and duplicates are included.

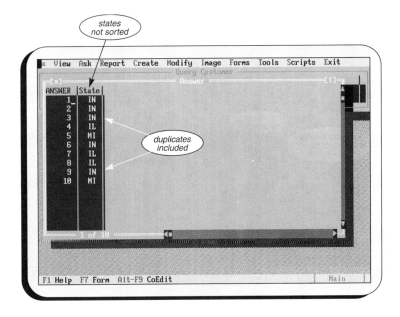

FIGURE 2-38

STEP 4: Press F8 to close the Answer table.

Sorting Data in a Query in Descending Sequence

In the final example of the use of checkmarks for sorting, the states are to be listed in reverse order. This requires **CheckDescending**. To use CheckDescending, press CTRL+F6 instead of F6.

TO REVERSE THE SORT ORDER

STEP 1: Be sure to have a clear Query form for the Customer table on the screen.

STEP 2: Move the cursor to the State field. Press CTRL+F6.

The State field contains a check-descending mark (✓▾) (Figure 2-39).

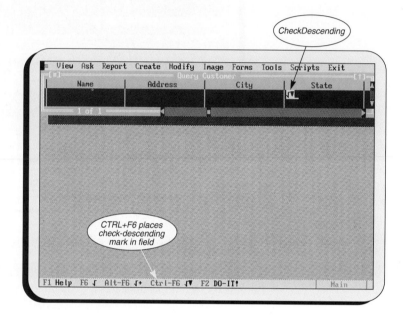

FIGURE 2-39

STEP 3: Press F2 to run the query.

The Answer table contains the state names from the database (Figure 2-40). They are sorted in reverse order. Duplicates have been eliminated.

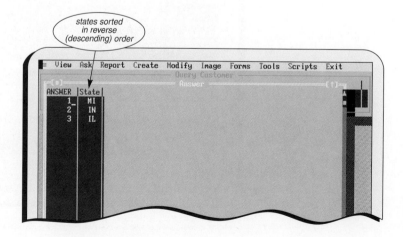

FIGURE 2-40

STEP 4: Press F8 to close the Answer table.

Sorting Data in a Query on Multiple Fields

Another approach to sorting, the one that offers maximum flexibility, is to sort the Answer table. To use this approach, choose the Sort command on the **Modify menu**.

The next example lists the number, name, address, city, and state for all customers. The data is to be sorted by city within state. The following steps accomplish this by first creating and then sorting the Answer table.

TO CREATE AND SORT THE ANSWER TABLE

STEP 1: Be sure to have a clear Query form for the Customer table on the screen.

STEP 2: Place checkmarks in the Customer Number, Name, Address, City, and State fields (Figure 2-41).

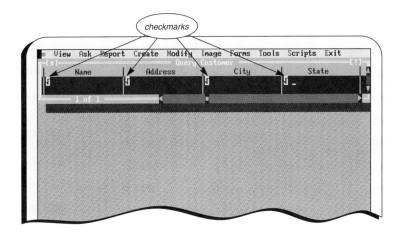

FIGURE 2-41

STEP 3: Press F2 to run the query.

The results display in the Answer table (Figure 2-42).

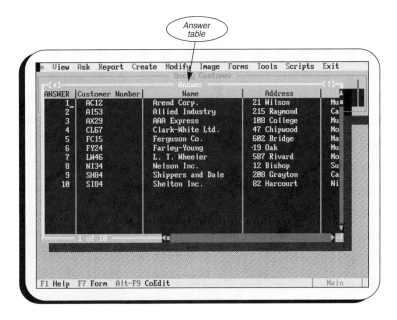

FIGURE 2-42

STEP 4: Press F10 and choose Modify | Sort (Figure 2-43).

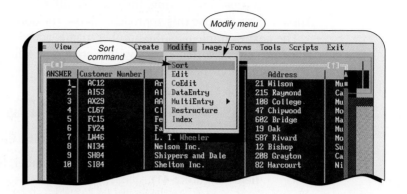

FIGURE 2-43

STEP 5: Choose the Answer table (Figure 2-44).

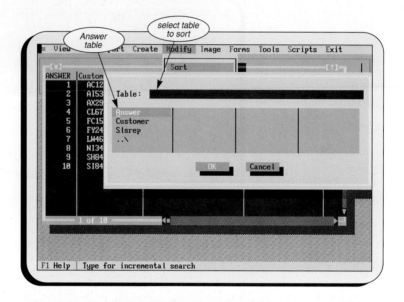

FIGURE 2-44

STEP 6: When the Paradox box asks for Same (if the result of the sorting is to be the same table, namely, Answer) or New (a different table), choose Same.

A list of the fields in the Answer table displays (Figure 2-45). To indicate a single sort key, place the number 1 in front of the field that is the sort key. To indicate two sort keys, as in this example, place the number 1 in front of the major key and the number 2 in front of the minor key.

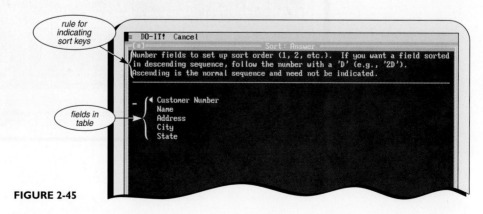

FIGURE 2-45

STEP 7: Press the DOWN ARROW key to move to the State field. Type the number 1, since State is the major sort key. Press the UP ARROW key to move to the City field and type the number 2, since city is the minor sort key.

The sort keys are indicated by the appropriate numbers (Figure 2-46).

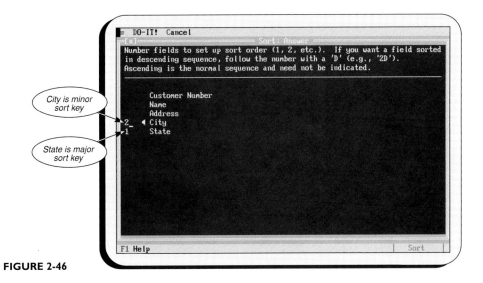

FIGURE 2-46

STEP 8: Press F2 to sort the Answer table, maximize the Answer table, and resize the columns so all columns are visible.

The data in the Answer table is sorted by state (Figure 2-47). Within each state the customers are sorted by city.

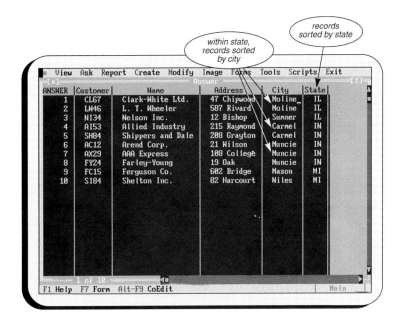

FIGURE 2-47

STEP 9: Press ALT+F8 to close the Answer table and the Query form window.

▼ JOINING TABLES

Suppose you want to list the number and name of each customer along with the number and name of the customer's sales rep. The customer name is in the Customer table, whereas the sales rep name is in the Slsrep table. Thus, this query cannot be satisfied using a single table. You need to **join** the tables; that is, to find records in the two tables that have identical values in matching fields (Figure 2-48). This example requires finding records in the Customer table and the Slsrep table that have the same value in the Sales Rep Number fields.

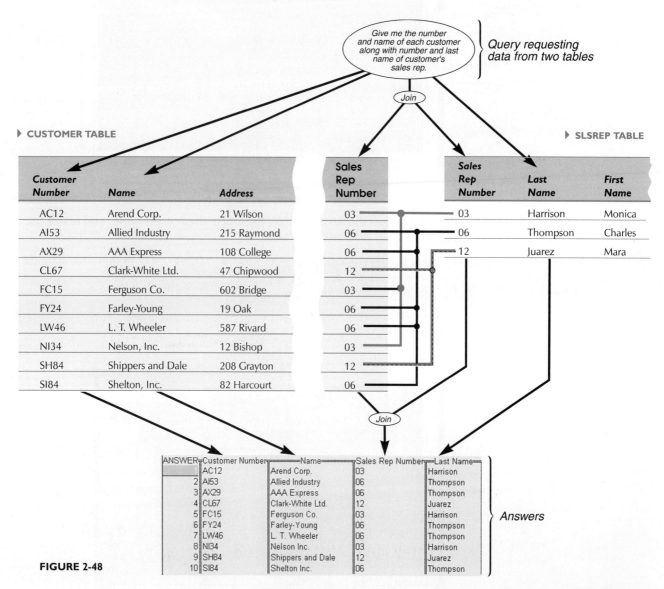

FIGURE 2-48

To join tables in Paradox, first bring Query forms for both tables to the screen. Choose all the necessary fields from both tables by placing checkmarks just as with a single table. Finally, indicate how the tables are related, that is, which fields in the tables must match. In choosing data from the Customer and Slsrep tables, for example, indicate that the Sales Rep Number fields in both tables must contain the same values.

To indicate that fields must match, use a special item called an example. An **example** is just a sample value. To indicate that it is an example, rather than a specific condition, press F5 before typing the entry. Paradox visually indicates that the entry represents an example by displaying it in a different color.

To indicate the matching fields, enter the *same* example in both fields. In the following steps, the number 99 will be used as the example in the Sales Rep Number fields. The choice of 99 is purely arbitrary. It really doesn't matter what number is used for the examples, as long as it is the same example in both fields.

Adding a Second Table to a Query

The first step is to add a second table to the query, that is, to bring a Query form for the second table to the screen.

TO ADD A TABLE TO A QUERY

STEP 1: Be sure to have a clear Query form for the Customer table on the screen.

STEP 2: Press F10 and move the cursor to the Ask menu option (Figure 2-49).

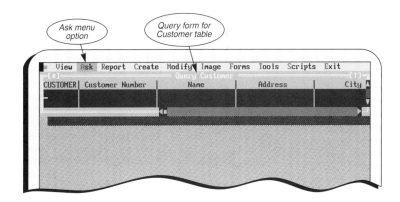

FIGURE 2-49

STEP 3: Choose Ask and then choose the Slsrep table.

The Query form window contains Query forms for both the Customer and Slsrep tables (Figure 2-50).

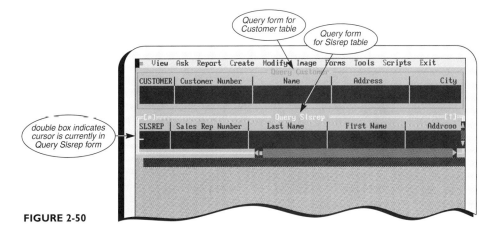

FIGURE 2-50

Joining the Tables

Once both Query forms are on the screen, fill them in appropriately to join the tables as the following steps illustrate.

TO JOIN TABLES

STEP 1: Press F3 to move to the Query form for the Customer table and then place checkmarks in the Customer Number and Name fields (Figure 2-51).

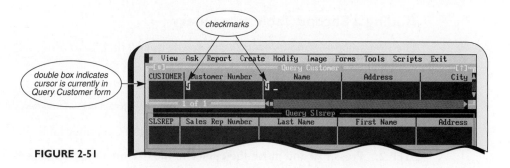

FIGURE 2-51

STEP 2: Move the cursor to the Sales Rep Number field. Press F5 and then type 99.

The example, 99, displays in the Sales Rep Number field in reverse video indicating it is an example (Figure 2-52).

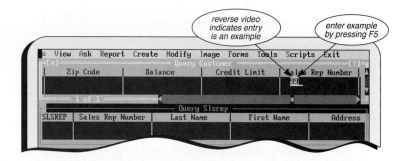

FIGURE 2-52

STEP 3: Press F4 to move to the Query form for the Slsrep table and then place a checkmark in the Sales Rep Number field. Press F5 and then type 99. Place a checkmark in the Last Name field.

The example, 99, displays in both Sales Rep Number fields (Figure 2-53).

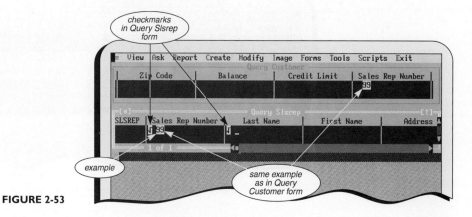

FIGURE 2-53

STEP 4:   **Press F2 to run the query.**

The answer contains data from both the Customer and Slsrep tables (Figure 2-54). Some of the data is not completely visible.

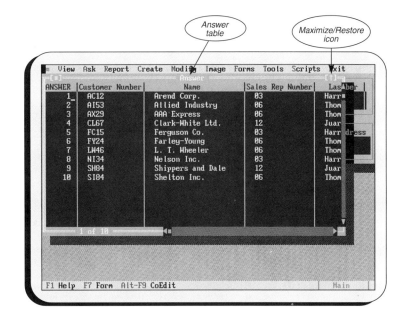

FIGURE 2-54

STEP 5:   **Maximize the window.**

The window is maximized (Figure 2-55). The answer contains data from both tables.

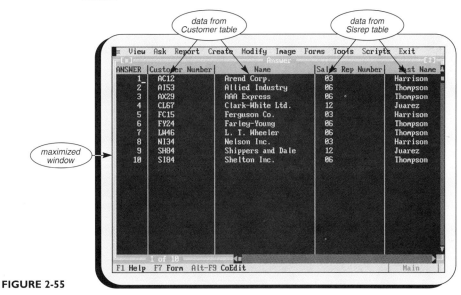

FIGURE 2-55

STEP 6:   **Close the Answer table but not the Query form window.**

Restricting Records in a Join

Sometimes you will want to join tables, but will not want to include all possible records. In such cases, you will include appropriate conditions in the queries to relate the tables as you did in the previous example. You will also enter additional conditions. To include the same fields as in the previous query, but only those customers whose credit limit is $8,000, make the same entries as before and then also enter the number 8000 in the Credit Limit field.

The following steps modify the Query forms from the previous instructions to restrict the records that will be included in the join.

TO RESTRICT THE RECORDS IN A JOIN

STEP 1: With both Query forms on the screen, press F3 to move up to the Query form for Customer. Press the LEFT ARROW key to move back to the Credit Limit field and then type 8000 (**Figure 2-56**).

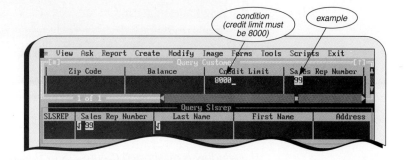

FIGURE 2-56

STEP 2: Press F2 to run the query and then maximize the window containing the Answer table.

The Answer table now contains only those customers who have a credit limit of $8,000 (Figure 2-57).

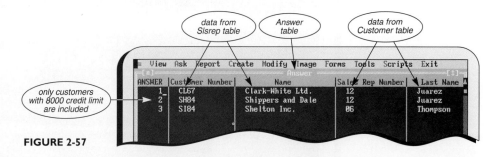

FIGURE 2-57

STEP 3: Close all windows by pressing ALT+F8.

▼   USING COMPUTED FIELDS

Suppose you want to find each customer's available credit. This poses a problem, because there is no field for available credit in the Customer table. It can be computed, however, because the available credit is equal to the credit limit minus the balance. Such a field is called a **computed field**. To include computed fields in queries, use examples.

Enter examples in each of the fields involved in the computation. Thus enter an example, such as 100, for Balance and a *different* example, such as 200, for credit limit. The values you use as examples are irrelevant. Then place the word calc followed by the appropriate expression in any field. (It doesn't matter which field is used for this purpose.)

The expression will use the examples that have already been created. In this case the expression would be the example created for credit limits followed by a minus sign (–), followed by the example created for balances.

Computations are not restricted to subtraction. Computations can involve addition (+), multiplication (*), and division (/), as well as parentheses.

The following steps use a computed field to display the number, name, and available credit of all customers.

TO USE A COMPUTED FIELD

STEP 1: **Be sure to have a clear Query form for the Customer table on the screen.**

STEP 2: **Place checkmarks in the Customer Number and Name fields. Move the cursor to the Balance field, press F5, and then type** 100 **as the example of a balance. Move the cursor to the Credit Limit field, press F5, and then type** 200 **as the example of a credit limit.**

Both the Balance field and the Credit Limit field contain examples (Figure 2-58).

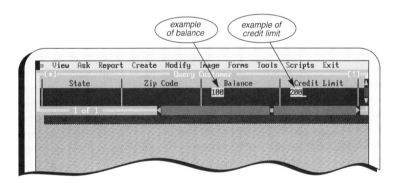

FIGURE 2-58

STEP 3: **Move the cursor to the Sales Rep Number field.**

STEP 4: **Type** calc **and press the SPACEBAR. Press F5 and then type** 200. **Type a minus sign (–). Press F5 and then type** 100.

The expression for calculating available credit displays in the Sales Rep Number field (Figure 2-59).

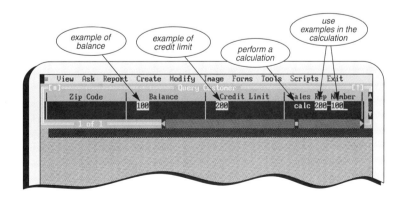

FIGURE 2-59

STEP 5: **Press F2 to run the query.**

The Answer table contains the two checked fields as well as the calculation (Figure 2-60). The parentheses around the 704, (704), indicate that it is negative.

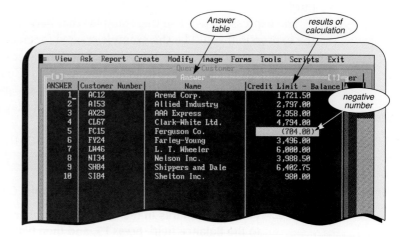

FIGURE 2-60

STEP 6: **Press F8 to close the Answer table.**

▼ CALCULATING STATISTICS

Most database systems, including Paradox, support the same collection of built-in functions: COUNT, SUM, AVERAGE, MAX (largest value), and MIN (smallest value). To use any of these in a query, precede it with the CALC operator, the same operator used for computed fields.

Calculating an Average

The following example illustrates how to use the built-in functions by calculating the average balance for all customers.

TO CALCULATE AN AVERAGE

STEP 1: Be sure to have a clear Query form for the Customer table on the screen.

STEP 2: Type `calc average` in the Balance field (Figure 2-61).

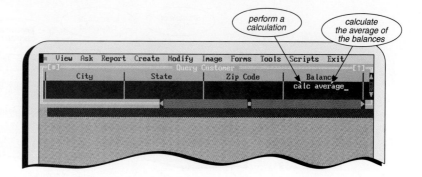

FIGURE 2-61

STEP 3: **Press F2 to run the query.**

The Answer table contains the average balance of all customers (Figure 2-62).

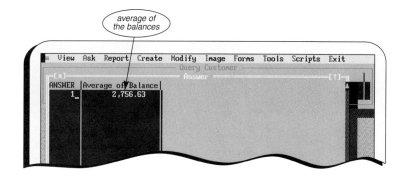

FIGURE 2-62

STEP 6: **Press F8 to close the Answer table.**

Grouping Similar Records

Sometimes calculating statistics for all the records in the table is appropriate. In other cases, however, you will need to calculate the statistics for groups of records. You may, for example, need to calculate the average balance for the customers of each sales rep. You will want the average for the customers of sales rep 03, the average for customers of sales rep 06, and so on.

This type of calculation involves **grouping**, which means creating groups of records that share some common characteristic. In grouping by sales rep number, the customers of sales rep 03 would form one group, the customers of sales rep 06 would be a second, and the customers of sales rep 12 form a third. The calculations are then made for each group. To indicate grouping in Paradox, place a checkmark in the field to be used for grouping. Do not place checkmarks in any other fields.

The following steps calculate the average balance for customers of each sales rep.

TO GROUP

STEP 1: **Be sure to have a clear Query form for the Customer table on the screen.**

STEP 2: **Enter** calc average **in the Balance field. Place a checkmark in the Sales Rep Number field.**

The calculation displays in the Balance field (Figure 2-63). A checkmark appears in the Sales Rep Number field indicating records are to be grouped by Sales Rep Number.

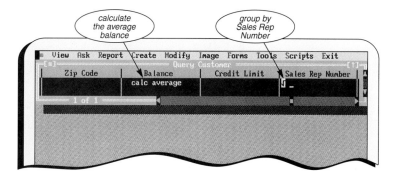

FIGURE 2-63

STEP 3:   Press F2 to run the query.

The Answer table shows each sales rep's number along with the average balance of the customers of that sales rep (Figure 2-64).

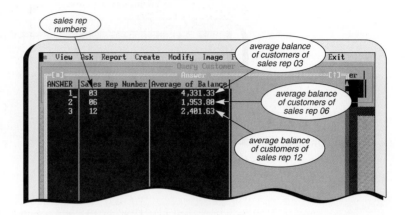

FIGURE 2-64

STEP 4:   Press F8 to close the Answer table.

▼   **SAVING A QUERY**

In some cases, you will construct a query that you will want to use again. You can avoid having to repeat all the entries by saving the query. To save the query, use the **QuerySave command** on the **Scripts menu**. The following steps illustrate the process by saving the query currently on the screen and calling it slsavg.

TO SAVE A QUERY

STEP 1:   Choose Scripts|QuerySave (Figure 2-65).

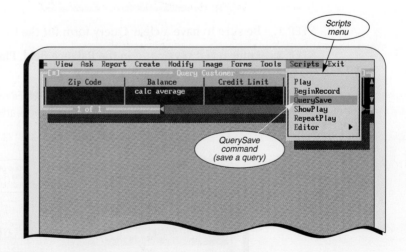

FIGURE 2-65

STEP 2:   Type slsavg **(Figure 2-66) and press the ENTER key.**

The query has been saved.

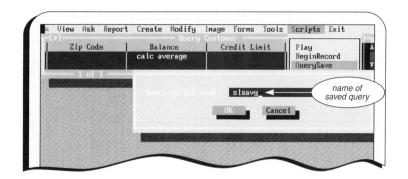

FIGURE 2-66

STEP 3:   Press F8 to remove the Query form window from the screen.

Using a Saved Query

Once the query has been saved, you can use it at any time in the future by *opening* it, which brings the completed Query form back to the screen, and then *running* it. This produces a new Answer table. The following steps illustrate the process.

TO USE A SAVED QUERY

STEP 1:   Press F10 and choose Scripts|Play (Figure 2-67).

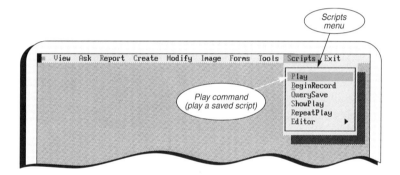

FIGURE 2-67

STEP 2:   Choose Slsavg (Figure 2-68).

The Query form displays.

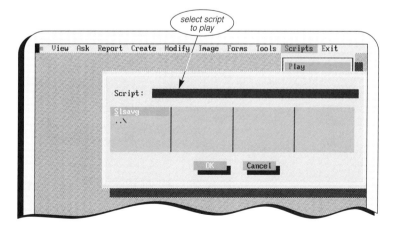

FIGURE 2-68

STEP 3:   Press F2 to run the query.

The Answer table displays on the screen (Figure 2-69).

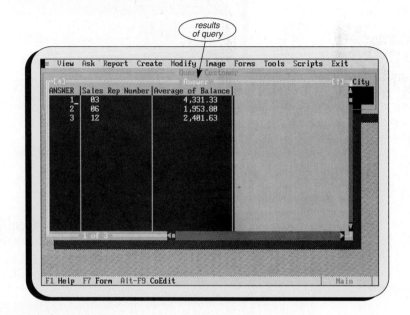

FIGURE 2-69

STEP 4:   Press ALT+F8 to close the Answer table and query.

▼ **PROJECT SUMMARY**

Project 2 introduced querying a database using Paradox. The project presented steps and techniques showing you how to create and run queries. You learned how to use various types of conditions. The project also illustrated joining tables using queries and showed you how to use calculated fields and statistics.

▼ **KEY TERMS**

AND condition *(P76)*
Ask menu *(P62)*
case-sensitive *(P70)*
Check (F6) *(P63)*
CheckDescending (CTRL+F6) *(P82)*
checkmark *(P63)*
CheckPlus (ALT+F6) *(P80)*
comparison operator *(P75)*
compound condition *(P75)*

computed field *(P90)*
example *(P87)*
grouping *(P93)*
join *(P86)*
LIKE operator *(P71)*
major key *(P79)*
minor key *(P79)*
OR condition *(P76)*
Modify menu *(P83)*
Play command *(P95)*

query *(P60)*
Query form *(P61)*
Query form window *(P61)*
QuerySave command *(P94)*
run the query *(P61)*
Scripts menu *(P94)*
sort *(P79)*
sort key *(P79)*
wildcards *(P71)*

• •

▼   ## QUICK REFERENCE

In Paradox, you can accomplish a task in a number of different ways. The following table provides a quick reference to each task presented in Project 2 with its available options. The commands listed in the Menu column can be executed using either the keyboard or the mouse.

Task	Mouse	Menu	Keyboard Shortcuts
Add a Table to a Query		From Main menu, choose Ask; choose the table	
Clear a Query Form			Press DELETE
Close a Query	Click Close box	From System menu, choose Close	Press F8
Close the Answer Table	Click Close box	From System menu, choose Close	Press F8
Create an AND Condition			Place conditions on same
Create an Example			Press F5
Create a New Query		From Main menu, choose Close	
Create an OR Condition			Enter condition, press DOWN ARROW, enter second condition
Enter a Condition	Click on the field for the condition, type condition		Press RIGHT ARROW or LEFT ARROW to move to the condition, type condition
Indicate Duplicates	Click CheckPlus		Press ALT+F8
Join Tables			Place the same example in the matching fields
Move the Cursor to a Field in a Query Form	Click the field		Press LEFT ARROW or RIGHT ARROW
Print the Answer to a Query		From Report menu, choose Output; choose Answer	Press ALT+F7
Place Checkmarks in			Press F6 with cursor under name of table
Place Checkmark in a Field			Press F6 with cursor under name of field
Run a Query	Click DO-IT! button	Choose DO-IT!	Press F2
Sort Data by Sorting		From Modify menu, choose Sort; choose Answer table	
Sort Data Using Checkmarks and Excluding Duplicates			Press F6 with cursor under name of field
Sort Data Using Checkmarks in Descending Order	Click CheckDescending		Press CTRL+F6 with cursor under name of field

SHORT ANSWER
ASSIGNMENTS

SHORT ANSWER ASSIGNMENT I
True/False

Instructions: Circle T if the statement is true or F if the statement is false.

T   F   1. To include all the fields in a record in a query, place a checkmark under the table name.

T   F   2. To list only certain records in a table, use a query.

T   F   3. To create a query in Paradox, choose Ask from the Main menu.

T   F   4. The answer to a query is placed in a special table called Answer.

T   F   5. When you have two or more Query forms on a screen, you can use the F3 key to move to the next form.

T   F   6. To run a query, press F2.

T   F   7. To clear all the entries in a query, press CTRL+D.

T   F   8. To indicate that a field is to be included in a query, place a checkmark in the field.

T   F   9. To place a checkmark in a field, press F3.

T   F   10. The wildcard symbols available for use in a query are .. and &.

T   F   11. To create a condition involving equals, type the equal sign (=).

T   F   12. To create a compound condition using AND, enter all conditions on the same line.

T   F   13. To create a compound condition using OR, type the word OR before the second condition.

T   F   14. To display credit limits in descending order, move to the Credit Limit field and press ALT+F6 for CheckDescending.

T   F   15. To enter an example instead of a condition in a field, press F5 before typing the entry.

T   F   16. To join two or more tables, use a query.

T   F   17. Paradox automatically eliminates duplicate records in the Answer table.

T   F   18. To obtain the average of the values in the Credit Limit field, type AVERAGE in the Credit Limit field of the Query form and run the query.

T   F   19. To group all records that have like values in the same field, place a checkmark in the field to be used for grouping and type the word GROUP.

T   F   20. To save a query, use the QuerySave command on the Scripts menu.

SHORT ANSWER ASSIGNMENT 2
Multiple Choice

Instructions: Circle the correct response.

1. To list only certain records in a table, use a(n) _____.

   a. list
   b. query
   c. question
   d. answer

2. The answer to a query is placed in a special table called _____.

   a. Query
   b. Solution
   c. Answer
   d. Result

3. To clear all the entries in a query, press _____.

   a. CTRL+D
   b. CTRL+DELETE
   c. CTRL+Y
   d. DELETE

4. The wildcard symbols available for use in a query are the _____ and the _____.

   a. double period (..), asterisk (*)
   b. question mark (?), ampersand (&)
   c. double period (..), at symbol (@)
   d. question mark (?), asterisk (*)

5. Equal to (=), less than (<), and greater than (>) are examples of _____.

   a. conditions
   b. comparison operators
   c. values
   d. compound conditions

6. When two or more conditions are connected with AND or OR, the result is called a _____.

   a. compound condition
   b. simple condition
   c. character condition
   d. pattern condition

7. To enter an example instead of a condition in a field, press _____ before typing the entry.

   a. F2
   b. F3
   c. F4
   d. F5

8. Use a query to _____ tables; that is, find records in two tables that have identical values in matching fields.

   a. merge
   b. match
   c. join
   d. combine

SHORT ANSWER ASSIGNMENT 2 (continued)

9. Press _____ to move from one Query form to the next.

   a. F2
   b. F3
   c. F4
   d. F5

10. To calculate the total of all balances in the Customer table, enter _____ in the Balance field of the Query form.

   a. sum
   b. sum all
   c. calc sum
   d. stat sum

SHORT ANSWER ASSIGNMENT 3
Understanding Query Forms

Instructions: Figure SA2-3, shows a Query form window with Query forms for the Slsrep and Customer tables. Use this figure to answer the following questions.

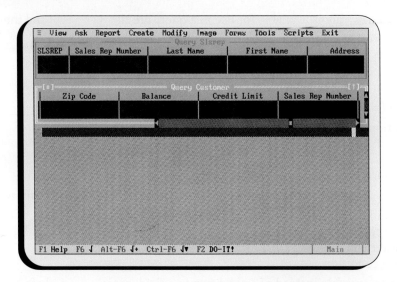

FIGURE SA2-3

1. Assume the cursor is in the Slsrep Query form. How can you move to the Customer Query form?

   _____

   _____

2. Explain the purpose of each function key listed on the bottom line of the screen.

   _____

   _____

   _____

3. How can you add the Query form for the Orders table to the window?

   _____

   _____

4. Assume that you have created and run a query. How can you save a query?

_____

_____

SHORT ANSWER ASSIGNMENT 4
Understanding Compound Conditions

Instructions: Figure SA2-4a shows a created query for the Customer table using a compound condition, and Figure SA2-4b lists the contents of the Customer table. In the space provided list the answer to this query.

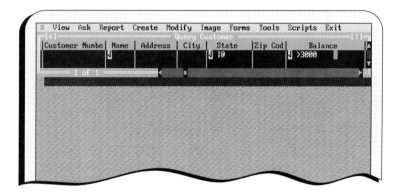

FIGURE SA2-4a

Customer Number	Name	Address	City	State	Zip Code	Balance	Credit Limit	Sales Rep Number
AC12	Arend Corp.	21 Wilson	Muncie	IN	47303	$4,278.50	$6,000.00	03
AI53	Allied Industry	215 Raymond	Carmel	IN	46032	$203.00	$3,000.00	06
AX29	AAA Express	108 College	Muncie	IN	47303	$42.00	$3,000.00	06
CL67	Clark-White Ltd.	47 Chipwood	Moline	IL	61265	$3,206.00	$8,000.00	12
FC15	Ferguson Co.	602 Bridge	Mason	MI	48854	$6,704.00	$6,000.00	03
FY24	Farley-Young	19 Oak	Muncie	IN	47303	$2,504.00	$6,000.00	06
LW46	L. T. Wheeler	587 Rivard	Moline	IL	61265	$0.00	$6,000.00	06
NI34	Nelson, Inc.	12 Bishop	Sumner	IL	62466	$2,011.50	$6,000.00	03
SH84	Shippers and Dale	208 Grayton	Carmel	IN	46032	$1,597.25	$8,000.00	12
SI84	Shelton, Inc.	82 Harcourt	Niles	MI	49120	$7,020.00	$8,000.00	06

FIGURE SA2-4b

_____

_____

_____

SHORT ANSWER ASSIGNMENT 5

Understanding Sorting Data in a Query

Instructions: Figure SA2-5 shows a query created to sort data in a particular order. In the space provided, list the answer to this query. Refer to Figure SA2-4b on the previous page for the contents of the Customer table.

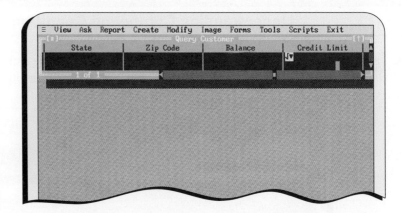

FIGURE SA2-5

_____

_____

_____

_____

SHORT ANSWER ASSIGNMENT 6

Understanding Statistics in Queries

Instructions: Figure SA2-6 shows a query created to calculate statistics. In the space provided, list the answer to this query. Refer to Figure SA2-4b on the previous page for the contents of the Customer table.

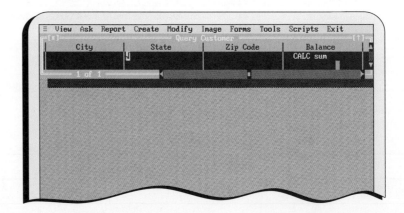

FIGURE SA2-6

_____

_____

_____

HANDS-ON EXERCISE 1
Using the Help Menu

Instructions: Perform the following tasks.

1. Start Paradox.
2. Press F1.
3. Press the F1 key again to see the Help Index.
4. Press CTRL+Z and enter query obtain help on queries.
5. Choose Ask from the Main menu, choose QueryForms, choose Calculations, and then choose Math.
6. Read the information and answer the following questions:
   a. What is the order of precedence for mathematical operations?

   _____

   _____

   b. How can you change the order of precedence?

   _____

   _____

   c. How do you separate "and" criteria for a field?

   _____

   _____

   d. How do you separate "or" criteria for a field?

   _____

   _____

7. Choose the Paradox command to exit the Help System.
8. Exit Paradox.

HANDS-ON EXERCISE 2
Sorting and Printing the Answer Table

Instructions: Perform the following tasks.

1. Start Paradox.
2. Create a new query for the Customer table.

HANDS-ON EXERCISE 2 (continued)

3. In the Query form window, place checkmarks in the Customer Number, Name, State, and Credit Limit fields.

4. Run the query. Print the Answer table as shown in Figure HOE 2-2.

```
10/11/94                    Standard Report                  Page   1


Customer Number  Name                    State  Credit Limit
---------------  --------------------    -----  ----------------
AC12             Arend Corp.             IN           6,000.00
AI53             Allied Industry         IN           3,000.00
AX29             AAA Express             IN           3,000.00
CL67             Clark-White Ltd.        IL           8,000.00
FC15             Ferguson Co.            MI           6,000.00
FY24             Farley-Young            IN           6,000.00
LW46             L. T. Wheeler           IL           6,000.00
NI34             Nelson Inc.             IL           6,000.00
SH84             Shippers and Dale       IN           8,000.00
SI84             Shelton Inc.            MI           8,000.00
```

FIGURE HOE 2-2

5. Choose Modify, then choose Sort and select the Answer table.

6. Sort the data by state within credit limit.

7. Print the Answer table.

8. Close the Answer table and the query.

9. Exit Paradox.

HANDS-ON EXERCISE 3
Performing Calculations in Queries

Instruction: The average balance for all customers is $2,756.63. Determine the difference between the actual balance and the average balance for each customer. Perform the following tasks.

1. Start Paradox.

2. Create a new query for the Customer table.

3. Place checkmarks in the Customer Number, Name, and Balance fields.

4. Enter the example 5000 in the Balance field.

5. Move to the State field and enter the formula to calculate the difference between the actual balance and the average balance. (Hint: Enter 5000 as an example and 2756.63 as an actual value.)

6. Run the query.

7. Print the Answer table as shown in Figure HOE 2-3.

```
10/11/94                    Standard Report                    Page   1


Customer Number  Name                 Balance           Balance - 2756.63
---------------  -------------------  ----------------  ----------------
AC12             Arend Corp.                 4,278.50           1,521.87
AI53             Allied Industry               203.00          (2,553.63)
AX29             AAA Express                    42.00          (2,714.63)
CL67             Clark-White Ltd.            3,206.00             449.37
FC15             Ferguson Co.                6,704.00           3,947.37
FY24             Farley-Young                2,504.00            (252.63)
LW46             L. T. Wheeler                   0.00          (2,756.63)
NI34             Nelson Inc.                 2,011.50            (745.13)
SH84             Shippers and Dale           1,597.25          (1,159.38)
SI84             Shelton Inc.                7,020.00           4,263.37
```

FIGURE HOE 2-3

8. Close the Answer table and the query.

9. Exit Paradox

LABORATORY ASSIGNMENT 1
Querying the Parts Database

Purpose: To provide practice in creating queries and using queries.

Problem: Query the Parts database in a variety of ways.

Instructions: Use the database created in Laboratory Assignment 1 of Project 1 for this assignment. Execute each task on the computer and print the answers.

1. Create a new query for the Parts table.

2. Display and print all the records in the table as shown in Figure LA 2-1 on the next page.

LABORATORY ASSIGNMENT I (continued)

```
10/11/94                    Standard Report                    Page   1


Part Number   Part Description   Units On Hand   Item Class Code   Warehouse Number
-----------   ----------------   -------------   ---------------   ----------------
AX12          IRON                   104         HW                3
AZ52          DARTBOARD               20         SG                2
BA74          BASKETBALL               0         SG                1
BH22          CORNPOPPER              95         HW                3
BT04          GAS GRILL               11         AP                2
BZ66          WASHER                  52         AP                3
CA14          GRIDDLE                 78         HW                3
CB03          BIKE                    44         SG                1
CX11          BLENDER                112         HW                3
CZ81          TREADMILL               68         SG                2
```

```
Price
----------------
          24.95
          12.95
          24.95
          29.95
         149.99
         399.99
          39.99
         299.99
          22.95
         349.95
```

FIGURE LA 2-1

3. Display and print the Part Number, Part Description, and Price for all records in the table.

4. Display and print the records for all parts that are classified as Sporting Goods.

5. Display and print the records for all parts where the part description begins with the letter B.

6. Display and print the records for all parts that sound like Cornpupper.

7. Display and print the records for all parts that have a price greater than 29.95.

8. Display and print the records for all parts that are classified as Sporting Goods and have a price greater than 29.95.

9. Display and print the records for all parts that are classified as Housewares or have a price of less than 24.95.

10. Display and print the average price of all parts.

11. Display and print the average price for each item class.

12. Join the Parts table and the Item Class table and display and print the Part Description, Units On Hand, Item Class Description, and Price for all records.

13. Sort the Answer table created in step 12 in ascending order by part description within item class description. Print the Answer table.

14. Restrict the records retrieved in step 12 to only those parts located in warehouse 3. Print the Answer table.

15. Calculate and display the on-hand value (units on hand * price) for all records in the database. Print the Answer table.

16. Close the Answer table, close the query without saving, and exit Paradox.

LABORATORY ASSIGNMENT 2
Querying the Employee Database

Purpose: To provide practice in creating queries and using queries.

Problem: Query the Employee database in a variety of ways.

Instructions: Use the database created in Laboratory Assignment 2 of Project 1 for this assignment. Execute the tasks on the computer and print the answers.

1. Create a new query for the Employee table.

2. Display and print all the records in the table as shown in Figure LA 2-2 on the next page.

3. Display and print the Employee Number, Employee Last Name, Employee First Name, and Pay Rate for all the records in the table.

4. Display and print the records for all employees who work in the department with a code 01.

5. Display and print the records for all employees whose last names start with the letter E.

6. Display and print the records for all employees whose last names sound like Benter.

7. Display and print the records for all employees whose pay rate is less than $8.00.

8. Display and print the records for all employees who work in the department with a code 03 and have a pay rate less than $8.00.

9. Display and print the records for all employees who work in department code 01 or whose pay rate is less $8.00.

10. Display and print the pay rates for all employees in ascending order.

11. Display and print the highest pay rate.

12. Display and print the lowest pay rate.

13. Display and print the average pay rate for each department.

LABORATORY ASSIGNMENT 2 (continued)

```
10/11/94                    Standard Report                    Page   1


Employee Number    Employee Last Name    Employee First Name    Department Code   Pay R
----------------   ------------------    -------------------    ---------------   -----
1011               Rapoza                Anthony                04
1013               McCormack             Nigel                  04
1016               Ackerman              David                  01
1017               Doi                   Chan                   03
1020               Castle                Mark                   04
1022               Dunning               Lisa                   02
1025               Chaney                Joseph                 01
1026               Bender                Helen                  03
1029               Anderson              Mariane                04
1030               Edwards               Kenneth                03
1037               Baxter                Charles                01
1041               Evans                 John                   02
1056               Andrews               Robert                 02
1057               Dugan                 Mary                   03
1066               Castleworth           Mary                   03
```

```
ate
-----------
    8.50
    8.25
    9.75
    6.00
    7.50
    9.10
    8.00
    6.75
    9.00
    8.60
   11.00
    6.00
    9.00
    8.75
    8.75
```

FIGURE LA 2-2

14. Join the Employee table and the Department table, and display and print the Employee Number, Employee Last Name, Employee First Name, Pay Rate, and Department Name.

15. Sort the Answer table created in step 14 in ascending order by employee last name within department name. Print the Answer table.

16. Display and print the Employee Number, Employee Last Name, Employee First Name, Department Name, and Pay Rate for all employees whose pay rate is greater than $9.00.

17. Close the Answer table, close the query without saving, and exit Paradox.

LABORATORY ASSIGNMENT 3
Querying the Movie Database

Purpose: To provide practice in creating queries and using queries.

Problem: Query the Movie database in a variety of ways.

Instructions: Use the database created in Laboratory Assignment 3 of Project 1 for this assignment. Execute the tasks on the computer and print the answers.

1. Create a new query for the Movie table.

2. Display and print all the records in the table as shown in Figure LA 2-3.

```
  10/11/94                    Standard Report                    Page    1


  Movie Number   Movie Title        Year Made   Movie Type   Length   Director Code
  ------------   ------------------  ---------   ----------   ------   -------------
  001            Ann Thompson        1977        COMEDY          93   01
  002            They Went Away      1964        COMEDY          93   04
  003            A Crack in Time     1971        SCI FI         136   04
  004            No Time for Henry   1959        SUSPEN         136   03
  005            The Dirty Car       1948        SUSPEN          80   03
  006            They Know Too Much  1969        HORROR         109   03
  007            The Old House       1978        DRAMA           95   01
  008            The Dervish         1960        HORROR         119   03
  011            Winston's Dog       1979        COMEDY          96   01
  012            Escape from Zero    1958        SUSPEN         128   03
  014            The Ninth Planet    1968        SCI FI         141   04
  021            A Single Bullet     1939        WESTER          99   02
  022            Rear Window         1954        SUSPEN         112   03
  024            Just Like Me        1940        DRAMA          128   02
```

FIGURE LA 2-3

3. Display and print the Movie Title, Year Made, and Movie Type for all the records in the table.

4. Display and print the Movie Number, Movie Title, Year Made, and Length for all movies with a movie type of COMEDY.

5. Display and print all the records for movies made after 1969.

6. Display and print all the records for movies with a movie type of SUSPEN and length greater than 100.

7. Display and print all the records for movies that have a movie title that begins with Th.

8. Display and print all the records for movies made before 1950 or longer than 100 minutes.

9. Display and print all the records for movies that are longer than 100 minutes and are either SUSPEN or HORROR movie types.

10. Sum the lengths of all movies. Print the results.

11. Count the number of movies each director has made. Print the results.

12. Display and print the average movie length for each director.

LABORATORY ASSIGNMENT 3 (continued)

13. Join the Movie table and the Director table, and display and print the Movie Number, Movie Title, Movie Type, and Director Name for all records.

14. Sort the Answer table created in step 13 in ascending order by movie title within director name. Print the Answer table.

15. Restrict the records retrieved in step 13 to only movies made after 1970 with a length longer than 100 minutes. Print the Answer table.

16. Display and print the Movie Title, Movie Type, Director Name, and the difference between the actual movie length and 100 minutes.

17. Close the Answer table, close the query without saving, and exit Paradox.

LABORATORY ASSIGNMENT 4
Querying the Book Database

Purpose: To provide practice in structuring, creating, and using queries.

Problem: You are the office manager for a local bookstore. The bookstore owner is gathering some facts to assist her in making plans for the next three months. She has sent you a memo outlining the type of information she needs. You are to supply her with the correct information.

Instructions: Use the database created in Laboratory Assignment 4 of Project 1 for this assignment.

Provide the following:

1. An inventory list sorted by author within publisher name.

2. The average price of all books and then the average price for each publisher.

3. The price of the most expensive and least expensive book in the inventory.

4. A list of which books are currently not in stock.

5. A list of all books that need to be reordered. Books with less than two copies need to be reordered. For reordering purposes, she would like the book title, author, publisher name, and price. She expects to ask for this list on a weekly basis.

6. The on-hand value of each book.

7. A chart showing the average price for each publisher.

8. A list of each different author in the inventory.

9. A count of the number of books grouped by book type.

10. The average price of books by book type.

Maintaining a Database

▼ OBJECTIVES

You will have mastered the material in this project when you can:

- Add records to a table
- Locate records
- Change the contents of records in a table
- Delete records from a table
- Restructure a table
- Change field characteristics
- Add a field
- Save the changes to the structure
- Update the contents of a single field
- Make the same change to all records

- Specify a range
- Specify a default value
- Specify a picture
- Specify legal values
- Specify referential integrity
- Update a table with validity checks
- Delete groups of records
- Make changes to groups of records
- Create single-field and multiple-field secondary indexes
- Use a secondary index

▼ INTRODUCTION

After creating and loading a database, you must be able to maintain it. Maintaining the database means modifying the data to keep it up-to-date, such as adding new records, changing the data for existing records, and deleting records. Updating can also include mass updates or mass deletions; that is, updating or deleting many records at the same time.

As needs in an organization change, the data may need to be restructured. For example, an organization may decide that customers are to be categorized by customer type, requiring the addition of a field for customer type to the Customer table. Characteristics of existing fields may also need to be changed. For example, the Name field might be too short to contain the name of a new customer, requiring a change in the field's width in the Customer table structure. To improve the efficiency of certain types of database processing, you can create **secondary indexes**, which are similar to indexes found in books.

Figure 3-1 summarizes the various types of activities involved in maintaining a database.

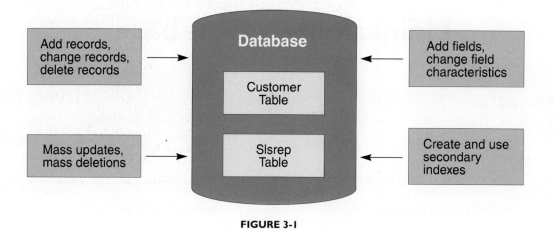

FIGURE 3-1

▼ ADDING, CHANGING, AND DELETING

Keeping the data in a database up-to-date requires three tasks: adding new records, changing the data in existing records, and deleting existing records.

Adding Records

In Project 1, you added records to a database using Table view, that is, as you were adding records, the records were displayed on the screen in the form of a table. When adding additional records, you can use the same techniques.

In Project 1, you viewed records using Form view. You can also use Form view to update the data in a table. Form view allows you to add new records, change existing records, or delete records. To perform these tasks, use the same techniques as in Table view. To add a record to the Customer table with a form, for example, use the following steps.

TO USE A FORM TO ADD RECORDS

STEP 1:   **Start Paradox. Choose View, select the Customer table, and maximize its window (Figure 3-2).**

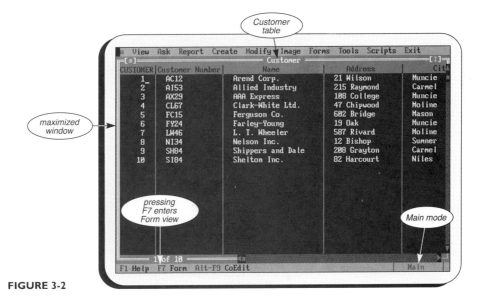

FIGURE 3-2

STEP 2:   **Press F7 to move to Form view.**

The screen displays the Standard Form (Figure 3-3).

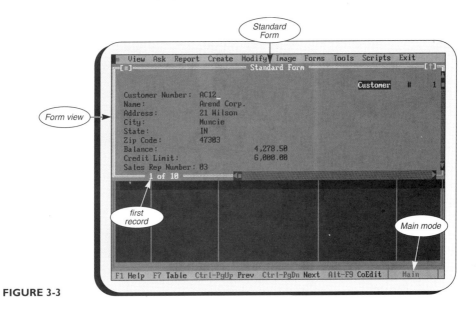

FIGURE 3-3

STEP 3: **Press F9 to enter Edit mode.**

The mode changes from Main to Edit as the status bar indicates (Figure 3-4). The menu at the top of the screen changes from the Main menu to the Edit menu. In Edit mode, you can make changes to the data in the table.

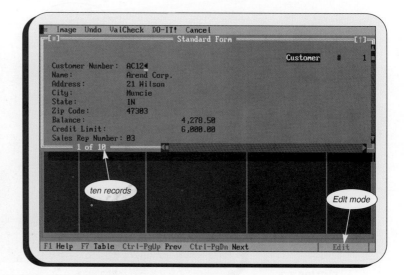

FIGURE 3-4

STEP 4: **Press the INSERT key to insert a blank record.**

The data portion of the form is blank (Figure 3-5). The blank record is the first record out of eleven.

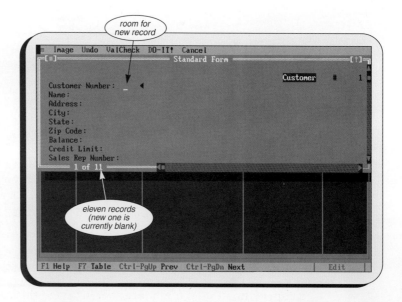

FIGURE 3-5

STEP 5:   **Type the data for the new record as shown in Figure 3-6, pressing the TAB key after entering the data in each field.**

After pressing the TAB key after the last field is entered, the record is added to the Customer table.

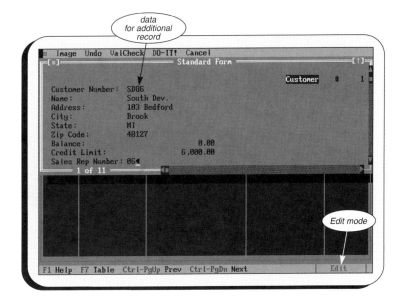

FIGURE 3-6

STEP 6:   **Press F2 to leave Edit mode and then press ALT+F8 to remove all windows from the screen.**

Originally, there were ten records in the Customer table. Now there are eleven records in the Customer table because of the addition of customer SD86.

Searching for a Record

In the database environment, **searching** means looking for records that satisfy some condition. Looking for all the customers whose sales rep number is 03 is an example of searching. The queries in Project 2 were examples of searching. Paradox had to locate those records that satisfied whatever condition was specified.

Searching is also required when using Form view or Table view. To update customer SD86, for example, you first need to find the customer. In a small table, repeatedly pressing the CTRL+PAGE DOWN or the DOWN ARROW key until customer SD86 displays on the screen may not be particularly difficult. In a large table with many records, this would be extremely cumbersome. It is important to be able to go directly to a record just by giving the value in some field. This is the function of the **Zoom command** on the **Image menu**. To use this command, first move the cursor to the field for the search. The following steps first move the cursor to the Customer Number field and then use the Zoom command to find the customer whose number is SD86.

TO LOCATE RECORDS

STEP 1: Make sure the Customer table is open and the Standard Form for the Customer table displays on the screen. Make sure the cursor is in the Customer Number field. Press F9 to enter Edit mode.

STEP 2: Choose the Image menu and move the cursor to the Zoom command. (Figure 3-7).

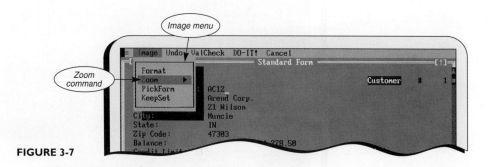

FIGURE 3-7

STEP 3: Choose the Zoom command and then move the cursor to the Value command.

The menu shown in Figure 3-8 displays. The cursor is on the Value command.

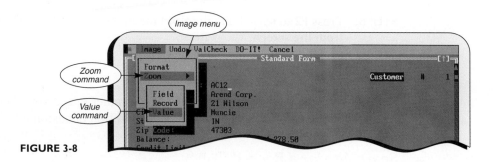

FIGURE 3-8

STEP 4: Choose the Value command and then press the ENTER key, because the cursor is already in the correct field. Type SD86 as the value (Figure 3-9) and then press the ENTER key.

Paradox locates the record on which the customer number is SD86 (Figure 3-10).

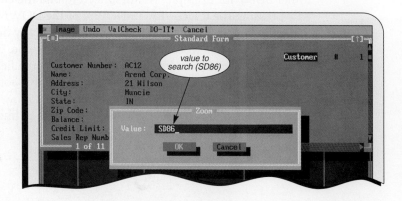

FIGURE 3-9

The three command choices on the Zoom menu are Field, Record, and Value. The **Field command** is used to move to a specific field. For example, choosing Field could be used to move the cursor to the Zip Code field. Unless there is a very large number of fields, the Field command is not particularly useful. The **Record command** finds a specific record by using the number of the record. This is only useful if you happen to know the number of the desired record. Most of the time, you will want to move to a record that contains a certain value in some field, which is the function of the Value command.

Sometimes, after having located a record that satisfies a condition, you will need to find the next record that satisfies the same condition. To do so, either repeat the process used to find the first record or press ALT+Z.

Changing the Contents of a Record

After locating the record to be changed, move the cursor to the field to be changed by using the TAB key.

Mouse Users: *Click the desired field.*

To change a field entry, you can simply type the new entry. Instead of retyping the entry in its entirety, however, you may prefer to make changes to the existing entry. To make changes to the existing entry, you must first enter a special view, called Field view, by pressing ALT+F5.

Use **Field view** within either **Table view** or **Form view**. The steps are exactly the same. In Field view, you can use the arrow keys to move within the field. You can also insert and delete individual characters. The following steps use Field View to change the name of customer SD86 to Southern Dev.

> **TO USE FIELD VIEW TO UPDATE THE CONTENTS OF A FIELD**

STEP 1:   **Make sure the Standard Form displays on the screen and the current record is customer SD86. Be sure you are in Edit mode. If not, press F9.**

The record for customer SD86 displays and the mode is Edit (Figure 3-10).

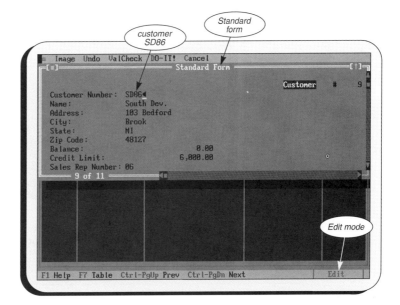

FIGURE 3-10

STEP 2: **Move to the Name field and then press ALT+F5 to enter Field View.**

The cursor becomes a rectangle (■) (Figure 3-11) indicating that Paradox is in Field view.

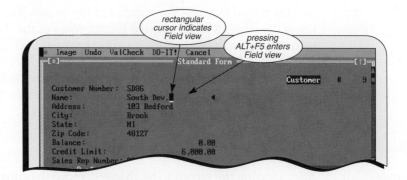

FIGURE 3-11

STEP 3: **Press the LEFT ARROW key to move the cursor to the space that follows** South **and then type** ern **as shown in Figure 3-12.**

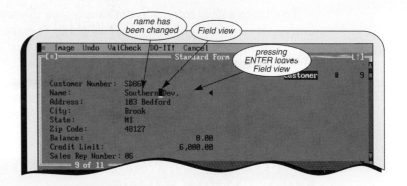

FIGURE 3-12

STEP 4: **Press the ENTER key to complete the entry and leave Field view.**

The name is changed (Figure 3-13) and the cursor returns to its normal shape (_) indicating that Paradox is no longer in Field view.

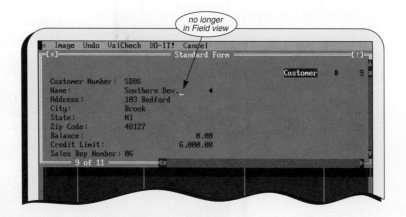

FIGURE 3-13

STEP 5: **Press F2 to leave Edit mode and then press ALT+F8 to remove all windows from the screen.**

Deleting Records

When records are no longer needed, they should be deleted (removed) from the table. If, for example, customer AI53 is no longer associated with the organization, that customer's record should be deleted. To delete a record, first locate it and then press the DELETE key. The following steps delete customer AI53.

TO DELETE A RECORD

STEP 1:   Make sure the Customer table is open and the window containing the table is maximized. Locate the record for customer AI53. Press F9 to enter Edit mode.

The Customer table is open (Figure 3-14). The mode is Edit and the cursor is on record 2.

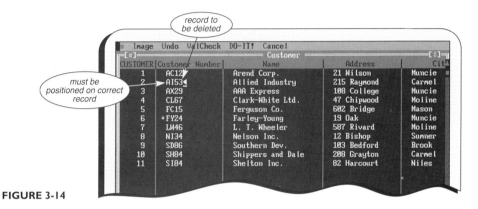

FIGURE 3-14

STEP 2:   Press the DELETE key to delete the record.

The record is deleted (Figure 3-15).

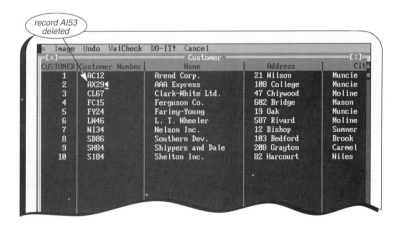

FIGURE 3-15

STEP 3:   Press F2 to leave Edit mode and then press F8 to close the table.

▼ CHANGING THE STRUCTURE

When you initially create a database, you define its **structure**; that is, you indicate the names, types, and widths of all the fields. If the structure you first defined would continue to be appropriate as long as the database is in use, there would be no reason to **restructure** it. However, a variety of reasons cause the structure of a table to change. Changes in the needs of users of the database might require additional fields to be added. For example, if it is important to store the type of a customer (such as regular, discount, or special), such a field would be added to the Customer table because it is not there already.

Characteristics of a given field might need to change. The Farley-Young customer name is stored incorrectly in this database. It should be changed to Farley-Young Industries. However, the Name field is not long enough to hold the correct name. To accommodate this change, the width of the Name field must be increased.

Fields become obsolete when they are no longer necessary. When a field occupies space and serves no useful purpose, it should be removed from the table.

The steps to restructure the database to accommodate these changes are explained on the following pages.

Changing the Size of a Field

To make any of the mentioned changes, open the Customer table and then use the **Restructure command** on the **Modify menu**. The following steps change the size of the Name field from 20 to 25.

TO CHANGE THE SIZE OF A FIELD

STEP 1: Choose Modify|Restructure and then select the Customer table. Press the TAB key five times to move to the Field Type column for the Name field.

The Restructure: Customer window displays (Figure 3-16). It contains the same information entered when the table was first created. The cursor is in the Field Type column for the Name field.

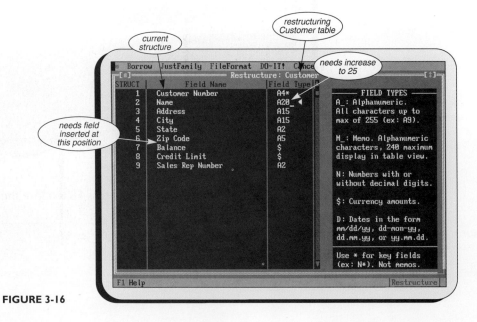

FIGURE 3-16

STEP 2:   Press the BACKSPACE key to delete the 0 **and then type** 5.

The new size displays (Figure 3-17).

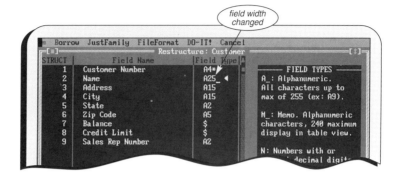

FIGURE 3-17

STEP 3:   Press the TAB key to complete the entry.

Adding a New Field

To add new field called Cust Type to the Customer table, use the techniques present-ed in the following steps. The field is to be used to indicate the customer type. The possible entries in this field are REG (regular customer), DSC (discount customer), and SPC (special customer). The new field follows the Zip Code in the list of fields; that is, it will be the *seventh* field in the restructured table. The current seventh field (Balance) will become the eighth field, Credit Limit will become the ninth field, and Sales Rep Number will become the tenth field.

TO ADD A FIELD TO THE CUSTOMER TABLE

STEP 1:   With the Restructure: Customer window displayed, press the TAB key until the cursor is in position for the new field (to the right of the 7 **in the first column) (Figure 3-18).**

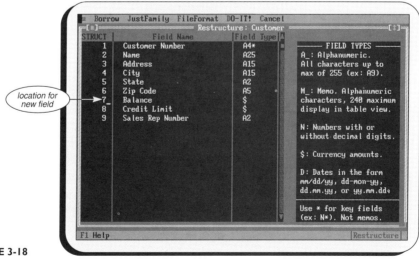

FIGURE 3-18

STEP 2:   **Press the INSERT key to insert a blank row.**

A blank row displays in the position for the new field (Figure 3-19).

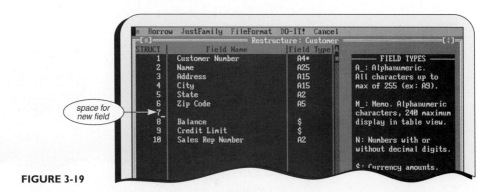

FIGURE 3-19

STEP 3:   **Press the TAB key to move to the Field Name column, type** Cust Type **(the field name), and press the TAB key. Type** A3 **(the field type) and press the TAB key.**

The entries for the new field are complete and the cursor advances to the next field (Figure 3-20).

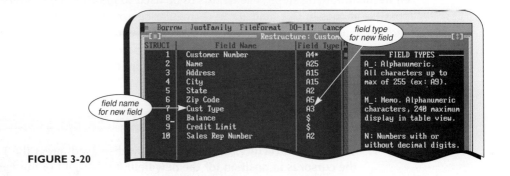

FIGURE 3-20

STEP 4:   **Press F2 to save the changes to the Customer table structure and then press F8 to close the table.**

Updating the Restructured Database

As soon as the structure is changed, the changes are immediately available. The customer name field is longer and the new customer type field is included.

You can make changes to a single field (like changing the name from Farley-Young to Farley-Young Industries) just as you did earlier; that is, you locate the record in either Table view or Form view, press F9 to enter Edit mode, locate the field to be changed, and then make the change. The following steps change the name of Farley-Young to Farley-Young Industries.

TO UPDATE THE CONTENTS OF A FIELD

STEP 1: **Make sure the Customer table is open and the window containing the table is maximized. Move the cursor to the field to be changed (the Name field on record 5) and press F9 to enter Edit mode.**

The cursor is in the correct field and the mode is Edit (Figure 3-21).

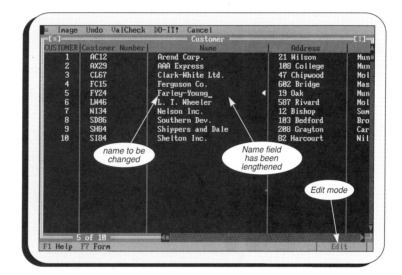

FIGURE 3-21

STEP 2: **Type** Farley-Young Industries **and press the ENTER key.**

The name is changed and the cursor moves to the Address field (Figure 3-22).

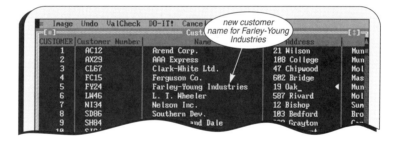

FIGURE 3-22

STEP 3: **Press F2 to leave Edit mode and then press F8 to remove the window from the screen.**

The name of customer FY24 is now Farley-Young Industries.

Updating the Contents of a New Field in a Table

The Cust Type field is blank on every record. One approach to updating the information in the field would be to step through the entire table, changing the value on each record to what it should be. If most of the customers have the same type, there is a simpler approach.

If most customers are type REG (regular), it is reasonable to initially set all the values to REG. The quickest and easiest way to accomplish this task is to use a special type of query called an **update query**. Later, you can individually change the type for the special and discount customers.

When an update query is run, Paradox creates a special table, called the **Changed table**. It contains all the records that were changed by the query as they appeared *before* the changes. This table automatically displays on the desktop. The following steps change the value in the Cust Type field for all the records to REG.

TO MAKE THE SAME CHANGE TO ALL RECORDS

STEP 1: **Choose Ask and then select the Customer table.**

A Query form for the Customer table displays (Figure 3-23).

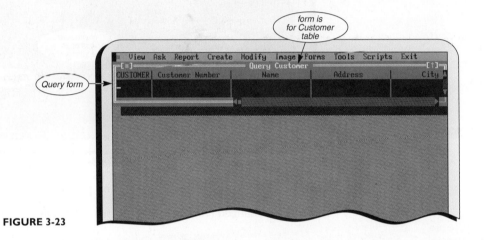

FIGURE 3-23

STEP 2: **Press the RIGHT ARROW key until the cursor is in the Cust Type field. Type** changeto REG**.**

The Cust Type field contains the appropriate entry (Figure 3-24).

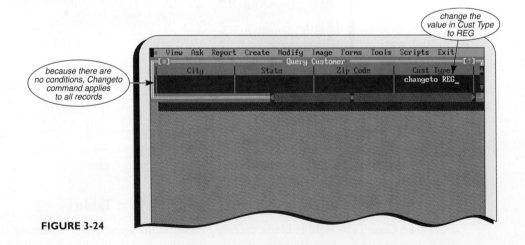

FIGURE 3-24

STEP 3:   **Press F2 to run the query.**

The Changed table displays on the screen (Figure 3-25). It contains all the records that were changed by the query. Because this query did not contain any conditions, the Changed table contains all the records from the Customer table.

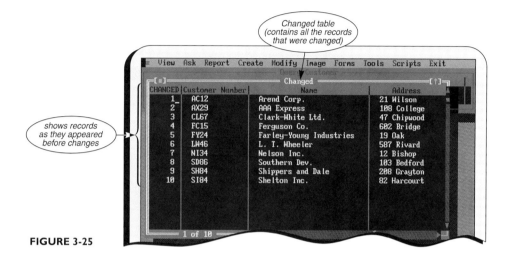

FIGURE 3-25

STEP 4:   **Press ALT+F8 to close all windows. Open the Customer table and maximize the window. Press the TAB key until the cursor is in the Cust Type field.**

The Customer table shows that all entries in the Cust Type field are now REG (Figure 3-26).

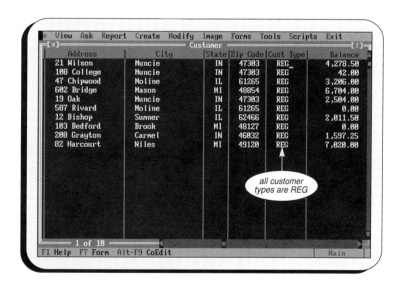

FIGURE 3-26

STEP 5:   **Press F8 to close the window.**

▼   CREATING VALIDITY CHECKS

Using the techniques presented in these projects, you have created, loaded, queried, and updated a database. No steps carried out so far, however, ensure that users only enter valid data. In this section, you will use the **ValCheck command** to create **validity checks**, that is, rules to be followed by a user when entering data. Paradox will prevent users from entering data not conforming to the rules.

Validity checks can be used to make sure an entry lies within a certain range of values; for example, that the values in the Balance field are between $0 and $20,000. Validity checks can be used to specify a default value, that is, a value that Paradox will display on the screen in a particular field before the user begins adding a record. Validity checks can also be used to specify a format for an entry; for example, that customer numbers must consist of two uppercase letters followed by a two-digit number.

To make data entry of customer numbers more convenient, you can use a validity check to have lowercase letters converted automatically to uppercase. Finally, validity checks can be used to specify a collection of acceptable values; for example, that the only legitimate entries for customer type are REG, SPC, and DSC.

Specifying a Range

Using the following steps, you are to specify that entries in the Balance field must be between $0 and $20,000 by declaring that the lowest value that can be entered is 0 and the highest value is 20000.

TO SPECIFY A RANGE

STEP 1:   **Make sure the Customer table is open and the window containing the table is maximized. Press F9 to enter Edit mode.**

The Customer table displays in a maximized window (Figure 3-27). The mode is Edit.

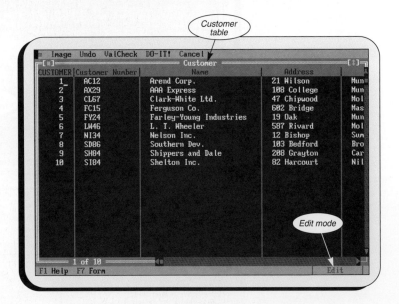

FIGURE 3-27

STEP 2:   Choose ValCheck.

The ValCheck menu displays (Figure 3-28). The **Define command** *defines a new validity check. The* **Clear command** *clears existing validity checks.*

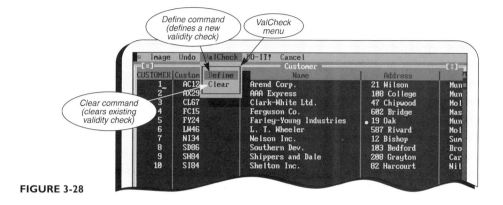

FIGURE 3-28

STEP 3:   Choose the Define command.

A message displays at the top of the screen instructing you to move the cursor to the field for the validity check and then press the ENTER key (Figure 3-29).

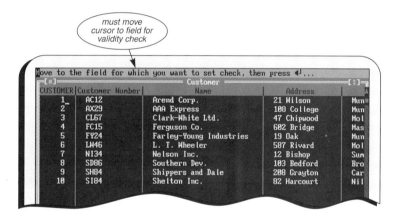

FIGURE 3-29

STEP 4:   Move the cursor to the Balance field and then press the ENTER key.

The menu of possible validity checks displays (Figure 3-30).

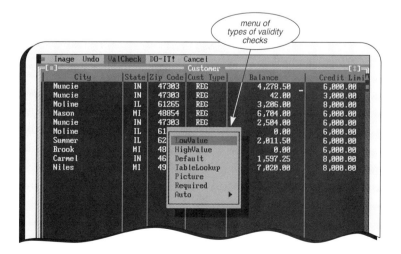

FIGURE 3-30

STEP 5:   Choose the LowValue command and type 0 (the minimum value) as shown in Figure 3-31. Press the ENTER key.

A message displays indicating the low value has been recorded.

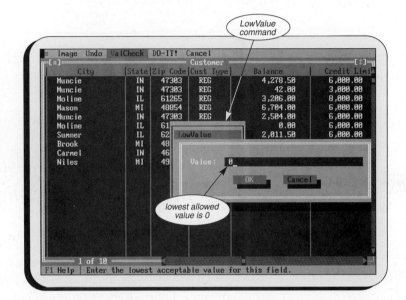

FIGURE 3-31

STEP 6:   Repeat Steps 2 through 4, then choose HighValue and type 20000 (the maximum value) as shown in Figure 3-32. Press the ENTER key.

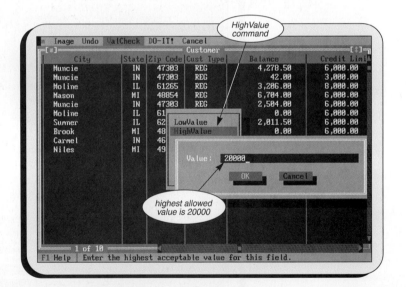

FIGURE 3-32

Users will now be prohibited from entering a balance that is either less than $0 or greater than $20,000.

Table 3-1 summarizes the commands on the Define command menu when specifying validity checks.

TABLE 3-1

Command	Function
LowValue	Specifies the lowest value the field can contain.
HighValue	Specifies the highest value the field can contain.
Default	Specifies a value to be used in case the user does not make an entry in the field.
TableLookup	Specifies that the data in the field is used to look up a record in another table, called the *lookup* table. If no such record exists, the data is considered to be invalid. Assists users in also finding values in the lookup table.
Picture	Uses picture symbols to specify the format that the data must follow.
Required	Indicates whether or not users must make an entry in the field.
Auto	Indicates that the cursor is to advance automatically to the next field as soon as this field is filled.

Specifying a Default Value

With Paradox, you can specify a default value when users are not required to enter a value for a particular field. The following steps specify a default value of $6,000 for the Credit Limit field. This procedure ensures that if users do not enter a credit limit, the credit limit will be $6,000.

TO SPECIFY A DEFAULT VALUE

STEP 1: Choose ValCheck│Define, move the cursor to the Credit Limit field, and then press the ENTER key. Choose the Default command and then type 6000 (the default value) as shown in Figure 3-33.

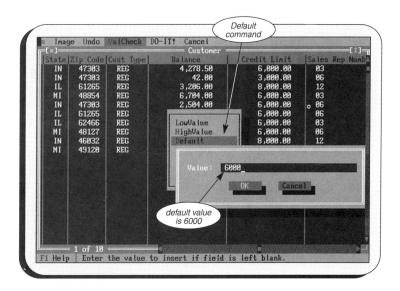

FIGURE 3-33

STEP 2: Press the ENTER key to complete the process.

From this point on, if users do not make an entry in the Credit Limit field, Paradox will set the credit limit to $6,000.

Specifying a Pattern

One way to govern data entry is to create a **template**, or pattern, that the data must follow. Such a template is a series of characters, one for each position in the field, that indicate how data is to be entered into the field. The characters used are called **picture symbols**. Paradox picture symbols are shown in Table 3-2.

TABLE 3-2

Symbol	Purpose
#	Accepts only a numeric digit.
?	Accepts any letter in either uppercase or lowercase.
&	Accepts any letter, but converts to uppercase.
@	Accepts any character.
!	Accepts any character, but converts any letters to uppercase.
*	Repeats the next symbol. If there is a number following the asterisk, repeats the next symbol that many times.
;	Interprets the following symbol as a literal character.
[ ]	Indicates item inside brackets is optional. Follows the rules for picture symbols, if entered.
{ }	Contains a list of the acceptable entries.
,	Separates entries within a list.

In Table 3-2, you can see the @ symbol indicates that Paradox will accept any character. The ? symbol indicates that Paradox will accept only alphabetic characters (letters). Thus, a template of ?????????? would prevent the user from entering numbers or special characters such as semicolons in the field. The & symbol indicates that letters are to be converted to uppercase. A template of &&&&&&&&& would cause any lowercase letters entered by the user to automatically be converted to uppercase letters. The ! symbol is similar in that it also converts letters to uppercase. The difference is that & only allows the user to enter letters, whereas ! allows the entry of any characters. The # symbol indicates that the only acceptable entries are numeric digits.

These symbols can be mixed. Suppose, for example, that the customer numbers must be two capital letters followed by a two-digit number (for example, XY18). To force the data to be entered in the correct fashion, use a template of &&##.

The steps on the nest page specify a picture for the Customer Number field in the Customer table. The picture requires that the customer number consist of two letters followed by two digits.

TO SPECIFY A PICTURE

STEP 1: Choose ValCheck|Define, move the cursor to the Customer Number field, press the ENTER key, and then move the cursor to Picture as shown in Figure 3-34.

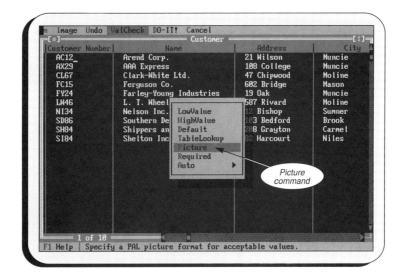

FIGURE 3-34

STEP 2: Press the ENTER key to choose the Picture command and then type &&## as shown in Figure 3-35.

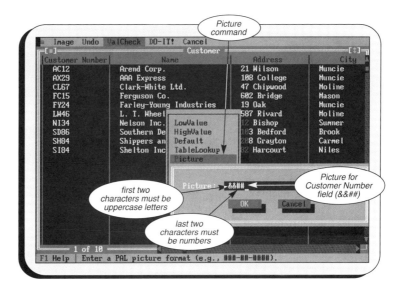

FIGURE 3-35

STEP 3: Press the ENTER key to complete the process.

Paradox will now only accept customer numbers for the Customer table that consist of two uppercase letters, followed by a two-digit number.

Specifying a Collection of Legal Values

When only certain values are required, you want to specify the **legal values**; that is the list of acceptable values. Curly brackets({ }), also called **braces**, contain a list of acceptable entries. The entries in the list are separated by commas. Using such a list prevents a user from entering an item not in the list. In addition, if you make sure the first letters in the various items are unique, users need to type only the first letter of the particular item. Paradox will automatically fill in the rest. You will use the { } picture symbols to force the user to enter REG, SPC, or DSC as the customer type.

TO SPECIFY LEGAL VALUES

STEP 1:   Choose ValCheck|Define, move the cursor to the Cust Type field, press the ENTER key, choose the Picture command, and then type {REG,SPC,DSC} as shown in Figure 3-36.

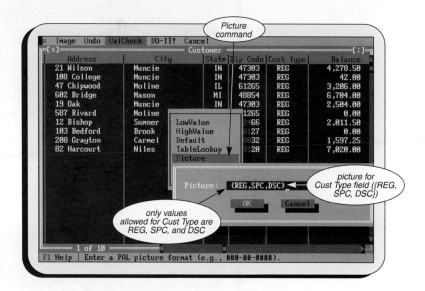

FIGURE 3-36

STEP 2:   Press the ENTER key to complete the process.

Paradox will only accept customer types for the Customer table that are equal to REG, SPC, or DSC.

····································

▼   SPECIFYING LOOKUPS

Another type of validity check, called **TableLookup,** is used to ensure that data in one table matches data in another. For example, this feature will be used to make sure that the sales rep number for any record in the Customer table actually matches the sales rep number on some row in the Slsrep table. It wouldn't make sense to have a customer whose sales rep number is 04 if there were no sales rep 04. The following steps specify a lookup.

TO SPECIFY A LOOKUP

STEP 1: Choose ValCheck|Define, move the cursor to the Sales Rep Number field, press the ENTER key, and then move the cursor to TableLookup as shown in Figure 3-37.

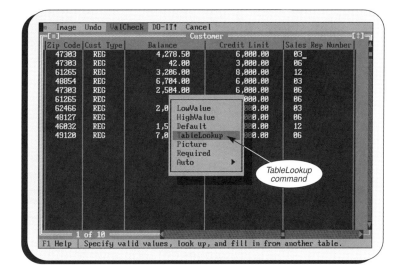

FIGURE 3-37

STEP 2: Press the ENTER key to choose the TableLookup command, press the ENTER key to produce a list of tables, and move the cursor to the Slsrep table (Figure 3-38).

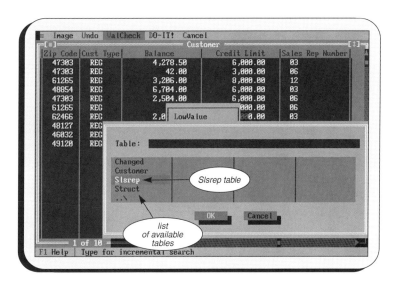

FIGURE 3-38

STEP 3: Press the ENTER key to choose the Slsrep table.

The menu shown in Figure 3-39 displays.

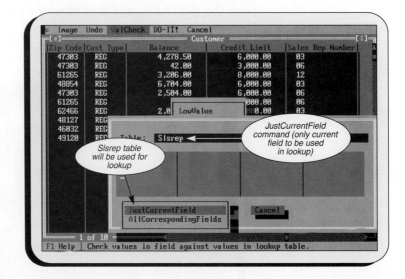

FIGURE 3-39

This menu contains two commands: **JustCurrentField** and **AllCorrespondingFields.** JustCurrentField is the most common. It indicates the lookup only involves the field on which the cursor is currently located. If, as is usual, this is the only field the two tables have in common, this is the only reasonable choice. If the tables have several fields in common, then a better choice is AllCorrespondingFields.

STEP 4: Choose the JustCurrentField command.

The menu shown in Figure 3-40 displays.

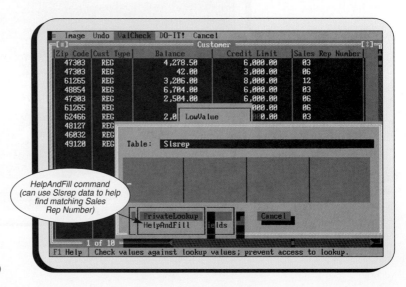

FIGURE 3-40

This is the final menu in defining a lookup. Its two commands are: PrivateLookup and HelpAndFill. **PrivateLookup** ensures the sales rep number entered by the user matches a sales rep in the Slsrep table. **HelpAndFill** also ensures that the sales rep number matches. It provides an additional feature, however. When the user is entering the sales rep number, he or she can press F1 to see the list of available sales reps and select from the list. It's often desirable to provide this extra level of help.

STEP 5:   Choose the HelpAndFill command.

The message "TableLookup Recorded" displays.

STEP 6:   Press F2 to leave Edit mode and then press F8 to close the window.

Paradox will now reject any number in the Sales Rep Number field in the Customer table that does not match a sales rep number in the Slsrep table.

▼ **UPDATING A TABLE THAT CONTAINS VALIDITY CHECKS**

When you update a table that contains validity checks, Paradox will not accept invalid data. Attempting to leave a required field blank, entering a number that is out of the required range, entering a value that has an incorrect format, or entering a value that is not one of the possible choices will produce an error message. You will not be able to update the database until you have fixed the error.

When a table has validity checks, it is possible to get stuck in a field. Perhaps you don't remember the validity check you created or perhaps the one you created was incorrect. In any case, if you have entered data that violates the validity check, you will not be able to leave the field. Pressing the ESCAPE key doesn't work, nor can you simply close the table.

The first action you should take is to enter an acceptable entry. If you find you cannot do this, repeatedly press the BACKSPACE key to erase the contents of the field. See if you can then leave the field. If neither of these actions works, your only recourse is to press the DELETE key to delete the record.

If you ever have to take such drastic action, you probably have a faulty validity check. Use the techniques found in the previous sections to correct the existing validity checks for the field. The following steps update a table that contains validity checks by changing some of the values in the Cust Type field.

STEP 1: Make sure the Customer table is open and the window containing the table is maximized. Press the TAB key until the cursor is in the Cust Type field (Figure 3-41).

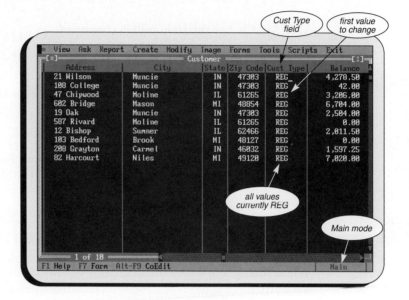

FIGURE 3-41

STEP 2: Press the DOWN Arrow key twice to move to the Cust Type field on the third record, press F9 to enter Edit mode, and then press the BACKSPACE key three times to erase the REG.

The previous value is deleted (Figure 3-42). The mode is Edit.

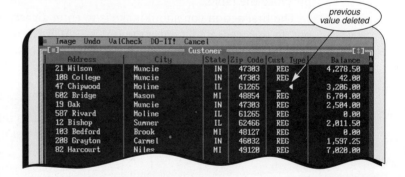

FIGURE 3-42

STEP 3: Type S and Paradox will automatically add PC.

STEP 4: Make the additional changes to customer types shown in Figure 3-43.

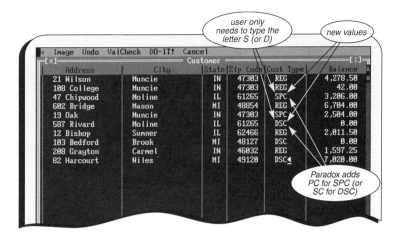

FIGURE 3-43

STEP 5: Press F2 to leave Edit mode and then press F8 to remove the window from the screen.

Using a Lookup

Once you have created a **lookup,** you can use it to assist you in the data entry process. The following steps use a lookup to change the sales rep number of a customer.

TO USE A LOOKUP

STEP 1: Make sure the Customer table is open and the window containing the table is maximized. Press the TAB key until the cursor is in the Sales Rep Number field. Use the DOWN Arrow key to move to the Sales Rep Number field on the last record, press F9 to enter Edit mode, and then press the BACKSPACE key twice to delete the sales rep number.

The previous value is deleted (Figure 3-44). The mode is Edit.

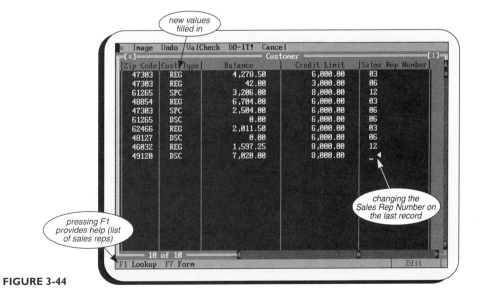

FIGURE 3-44

At this point, you could simply type a sales rep number. If so, Paradox would check to make sure the number matches the number of a sales rep currently in the Slsrep table. If not, Paradox would display a message and force you to make a correction. As an alternative to typing the number, press F1 and select the number directly from the Slsrep table.

STEP 2:   Press F1.

A window displays showing the records currently in the Slsrep table (Figure 3-45). To select one, move the cursor to that sales rep's row and press F2.

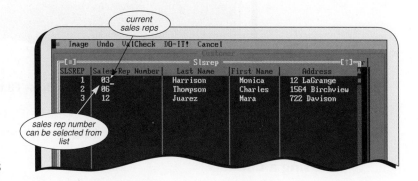

FIGURE 3-45

STEP 3:   Move the cursor to sales rep 12 and press F2.

The change is made and the window containing the Slsrep table no longer displays.

STEP 4:   Press F2 to leave Edit mode and then press F8 to close the window containing the Customer table.

▼   **MASS UPDATES**

Earlier in this project, you used an update query to change all the entries in the Cust Type field to **REG**. It is possible to be much more selective when making mass changes with update queries. An update query can delete all the records that satisfy some condition. An update query can also make the same change to all records satisfying a condition.

When an update query makes deletions, Paradox places the records that were deleted in a special table called **Deleted.** When an update query makes changes, Paradox places the records that were changed by the query as they appeared before the changes in the special table called Changed. These tables will automatically display on the screen. Both the Deleted table and the Changed table are temporary. Paradox will automatically overwrite them whenever another update query is run. It will delete them when you leave Paradox.

Deleting Groups of Records

In some cases, you may need to delete several records at a time. If, for example, territories change and customers whose Zip Code is 46032 are assigned to a different organization, the customers with the zip code should be deleted. Instead of deleting these customers individually, which could be very cumbersome, delete them in one operation by using an update query. The following steps use an update query to delete all customers whose Zip Code is 46032.

TO DELETE GROUPS OF RECORDS

STEP 1:   Choose Ask, press the ENTER key, and then move the cursor to the Customer table (Figure 3-46).

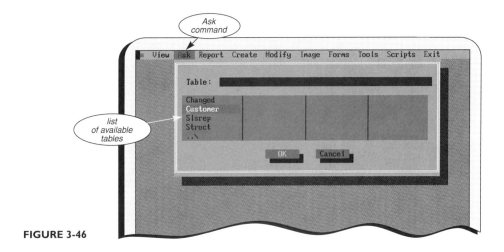

FIGURE 3-46

STEP 2:   Select the Customer table by pressing the ENTER key. Type `delete` under the name of the table in the Query form that displays.

A Query form for the Customer table displays (Figure 3-47). The word delete appears under the name of the table indicating that the purpose of the query is to delete records.

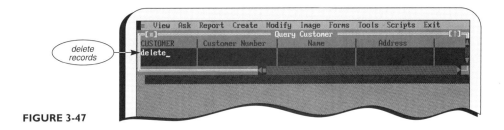

FIGURE 3-47

STEP 3:   Press the TAB key until the cursor is in the Zip Code field and then type `46032` (Figure 3-48).

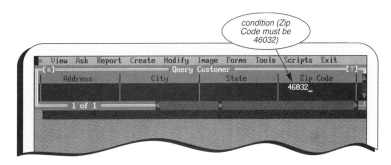

FIGURE 3-48

STEP 4: Press F2 to run the query.

The query is executed. The records that were deleted by the query are placed in a special table called Deleted, which is displayed on the screen (Figure 3-49).

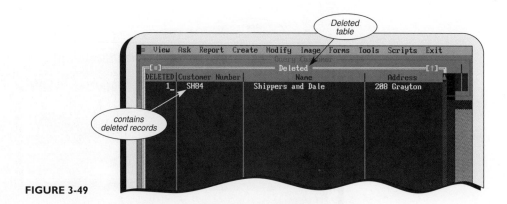

FIGURE 3-49

STEP 5: Press ALT+F8 to close all windows.

All customers with the Zip Code 46032 (there is only one) have now been removed from the table.

Changing Groups of Records

Just as you may need to delete several records at once, you may also need to change several records at a time. To change the credit limit of all customers whose credit limit is currently $3,000 to $4,000 would be very cumbersome, if each change had to be made individually. Again, use an update query to simplify the process. The following steps use an update query to change the credit limit to $4,000 of all customers whose current credit limit is $3,000.

TO MAKE CHANGES TO GROUPS OF RECORDS

STEP 1: Choose Ask and then the Customer table.

STEP 2: Press the TAB key until the cursor is in the Credit Limit field and then type `3000,changeto 4000`.

The condition and the changeto operator are both entered in the Credit Limit field (Figure 3-50).

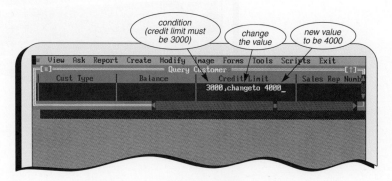

FIGURE 3-50

STEP 3: **Press F2 to run the query.**

The query is executed. The list of records that were changed by the query is placed in the special table called Changed, which is displayed on the screen (Figure 3-51). The Changed table shows the records as they appeared before the changes.

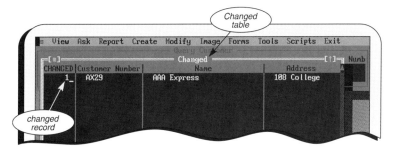

FIGURE 3-5I

STEP 4: **Press ALT+F8 to close all windows.**

Undoing Mass Changes

If you accidentally enter the wrong condition when you are making mass deletions or changes, you may incorrectly delete or change a large number of records. If this happens, you can undo the change by using the Deleted or Changed tables as follows:

TO UNDO A MASS CHANGE

STEP 1: **Choose Tools|More|Add.**

STEP 2: **Select the Changed table.**

STEP 3: **Select the table in which records were changed as the Target table.**

STEP 4: **Select Update.**

TO UNDO A MASS DELETE

STEP 1: **Choose Tools|More|Add.**

STEP 2: **Select the Deleted table.**

STEP 3: **Select the table from which the records were deleted as the Target table.**

STEP 4: **Select NewEntries.**

▼ **CREATING AND USING INDEXES**

You are already familiar with the concept of an index. The index in the back of a book contains important words or phrases together with a list of pages on which the given words or phrases can be found. An index for a database table is similar. Figure 3-52, for example, shows the Customer table along with an index built on customer names. In this case, the items of interest are customer names rather than key words or phrases as is the case in the back of this book.

▶ **INDEX ON NAME FIELD** ▶ **CUSTOMER TABLE**

Name	Record Number
AAA Express	2
Arend Corp.	1
Clark-White Ltd.	3
Farley-Young Industries	5
Ferguson Co.	4
L. T. Wheeler	6
Nelson Inc.	7
Shelton Inc.	9
Southern Dev.	8

Record Number	Customer	Name	Address	City	State
1	AC12	Arend Corp.	21 Wilson	Muncie	IN
2	AX29	AAA Express	108 College	Muncie	IN
3	CL67	Clark-White Ltd.	47 Chipwood	Moline	IL
4	FC15	Ferguson Co.	602 Bridge	Mason	MI
5	FY24	Farley-Young Industries	19 Oak	Muncie	IN
6	LW46	L. T. Wheeler	587 Rivard	Moline	IL
7	NI34	Nelson, Inc.	12 Bishop	Sumner	IL
8	SD86	Southern Dev.	103 Bedford	Brook	MI
9	SI84	Shelton, Inc.	82 Harcourt	Niles	MI

FIGURE 3-52

Each customer name occurs in the index along with the number of the record on which the customer name is located. Further, the names appear in the index in alphabetical order. If Paradox were to use this index to find Ferguson Co., for example, it could rapidly scan the names in the index to find Ferguson Co. Once it did, it would determine the corresponding record number (5) and then go immediately to record 5 in the Customer table, thus finding the customer much more rapidly than if it had to look through the entire Customer table one record at a time. Thus, indexes make the process of retrieving records very fast and efficient.

There is another benefit of indexes. Indexes provide an efficient alternative to sorting. That is, if the records are to appear in a certain order, you can use an index instead of having to physically rearrange the records in the table. Physically rearranging the records in a different order, which is called sorting, can be a very time-consuming process.

To see how indexes can be used for this purpose, look at the record numbers in the index (Figure 3-52) and use these to list all customers. That is, simply follow down the record number column, listing the corresponding customers as you go. In this example, Paradox would first list the customer on record 2 (AAA Express), then the customer on record 1 (Arend Corp.), then the customer on record 3 (Clark-White Ltd.), and so on. The customers would be listed in Name order without Paradox actually sorting the table.

To gain the benefits from an index, you must first create one. In the process, you must specify the **index key**, that is, the field or fields on which the index will be built. Paradox automatically creates an index on the **primary key**. In this index, which is called the **primary index**, the primary key you specified for the table is also the index key. The other indexes are called **secondary indexes**. You must create the secondary indexes. To create the secondary indexes, indicate the field or fields on which the index is built. You must also assign a name to the index.

Usually secondary indexes will be created for a single field (like Name). In other words, the index key is usually a single field. In this case, it is a good idea to make the name of the index the same as the name of the field. In fact, if you don't specify a name, Paradox automatically uses the name of the field.

Although the index key will usually be a single field, it can be a combination of fields. In Project 2, for example, the Answer table was sorted by city *within* state. In other words, the records were ordered by a combination of fields: State and City. An index can be used for the same purpose by using a combination of fields for the index key. The steps in creating such an index are very similar to those used when the index is a single field. In this case, assign a name that represents the combination of fields. For example, for the index built on the combination of credit limit and balance, you will use the name credbal.

Creating Single-Field Indexes

In the following steps, you are to create two single-field secondary indexes. In the first one, the index key will be the Name field. In the second, the index key will be the Zip Code field. You will then create a multiple-field index, in which the index key will be the combination of the Credit Limit field and the Balance field.

TO CREATE SINGLE-FIELD SECONDARY INDEXES

STEP 1: Choose Modify from the Main menu and then move the cursor to Index (Figure 3-53).

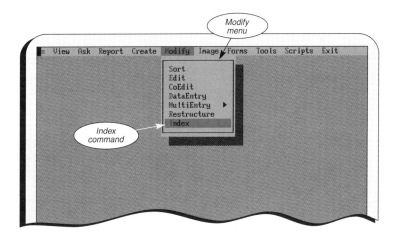

FIGURE 3-53

STEP 2: **Choose the Index command by pressing the ENTER key and then select the Customer table.**

The Secondary Index: Customer window displays (Figure 3-54).

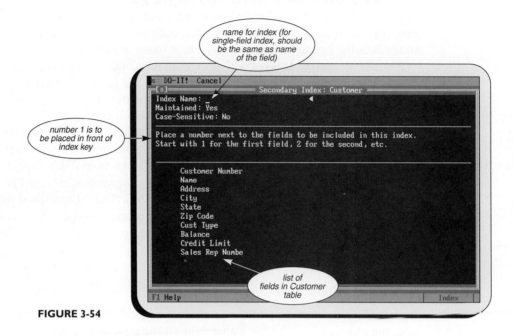

FIGURE 3-54

Use the first line in the window to give a name to the index. If it is left blank, Paradox uses the name of the field as the Index Name. Use the second line to indicate whether Paradox should keep the index up-to-date. If you choose Yes, Paradox makes appropriate changes to this index whenever the Customer table is updated. If you choose No, Paradox does not make such changes. Instead, it recreates the index from scratch whenever it is necessary. Usually you will choose Yes.

On the third line, indicate whether the index is to be **case-sensitive**. If the answer is Yes, Martin will be considered different from MARTIN. If the answer is No, they will be the same; that is, Paradox will ignore differences in case. Usually you will choose No.

To indicate the field or fields that make up the index, place numbers in front of the fields. To indicate a single field, place the number 1 in front of the field. To indicate an index on two fields, place the number 1 in front of the more important field and the number 2 in front of the other.

STEP 3: **Use the DOWN Arrow key to move the cursor so it is positioned in front of the Name field and then type the number 1 (Figure 3-55).**

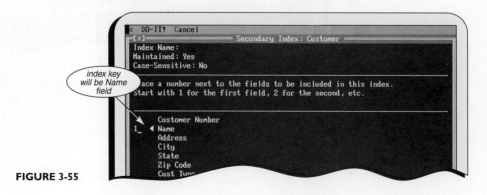

FIGURE 3-55

STEP 4:   Press F2 to create the secondary index.

STEP 5:   Use the techniques described in Steps 1 through 4 to create a secondary index for the Zip Code field. For this index, the number 1 should be placed in front of Zip Code instead of Name (Figure 3-56).

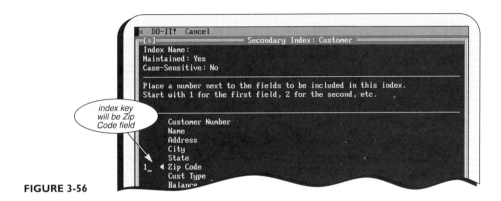

FIGURE 3-56

The indexes on the Name and Zip Code fields have now been created and are ready for use.

Creating Multiple-Field Indexes

Creating multiple-field secondary indexes is similar to creating indexes for single fields. The following steps create a multiple-field secondary index with the name credbal. The key will be the combination of the Credit Limit field and the Balance field.

TO CREATE A MULTIPLE-FIELD SECONDARY INDEX

STEP 1:   Choose Modify|Index and choose the Customer table. Type `credbal` as the Index Name, type 1 in front of the Credit Limit field and 2 in front of the Balance field (Figure 3-57).

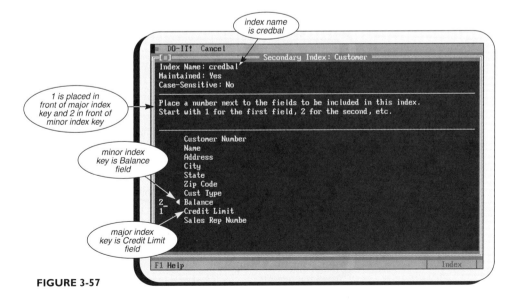

FIGURE 3-57

STEP 2:   Press F2 to create the secondary index.

Using an Index to Order Records

Recall from previous discussions that Paradox sequences the records by customer number because customer number is the primary key. The following steps use the Name secondary index to change the order in which Paradox sequences the records so they are displayed alphabetically by customer name.

TO SELECT A SECONDARY INDEX FOR ORDERING RECORDS

STEP 1: Be sure the Customer table is open and the window containing the table is maximized. Choose Image and then move the cursor to OrderTable (Figure 3-58).

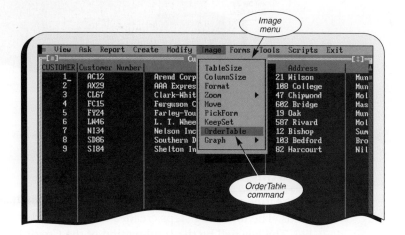

FIGURE 3-58

STEP 2: Choose the OrderTable command by pressing the ENTER key, then move the cursor to the Name field, and press the ENTER key again.

The Indexes box displays with a list of available indexes for the Name field (Figure 3-59). There is currently only one.

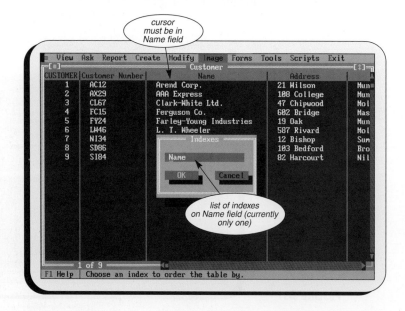

FIGURE 3-59

STEP 3:   **Select the Name index by pressing the ENTER key.**

The records appear in the Customer table displayed alphabetically by the customer name (Figure 3-60).

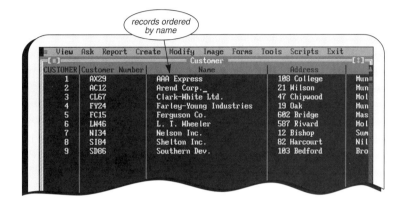

FIGURE 3-60

Changing the Secondary Index

Use the Credbal secondary index to order the records by credit limit and balance by performing the following steps.

TO CHANGE THE SECONDARY INDEX

STEP 1:   **Be sure the Customer table is open and the window containing the table is maximized. Choose Image|OrderTable. Move the cursor to the Credit Limit field (the more important index key), and press the ENTER key.**

The Indexes box displays with a list of available indexes for the Credit Limit field (Figure 3-61). There are currently two: the Credbal index just created and a second one called Credit Limit. (The index on Credit Limit displays in a different color. This indicates that such an index does not currently exist. If you select this index, Paradox will create one and then use it for sorting.)

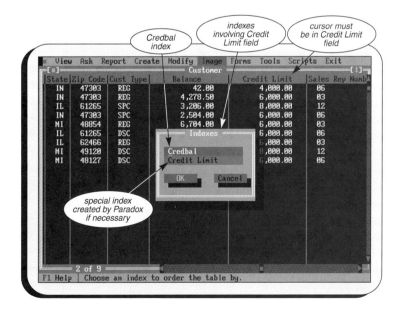

FIGURE 3-61

STEP 2: **Choose the Credbal index.**

The records are ordered by credit limit (Figure 3-62). Within any group of customers who have the same credit limit, the records are ordered by balance.

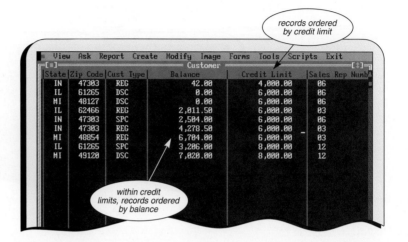

FIGURE 3-62

STEP 3: **After viewing the Customer table, close the window by pressing F8.**

▼ PROJECT SUMMARY

Project 3 covered the issues involved in maintaining a database and presented the steps on how to create and use both indexes and validity checks. The project explained how to change the structure of a table and how to specify lookups. You learned to use Form view to add records and also how to search for the next record satisfying some condition. Finally, the project showed you how you make mass changes to a table.

▼ KEY TERMS

AllCorrespondingFields command *(P134)*
Auto command *(P129)*
braces *(P132)*
case-sensitive *(P144)*
Changed table *(P124)*
Clear command *(P127)*
Default command *(P129)*
Define command *(P127)*
Deleted table *(P138)*
Field command *(P117)*
Field view *(P117)*
Form view *(P117)*
HelpAndFill command *(P135)*
HighValue command *(P128)*
Image menu *(P115)*
Index command *(P144)*

index key *(P143)*
JustCurrentField command *(P134)*
legal values *(P132)*
lookup *(P137)*
LowValue command *(P128)*
Modify menu *(P120)*
multiple-field index *(P145)*
Order Table command *(P146)*
Picture command *(P129)*
picture symbols *(P130)*
primary index *(P143)*
primary key *(P143)*
PrivateLookup command *(P135)*
queries *(P124)*
Record command *(P117)*
Required command *(P129)*
restructure *(P120)*

Restructure command *(P120)*
searching *(P115)*
secondary indexes *(P112, P143)*
single-field secondary indexes *(P143)*
structure *(P120)*
TableLookup *(P132)*
TableLookup command *(P129)*
Table view *(P117)*
template *(P130)*
update query *(P124)*
ValCheck command *(P126)*
validity check *(P126)*
Value command *(P116)*
Zoom command *(P115)*

▼　**QUICK REFERENCE**

In Paradox, you can accomplish a task in a number of different ways. The following table provides a quick reference to each task presented in this project with its available options. The commands listed in the Menu column can be executed using either the keyboard or the mouse.

Task	Mouse	Menu	Keyboard Shortucts
Add a Field			Press INSERT
Change a Field Characteristic			Type new value, press TAB
Change a Group of Records			Type the word changeto followed by the new value
Change to Field			Press ALT+F5
Create a Secondary Index		From Modify menu, choose Index	
Delete a Field			Press DELETE
Delete a Group of Records			Type delete under the name of the table in the Query form
Delete a Record			Press DELETE
Restructure a Table		From Modify menu, choose Restructure	
Search for a Record		From Image menu, choose Zoom; choose Value	Press CTRL+Z
Specify a Default Value		From ValCheck menu, choose	
Specify a Picture		From ValCheck menu, choose	
Specify a Range		From ValCheck menu, choose Default|LowValue; choose	
Specify Legal Values			Type a picture containing the legal values
Specify Lookup		From ValCheck menu, choose	
Use an Index to Order Records		From Image menu, choose OrderTable	

SHORT ANSWER ASSIGNMENTS

SHORT ANSWER ASSIGNMENT 1
True/False

Instructions: Circle T if the statement is true or F if the statement is false.

T F 1. Paradox automatically sorts records by the primary index.

T F 2. Paradox allows secondary indexes on single fields only.

T F 3. Indexes provide an efficient alternative to sorting.

T F 4. To create a secondary index, choose Secondary Index from the Modify menu.

T F 5. To arrange the data in a table in order by a secondary index, choose the OrderTable command from the Image menu.

T F 6. The quickest and easiest way to make the same change to all records is to use a query.

T F 7. A template is a series of characters, one for each position in a field, that indicates how data is to be entered in a field.

T F 8. Only currency and numeric fields can be assigned default values.

T F 9. To force all letters in a field to display as uppercase, use the ? symbol in the template.

T F 10. A field has the picture {HW,SG,AP}. To enter the value HW in the field, a user only needs to type the letter H.

T F 11. The TableLookup validity check is used to ensure that data in one table matches data in another.

T F 12. If you choose the HelpAndFill command associated with the TableLookup validity check, you can, when you edit the field, press F2 to see a list of available choices for the field.

T F 13. To add records to a table in Form view, move to the last record in the table before you press the INSERT key.

T F 14. You can add and change records using Form view but you can only delete records using Table view.

T F 15. To delete a record from a table, move to any field in the record and press CTRL+D.

T F 16. To search for a specific record in a table, use the Zoom command from the Image menu.

T F 17. To delete a group of records that satisfy a condition, use a query.

T F 18. In a query to delete records, any deleted records are placed in a permanent table called Deleted.

T F 19. To delete records that satisfy some condition using a query, enter the word DEL followed by the condition in the appropriate column.

T F 20. In a query, use the changeto operator to replace one value with another in a field.

SHORT ANSWER ASSIGNMENT 2
Multiple Choice

Instructions: Circle the correct response.

1. Indexes _____.
   a. provide an efficient alternative to sorting
   b. allow rapid retrieval of records
   c. allow rapid retrieval of tables
   d. both a and b

2. To create a secondary index, choose the _____ command from the Modify menu.
   a. Index
   b. Define Index
   c. Define Secondary Index
   d. Secondary Index

3. To arrange the data in a table in order by a secondary index, choose the _____ command from the Image menu.
   a. Set Index
   b. Sort/Order
   c. Order/Range
   d. OrderTable

4. A(n) _____ is a series of characters, one for each position in a field, that indicates how data is to be entered in a field.
   a. object
   b. template
   c. picture function
   d. character set

5. To force all letters in a field to display as uppercase, use the _____ symbol in the template.
   a. ?
   b. #
   c. @
   d. &

6. To create a validity check for a field, choose the _____ command from the ValCheck menu.
   a. Create
   b. Define
   c. New
   d. Add

7. To move from Table view to Form view, press _____.
   a. F6
   b. F7
   c. ALT+F6
   d. ALT+F7

8. To search for a specific record, use the Zoom command from the _____ menu.
   a. Image
   b. Record
   c. Search
   d. Select

SHORT ANSWER ASSIGNMENT 2 (continued)

9. Assume that you have located a record by using the Zoom command. To locate the next record that satisfies the same condition, press _____.

    a. ALT+I

    b. ALT+Z

    c. CTRL+I

    d. CTRL+Z

10. In a query, use the _____ operator to replace one value with another in a field.

    a. with

    b. by

    c. changeto

    d. replace

SHORT ANSWER ASSIGNMENT 3
Understanding Menu Commands

Instructions: In this project, you have used several different menu commands to change the structure of a table, define validity checks, create secondary indexes, and locate records. For each of the situations below, identify the menu command you would use. Also indicate whether you need to be in Edit mode to access the menu. Assume that all questions refer to the Customer table.

1. Change the width of the Address field to 20.

    _____

    _____

2. Create an index on the City field.

    _____

    _____

3. Locate the first record with the zip code 61265.

    _____

    _____

4. Order records by city.

    _____

    _____

5. Convert all entries for the state to uppercase.

    _____

    _____

SHORT ANSWER ASSIGNMENT 4
Understanding Templates

Instructions: In the space provided, indicate what the effect will be when the template in column 2 is applied to the data in column 1. If valid, write the corresponding value and if invalid, write INVALID.

database	????????	
database	&???&???	
12ab45	##!!##	
93	??	
8934x	####?	
8174x	####&	
197a	####	
FIC	@@@	
mi	&&	
346 Magee	!!!!!!!!!	

SHORT ANSWER ASSIGNMENT 5
Using Queries to Update a Table

Instructions: The Customer table needs to be updated using queries. For each of the following changes to the Customer table, list the column and the appropriate expression necessary to make the change. Use the table below to help identify the column headings.

CUSTOMER	Customer Number	Name	Address	City	State	Zip Code	Cust Type	Balance	Credit Limit	Sales Rep Number

1. Change the city for all records from Mason to Manitowc.

_____

_____

2. Change the sales rep number for all records from 03 to 06.

_____

_____

3. Change the credit limit for all records from $8,000 to $9,000.

_____

_____

4. Delete all records where the Cust Type is SPC.

_____

_____

SHORT ANSWER ASSIGNMENT 6
Understanding Adding, Changing, and Deleting

Instructions: Figure SA3-6 shows the Form view screen for the first record in the Customer table. Use this figure to explain how to perform the following tasks in Form view.

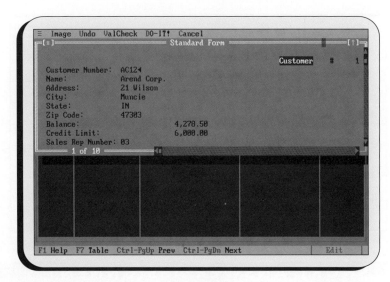

FIGURE SA3-6

1. Add a new record to the Customer table.

_____

_____

_____

2. Change the address from 21 Wilson to 21 S. Wilson.

_____

_____

_____

3. Delete the record with Customer Number LW46.

_____

_____

_____

4. Locate the record that contains the value Moline in the City field.

_____

_____

_____

5. Locate the next record that contains the value Moline in the City field.

_____

_____

_____

HANDS-ON
EXERCISES

HANDS-ON EXERCISE 1
Using the Help Menu

Instructions: Perform the following tasks.

1. Start Paradox.

2. Open the Customer table and enter Edit mode.

3. Choose the ValCheck menu.

4. Press F1.

5. Choose LookupTables.

6. Read the information and answer the following:

   a. Name the two requirements for creating lookup tables.

   _____

   _____

   b. How can you get the best performance when you use a lookup table?

   _____

   _____

7. Choose Paradox.

8. Press the ESCAPE key to remove the ValCheck menu.

9. Choose Cancel|Yes.

10. Press F8 to close the window.

11. Exit Paradox.

HANDS-ON EXERCISE 2
Creating and Using Secondary Indexes

Instructions: Perform the following tasks.

1. Start Paradox.

2. Open the Customer table.

3. Choose Index from the Modify menu.

4. Create a multiple-field index on the combination of the state and city fields.

5. Name the index statcity.

6. Order the records by the statcity index.

HANDS-ON EXERCISE 2 (continued)

7. List the first record and the last record in the reordered table.

_____

_____

8. Close the table.
9. Exit Paradox.

HANDS-ON EXERCISE 3
Creating Validity Checks

Instructions: Perform the following tasks.

1. Start Paradox.

2. Open the Slsrep table and enter Edit mode.

3. Choose Define from the ValCheck menu.

4. Assign a minimum value of .04 and a maximum value of .09 to the Commission Rate field. List the steps involved.

_____

_____

5. Create a template for the State field to convert the two character state code to uppercase. List the steps involved.

_____

_____

6. Assign a default value of .05 to the Commission Rate field. List the steps involved.

_____

_____

7. Save the validity checks and close the Slsrep table.

8. Exit Paradox.

LABORATORY
ASSIGNMENTS

LABORATORY ASSIGNMENT 1
Maintaining the Parts Database

Purpose: To provide practice in maintaining a database.

Problem: The user of the Parts database has discovered that the structure of the database needs to be changed to accommodate some new requirements. In addition, some invalid data has been entered into the database and the user would like to prevent this from happening in the future. Finally, to make things more efficient, the user would like some secondary indexes created.

Instructions: Use the database created in Laboratory Assignment 1 of Project 1 for this assignment. Execute each task on the computer and print the results.

1. Start Paradox.

2. Choose Modify|Restructure and select the Part table.

3. Change the field width of the Part Description field to 19.

4. Save the change.

5. Open the Part table and enter Edit mode.

6. Change the part description for Part Number BZ66 from WASHER to WASHING MACHINE.

7. Print the table as shown in Figure LA 3-1.

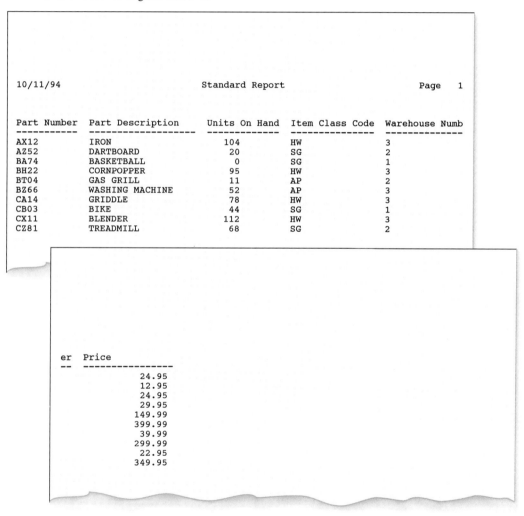

```
10/11/94                    Standard Report                    Page   1


Part Number  Part Description    Units On Hand  Item Class Code  Warehouse Numb
-----------  ------------------  -------------  ---------------  --------------
AX12         IRON                     104       HW               3
AZ52         DARTBOARD                 20       SG               2
BA74         BASKETBALL                 0       SG               1
BH22         CORNPOPPER                95       HW               3
BT04         GAS GRILL                 11       AP               2
BZ66         WASHING MACHINE           52       AP               3
CA14         GRIDDLE                   78       HW               3
CB03         BIKE                      44       SG               1
CX11         BLENDER                  112       HW               3
CZ81         TREADMILL                 68       SG               2
```

```
er  Price
--  ----------------
          24.95
          12.95
          24.95
          29.95
         149.99
         399.99
          39.99
         299.99
          22.95
         349.95
```

FIGURE LA3-1

8. Create and save the following validity checks for the Part table. List the steps involved.

   a. Require a minimum value of 0 and a maximum value of 999 for Units On Hand.

LABORATORY ASSIGNMENT I (continued)

    b. Create a template so part numbers must be two uppercase letters followed by a two-digit number.

_____

_____

    c. Use picture symbols to force the user to enter HW, SG, or AP for the Item Class Code field.

_____

_____

    d. Ensure that the data in the Item Class Code field in the Part table matches the data in the Class table. Have the values in the Class table display when data is entered into the Item Class Code field in the Part table.

_____

_____

9. Create a secondary index for the Part Description field.

10. Create a secondary index on the combination of the Item Class Code and Part Description fields. Name the index Classpart.

11. Order the records in the Part table by the Classpart index.

12. List the first record and the last record in the reordered table.

_____

_____

13. Change from Table view to Form view.

14. Using the Form view screen, add the following record to the Part table.

CP03	POOL TABLE	2	SG	1	299.99

15. Return to Table view and print the table.

16. Using a query, delete all records in the Part table where the Part Description starts with the letter P.

    (Hint: Use the Wildcards described in Project 2.)

17. Close the query without saving it.

18. Print the Part table.

19. Exit Paradox

LABORATORY ASSIGNMENT 2
Maintaining the Employee Database

Purpose: To provide practice in maintaining a database.

Problem: The user of the Employee database has discovered that the structure of the database needs to be changed to accommodate some new requirements. In addition, some invalid data has been entered into the database and the user would like to prevent this from happening in the future. Finally, to make things more efficient, the user would like some secondary indexes created.

Instructions: Use the database created in Laboratory Assignment 2 of Project 1 for this assignment. Execute each task on the computer and print the results.

1. Start Paradox.

2. Choose Modify|Restructure and select the Employee table.

3. Add the field Union Code to the Employee Table. Insert the Union Code field after the Department Code field. Define the field as Alphanumeric with a width of 3. This field will contain data on whether the employee is a union member (UNM) or non-union (NON). Save the changes to the Employee table.

4. Using a query, change all the entries in the Union Code field to UNM. This will be the status of most employees.

5. Close the query without saving.

6. Print the Employee table as shown in Figure LA 3-2.

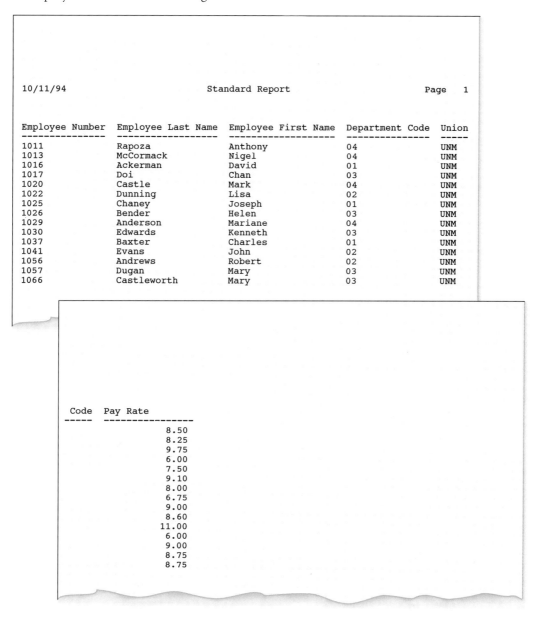

```
10/11/94                    Standard Report                    Page    1


Employee Number   Employee Last Name   Employee First Name   Department Code   Union
---------------   ------------------   -------------------   ---------------   -----
1011              Rapoza               Anthony               04                UNM
1013              McCormack            Nigel                 04                UNM
1016              Ackerman             David                 01                UNM
1017              Doi                  Chan                  03                UNM
1020              Castle               Mark                  04                UNM
1022              Dunning              Lisa                  02                UNM
1025              Chaney               Joseph                01                UNM
1026              Bender               Helen                 03                UNM
1029              Anderson             Mariane               04                UNM
1030              Edwards              Kenneth               03                UNM
1037              Baxter               Charles               01                UNM
1041              Evans                John                  02                UNM
1056              Andrews              Robert                02                UNM
1057              Dugan                Mary                  03                UNM
1066              Castleworth          Mary                  03                UNM
```

```
Code   Pay Rate
-----  ----------------
               8.50
               8.25
               9.75
               6.00
               7.50
               9.10
               8.00
               6.75
               9.00
               8.60
              11.00
               6.00
               9.00
               8.75
               8.75
```

FIGURE LA3-2

LABORATORY ANSWER ASSIGNMENT 2 (continued)

7. Open the Employee table and enter Edit mode.

8. Create and save the following validity checks for the Employee table. List the steps involved.

   a. Assign a minimum value of $6.00 and a maximum value of $13.00 to the Pay Rate field.

   _____

   _____

   b. Create a template so employee numbers must be four digits.

   _____

   _____

   c. Use picture symbols to force the user to enter UNM or NON for the Union Code field.

   _____

   _____

   d. Ensure that the data in the Department Code field in the Employee table matches the data in the Dept table. Have the values in the Dept table display when data is entered into the Department Code field in the Employee table.

   _____

   _____

9. Create a secondary index for the Employee Last Name field.

10. Create a secondary index on the combination of the Department Code and Employee Last Name fields. Name the index Deptname.

11. Order the records in the Employee table by the Deptname index.

12. List the first record and the last record in the reordered table.

   _____

   _____

13. Create a secondary index on the combination of the Pay Rate and Employee Last Name fields. Name the index Payname.

14. Order the records in the Employee table by the Payname index.

15. List the first record and the last record in the reordered table.

   _____

   _____

16. Change from Table view to Form view.

17. Using the Form view screen, add the following record to the Employee table.

| 1070 | Fisher | Ella | 02 | NON | 9.30 |

18. Locate the employees with Employee Numbers 1016, 1022, and 1037 and change the Union Code for each record to NON.

19. Return to Table view and print the table.

20. Using a query, delete all records in the Employee table where the employee's last name starts with the letter F. (Hint: Use the Wildcards described in Project 2)

21. Close the query without saving it.

22. Print the Employee table.

23. Exit Paradox

LABORATORY ASSIGNMENT 3
Maintaining the Movie Database

Purpose: To provide practice in maintaining a database.

Problem: The user of the Movie database has discovered that the structure of the database needs to be changed to accommodate some new requirements. In addition, some invalid data has been entered into the database and the user would like to prevent this from happening in the future. Finally, to make things more efficient, the user would like some secondary indexes created.

Instructions: Use the database created in Laboratory Assignment 3 of Project 1 for this assignment. Execute each task on the computer and print the results.

1. Start Paradox.

2. Choose Modify|Restructure and select the Movie table.

3. Change the field width of the Movie Title to 20.

4. Add the field Color Type to the Movie table. Insert the Color Type field after the Length field. Define the field as Alphanumeric with a width of 5. This field will contain data on whether the movie is in color (COLOR) or black and white (BW). Save the changes to the Movie table.

5. Using a query, change all the entries in the Color Type column to COLOR. This will be the status of most movies.

6. Close the query without saving.

7. Print the Movie table as shown in Figure LA 3-3 on the next page.

8. Open the Movie table and enter Edit mode.

9. Change the title for the movie, The Dervish, to The Whirling Dervish.

10. Create and save the following validity checks for the Movie table. List the steps involved:

   a. Create a template so the movie numbers must be three digits.

   _____

   _____

   b. Use picture symbols to force the user to enter COLOR or BW for the Color Type field.

   _____

   _____

   c. Ensure that the data in the Director Code field in the Movie table matches the data in the Director table. Have the values in the Director table display when data is entered into the Director Code field in the Movie table.

   _____

LABORATORY ASSIGNMENT 3 (continued)

    d. Assign a default value of COLOR to the Color Type field.

_____

_____

```
10/11/94                        Movie Report                    Page    1

  Movie                           Year   Movie      Color
 Number   Movie Title             Made   Type       Type
 ------   --------------------    ----   ------     -----
  001     Ann Thompson            1977   COMEDY     COLOR
  002     They Went Away          1964   COMEDY     COLOR
  003     A Crack in Time         1971   SCI FI     COLOR
  004     No Time for Henry       1959   SUSPEN     BW
  005     The Dirty Car           1948   SUSPEN     COLOR
  006     They Know Too Much      1969   HORROR     COLOR
  007     The Old House           1978   DRAMA      COLOR
  008     The Whirling Dervish    1960   HORROR     COLOR
  011     Winston's Dog           1979   COMEDY     COLOR
  012     Escape from Zero        1958   SUSPEN     COLOR
  014     The Ninth Planet        1968   SCI FI     COLOR
  021     A Single Bullet         1939   WESTER     BW
  022     Rear Window             1954   SUSPEN     COLOR
  024     Just Like Me            1940   DRAMA      BW
```

FIGURE LA3-3

11. Create a secondary index for the Movie Title field.

12. Create a secondary index on the combination of the Movie Type and Movie Title fields. Name the index Typetitle.

13. Order the records in the Movie table by the Typetitle index.

14. List the first record and the last record in the reordered table.

_____

_____

15. Change from Table view to Form view.

16. Using the Form view screen, add the following record to the Movie table.

023	Mojave	1937	WESTER	97	BW	02

17. Locate the Movies with Movie Numbers 024, 021, and 004 and change the Color Type for each record to BW.

18. Return to Table view and print the table.

19. Using a query, delete all records in the Movie table where the movie was made in 1937.

20. Close the query without saving it.

21. Print the Movie table.

22. Exit Paradox

LABORATORY ASSIGNMENT 4
Maintaining the Book Database

Purpose: To provide practice in maintaining a database.

Problem: The owner of the bookstore where you are employed is very pleased with the work you have done so far on the Book database. Because the business is expanding rapidly, she would like to make some changes to the database. She has sent you a list of recommended changes and asked if you can implement them.

Instructions: Use the database created in Laboratory Assignment 4 of Project 1 for this assignment. Provide printed output and/or a written explanation that confirms the changes to the database.

The following are recommended changes to the Book database:

1. The title for book code 2295 is really, "The Thing Struck Twice" not "It Struck Twice." Change the size of the field to accommodate the correct title.

2. Customer queries can be answered more efficiently if the books can be displayed in various orders. List the books in author order. In order by title within publisher. In order by title within book type.

3. Most books in inventory are paperback but there are a few hardback books. Add a new field with values such as SOFT (paperback) and HARD (hardback) to indicate the cover type.

4. Currently, the only hardback books in stock are those books with a price greater than $14.99. Use a more efficient method than changing each record individually to make these corrections to the database.

5. Various personnel in the bookstore are updating the database. Improve the accuracy of the data entry process by adding some validity checks to the database. The following are examples.

   a. No book is priced less than $1.99 or more than $49.99.
   b. All book type and publisher code entries are in uppercase.
   c. Publisher code entries should match the entries in the Publish table.
   d. SOFT and HARD are the only choices for the cover type. Most books are paperback.
   e. Any letters entered in the Book Code field are in uppercase.

6. Three copies of a new paperback book (code 6781) have just arrived that should be added to the database. However, the book publisher is not in the Publish table. Add the book to the database. The publisher is Fraser Books (FR). The book is "The Runaway" by Megan Rust and it is a mystery. The price is $5.95.

7. The store will no longer carry science fiction (SFI) books. Delete all science fiction books from the database.

PARADOX 4.5

PROJECT
4

Presenting Data:
Reports and Forms

▼ OBJECTIVES

You will have mastered the material in this project when you can:

■ Create a report

■ Understand the function of report bands

■ Change column headings and widths

■ Remove columns

■ View a report on the screen

■ Save a report

■ Print a report

■ Add a column and field to a report

■ Add a group band to a report

■ Include fields from other files in a report

■ Add totals and subtotals to a report

■ Know the principles of good report design

■ Create a form

■ Modify the design of a form

■ Move fields and prompts on a form

■ Add boxes to a form

■ View data using a form

■ Assign a form as the default form

▼ INTRODUCTION

In the previous projects, you learned how to create a database, query a database, and maintain a database. Project 4 introduces you to presenting the data in a database in a pleasing and useful way, either on paper or on the screen.

Reports generated on a printer represent one way of presenting data. Figure 4-1 shows a report that lists the customer number, name, address, city, state, and zip code of all customers. This report is similar to the report you produced earlier by selecting Report|Output. It does not contain all the fields, however, and has a special title.

```
                    ╭─────────╮                      ╭────────╮
                    │ system  │                      │  page  │
                    │  date   │                      │ number │
                    ╰─────────╯                      ╰────────╯
   10/06/94  ◄─────           Customer Address List           ►Page   1


   Cust                                                          Zip
   Numb    Name                 Address          City     State  Code
   ----    ----------------     ----------       ------   -----  -----
   AC12    Arend Corp.          21 Wilson        Muncie   IN     47303
   AX29    AAA Express          108 College      Muncie   IN     47303
   CL67    Clark-White Ltd.     47 Chipwood      Moline   IL     61265
   FC15    Ferguson Co.         602 Bridge       Mason    MI     48854
   FY24    Farley-Young Industries  19 Oak       Muncie   IN     47303
   LW46    L. T. Wheeler        587 Rivard       Moline   IL     61265
   NI34    Nelson Inc.          12 Bishop        Sumner   IL     62466
   SD86    Southern Dev.        103 Bedford      Brook    MI     48127
   SI84    Shelton Inc.         82 Harcourt      Niles    MI     49120
```

FIGURE 4-1

The report shown in Figure 4-2 contains a special feature, grouping. **Grouping** means creating separate collections of records sharing some common characteristic. In the report in Figure 4-2, for example, the records have been grouped by sales rep number. There are three separate groups: one for sales rep 03, one for sales rep 06, and one for sales rep 12. The appropriate sales rep name appears before each group and the total of the balances for the customers in the group (called a **subtotal**) appears after. At the bottom of the report is a total of the balances (30,234.00) for all the customers.

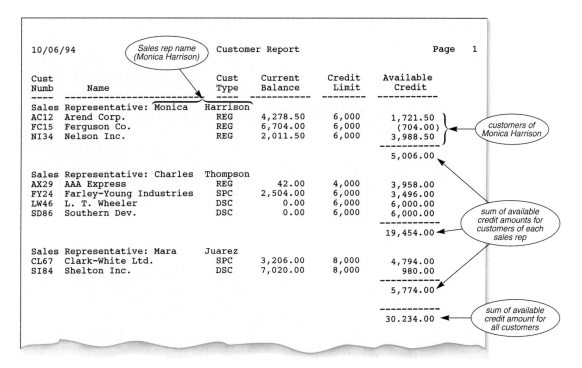

FIGURE 4-2

Another way of presenting data is by displaying custom forms on the screen. You have already used the Form view screen to view records in a table as well as to update records. When you did, you used a standard display form automatically generated by Paradox. Rather than simply using the form Paradox creates, you can design and use your own custom forms like the one shown in Figure 4-3.

This project covers the design and creation of reports and forms.

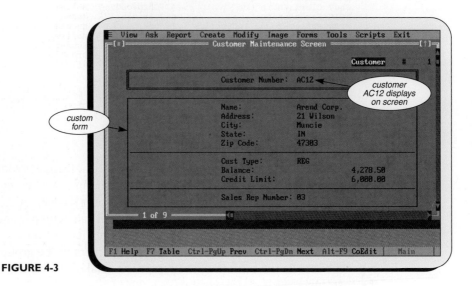

FIGURE 4-3

....

▼ **CREATING A REPORT**

To create a report, you use a special window, called the **Report Designer window**. In this window, you indicate exactly what you want the report to look like. Once you have designed the report, you can print the report when you want. Whenever you print the report, Paradox will produce a report containing the data currently in the table in a format that matches the design you created.

Beginning the Report Creation

To create a new report, use the **Design command** of the Report menu. The following steps begin the report creation.

TO BEGIN CREATING A REPORT

STEP 1: Choose Report and then move the cursor to the Design command (Figure 4-4).

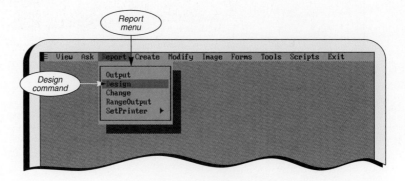

FIGURE 4-4

STEP 2: **Choose the Design command, press the ENTER key, and move the cursor to Customer in the dialog box.**

The Design command is chosen and the cursor is on Customer in the dialog box (Figure 4-5).

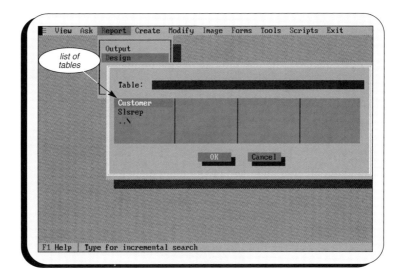

FIGURE 4-5

STEP 3: **Press the ENTER key to select the Customer table. In the Report Designer box, select 1-Unused report. Type** `Customer Address List` **in the Report description box, and press the ENTER key.**

A list of available reports for the Customer table displays (Figure 4-6). Fourteen reports, numbered 1-14, are available. Report 1 is selected. The report description is Customer Address List. The cursor is on Tabular.

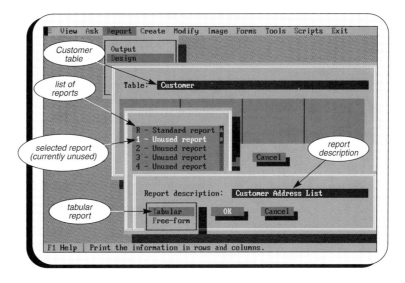

FIGURE 4-6

STEP 4: Choose Tabular.

The Report Designer window displays an initial report layout (Customer.R1) (Figure 4-7).

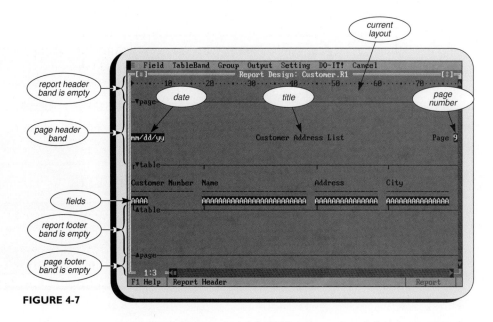

FIGURE 4-7

Notice in Figure 4-6 that there are two report types: tabular and free-form. In a **tabular report**, data displays in columns, much like in Table view. The standard report you saw in Project 1 on page P3. is an example of a tabular report. By contrast, a **free-form report** looks more like a form. For example, you could create a free-form report that looks like the form shown in Figure 4-3 on the page P166. The report you are creating is a tabular report. Thus, tabular was chosen in Step 4.

Report Bands

Each of the different portions of the report is described in what is often termed a **band**. These specific bands are the **page header band**, **table band** (which is used for detail lines), and **report footer band**, all of which correspond to sections of a report. Two additional bands are the **report header band** and **page footer band**. A **report header** appears once at the beginning of a report, regardless of how many pages the report contains. A **page footer** appears at the bottom of each page. Neither the report header nor the page footer bands are commonly used, but they are advantageous when you are to create a report that requires them, such as identifying the name of the person to whom the report goes in the report header.

To design a report, you need to describe each of the bands to be included in the report. At any given time during the design process, you will be working with only one band. The name of the band will appear on the line at the bottom of the screen. For example, in Figure 4-7 the cursor is in the report header band. To move from one band to another, use the UP ARROW and DOWN ARROW keys.

The block of space that follows the word page at the top of the screen is the **page header** that prints at the top of each page. The report header band, the page footer band, and the report footer band are currently empty (Figure 4-7).

In many band-oriented report tools, the table band (sometimes called the **detail band**) contains just the data that is to be printed in the **detail line**. The detail line represents the line that will be used to print each record in the table. In Paradox, the table band contains both the data for the detail line and the column headings.

In the page header band, you see an area for the system date (mm/dd/yy), the title, Customer Address List, and the report page number title, Page. These are printed in the page heading exactly as they are shown in exactly the same position. The mm/dd/yy is replaced in the printout with the system date and the 9 following the report page number title, Page, is replaced by the page number. Thus, Customer Address List will be printed four lines down on the page. It is centered on the line. Page will print on the right-hand side of the same line. Two blank lines will follow the line containing the heading, Customer Address List.

In the table band, the detail line starts with AAAA. The A symbols indicate the position at which the data in some particular field will be printed and what it will look like. The 9 following the word Page indicates that the field is numeric, and the A in the detail line indicates the field is a character field. The number of 9s or As indicates how many positions the field will occupy. Decimal points or commas in a group of 9s indicate the position at which the decimal point or comma will appear when the field is displayed on the report. A group of 9s surrounded by parentheses indicates that negative numbers are to be enclosed in parentheses on the report. (To see how this appears, look at the available credit amount for customer FC15 on the report in Figure 4-2 on page P165.)

TABLE 4-1

Key	Purpose
UP ARROW	Moves the cursor up one row.
DOWN ARROW	Moves the cursor down one row.
RIGHT ARROW	Moves the cursor one position to the right.
LEFT ARROW	Moves the cursor one position to the left.
HOME	Moves the cursor to the beginning of the line.
END	Moves the cursor to the end of the line.
CTRL+HOME	Moves the cursor to the first line on the screen.
CTRL+END	Moves the cursor to the last line on the screen.
PAGE DOWN	Moves down one screen.
PAGE UP	Moves up one screen.
INSERT	Turns insert mode on and off.
DELETE	Deletes the character at the cursor position.
BACKSPACE	Moves the cursor one position to the left and deletes the character in that position.
ENTER	Inserts a blank line (must be in insert mode).
CTRL+RIGHT	Moves right one-half screen.
CTRL+LEFT	Moves left one-half screen.
CTRL+Y	Deletes all characters to the right of the cursor. If the cursor is in the first position, also removes the line.
CTRL+V	Turns a vertical ruler on and off. Useful if there are many lines in a band.

In modifying the contents of the table band, you work with columns using the **TableBand menu**. Use this menu to remove columns, add new ones, resize columns, and move columns. By using the **Field menu**, you can also work with the fields within the columns. Use this menu to delete fields, add new fields, or change the format of existing fields. Use these two menus to transform the table band. In changing the report design, you can also use the keys shown in Table 4-1 on the previous page.

Changing Column Headings and Widths

In the initial design presented by Paradox (Figure 4-7 on page p168), some of the columns are wider than they need to be because the field name is considerably longer than the data in the field. Customer numbers, for example, are only four characters. The field name, Customer Number, however, is 15 characters, so the column must be 15 characters wide. One way to remedy this situation is to shorten the heading and also to extend it over two lines. For example, you could place Cust on one line and Numb on the next.

Changing a Column

Two types of changes you can make to a column are: (1) changing the heading in the column; and (2) changing the size of the column. The following steps change the column heading.

TO CHANGE THE COLUMN HEADINGS

STEP 1: Move the cursor to the first position in the first line of the table band (one line above the C of Customer) and type `Cust`.

STEP 2: Move the cursor to the beginning of the second line (the C of Customer), press the DELETE key until Customer Number has been deleted, and type `Numb`.

STEP 3: Move the cursor to the beginning of the third line (the first hyphen) and press the DELETE key until only four hyphens remain.

The column heading has been changed (Figure 4-8).

The final step is to resize the column by using the **Resize command** on the TableBand menu. The steps on the following two pages resize the column.

TO CHANGE THE SIZE OF COLUMNS

STEP 1:   Choose TableBand and move the cursor to the Resize command (Figure 4-8).

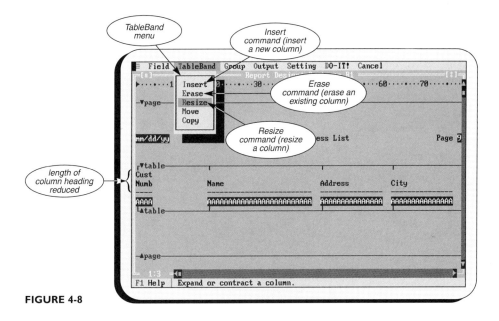

FIGURE 4-8

STEP 2:   Press the ENTER key to choose the Resize command. Use the arrow keys to move the cursor to the rightmost position in the first column (immediately preceding the N of Name) and press the ENTER key.

STEP 3:   Press the LEFT ARROW key until only one space appears between the b of Numb and the N of Name. Press the ENTER key.

The column has been resized (Figure 4-9).

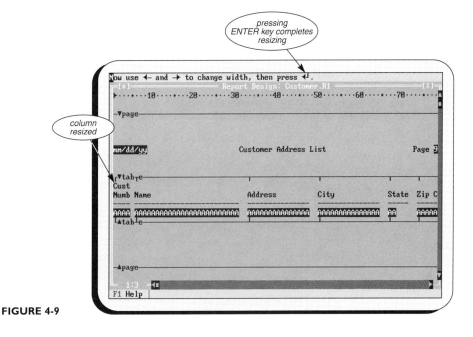

FIGURE 4-9

STEP 4: Use the TableBand|Resize command to resize the Name, Address, City, and State columns to the size shown in Figure 4-10, and then change the heading for the Zip Code field to the one shown in the figure (Zip on one line and Code on the next). Resize the Zip Code field so only one space follows the final hyphen.

The Customer Number, Name, Address, City, State, and Zip Code columns are all resized (Figure 4-10).

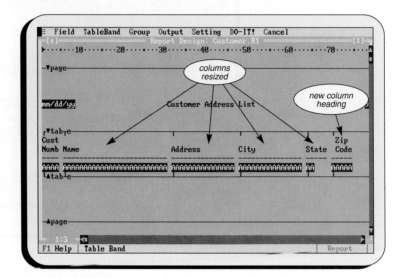

FIGURE 4-10

Mouse Users: *After choosing TableBand|Resize, position the mouse pointer on the rightmost position in the column you want to change and drag to the left to reduce the column width; drag to the right to increase the column width.*

Removing Columns

The report currently contains all the columns. The only columns that are supposed to be included, however, are Customer Number, Name, Address, City, State, and Zip Code. The others need to be removed. To remove a column, use the Erase command of the TableBand menu as shown in the following steps.

TO REMOVE COLUMNS

STEP 1: Choose the TableBand menu and move the cursor to Erase.

The TableBand menu displays (Figure 4-11). The cursor is on Erase, the command to remove a column.

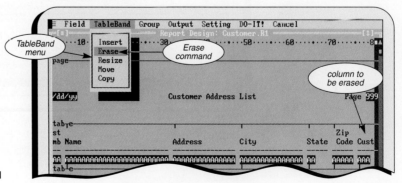

FIGURE 4-11

STEP 2: Choose the Erase command, move the cursor to the column containing the Cust Type field, and press the ENTER key.

The Cust Type field is removed from the report design (Figure 4-12).

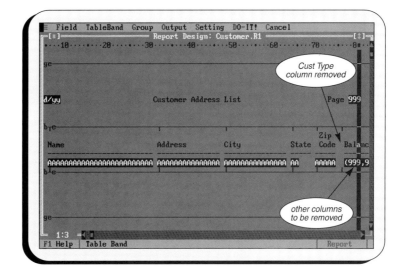

FIGURE 4-12

STEP 3: Use the procedure illustrated in Steps 1 and 2 to remove the Balance, Credit Limit, and Sales Rep Number columns from the report design.

The Balance, Credit Limit, and Sales Rep Number columns are removed (Figure 4-13).

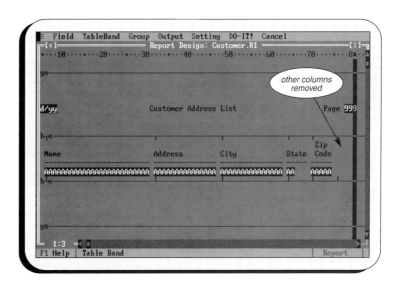

FIGURE 4-13

Mouse Users: *After choosing the TableBand|Erase command, click the column you want to delete.*

Viewing the Report

When working on a report, it is often helpful to be able to view the report on the screen. To view the report on the screen, use the Output|Screen command. The steps on the following page display the report on the screen.

TO VIEW A REPORT ON THE SCREEN

STEP 1: Choose the Output menu and move the cursor to the Screen command (Figure 4-14).

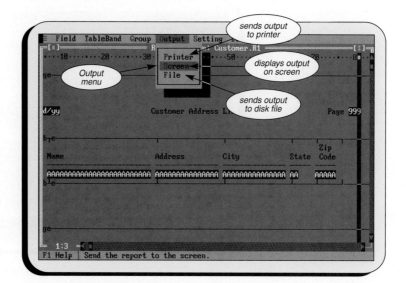

FIGURE 4-14

STEP 2: Choose the Screen command.

The report displays (Figure 4-15). You can use the arrow keys, PAGE UP key and PAGE DOWN key to move around in the report.

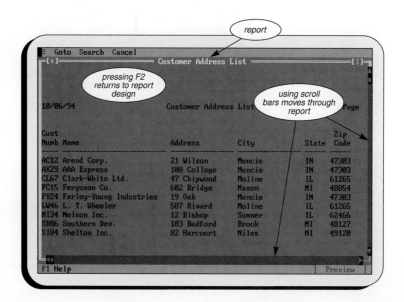

FIGURE 4-15

Mouse Users: *To move around in the report after choosing Output|Screen, use the horizontal and vertical scroll bars.*

STEP 3: When you have finished looking at the report, press F2 to return to the report design.

The Report Design window once again displays.

Correcting Mistakes

Before saving the report, check to make sure it is correct by comparing it with Figure 4-15. If not, you can use the following guidelines to correct it.

1. To delete a line, make sure the cursor is in the first position in the line and press CTRL+Y. (If the cursor is not in the first position, pressing CTRL+Y deletes any characters from the cursor to the end of the line.)
2. To insert a blank line, make sure you are in insert mode and positioned at the left margin. Then press the ENTER key.
3. To delete a field, choose the Field|Erase command. To insert a new field, choose the Field|Place command. In both cases follow the directions given on the screen.
4. To delete an entire column from the table band, choose the TableBand|Erase command. To insert a new column into the table band, choose the TableBand|Insert command. In both cases follow the directions given on the screen.

Occasionally, you might decide that it would be simpler to start over than to make a number of individual corrections. If this is the case, choose Cancel. Paradox then asks you if you are sure you want to abandon the changes. To abandon the changes, choose Yes. After choosing Yes, you are returned to the Main menu without any of your work being saved. You can now start the process again.

Saving a Report

To save a report design, press F2. The following step saves the report design.

TO SAVE A REPORT DESIGN

STEP 1: Press F2.

The report design is saved on disk using the filename Customer.R1. The file is linked to the Customer table in such a way that it is available to you whenever you open the Customer table.

When you save a report, Paradox automatically uses the table name (Customer) and an extension equal to the report number (R1).

Printing a Report

From the Report Design window, you can print a report by selecting the Output|Printer command. Most of the time, however, it will be simpler to print the report from the Main menu. The technique for doing this is the same as the technique for printing the standard report you encountered in Project 1. Follow the steps to print the report you just designed.

TO PRINT A REPORT

STEP 1: **Choose Report|Output, select the Customer table, and select Report 1, Customer Address List.**

The menu of available destinations for the report displays along with the Table name box and the Report box (Figure 4-16).

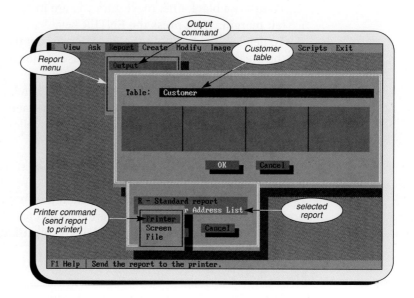

FIGURE 4-16

STEP 2: **Choose Printer.**

The report shown in Figure 4-1 on page P165 prints.

▼ GROUPING

Sometimes you want to **group** records in a report; that is, you want to create separate collections of records sharing some common characteristic. In the report in Figure 4-2 on page P165, for example, the records are grouped by sales rep. There are three separate groups: one for each sales rep.

When you group, you typically include in the report two other types of bands: a group header and a group footer. A **group header** is printed before the records in a particular group and a **group footer** is printed after. In Figure 4-2, the group header indicates the sales rep. The group footer includes the total of the balances for the customers of that sales rep. As indicated earlier, such a total is called a subtotal, because it is just a subset of the overall total of the balances.

To group records in Paradox, you need to add a special band, called a **group band** to your report design. The report design in this project requires such a band.

Creating a Report

To begin creating a report that includes grouping, you start with the same steps you used to create other reports. The report creation steps follow.

STEP 1: Choose Report|Design and select the Customer table. Choose report 2 in the Report box, type `Customer Report` in the Report description box, and press the ENTER key.

Report 2 of the Customer table is chosen (Figure 4-17). Its description is Customer Report. The cursor is positioned on Tabular.

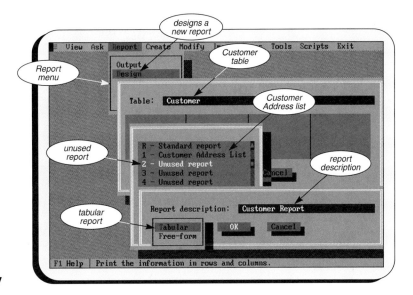

FIGURE 4-17

STEP 2: Choose Tabular.

The Report Design window displays with an initial tabular report layout (Figure 4-18).

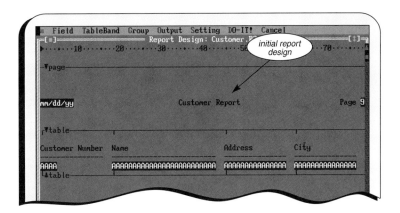

FIGURE 4-18

Changing and Deleting Columns

Throughout the report creation process, you have seen how to change column headings and column sizes, as well as how to delete columns. The following step makes appropriate changes to columns and also deletes the columns that need to be removed for the report.

TO CHANGE AND DELETE COLUMNS

STEP 1:   Make the modifications shown in Figure 4-19 by changing the column headings and widths for the Customer Number and Cust Type columns. In addition, delete the Address, City, State, and Zip Code columns.

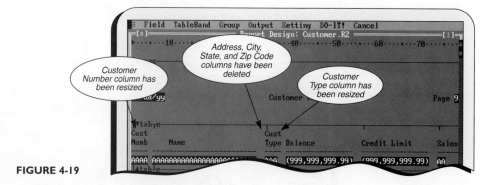

FIGURE 4-19

Reformatting Fields

Changing field sizes and other field characteristics is part of the process called **reformatting**. To reformat a field, use the **Reformat command** on the Field menu, as
shown in the following steps.

TO REFORMAT FIELDS

STEP 1:   Select the Field menu and move the cursor to Reformat.

*The Field menu displays (Figure 4-20). The cursor is on Reformat, the command to
change the format of a field.*

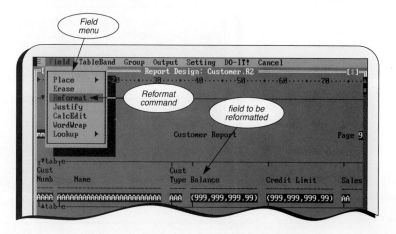

FIGURE 4-20

STEP 2:   Choose the Reformat command, use the arrow keys to move the cursor to the
Balance field (the 9s that represent the Balance), and then press the ENTER
key.

*The reformatting choices display as shown in Figure 4-21. Using the **Sign-
Convention command** changes the way negative numbers are represented. Using
the **Commas command** changes the way commas will be used. The majority of
the reformatting of fields will be accomplished using the **Digits command** to
change the size; that is, to change the number of digits that the field occupies.*

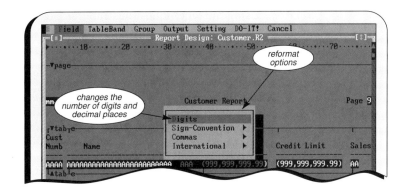

FIGURE 4-21

STEP 3: Choose Digits. Press the LEFT ARROW key until 99,999 displays in the Balance column (Figure 4-22).

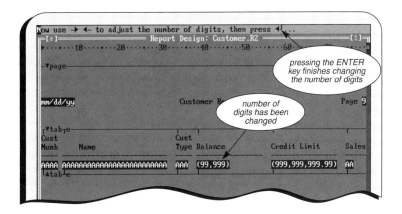

FIGURE 4-22

STEP 4: Press the ENTER key.

Paradox displays instructions indicating you are to use the arrow keys to adjust the number of decimal places.

STEP 5: Make sure there are two decimal places showing and press the ENTER key.

The size of the Balance field is changed.

STEP 6: Change the column headings and column size for the Balance column to the ones shown in Figure 4-23.

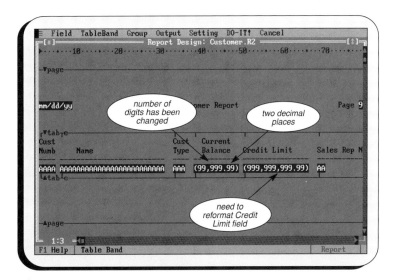

FIGURE 4-23

STEP 7: Using the techniques illustrated in Steps 1 through 4, change the field size, column headings and column size of the Credit Limit column to the ones shown in Figure 4-24.

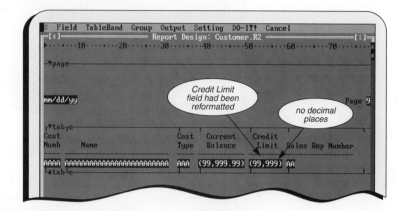

FIGURE 4-24

Mouse Users: *After choosing Field | Reformat | Commas, drag the rightmost 9 in a numeric field to the left or right. Release the mouse button to insert a decimal point. Continue to drag to add additional decimal places.*

The Sales Rep Number field is not included in this report, so the column containing Sales Rep Number is to be removed. The following step removes the Sales Rep Number column.

TO REMOVE A COLUMN

STEP 1: Choose TableBand | Erase, move the cursor to the Sales Rep Number column, and then press the ENTER key.

The column containing the Sales Rep Number field has been removed (Figure 4-25).

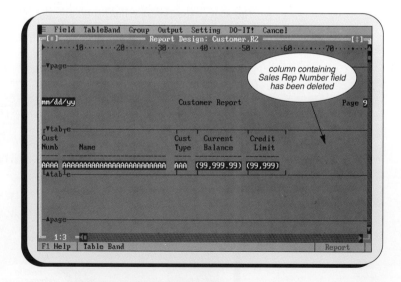

FIGURE 4-25

Adding a Field and Column

To add a column to a report, first use the TableBand menu and **Insert command** to add a new column. Next, use the Field menu and **Place command** to add the field. Finally, enter the appropriate column headings.

The possible field types on the Place command menu are described in Table 4-2.

TABLE 4-2

Command	Function
Regular	Adds a field from a table.
Summary	Adds a summary computation (sum, average, and so on).
Calculated	Adds a field that is calculated from other fields.
Date	Adds a field that will always print the current date.
Time	Adds a field that will always print the current time.
Page	Adds a field that will always print the appropriate page number.
#Record	Adds a field that will always print the record number.

Use the following steps to add the available credit field and column to the report.

TO ADD A COLUMN AND FIELD

STEP 1: **Choose TableBand.**

The TableBand menu displays (Figure 4-26). The cursor is on Insert, the command to insert a new column.

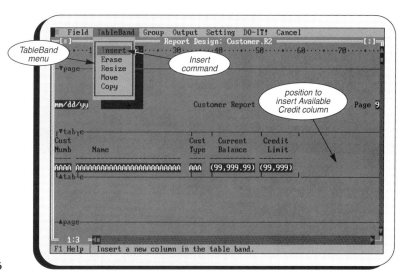

FIGURE 4-26

STEP 2: **Press the ENTER key to choose the Insert command, move the cursor to the position for the new column (the blank area at the far right end of the table band), and press the ENTER key.**

The column is added.

STEP 3:   **Choose Field.**

The Field menu displays. The cursor is on Place, the command to place a new field (Figure 4-27).

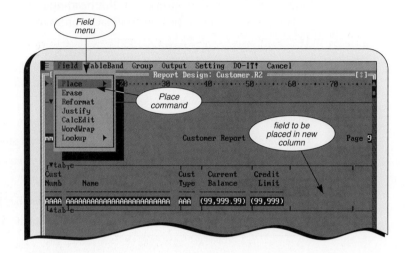

FIGURE 4-27

STEP 4:   **Press the ENTER key to choose the Place command and move the cursor to Calculated.**

The Place command menu of field types displays (Figure 4-28).

*The field to be added, available credit, is a calculation (credit limit minus balance). Thus, the **Calculated command** is the appropriate command to use.*

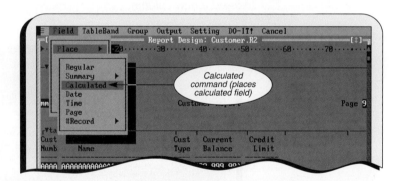

FIGURE 4-28

STEP 5:   **Choose Calculated and then type** [Credit Limit] - [Balance] **(Figure 4-29). The square brackets are necessary.**

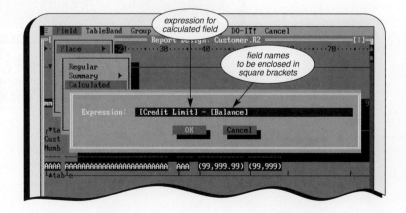

FIGURE 4-29

STEP 6: Press the ENTER key and then move the cursor to the position where the field should be placed (at the beginning of the last line in the new column). Press the ENTER key again.

STEP 7: Press the LEFT or RIGHT arrow key as necessary to make sure five digits are showing and then press the ENTER key.

STEP 8: Press the LEFT or RIGHT arrow key to make sure exactly two decimal places are showing and press the ENTER key.

The field is now added to the column (Figure 4-30). Next, you need to complete the column heading.

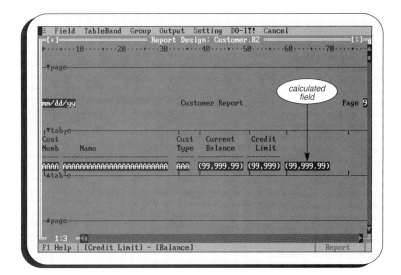

FIGURE 4-30

STEP 9: Type `Available Credit` and `- - - - - - - - - - -` (11 hyphens) in the positions shown in Figure 4-31.

The table band is now complete.

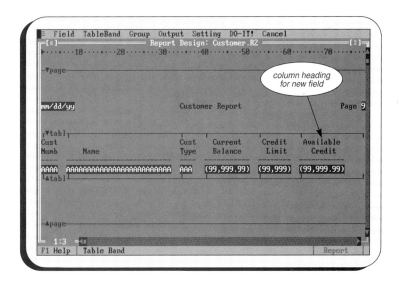

FIGURE 4-31

Saving the Report Design

Although the design is not complete at this point, you have already made several changes. Before going any further, it would be a good idea to save your work. The following step saves the current report design.

TO SAVE THE REPORT DESIGN

STEP 1: Press F2.

The design is saved on your disk using the filename Customer.R2 and the report design is removed from the screen. Here again, the report is available whenever you open the Customer table.

Modifying an Existing Report

To modify an existing report, you first choose Report as you did before. You do not choose the Design command, however. The Design command is only appropriate when you are creating the report initially. You need the **Change command** as shown in the following steps.

TO MODIFY AN EXISTING REPORT

STEP 1: Choose Report and move the cursor to Change.

The Report menu displays (Figure 4-32). The cursor is on Change, the command to change an existing report design.

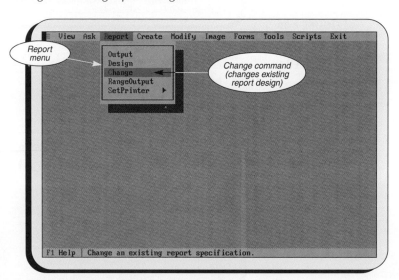

FIGURE 4-32

STEP 2: Choose the Change command, select the Customer table, and move the cursor to report 2 - Customer Report.

The Customer table is selected (Figure 4-33) and the cursor is on report 2, the report to be modified.

STEP 3:   Press the ENTER key to select report 2 and then press the ENTER key a second time to see the report.

The Report Designer window displays, containing the current design (Figure 4-33).

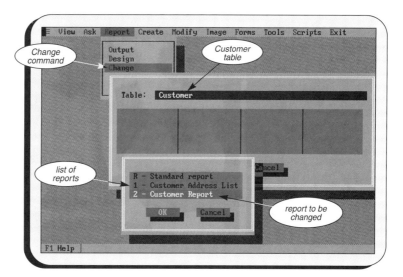

FIGURE 4-33

Adding a Group Band

To calculate and display subtotals, the records must be grouped. This involves the use
of a new band, called a group band.

To add the necessary group band to the report, position the cursor in the page band
and then use the Group|Insert command. Next, choose the type of grouping that is
appropriate for the report. The following steps add a group band where the records
are to be grouped by Sales Rep Number.

TO ADD A GROUP BAND

STEP 1:   Move the cursor anywhere within the page header band, the portion between
the word page near the top of the screen and table near the middle of the
screen.

STEP 2:   Choose Group.

*The Group menu displays (Figure 4-34). The cursor is on Insert, which is the com-
mand to insert a new group.*

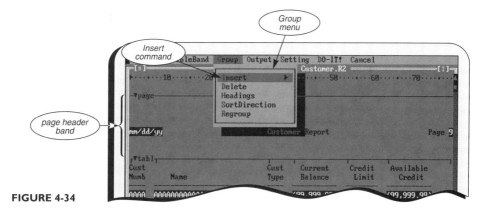

FIGURE 4-34

STEP 3:   Choose Insert and then choose the Field command. Move the cursor to the Sales Rep Number field.

Group | Insert | Field is chosen (Figure 4-35). The cursor is on the Sales Rep Number field, which is the field that will be used for grouping.

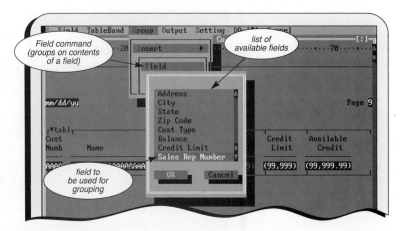

FIGURE 4-35

STEP 4:   Select the Sales Rep Number field and then press the ENTER key to place the band.

A group band is inserted (Figure 4-36). The grouping will take place on the Sales Rep Number field. This means that the collection of customers who all have the same sales rep number are considered to be a group.

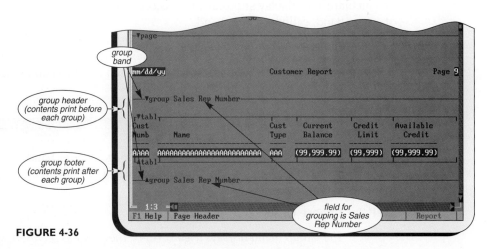

FIGURE 4-36

The portion of the band before the table band is the group header. The contents of the group header will print before each group. The portion of the band after the table band is the group footer. The contents of the group footer will print immediately after each group.

Including Fields from Other Tables

Two fields in this report are not in the Customer table; namely, the first and last names of the sales representative. To include fields from another table, you must first link the tables together. This will only be possible if a field in the table you are working on matches the key field in the other table. In this case, the Sales Rep Number field in the Customer table matches the key field of the Slsrep table.

To link the tables, use the **Lookup command** on the Field menu. The following steps use the Lookup command to link the tables.

TO LINK THE TABLES

STEP 1:   Choose Field|Lookup.

*The menu of linking commands displays (Figure 4-37). It contains three commands: Link, Unlink, and Relink. To create a link between tables, use the **Link command**. To remove an existing link, choose the **Unlink command**. The **Relink command** is used to change an existing link.*

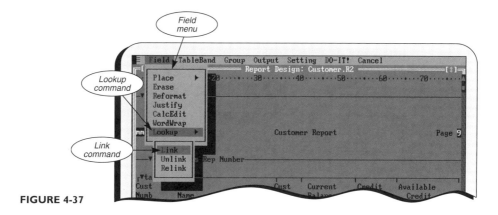

FIGURE 4-37

STEP 2:   Choose Link and then select the Slsrep table. Move the cursor to the Sales Rep Number field.

A list of fields from the Customer table displays (Figure 4-38). You need to select the one that will match the Sales Rep Number in the Slsrep table (the key). The cursor is pointing to the Sales Rep Number field in the Customer table, the correct field.

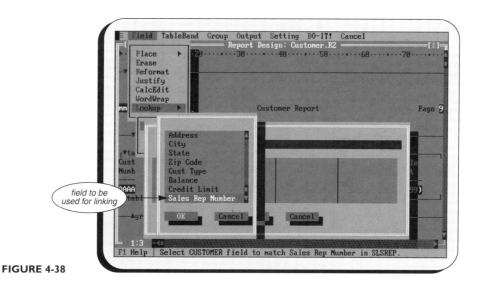

FIGURE 4-38

STEP 3:   Select Sales Rep Number by pressing the ENTER key.

The tables are now linked. You can now place fields from the Slsrep table on the report just as though they were in the Customer table.

Modifying the Group Header

Now that the tables are linked, you can include the first and last name of the sales representative in the group header. You also need to include the text ,Sales Representative: in the header. The following steps add text to the group header.

TO ADD TEXT TO THE GROUP HEADER

STEP 1: Move the cursor to the leftmost position in the group header.

STEP 2: Type `Sales Representative:` and press the RIGHT ARROW key once to leave a space after the colon.

The following steps add fields to the group header.

TO ADD FIELDS TO THE GROUP HEADER

STEP 1: Choose Field|Place|Regular and then move the cursor to [Slsrep->].

A list of the fields in the Customer table displays (Figure 4-39). The cursor is on the last entry, [Slsrep->], which represents the Slsrep table. If this is selected, a list of fields from the Slsrep table will display.

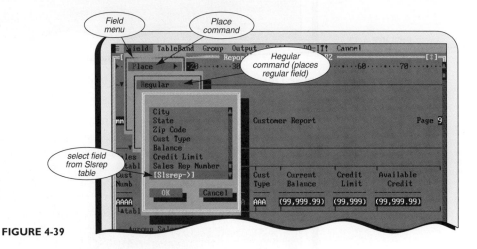

FIGURE 4-39

STEP 2: Select [Slsrep->] by moving the cursor to it and pressing ENTER. Then move the cursor to First Name.

A list of the fields from the Slsrep table displays (Figure 4-40). The cursor is on the First Name field.

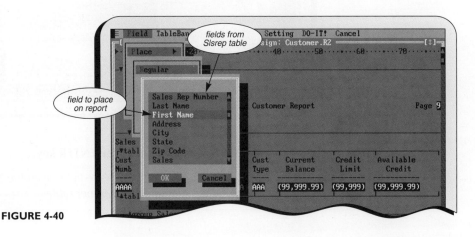

FIGURE 4-40

STEP 3: Select First Name and then press the ENTER key to place the field on the report. Press the ENTER key a second time to accept the normal width for the field (Figure 4-41).

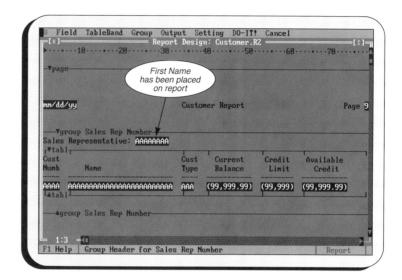

FIGURE 4-41

STEP 4: Use the techniques illustrated in Steps 1 through 3 to place the Last Name field in the position indicated in Figure 4-42.

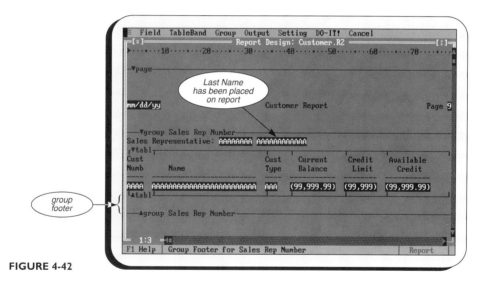

FIGURE 4-42

Modifying the Group Footer

Three changes are to be made to the group footer. It needs to be enlarged by one line and hyphens are to be added to emphasize that it includes a total. You also need to add the sum of the available credit amounts. The following steps modify the group footer.

TO MODIFY THE GROUP FOOTER

STEP 1: Add an extra line to the group footer. To do so, make sure you are in insert mode. (If you are not in insert mode, you will see a blinking block cursor). If you are not in insert mode, press the INSERT key. Then move the cursor (a narrow blinking cursor) to the first position of the group footer and press the ENTER key.

STEP 2: Type the hyphens in the positions shown in Figure 4-43.

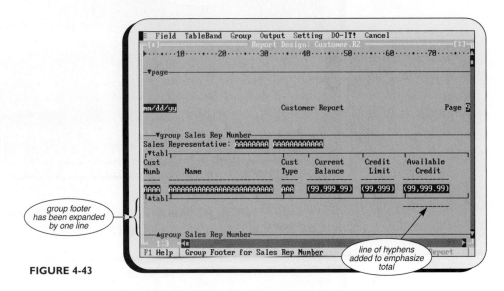

FIGURE 4-43

STEP 3: Choose Field|Place|Summary|Calculated and type `[Credit Limit] - [Balance]` as the expression. Press the ENTER key. Choose Sum.

*Field|Place|Summary|Calculated is chosen, the expression for available credit is entered, and Sum is chosen (Figure 4-44). The cursor is on the **PerGroup** which means that the sum is to be calculated for each group.*

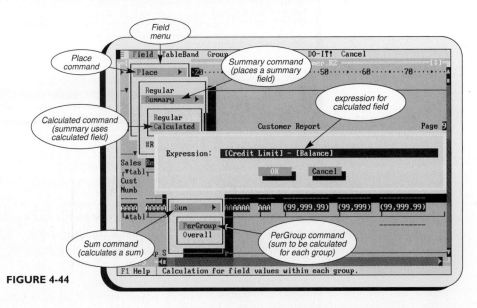

FIGURE 4-44

STEP 4:   Choose the PerGroup command.

STEP 5:   Place the field in the position shown in Figure 4-45 and adjust the size to match the size of the field shown in the figure.

The group footer is complete (Figure 4-45).

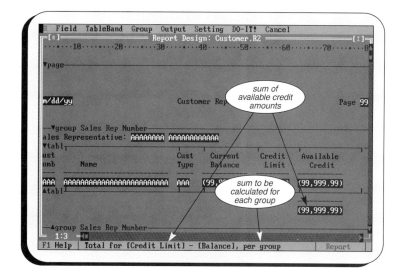

FIGURE 4-45

Modifying the Report Footer

The report is to contain a grand total of the available credit amounts. Because this total should display once at the end of the report, it should appear in the report footer. In addition, the report footer should include a line of hyphens above the total, emphasizing that it is indeed a total. The following steps modify the report footer.

TO MODIFY THE REPORT FOOTER

STEP 1:   Move the cursor to the report footer band so it is lined up with the first hyphen in the Available Credit column.

STEP 2:   Type - - - - - - - - - - - (eleven hyphens) (Figure 4-46).

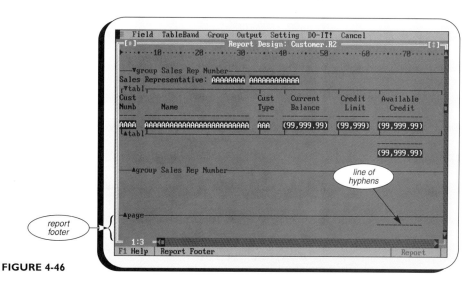

FIGURE 4-46

STEP 3: Make sure Paradox is in insert mode and press the ENTER key to add an extra line to the report footer band. Move the cursor so it is under the first hyphen.

STEP 4: Choose Field|Place|Summary|Calculated. Type `[Credit Limit] - [Balance]` as the calculation to summarize and press the ENTER key.

STEP 5: Choose Sum|Overall.

STEP 6: Place the field in the position shown in Figure 4-47 and adjust the size so it matches the one shown in the figure.

The report footer is complete.

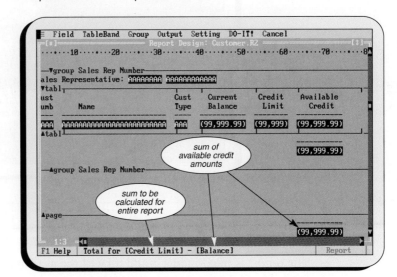

FIGURE 4-47

Saving the Report

The following step saves the report.

TO SAVE THE REPORT

STEP 1: Press F2.

The design is saved using the filename Customer.R2. Recall that the previous steps modified Customer.R2.

▼ REPORT DESIGN CONSIDERATIONS

As you design and create reports, keep in mind the following guidelines.

1. The purpose of any report is to provide certain information. Ask yourself if the report you have designed conveys this information effectively. Is the meaning of the rows and columns in the report clear? Are the column headings easily understood? Are there any abbreviations on the report that would not be clear to those looking at the report?

2. Be sure to allow sufficient white space between groups. You can accomplish this by enlarging the group footer.

3. Be consistent in your reports. Once you have decided on a general style, stay with it.

▼   CREATING AND USING CUSTOM FORMS

To add new records to a table as well as to change existing records, you used the Form view screen. When you did, you used a standard display form generated automatically by Paradox. Although the form did provide you some assistance in the task, the form was not particularly pleasing. The Standard Form stacked fields on top of each other at the left side of the screen. In this section, you will learn about **custom forms**, forms that you design. You can use custom forms in place of those normally supplied by Paradox. To create a form, you use a special window, called the **Form Designer window**. You indicate in this window exactly what you want the form to look like. Once you have done so, you can use the form to view or update data in place of the Standard Form whenever you want.

Creating an Initial Form Design

For each table, Paradox creates a Standard Form design, called form F. This is the form you have seen when you used Form view. One way to create custom forms is to use this Standard Form design as a basis, making the necessary modifications to create precisely the form you want.

There are two ways to accomplish this. The first is to modify the Standard Form itself. The problem with this approach is that you will lose the original standard layout. It's a good idea to retain that original layout in case you need it in the future.

There is another approach. First create an initial form by copying the Standard Form to one of the other available forms. Then modify the new form. To copy the form, use the **Copy command** on with the Tools menu. The following steps copy the Standard Form.

TO COPY THE STANDARD FORM

STEP 1:   Choose Tools|Copy|Form.

Tools|Copy|Form is selected (Figure 4-48). The next step is to indicate whether the copy is to the same table or a different table.

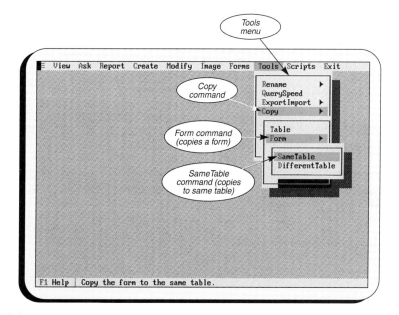

FIGURE 4-48

STEP 2: **Choose SameTable and then type** `Customer` **as the name of the table. Press the ENTER key.**

A list of forms currently defined for the Customer table displays (Figure 4-49).

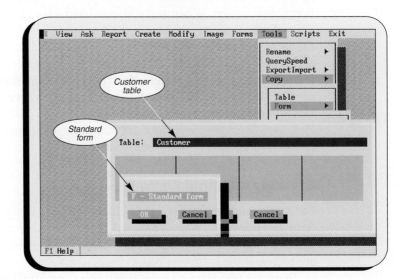

FIGURE 4-49

STEP 3: **Select form F (Standard form).**

A list of available forms for the Customer table displays (Figure 4-50). Fourteen other forms are available, numbered 1 through 14.

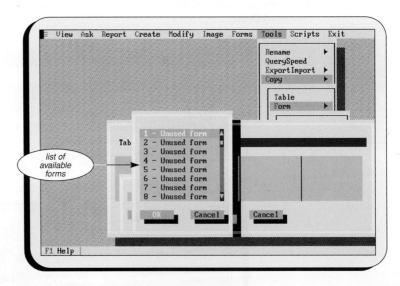

FIGURE 4-50

STEP 4: **Select 1.**

Form 1 is now defined. At this point, it has exactly the same design as the Standard Form.

Modifying a Form Design

To modify a form design, use the **Forms menu**. The two commands on the Forms menu are: Design and Change. Use Design to create a brand-new form design. To work on an existing design, choose the Change command. Because work is to be performed on an existing design (form 1), use the Change command as illustrated in the following steps.

TO MODIFY A FORM DESIGN

STEP 1: Choose the Forms menu and move the cursor to Change (Figure 4-51).

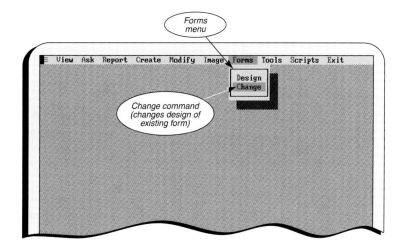

FIGURE 4-51

STEP 2: Choose the Change command. Type `Customer` as the name of the table and press the ENTER key. Move the cursor to form 1 (Figure 4-52).

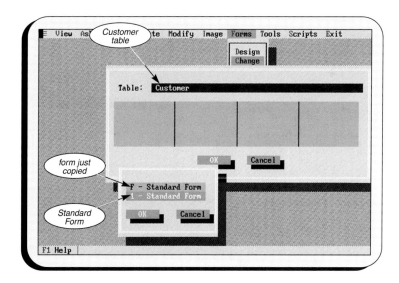

FIGURE 4-52

STEP 3: **Choose form 1.**

A dialog box displays requesting a form description (Figure 4-53). The form description currently reads Standard Form because it is the description of the form that was copied.

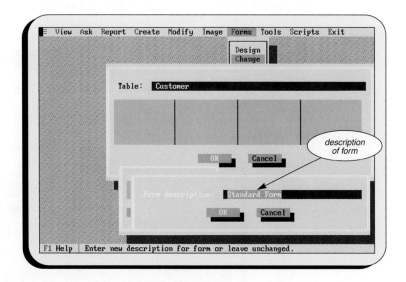

FIGURE 4-53

STEP 4: **Use the BACKSPACE key to erase the current description, type** Customer Maintenance Screen **as the new form description, and press the ENTER key.**

The current form description, Form Design:Customer.F1, displays in the Form Design window (Figure 4-54).

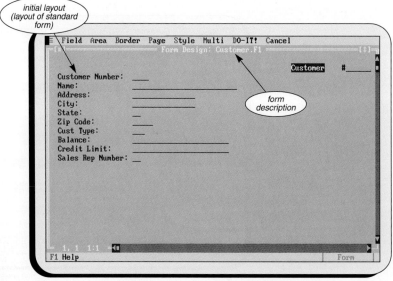

FIGURE 4-54

In the process of modifying the design, you can use the keys shown in Table 4-3.

TABLE 4-3

Key	Purpose
UP ARROW	Moves the cursor up one row.
DOWN ARROW	Moves the cursor down one row.
RIGHT ARROW	Moves the cursor one position to the right.
LEFT ARROW	Moves the cursor one position to the left.
HOME	Moves the cursor to the beginning of the line.
END	Moves the cursor to the end of the line.
CTRL+HOME	Moves the cursor to the first line on the screen.
CTRL+END	Moves the cursor to the last line on the screen.
INSERT	Turns insert mode on and off.
DELETE	Deletes the character at the cursor position.
BACKSPACE	Moves the cursor one position to the left and deletes the character in that position.
CTRL+Y	Deletes all characters to the right of the cursor. If the cursor is in the first position, also removes the line.

Moving Fields and Prompts

To ensure the form corresponds to the one in Figure 4-3 on page P166, you need to move existing fields and prompts. The fields are represented on the screen by the underscores. Whenever you move the cursor into the group of underscores representing a field, the name of the field displays at the left edge of the status bar. A **prompt** is the text that precedes the field on the screen. For example the words Customer Number: (including the colon) are the prompt for the Customer Number field.

To move the fields and their prompts, use the **Area menu** as the following steps illustrate.

TO MOVE THE FIELDS AND PROMPTS

STEP 1: **Use the arrow keys to move the cursor to the S in Sales Rep Number: and then select Area.**

*The Area menu displays (Figure 4-55). The cursor is on the **Move command**, which is used to move an area of the form from one position to another.*

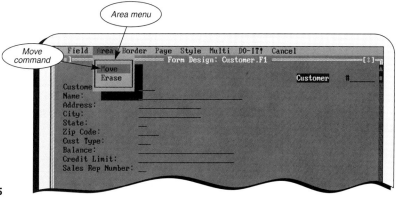

FIGURE 4-55

STEP 2: **Choose Move.**

You now need to indicate the area of the screen to be moved by selecting two opposite corners. If the area consists of a single field, this means you need to select the first and last positions in the field.

STEP 3: **Make sure the cursor is on the S of Sales Rep Number: and press the ENTER key. Use the arrow keys to move the cursor to the last underscore in the Sales Rep Number field and press the ENTER key again.**

The area to be moved has been selected.

STEP 4: **Use the arrow keys to move the field (it will appear as a highlighted box) to the position shown in Figure 4-56 and then press the ENTER key.**

The field is moved to the new position.

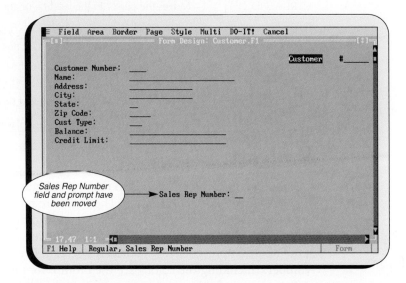

FIGURE 4-56

STEP 5: **Use the techniques illustrated in Steps 1 through 4 to move the Cust Type, Balance, and Credit Limit fields to the positions shown in Figure 4-57. When you select the area, first move the cursor to the C of Cust Type press the ENTER key, then move the cursor to the last underscore in the Credit Limit field, and press the ENTER key again. By doing this, you will be able to move all three fields as a single area.**

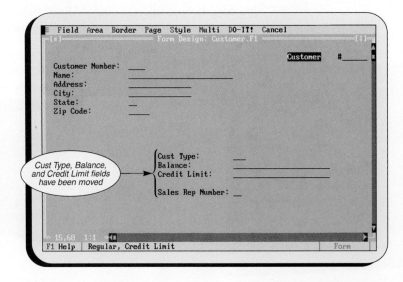

FIGURE 4-57

STEP 6:   Move the Name, Address, City, State, and Zip Code fields to the positions shown in Figure 4-58. Then move the Customer Number field to the position shown in the figure. Notice that you have left blank lines between various logical groups of fields. This groups the Name, Address, City, Street, and Zip Code fields, for example. It also groups the Cust Type, Balance, and Credit Limit fields.

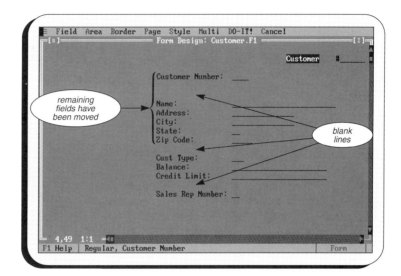

FIGURE 4-58

When you are designing forms, you occasionally will need to insert or remove lines. Paradox contains no commands for doing so. You can effectively insert or remove lines, however, by using the Area menu to either move or erase areas on the screen.

Mouse Users: *After you choose Area|Move, drag over the field to move (Paradox will highlight the selection in blue) and release the left mouse button. Drag the blue highlight to the desired location on the screen.*

Adding Borders

By adding borders to set off important portions, you can improve the look of a form. In this form, you will place a double border around the customer number and a single border around the other fields. To place a border, use the **Border menu**, as the following steps illustrate.

TO PLACE BORDERS ON A FORM

STEP 1:   Choose Border.

The Border menu displays (Figure 4-59). The cursor is on Place, the command to place a border.

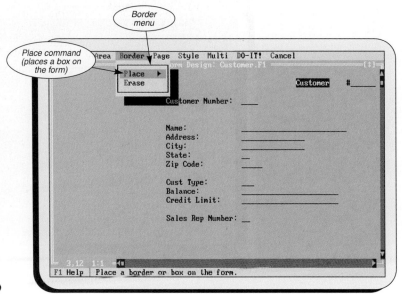

FIGURE 4-59

STEP 2:   Choose the Place command and move the cursor to Double-line.

The menu of border styles displays (Figure 4-60). The cursor is on Double-line.

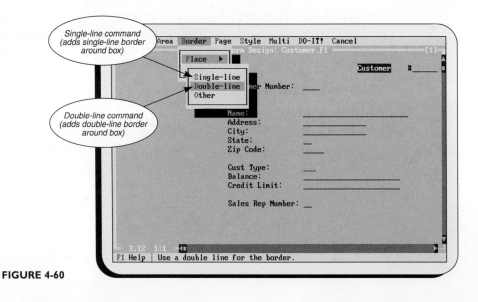

FIGURE 4-60

STEP 3:   Choose Double-line.

STEP 4:   Move the cursor five spaces to the right from the left margin of the line above the line containing the customer number and press the ENTER key.

The upper left-hand corner of the border is selected.

STEP 5: Move the cursor five spaces to the left from the right margin of the line below the line that contains the customer number and press the ENTER key.

The double-line border is now in place (Figure 4-61).

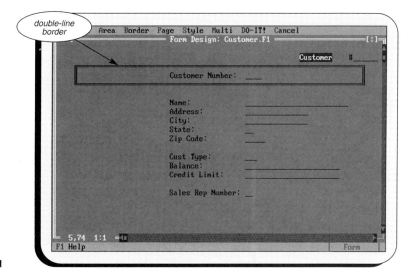

FIGURE 4-61

STEP 6: Use the techniques illustrated in Steps 1 through 5 to add the single-line border shown in Figure 4-62. Be sure to choose Single-line rather than Double-Line.

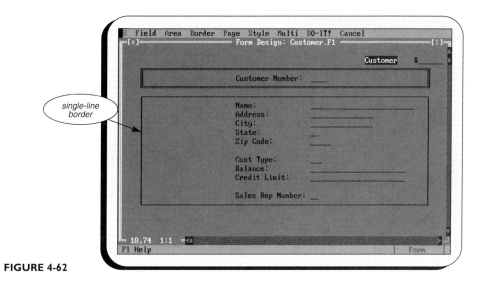

FIGURE 4-62

STEP 7:   Use the techniques illustrated in Steps 1 through 5 to add each of the additional borders shown in Figure 4-63. To add each line, use the same Border option as when you added a border. Simply keep both corners of the border on the same line on the screen.

The border and lines have all been added.

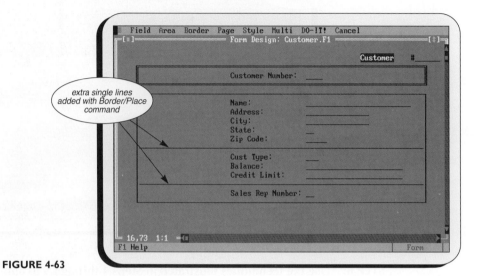

FIGURE 4-63

Mouse Users: *Drag from one corner to the diagonally opposite corner to form the rectangle around which the border is to be placed.*

Saving the Form

To save the form, press F2. If you decide you don't want to save it, you can cancel the changes by selecting Cancel and then selecting Yes. The following step saves the form.

TO SAVE THE FORM

STEP 1:   Press F2.

The form is saved using the filename Customer.F1. This form is available whenever you use the Customer table.

Using the Form

To use a form, first view the table. Then use the **PickForm command** on the Image menu as illustrated in the following steps.

TO USE A FORM

STEP 1:   Choose View and select the Customer table.

STEP 2:   Choose the Image menu and move the cursor to PickForm.

The Customer table displays in Table view (Figure 4-64). The Image menu displays and the cursor is on PickForm, the command to select one of the available forms.

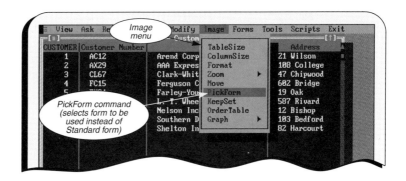

FIGURE 4-64

STEP 3: **Choose the PickForm command and move the cursor to form 1, the Customer Maintenance Screen.**

The list of forms for the Customer table displays (Figure 4-65). The cursor is on form 1.

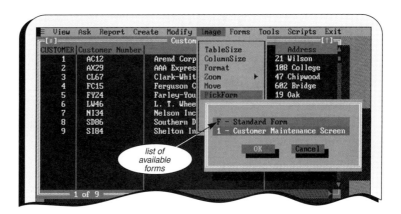

FIGURE 4-65

STEP 4: **Choose form 1.**

The custom form you selected displays in Form view (Figure 4-66). You can now use this form in the same ways you previously used the Standard Form. By pressing the PAGE UP or PAGE DOWN key, you can move from record to record. You can transfer to Edit mode by pressing F9 and then edit data using the form. In other words, the techniques aren't new. The form is just nicer looking.

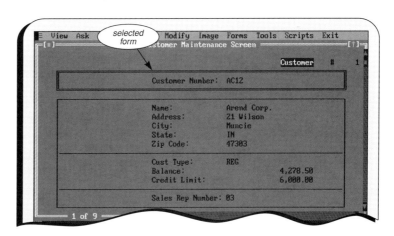

FIGURE 4-66

Assigning the Form as the Default Form

Having to select the custom form every time you want to use it would be very cumbersome. In Paradox, it is easy to use the custom form as the default form. That way, whenever you transfer to Form view, you will see the form you created.

The **KeepSet command**, on the Image menu, saves the current settings for the table. In particular, if you have selected a special form, it will save this information. The next time you access this table through Form view, Paradox will automatically use the custom form. The following steps use the KeepSet command to make the custom form that you created the default form for the Customer table.

TO ASSIGN A CUSTOM FORM AS THE DEFAULT FORM

STEP 1: **Choose Image and move the cursor to KeepSet.**

The Image menu displays (Figure 4-67). The cursor is on KeepSet.

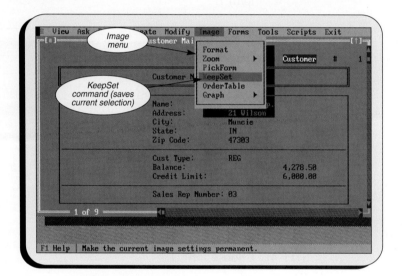

FIGURE 4-67

STEP 2: **Choose the KeepSet command.**

The current settings have now been recorded.

The following step removes all windows from the screen.

TO CLOSE ALL WINDOWS

STEP 1: **Press Alt-F8.**

All windows are removed from the screen.

▼ FORM DESIGN CONSIDERATIONS

As you design and create custom forms, keep in mind the following guidelines.

1. Remember that someone using your form may be looking at the form for several hours at a time. Forms that are excessively cluttered can become very difficult on the eyes.
2. Place the fields in logical groupings. Fields that relate to each other should be close to each other on the form. Consider using borders to emphasize the groupings of related fields.
3. If the data that a user will enter comes from a paper form, make the screen form resemble the paper form as closely as possible.

▼ PROJECT SUMMARY

Project 4 covered the issues involved in presenting the data in a database. In the project, you learned how to create and print reports. Steps and techniques illustrated the purpose of the various bands and how to modify their contents. Using group bands, you also learned how to group in a report. You learned how to create and use custom forms. By performing logical steps, you learned how to move fields, as well as how to add borders and text. Using a form, you viewed and updated data and assigned a custom form as the default form. Finally, you learned some general principles to help you design effective reports and forms.

▼ KEY TERMS

Area menu *(P191)*
#Record command *(P181)*
band *(P168)*
Border menu *(P199)*
Calculated command *(P181, P182)*
Change command *(P185)*
Commas command *(P178)*
Copy command *(P193)*
custom form *(P193)*
Date command *(P181)*
Design command *(P166)*
detail band *(P169)*
detail line *(P169)*
Digits command *(P178)*
Double-line command *(P200)*
Erase command *(P171)*
Field command *(P186)*
Field menu *(P170)*
Form command *(P193)*
Form Designer window *(P193)*
Forms menu *(P195)*
free-form report *(P168)*

group *(P176)*
group band *(P176)*
group footer *(P176)*
group header *(P176)*
Group menu *(P185)*
grouping *(P165)*
Insert command *(P181)*
KeepSet command *(P204)*
Link command *(P187)*
Lookup command *(P187)*
Move command *(P197)*
Output menu *(P173)*
Page command *(P181)*
page footer *(P168)*
page footer band *(P168)*
page header *(P168)*
page header band *(P168)*
PerGroup command *(P190)*
PickForm command *(P202)*
Place command *(P181, P188)*
prompt *(P197)*
Reformat command *(P178)*

reformatting *(P178)*
Regular command *(P181, P188)*
Relink command *(P187)*
Report Designer window *(P166)*
report footer band *(P168)*
report header *(P168)*
report header band *(P168)*
Resize command *(P170)*
SameTable command *(P193)*
Screen command *(P174)*
Sign-Convention command *(P178)*
Single-line command *(P200)*
subtotal *(P165)*
Sum command *(P190)*
Summary command *(P181, P190)*
table band *(P168)*
TableBand menu *(P170)*
tabular report *(P168)*
Time command *(P181)*
Tools menu *(P193)*
Unlink command *(P187)*

....

▼   **QUICK REFERENCE**

In Paradox, you can accomplish a task in a number of different ways. The following table (on the next page) provides a quick reference to each task presented in this project with its available options. The commands listed in the Menu column can be executed using either the keyboard or the mouse.

Task	Mouse	Menu	Keyboard Shortcuts
Add Borders to a Form		From Border menu, choose Place	
Add a Column to a Report		From TableBand menu, choose Insert	
Add a Field to a Report		From Field menu, choose Place; choose type of field	
Add a Group Band to a Report		From Group menu, choose Insert; choose field for grouping	
Add a Line to a Report			Make sure you are in Insert mode and press the ENTER key
Add a Total or Subtotal		From Field menu, choose Place|Summary	
Assign a Form as the Default Form		From Image menu, choose KeepSet	
Change Column Headings			Use arrow keys to move the heading, and then make the change
Change Column Widths	Drag righthand edge of column	From TableBand menu, choose Resize	
Copy a Form		From Tools menu, choose Copy|Form	
Create a Form		Copy Standard Form, then use Form|Change	
Create a Report		From Report menu, choose Design	
Modify a Form or Report Design		From Form or Report menu, choose Change	
Move Fields and Prompts	Drag field or prompt	From Area menu, choose Move	
Print a Report		From Report menu, choose Output	
Reformat a Field		From Field menu, choose Reformat	
Reformat a Column	Click column after selecting	From TableBand menu, choose Erase	
Return to Report or Form Design while Viewing Data		From Exit meu, choose Cancel	Press F2
Save a Form or Report		From Form or Report menu, choose DO-IT!	Press F2
View Data when Designing a		From Output menu, choose Screen	

SHORT ANSWER ASSIGNMENTS

SHORT ANSWER ASSIGNMENT 1
True/False

Instructions: Circle T if the statement is true or F if the statement is false.

T   F   1. To create a report in Paradox, use the Design command on the Report menu.

T   F   2. The initial report design includes all the fields from a table.

T   F   3. To remove a column from a report, use the Remove command on the TableBand menu.

T   F   4. To change the size of a column, use the Resize command on the TableBand menu.

T   F   5. The contents of a Report footer will appear only once on a report.

T   F   6. The Report Designer window uses 9s to indicate that a field is numeric and Xs to indicate that a field is a character field.

T   F   7. To delete a line in a report, make sure the cursor is in the first position in the line and press CTRL+DELETE.

T   F   8. To view a report on the screen, use the View command on the Output menu of the Report Designer window.

T   F   9. To insert a new column into a table band, use the Insert command on the TableBand menu.

T   F   10. To change the number of digits in a numeric field, use the Format command on the Field menu.

T   F   11. To add a field to a report, use the Place command on the Field menu.

T   F   12. To modify an existing report, use the Modify command on the Report menu.

T   F   13. Group bands are used to specify subtotals when you are using the Paradox report feature.

T   F   14. To add a group band to a report, use the Add command on the Group menu.

T   F   15. To include fields from other files in a report, use the Lookup command on the Field menu.

T   F   16. To add borders to a form, use the Position command on the Border menu.

T   F   17. To move fields and prompts on a form, use the Move command on the Area menu.

T   F   18. To assign a custom form as the default form, use the KeepSet command on the Image menu.

T   F   19. To change a form design, use the Modify command on the Forms menu.

T   F   20. To use a custom form to view or update data in a table, choose the Form command from the Image menu.

SHORT ANSWER ASSIGNMENT 2
Multiple Choice

Instructions: Circle the correct response.

1. The process of creating separate collections of records sharing some common characteristic is known as _____.
   a. collecting
   b. matching
   c. grouping
   d. categorizing

2. To create a new report, use the _____ command on the Report menu.
   a. Create
   b. Design
   c. New
   d. Image

3. To remove a column from a report, use the _____ command on the TableBand menu.
   a. Delete
   b. Erase
   c. Remove
   d. Cancel

4. The portions of the Report Designer window (such as report header, page header) are called _____.
   a. segments
   b. areas
   c. portions
   d. bands

5. To delete a line in a report, make sure the cursor is in the first position in the line, and press _____.
   a. CTRL+DELETE
   b. CTRL+Y
   c. CTRL+D
   d. DELETE

6. To view a report on the screen, use the _____ command on the Output menu of the Report Designer window.
   a. View
   b. Screen
   c. ViewData
   d. Display

7. To add a field to a report, use the _____ command on the Field menu.
   a. AddField
   b. Insert
   c. Place
   d. Add

8. To include fields from other files in a report, use the _____ command on the Field menu.
   a. Lookup
   b. TableLookup
   c. FileLookup
   d. AddFile

9. To move fields and prompts on a form, use the Move command on the _____ menu.
   a. Field
   b. Image
   c. Design
   d. Area

10. To assign a custom form as the default form, use the _____ command on the Image menu.
    a. SaveForm
    b. Save
    c. Keep
    d. KeepSet

SHORT ANSWER ASSIGNMENT 3
Understanding the Report Designer Window

Instructions: Figure SA4-3 shows the completed Report Design window for the Customer Report. Use Figure SA4-3 to answer the following questions.

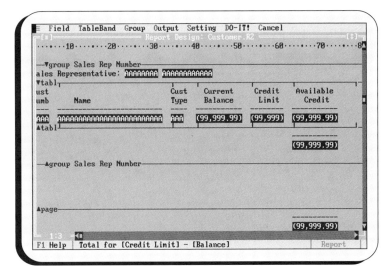

FIGURE SA4-3

1. How many times will the data in the table band print?

   _____

2. How many times will the data in the group header band print?

   _____

3. Which values will print once at the top of every page?

   _____

   _____

4. Which values will print in the report footer?

   _____

   _____

5. Which values will print in the group footer?

   _____

SHORT ANSWER ASSIGNMENT 4
Understanding the Form Designer Window

Instructions: Figure SA4-4 shows the completed design for the Customer Maintenance Form. Use Figure SA4-4 to answer the following questions.

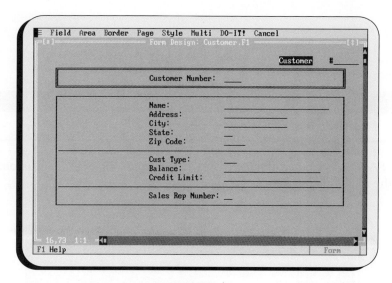

FIGURE SA4-4

1. What are prompts?

_____

_____

2. What are borders ?

_____

_____

3. What command allows you to move fields and prompts?

_____

_____

4. What command saves the form?

_____

_____

5. Are there command(s) to insert and remove lines? What command(s)?

_____

_____

SHORT ANSWER ASSIGNMENT 5

Using the Report Designer Window

Instructions: Figure SA4-5 shows the initial Report Design window for the Slsrep table. Use Figure SA4-5 to explain how to perform the following tasks on the Report Designer window.

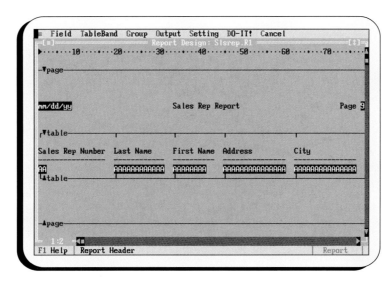

FIGURE SA4-5

1. Change the heading for Sales Rep Number so Sales Rep is on the first line and Number is on the second line.

_____

_____

_____

2. Reduce the width of the Sales Rep Number column.

_____

_____

_____

3. View the report on the screen.

_____

_____

_____

4. Adjust the number of digits in the Commission Rate field.

_____

_____

_____

5. Add a field to the Report footer band to total the sales for all sales reps.

_____

_____

SHORT ANSWER ASSIGNMENT 6
Using the Form Designer Window

Instructions: Figure SA4-6 shows the initial Form Design window for the Slsrep table. Use Figure SA4-6 to explain how to perform the following tasks on the Form Designer window.

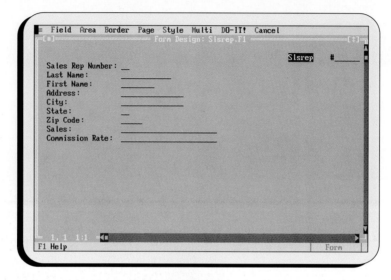

FIGURE SA4-6

1. Place two blank lines between the Sales Rep Number field and the remaining fields on the form.

_____

_____

_____

2. Place a double-line border around the Sales Rep Number.

_____

_____

_____

3. Place a single-line border around the remaining fields.

_____

_____

_____

4. Use the form with the Slsrep table.

_____

_____

_____

5. Make the form the default form for the Slsrep table.

_____

_____

HANDS-ON EXERCISE 1
Using the Help System

Instructions: Perform the following tasks.

1. Start Paradox.

2. Choose the Report|Change command, choose the Customer table, and select the Customer Report to bring the Report Designer window to the screen.

3. Choose the Field menu and with the Field menu on the screen, press the F1 key to access the Help system. The Help window shown in Figure HOE4-1 displays on the screen.

4. Choose Lookup and then choose Link from the menus.

5. Read the information and answer the following question.
   a. Where in a report can you place fields from the Lookup table?

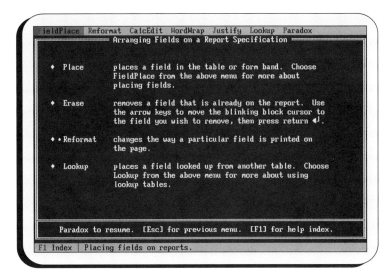

FIGURE HOE 4-1

_____

_____

_____

6. Choose Glossary.

7. Read the information and answer the following question.
   a. What is a dynamic link?

_____

_____

_____

8. Choose Paradox to exit the Help system.

9. Choose Cancel|Yes to close the Report Designer window.

10. Exit Paradox.

HANDS-ON EXERCISE 2

Creating a Report for the Slsrep Table

Instructions: Figure HOE4-2 shows a report design for the Slsrep table. Create the Sales Rep report by performing the following tasks.

1. Start Paradox.

2. Create a report for the Slsrep table. Use SalesRep Report as the report description.

3. Delete the Address, City, State, and Zip Code fields.

4. Design the report so it looks like Figure HOE4-2. Use the guidelines and techniques presented in Project 4.

5. Include a report footer with a total of all sales.

6. Save the report.

7. Print the report.

8. Exit Paradox.

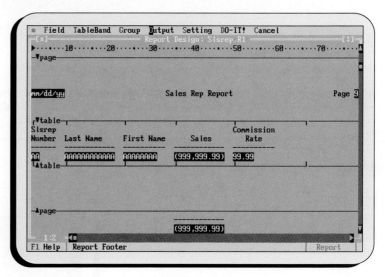

FIGURE HOE 4-2

HANDS-ON EXERCISE 3

Creating a Form for the Slsrep Table

Instructions: Figure HOE4-3 shows a form design for the Slsrep table. Create the Sales Rep form by performing the following tasks.

1. Start Paradox.

2. Copy the Standard Form for the Slsrep table. Change the form description to Sales Rep Maintenance Form.

3. Design the form so it looks like the form in Figure HOE4-3. Use the guidelines and techniques presented in Project 4.

4. Print the form. (Use the SHIFT+PRINT SCREEN keys.)

5. Save the form.

6. Exit Paradox.

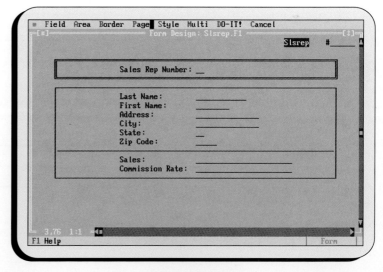

FIGURE HOE 4-3

LABORATORY ASSIGNMENT 1

Presenting Data in the Parts Database

Purpose: To provide practice in creating reports and forms.

Problem: The user of the Parts database needs to be able to present the data in the database as a report and also by using a form on the screen.

Instructions: Use the database created in Laboratory Assignment 1 of Project 1 for this assignment. Execute each task on the computer and print the results.

1. Create a report for the Part table. Use Part Report as the report title.

2. Include all fields in the report. Follow the design guidelines and procedures presented in Project 4 to produce an attractive report similar to the one in Figure LA4-1.

```
10/11/94                      Part Report                      Page   1


Part                          Units    Item   Whouse   Unit
Numb   Part Description      On Hand   Class   Number   Price
----   ------------------    -------   -----   ------   ----------
AX12   IRON                    104      HW       3         24.95
AZ52   DARTBOARD                20      SG       2         12.95
BA74   BASKETBALL                0      SG       1         24.95
BH22   CORNPOPPER               95      HW       3         29.95
BT04   GAS GRILL                11      AP       2        149.99
BZ66   WASHING MACHINE          52      AP       3        399.99
CA14   GRIDDLE                  78      HW       3         39.99
CB03   BIKE                     44      SG       1        299.99
CX11   BLENDER                 112      HW       3         22.95
CZ81   TREADMILL                68      SG       2        349.95
                             ----
                              584
```

FIGURE LA 4-1

3. Include a total of the number of Units on Hand in the report footer.

4. Save the report.

5. Print the report.

6. Copy the Standard Form for the Part table. Change the form description to Part Maintenance Screen.

7. Follow the design guidelines and procedures presented in Project 4 to produce an attractive form.

8. Print the form. (Use the SHIFT+PRINT SCREEN keys.)

9. Save the form.

10. Exit Paradox.

LABORATORY ASSIGNMENT 2
Presenting Data in the Employee Database

Purpose: To provide practice in creating reports and forms.

Problem: The user of the Employee database needs to be able to present the data in the database using two different reports and also by using a form on the screen.

Instructions: Use the database created in Laboratory Assignment 2 of Project 1 for this assignment. Execute each task on the computer and print the results.

1. Create a report for the Employee table. Use Employee Report as the report title.

2. Include all fields except Union Type in the report. Follow the design guidelines and procedures presented in Project 4 to produce an attractive report similar to the one in Figure LA 4-2.

```
10/11/94                        Employee Report                    Page    1


  Emp       Employee       Employee      Dept       Pay
  Numb      Last Name      First Name    Code       Rate
  ----      ---------      ----------    ----       ------
  1011      Rapoza         Anthony        04         8.50
  1013      McCormack      Nigel          04         8.25
  1016      Ackerman       David          01         9.75
  1017      Doi            Chan           03         6.00
  1020      Castle         Mark           04         7.50
  1022      Dunning        Lisa           02         9.10
  1025      Chaney         Joseph         01         8.00
  1026      Bender         Helen          03         6.75
  1029      Anderson       Mariane        04         9.00
  1030      Edwards        Kenneth        03         8.60
  1037      Baxter         Charles        01        11.00
  1041      Evans          John           02         6.00
  1056      Andrews        Robert         02         9.00
  1057      Dugan          Mary           03         8.75
  1066      Castleworth    Mary           03         8.75
                                                     ------
                                                      8.33
```

FIGURE LA 4-2

3. Include the average pay rate of all employees in the report footer.

4. Save the report.

5. Print the report.

6. Create a report that groups records by department code. Use Employee by Dept Report as the report title.

7. Display the department name in the group header. Calculate the average pay rate for each department.

8. Save and print the report.

9. Copy the Standard Form for the Employee table. Change the form description to Employee Maintenance Screen.

10. Follow the design guidelines and procedures presented in Project 4 to produce an attractive form.

11. Print the form. (Use the SHIFT+PRINT SCREEN keys.)

12. Save the form.

13. Exit Paradox.

LABORATORY ASSIGNMENT 3
Presenting Data in the Movie Database

Purpose: To provide practice in creating reports and forms.

Problem: The user of the Movie database needs to be able to present the data in the database using two different reports and also by using a form on the screen.

Instructions: Use the database created in Laboratory Assignment 3 of Project 1 for this assignment. Execute each task on the computer and print the results.

1. Create a report for the Movie table. Use Movie Report as the report title.

2. Include all fields except Length and Director Code in the report. Follow the design guidelines and procedures presented in Project 4 to produce an attractive report similar to the one in Figure LA 4-3.

```
10/11/94                      Movie Report                      Page    1


  Movie                         Year    Movie     Color
  Number    Movie Title         Made    Type      Type
  ------    --------------------  ----    ------    -----
  001       Ann Thompson        1977    COMEDY    COLOR
  002       They Went Away      1964    COMEDY    COLOR
  003       A Crack in Time     1971    SCI FI    COLOR
  004       No Time for Henry   1959    SUSPEN    BW
  005       The Dirty Car       1948    SUSPEN    COLOR
  006       They Know Too Much  1969    HORROR    COLOR
  007       The Old House       1978    DRAMA     COLOR
  008       The Whirling Dervish 1960   HORROR    COLOR
  011       Winston's Dog       1979    COMEDY    COLOR
  012       Escape from Zero    1958    SUSPEN    COLOR
  014       The Ninth Planet    1968    SCI FI    COLOR
  021       A Single Bullet     1939    WESTER    BW
  022       Rear Window         1954    SUSPEN    COLOR
  024       Just Like Me        1940    DRAMA     BW
```

FIGURE LA 4-3

3. Save the report.

4. Print the report.

5. Create a report that groups records by Director Code. Use Movie by Director Report as the report title.

6. Display the Director Name in the group header.

7. Save the report.

8. Print the report.

9. Copy the Standard Form for the Movie table. Change the form description to Movie Maintenance Screen.

10. Follow the design guidelines and procedures presented in Project 4 to produce an attractive form.

11. Print the form. (Use the SHIFT+PRINT SCREEN keys.)

12. Save the form.

13. Copy the Standard Form for the Director table. Change the form description to Director Maintenance Screen.

LABORATORY ASSIGNMENT 3 (continued)

14. Follow the design guidelines and procedures presented in Project 4 to produce an attractive form.

15. Print the form. (Use the SHIFT+PRINT SCREEN keys.)

16. Save the form.

17. Exit Paradox.

LABORATORY ASSIGNMENT 4
Presenting Data in the Book Database

Purpose: To provide practice in creating reports and forms.

Problem: Now that the database in the bookstore where you are employed is totally functional, the owner would like the capability to present the data in the database using reports and also by using attractive screen forms.

Instructions: Use the database created in Laboratory Assignment 4 of Project 1 for this assignment. Execute each task on the computer and print the results.

The bookstore owner has asked you to prepare the following reports:

1. A report of all books in the database. The report does not need to include the cover type, but the owner would like to know the average price of all books in the database.

2. A report of all books grouped by publisher and a report with books grouped by book type. She would like to know the average price of all books in the database and the average by publisher and book type.

The owner has also asked you to provide her with attractive data screens for both the Book and the Publisher tables.

Graphing in Paradox

▼ ## OBJECTIVES

You will have mastered the material in this project when you can:

- Create a graph
- Print a graph
- Change the graph type
- Understand the purpose of a crosstab
- Create a crosstab
- Select different row and column labels for a crosstab
- Create a graph from a crosstab
- Change the titles on a graph

- Change the sizes and fonts on a graph
- Change legends and labels on a graph
- Change fill patterns and markers on a graph
- Explode slices on a pie graph
- Save graph settings
- Create a script to use saved graph settings
- Use a script to display a graph

▼ ## INTRODUCTION

Reports and forms represent important ways of presenting data. In certain circumstances, however, the best way to present data is visually, in the form of a **graph**, also called a **chart**, such as the one shown in Figure 5-1 on the next page. In this graph, there is a bar for each sales representative. The height of the bar represents the total sales for the sales rep. As the graph clearly demonstrates, sales rep 06 has significantly higher sales than either of the other two. This project shows you how to create and modify such graphs.

Another way of presenting data is to summarize data. The data in Figure 5-2 on the following page, for example, shows sales information over three sales periods (for example, over three months). The first column gives the Sales Rep Number of the sales representative who made the sale. The second column gives the Item Class (category) of the part that he or she sold. The possible item classes are AP (appliances), HW (housewares), and SG (sporting goods). The third column gives the Period in which the sale took place. Finally, the fourth column gives the Amount of the sale.

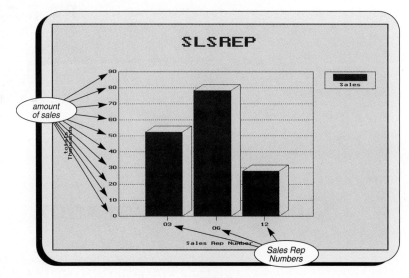

FIGURE 5-1

▶ **SALES INFORMATION**

Sales Rep Number	Item Class	Period	Amount
03	HW	1	15,000.00
03	SG	2	1,280.00
03	HW	2	3,085.56
03	HW	3	5,896.24
03	HW	3	2,000.00
03	SG	1	4,180.95
03	SG	3	5,608.00
03	AP	1	2,108.00
03	AP	3	4,652.00
06	HW	1	8,956.44
06	HW	2	1,406.00
06	HW	3	2,495.50
06	AP	1	5,600.00
06	AP	2	2,106.50
06	SG	1	5,680.00
06	SG	2	0.00
06	SG	3	4,200.00
12	HW	1	3,500.00
12	HW	2	6,504.50
12	HW	3	7,500.25
12	SG	1	4,208.50
12	SG	2	2,680.00
12	SG	3	8,702.00
12	AP	2	5,176.50
12	AP	3	1,248.00

Callouts: Item Class HW (hardware); Sales Rep Number 03; Period 1; Amount of Sales

FIGURE 5-2

The first row in the table in Figure 5-2 indicates that sales rep 03 sold $15,000.00 worth of housewares (Item Class HW) in Period 1. The third row indicates that the same sales rep sold $3,085.56 worth of housewares in Period 2.

If you only want to know the total sales for each sales rep in each period, there is too much data in Figure 5-2. It would be more helpful to view the data in the form shown in Figure 5-3. In Paradox, this type of summary of data is called Crosstab, which stands for *cross-tab*ulation. This project covers the creation and use of Crosstab tables.

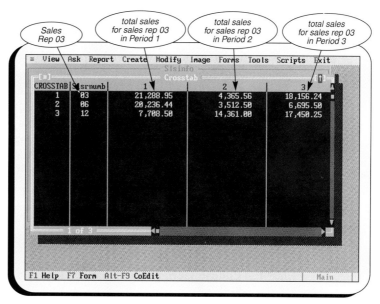

FIGURE 5-3

Just as with data in a regular table, you can graph the data in a Crosstab table you have created. Figure 5-4, for example, shows a graph of the data in the Crosstab table from Figure 5-3. In this figure, each sales rep has three bars, one for each period. Just as with the graph in Figure 5-1, the heights of the bars represent the sales amounts. This project shows how to graph the contents of a Crosstab table as well as how to customize the resulting graph in a variety of ways.

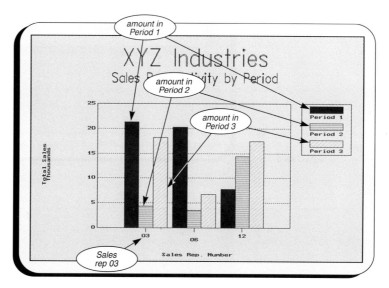

FIGURE 5-4

▼ GRAPHS

In Paradox, creating, modifying, displaying, and printing graphs are all accomplished through the **Graph command** on the Image menu.

Creating a Graph

In this section, you will create the graph shown in Figure 5-1. This graph has sales rep numbers along the **x-axis** (horizontal). The **y-axis** (vertical) represents dollars. The bars on the graph represent sales amounts.

For values on the x-axis, Paradox uses the values in the first column of the table. Because the first column of the Slsrep table is Sales Rep Number, which is correct, no special action needs to be taken.

For the bars, you must use columns that contain numbers. The value of the numbers determine the height of the bars. Because the column for the y-axis, Sales, is a currency type, which is considered numeric, this is not a problem. You do need to indicate the column, however, by moving the cursor to it *before* creating the graph.

To create and view a graph, use the Graph|ViewGraph command on the Image menu. From there, you indicate whether you want to see the graph on the screen, to print it, or to send it to a file. The following steps create a quick graph for the Slsrep table.

TO CREATE A GRAPH

STEP 1: Choose View, press the ENTER key, and move the cursor to Slsrep (Figure 5-5).

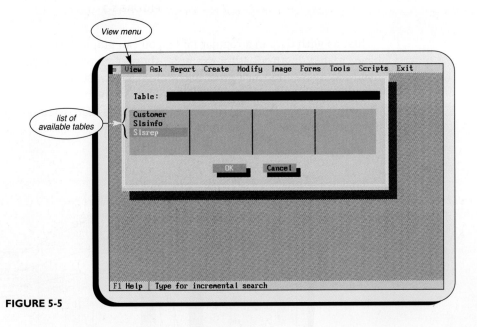

FIGURE 5-5

STEP 2: **Press the ENTER key to select the Slsrep table and then move the cursor to the Sales column. Choose the Image|Graph|ViewGraph command.**

The Slsrep table and the Image menu display (Figure 5-6). The Graph and ViewGraph commands are both selected. The cursor is on the Screen command.

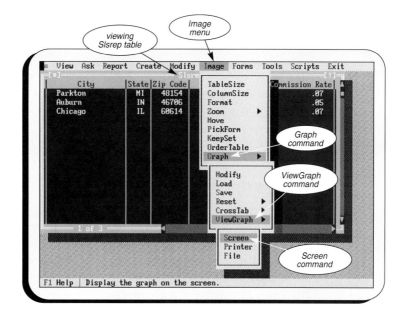

FIGURE 5-6

STEP 3: **Choose the Screen command by pressing the ENTER key.**

The graph displays (Figure 5-7). For each sales representative, there is a bar, representing the amount of sales for that sales representative.

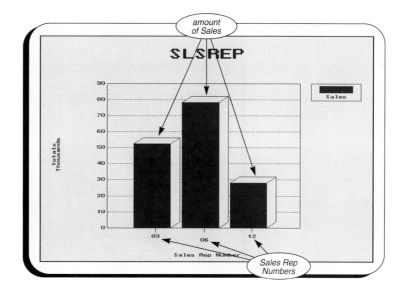

FIGURE 5-7

STEP 4: **Press the ESC key to remove the graph from the screen.**

In general, Paradox includes in the graph the field on which the cursor is located, provided the field is numeric. If it is not numeric, an error message displays. The graph also includes up to four additional fields to the right of the cursor field. The graph will include all the fields until it reaches the end of the list of fields or it reaches a field it cannot include, such as a field that does not contain numbers. In the creation of the graph in the previous steps, that didn't appear to happen. The field immediately to the right of the Sales field is the Commission Rate, which is also numeric, but commission rate is not included in the graph.

To understand why Paradox cannot include the Commission Rate field, consider the values. Because of the range of values in the Sales field, Paradox is forced to use a scale on the y-axis that has a top value of 90,000. The first mark on the y-axis represents 10,000. The values of Commission Rate are .07, .05, and .07. None of these values is large enough to even appear on the graph. Thus, Paradox does not include this field.

Printing the Graph

Printing a graph is accomplished in the same way as displaying one on the screen. Instead of selecting Screen from the Image|Graph|ViewGraph menu commands, you select Printer. (To print appropriately, your printer must have already been selected using the Paradox custom configuration program. Your instructor can tell you if this has already been done. For details on this program, consult the Paradox manuals.) The following steps print the graph.

TO PRINT THE GRAPH

STEP 1: Make sure the Slsrep table is active and the cursor is in the Sales column, then select Image|Graph|ViewGraph and move the cursor to Printer (Figure 5-8).

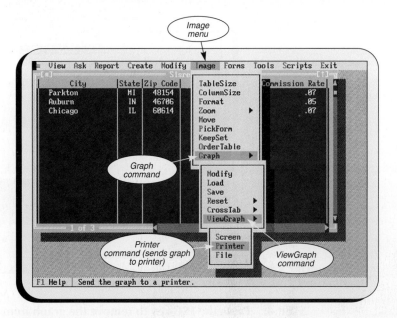

FIGURE 5-8

STEP 2: Select the Printer command by pressing the ENTER key.

A message displays indicating the graph is printing and informing you that you can interrupt printing by pressing the ESC key. The printed graph looks like the one in Figure 5-9.

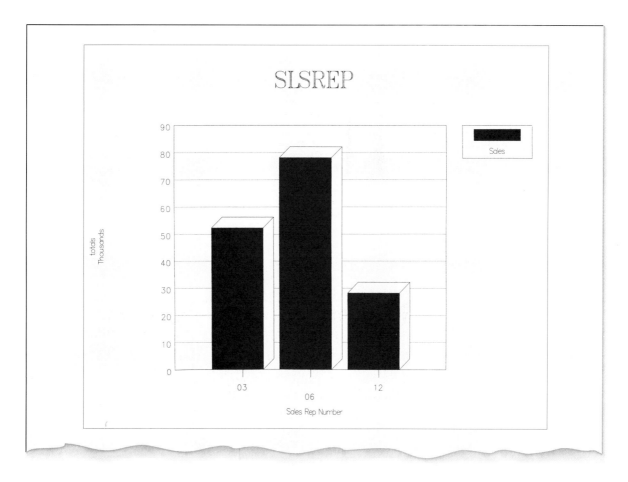

FIGURE 5-9

Changing the Graph Type

To change the characteristics of the graph, use the Image|Graph|Modify command. The following steps change the graph to a **Pie graph**.

TO CHANGE THE GRAPH TYPE

STEP 1: Choose the Image|Graph command and position the cursor on the Modify command (Figure 5-10).

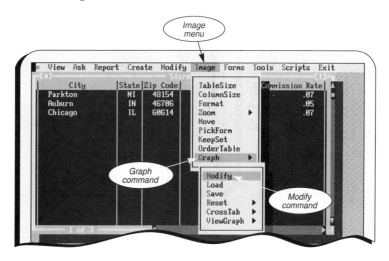

FIGURE 5-10

STEP 2:   Choose the Modify command.

The Customize Graph Type form displays (Figure 5-11). The available graph types display in the Basic Graph Types area on the right of the window. To select a graph type, type the indicated letter. To select Pie Graph, for example, type the letter P.

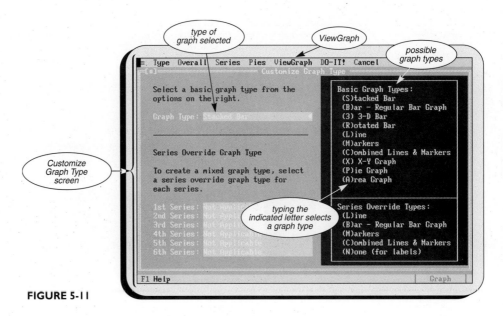

FIGURE 5-11

To return to the regular Paradox screen, you could now press F2 or select DO-IT!, and then select Image|Graph|ViewGraph as you did before. The preferred way, however, is to choose the ViewGraph menu on the menu bar of the Customize Graph Type form.

STEP 3:   Type P **(for Pie Graph) and then choose ViewGraph.**

The graph type is changed to Pie (Figure 5-12). The ViewGraph menu displays and the cursor is on the Screen command.

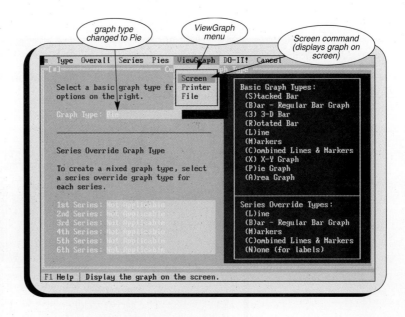

FIGURE 5-12

STEP 4:   Choose the Screen command.

*A pie graph representing the data displays (Figure 5-13). The sales amounts cur-
rently display as asterisks, because the actual numbers will not fit in the space
Paradox has allocated. Later in the project, you will see how to change this.*

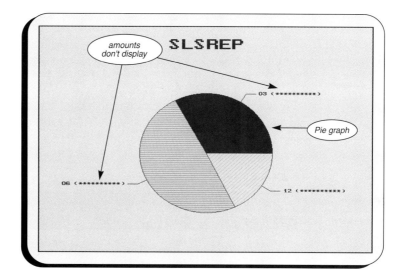

FIGURE 5-13

STEP 5:   Press the ESC key to remove the graph from the screen.

**STEP 6:   Choose Cancel|Yes to remove the Customize Graph Type form from the
            screen.**

▼   **CROSSTABS**

The Need for Crosstabs

Suppose you want to keep sales totals for sales reps over three sales periods (for
example, the first three months of the year). The sales are to be broken down by item
class. That is, you want to record the sales amount for each sales rep in the three item
classes within the organization: appliances (AP), housewares (HW), and sporting
goods (SG). You ultimately want to represent this information graphically. With all
this in mind, how do you structure the data?

One possibility would be to create a table with a single row for each sales rep. In
each row, there would be a sales amount in Period 1 for appliances, a sales amount in
Period 1 for housewares, and a sales amount in Period 1 for appliances. There would
also be similar amounts for Period 2 and for Period 3. Altogether there would be nine
sales amounts.

While this structure might be appropriate for graphing, it is certainly cumbersome.
Further, if you decide to extend the number of periods from three to six, the structure
becomes insufficient. You would have to add several more columns to it. The same
thing would happen if you add additional item classes.

A better approach is to use the structure shown in Figure 5-14 on the next page.
For each sale, there is a row to this table consisting of the sales rep number
(Slsrnumb), the item class (Itemclss), the period in which the sale took place, and the
amount.

▶ **STRUCTURE OF SLSINFO TABLE**

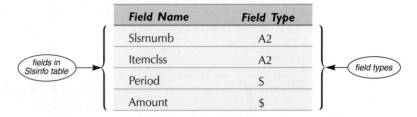

Field Name	Field Type
Slsrnumb	A2
Itemclss	A2
Period	S
Amount	$

FIGURE 5-14

Figure 5-15 shows the data for this table. The first row indicates that Sales Rep 3 sold $15,000.00 worth of housewares (HW) in Period 1. The last row indicates that Sales Rep 12 sold $1,248.00 worth of appliances (AP) in Period 3.

▶ **SALES INFORMATION**

Sales Rep Number	Item Class	Period	Amount
03	HW	1	15,000.00
03	SG	2	1,280.00
03	HW	2	3,085.56
03	HW	3	5,896.24
03	HW	3	2,000.00
03	SG	1	4,180.95
03	SG	3	5,608.00
03	AP	1	2,108.00
03	AP	3	4,652.00
06	HW	1	8,956.44
06	HW	2	1,406.00
06	HW	3	2,495.50
06	AP	1	5,600.00
06	AP	2	2,106.50
06	SG	1	5,680.00
06	SG	2	0.00
06	SG	3	4,200.00
12	HW	1	3,500.00
12	HW	2	6,504.50
12	HW	3	7,500.25
12	SG	1	4,208.50
12	SG	2	2,680.00
12	SG	3	8,702.00
12	AP	2	5,176.50
12	AP	3	1,248.00

Item Class HW (hardware)

Sales Rep Number 03

Period 1

Amount of Sales

data in Slsinfo Table

FIGURE 5-15

Look at the fourth and fifth rows. The fourth indicates that Sales Rep 3 sold $5,896.24 worth of housewares in Period 3. The fifth indicates that the same sales rep sold $2,000.00 of the same item class in the same period. To obtain the total amount of housewares Sales Rep 3 sold in Period 3, you would need to add these two amounts together, resulting in $7,896.24.

While this may be the best way to store the data, this form is certainly not suitable for graphing. Fortunately, Paradox furnishes a way to convert this data to a form that is suitable. To do so, you create a Crosstab table.

In the first Crosstab you will create, there is to be a row for each sales rep. Another way of saying this is that the sales rep numbers will be the **Crosstab row labels**. This first Crosstab totals the sales amounts in each item class, without regard for the periods in which the sales took place. In other words, the values in the Itemclss field will be the column labels.

Creating a Crosstab

Although Crosstabs are a valuable tool in general, they are most useful in connection with graphs. Thus, the option to create Crosstabs appears on the Image|Graph menu. The following steps create a Crosstab table.

TO CREATE A CROSSTAB

STEP 1: Create the Slsinfo table using the structure shown in Figure 5-14 and the data shown in Figure 5-15. (You can also load it from the PDOX45 subdirectory on the Student Diskette). Open the Slsinfo table.

The Slsinfo table displays in a window (Figure 5-16).

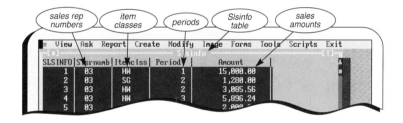

FIGURE 5-16

STEP 2: Choose the Image|Graph command and move the cursor to the CrossTab command (Figure 5-17).

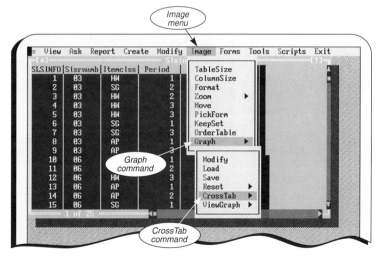

FIGURE 5-17

STEP 3:   Choose the CrossTab command.

A list of commands displays from which you can choose how values are to be combined (Figure 5-18). You can choose to add them together (Sum), take the smallest (Min), take the largest (Max), or simply count them (Count). In this case, they should be added together, so choose Sum. In most cases, the common choice is Sum.

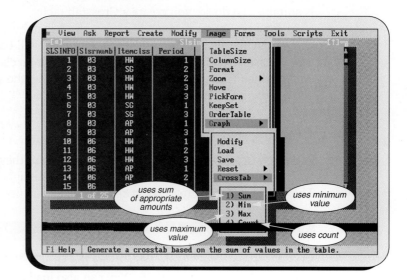

FIGURE 5-18

STEP 4:   Choose Sum.

A Paradox message instructs you to move to the column to be used for row labels and then press ENTER (Figure 5-19).

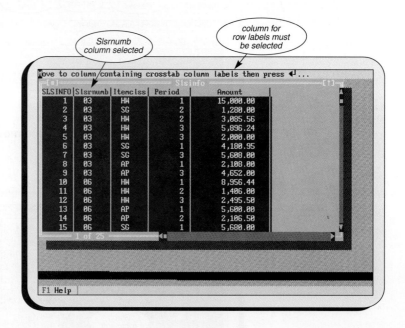

FIGURE 5-19

STEP 5:   Move the cursor to the Slsrnumb column and then press the ENTER key.

A Paradox message instructs you to move to the column containing the crosstab column labels and then press ENTER (Figure 5-20).

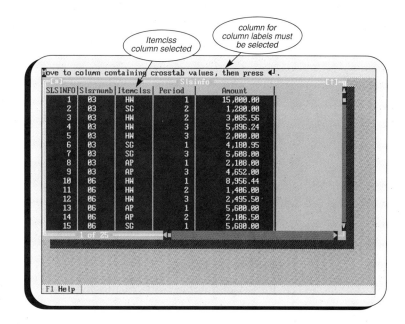

FIGURE 5-20

STEP 6:   Move the cursor to the Itemclss column and then press the ENTER key.

A Paradox message instructs you to move to the column containing the crosstab values.

STEP 7:   Move the cursor to the Amount column and press the ENTER key.

The Crosstab table displays (Figure 5-21). There is a row for each sales rep. The item classes are the column labels. Paradox has automatically combined the three periods and calculated the appropriate totals.

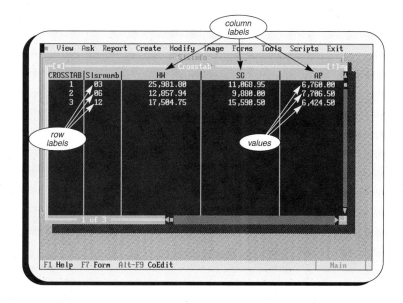

FIGURE 5-21

STEP 8:   Press F8 to remove the image of the Crosstab table from the screen.

Using a Crosstab

The results of creating a Crosstab are placed in a temporary table called Crosstab. It is similar in many ways to the Answer table you obtained earlier from queries. It exists only until you leave Paradox or create another Crosstab. In Project 2, you learned how to create and use reports for the Answer table for a particular query. You also saw how to automate the process with scripts. The same techniques apply to the Crosstab table.

Creating Additional Crosstabs

From the data in the Slsinfo table, you can create a variety of Crosstabs. The following steps create additional Crosstabs that summarize the data in a variety of ways.

TO CREATE ADDITIONAL CROSSTABS

STEP 1:   The Slsinfo table should still be on the screen. If not, use the View command to open it.

STEP 2:   Choose the Image|Graph|CrossTab command.

STEP 3:   Choose Sum.

STEP 4:   Select the row labels by moving the cursor to the Slsrnumb column and then pressing the ENTER key.

STEP 5:   Select the column labels by moving the cursor to the Period column and then pressing the ENTER key.

STEP 6:   Select the Crosstab values by moving the cursor to the Amount column and pressing the ENTER key.

The Crosstab displays (Figure 5-22). The period numbers are now used as the column labels.

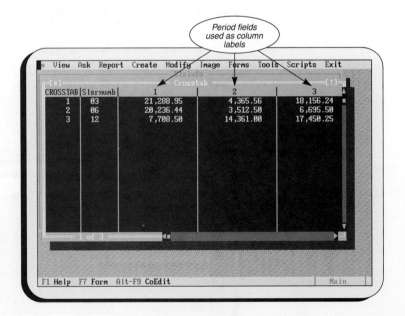

FIGURE 5-22

STEP 7: Press F8 to remove the Crosstab from the screen. Create a Crosstab, this time selecting Itemclss for the row labels, Period for the column labels, and Amount for the crosstab values.

The Crosstab displays (Figure 5-23). The row labels are not just the item classes, but the combination of sales rep numbers and item classes.

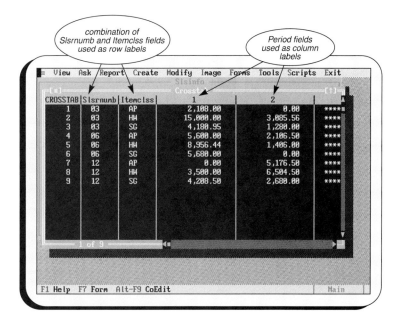

FIGURE 5-23

The combination of sales rep numbers and item classes used for row labels is due to the scheme Paradox uses to determine row labels. It takes the column you select along with any columns to its left. Because Slsrnumb is the first column, this rule did not affect the previous Crosstabs. This time, however, it gives the combination you see in Figure 5-23.

If you wanted sales figures by the sales rep/item class combination, then the Crosstab you just created is correct. If you only want sales by item class, however, they would not be. You need to make Itemclss the first column in the table. Fortunately, there is an easy way to change the order of columns.

Pressing CTRL+R rotates the collection of columns consisting of the column in which the cursor is located and all columns to its right. You can use this property to change the order of the columns to any order you want. Move the cursor to the first column and press CTRL+R until the column that you want to be first has moved into position. You could, if need be, then move to the second column and repeat the process, and so on.

In this case, the only thing that is important is that the Itemclss column is first. The order of the remaining columns is not critical for the creation of the Crosstab.

STEP 8: Press F8 to remove the Crosstab from the screen. Move the cursor to the Slsrnumb column. Press CTRL+R until the Itemclss column is at the beginning of the table.

STEP 9: Once again create a Crosstab, selecting Itemclss for the row labels and Period for the column labels.

The Crosstab displays (Figure 5-24). The Crosstab contains only item classes for the row labels.

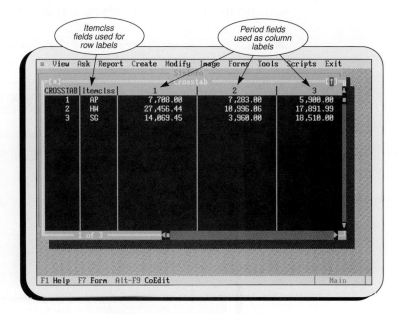

FIGURE 5-24

STEP 10: Press F8 to remove the Crosstab table from the screen.

As a final example, you want to break down item class sales figures by sales rep instead of by period. Thus, sales rep numbers will be used for column labels.

STEP 11: Create a Crosstab, selecting Itemclss for the row labels and Slsrnumb for the column labels.

The Crosstab displays (Figure 5-25).

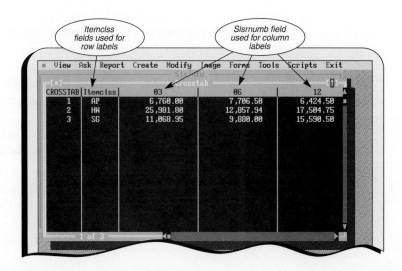

FIGURE 5-25

STEP 12: Press F8 to remove the image of the Crosstab table from the screen.

▼   **ADVANCED GRAPHING**

When creating a graph, be guided by the following general procedure.

1. Activate the table you will use for the graph. If you need a Crosstab for the graph, create the Crosstab.
2. Make sure the column to be used for the x-axis is the first column in the table. If it is not, use CTRL+R to rotate the columns appropriately.
3. Make sure the cursor is in the first numeric column to be used for values in the graph. If other numeric columns are also to be used, make sure they immediately follow the first one. If not, use CTRL+R to move the columns appropriately.
4. Choose Image|Graph|Modify.

Creating the Initial Graph

The following examples use the Crosstab shown in Figure 5-26. Performing the steps creates the necessary Crosstab.

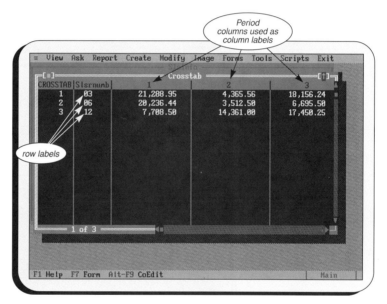

FIGURE 5-26

TO CREATE THE CROSSTAB

STEP 1:   **Make sure the Slsrnumb column is at the beginning of the Slsinfo table. If not, use CTRL+R to get it there.**

STEP 2:   **Create the crosstab shown in Figure 5-26. It uses the Slsinfo table. The row labels come from the Slsrnumb column and the column labels come from the Period column.**

The values in the Slsrnumb column will be used for the x-axis. Because Slsrnumb is already the first column, no movement of columns is necessary. The values in the columns labeled 1, 2, and 3 will be used for the y-axis. Because these columns are already next to each other, you need only to make sure the cursor is in the first of the columns. The following steps create an initial bar graph.

TO CREATE THE INITIAL BAR GRAPH

STEP 1:   Make sure the cursor is in the column labeled 1.

STEP 2:   Choose the Image|Graph command (Figure 5-27).

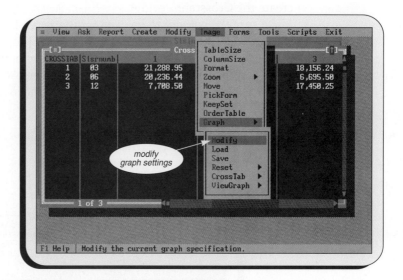

FIGURE 5-27

STEP 3:   Choose the Modify command and then type the letter B to change the graph type to Bar.

The Customize Graph Type form displays (Figure 5-28). The graph type is Bar.

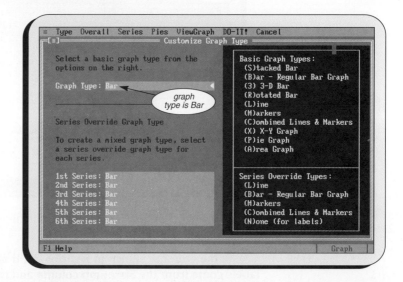

FIGURE 5-28

STEP 4:   View the graph by selecting the ViewGraph|Screen command.

*The graph displays (Figure 5-29). The title at the top of graph indicates that the data comes from the Crosstab table. The series elements, or descriptions, in the small box on the right are called the **legend**. The legend indicates the meaning of the different types of shading in the bars. The first category (the number 1 under the first small strip), for example, indicates that the bars with the dark shading represent sales for Period 1.*

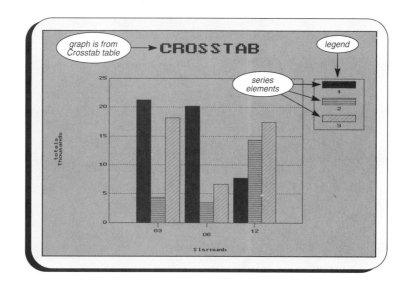

FIGURE 5-29

Changing Titles

In the initial graph design, the title of the graph, CROSSTAB, and the titles for the x-axis and y-axis are not particularly descriptive. To change the titles, use the **Titles command** on the **Overall menu** as shown in the following steps.

TO CHANGE THE TITLES

STEP 1:   Press the ESC key to remove the graph from the screen. Choose Overall from the menu bar on the Customize Graph Type form.

The Overall menu displays and the cursor is on Titles (Figure 5-30).

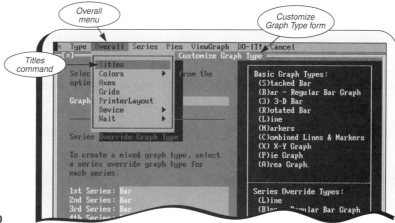

FIGURE 5-30

STEP 2:   Choose the Titles command.

The Customize Graph Titles form displays (Figure 5-31). On this form, you can enter a first and second line of titles for the graph; you can also enter titles for the x and y axes; you can change the size of the titles; and you can change the font for the main titles. The Fonts box lists the available font styles, and the Sizes box lists the available font sizes.

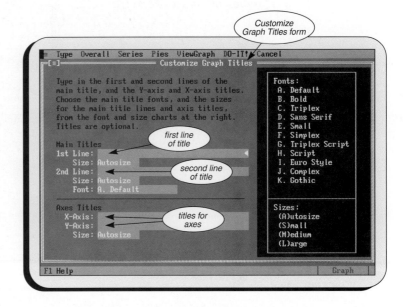

FIGURE 5-31

STEP 3:   Enter the 1st line title, the 2nd line title, the x-axis title, and the y-axis title as shown in Figure 5-32 pressing the TAB key after making each entry.

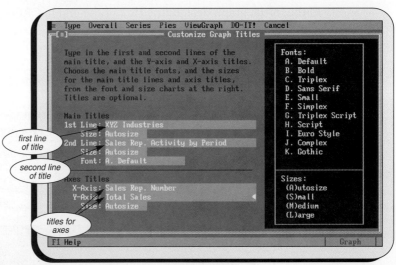

FIGURE 5-32

STEP 4: Choose ViewGraph|Screen to view the result.

The graph displays (Figure 5-33). The titles have been changed.

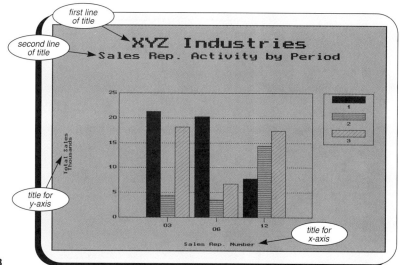

FIGURE 5-33

Changing Sizes and Fonts

To enhance the appearance of a graph, you can change the size of the characters in the titles as well as the **fonts** used for the titles. The following steps change the sizes and fonts (shapes of the characters) for the titles in the graph.

TO CHANGE SIZES AND FONTS

STEP 1: Press the ESC key to remove the graph from the screen.

STEP 2: Change the sizes and fonts for the main titles to those shown in Figure 5-34.

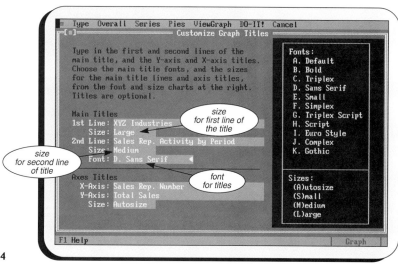

FIGURE 5-34

STEP 3: **Choose ViewGraph|Screen.**

The graph displays (Figure 5-35). The letters in the main titles appear with a different font and a different size from before.

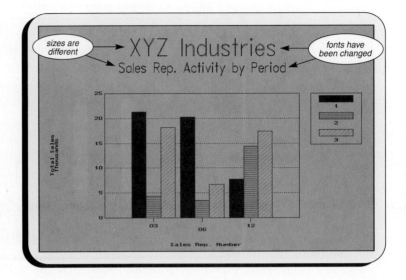

FIGURE 3-35

STEP 4: **Press the ESC key to remove the graph from the screen.**

Special Customizations

To further customize a graph, you can change the color scheme used on the screen by choosing Overall|Colors|Screen (Figure 5-36).

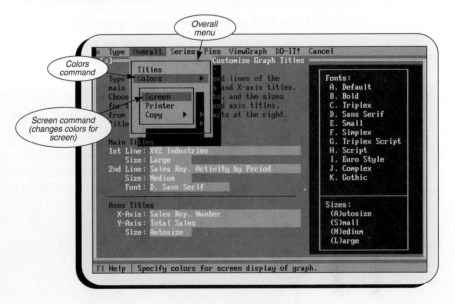

FIGURE 5-36

The Customize Graph Screen Colors form displays as shown in Figure 5-37. To change the color of any portion of the screen, use the arrow keys to move the cursor to the appropriate position and type the letter corresponding the color you want.

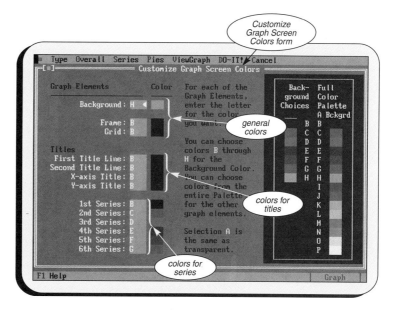

FIGURE 5-37

To change the characteristics of the axes, choose Overall|Axes (Figure 5-38). On the Customize Graph Axes form, you can then change the scaling of either axis. You can also change the way the tick marks on the axes are formatted.

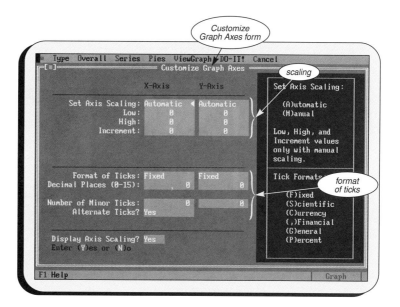

FIGURE 5-38

By choosing Overall|Grids, you can change the use of grid lines as well as the framing of the graph (Figure 5-39). On the Customize Grids and Frames form, you make changes by moving the cursor to the appropriate location and then typing the letter or number of your choice.

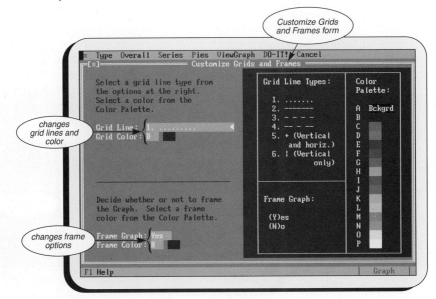

FIGURE 5-39

To customize the way the graph will be printed on the printer, choose Overall|Device|Print (Figure 5-40).

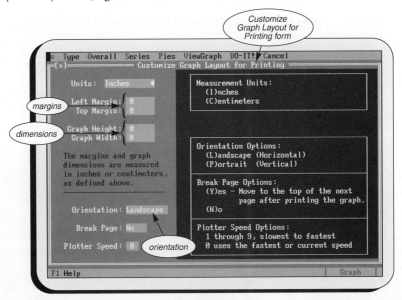

FIGURE 5-40

Customizing Legends and Labels

The legend contains the descriptions given for the various bars in the graph. **Labels** are the specific amounts the bars represent. Placing labels on a graph means that the number the bar represents will appear on the graph near the bar. To customize legends or labels, use the **Series|LegendsAndLabels command** as illustrated in the following steps.

TO CUSTOMIZE LEGENDS AND LABELS

STEP 1:   Choose Series|LegendsAndLabels.

The Customize Series Legends and Labels form displays (Figure 5-41).

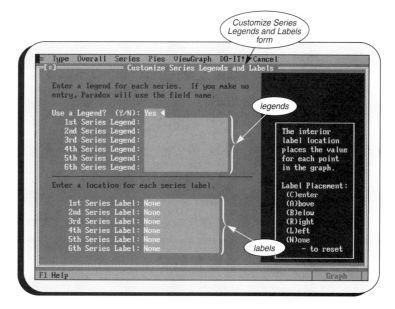

FIGURE 5-41

STEP 2:   Type the legends shown in Figure 5-42.

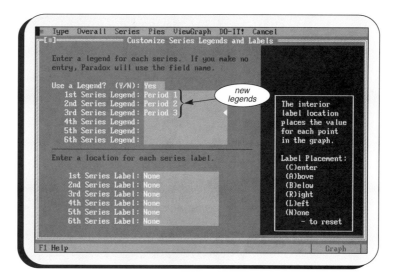

FIGURE 5-42

STEP 3: **Choose ViewGraph|Screen.**

The graph displays (Figure 5-43). The series legends you entered display in the legend box to the right of the graph.

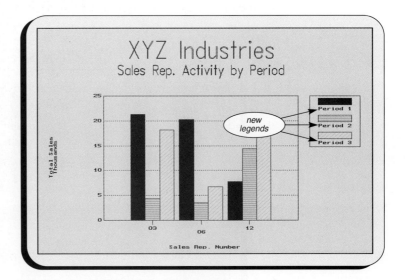

FIGURE 5-43

Customizing Fill Patterns

To customize the patterns that Paradox uses for the series bars, called **fill patterns,** choose Series|MarkersAndFills. The Customize Series Markers and Fills form displays. You change a fill pattern for a series by typing the letter of the new fill pattern.

TO CUSTOMIZE FILL PATTERNS

STEP 1: **Press the ESC key to remove the graph from the screen.**

STEP 2: **Choose Series and move the cursor to MarkersAndFills.**

The Series menu displays (Figure 5-44). The cursor is on MarkersAndFills.

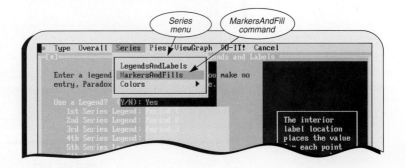

FIGURE 5-44

STEP 3: **Choose the MarkersAndFills command.**

The Customize Series Markers and Fills form displays (Figure 5-45).

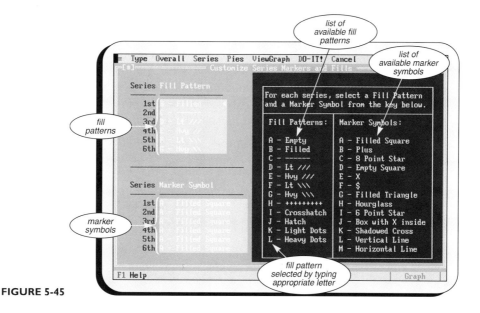

FIGURE 5-45

STEP 4:   Change the fill patterns to the ones shown in Figure 5-46.

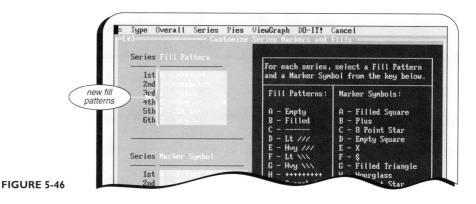

FIGURE 5-46

STEP 5:   Choose ViewGraph|Screen.

The graph displays (Figure 5-47). It includes the new fill patterns.

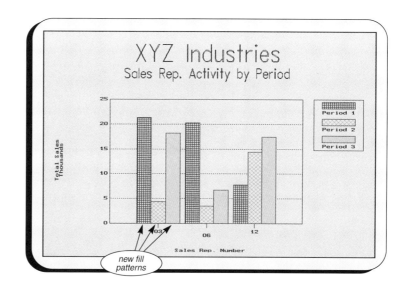

FIGURE 5-47

The various changes made to the bar graph apply to graphs of other types as well. To see this, press the ESC key to remove the graph from the screen, choose **Type**, to change the graph type, and then choose ViewGraph|Screen. The following figures illustrate the results.

Figure 5-48 shows a **stacked bar graph**. The bars representing a sales rep's sales in each of the three periods are *stacked* on top of each other. The height of the resulting bar then represents the total sales for the sales rep.

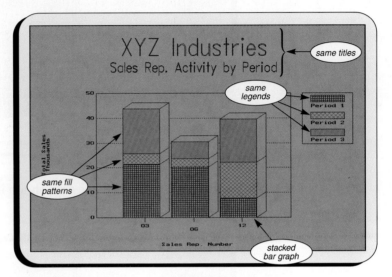

FIGURE 5-48

Figure 5-49 shows a **3D bar graph**. **3D** stands for three-dimensional.

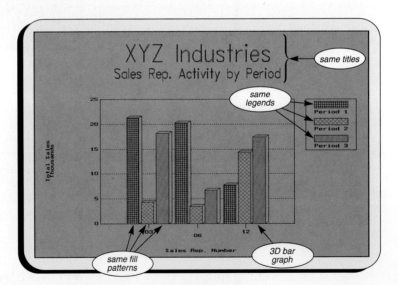

FIGURE 5-49

Figure 5-50 shows a **rotated bar graph**. The graph has been rotated 90 so the roles of the x-axis and y-axis axes are reversed.

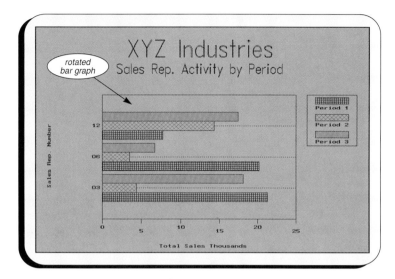

FIGURE 5-50

Instead of representing the values with bars, they can be represented by points which are then joined by lines. Such a graph, called a **line graph**, is shown in Figure 5-51.

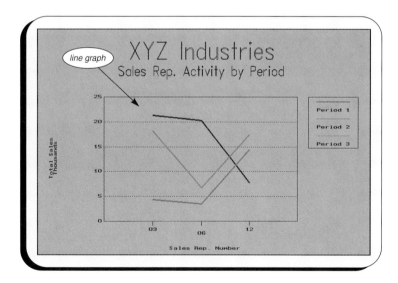

FIGURE 5-51

In some graphs, the points without the lines are important. You can often emphasize the points by representing them with special symbols called **markers**. This type of graph is called a **markers graph** (Figure 5-52 on the next page). In the markers graph, the differences in fill patterns are not particularly obvious. You can make them more noticeable by changing the marker symbols as shown in the following steps.

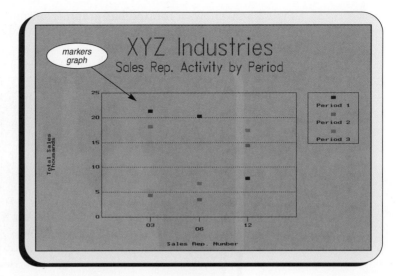

FIGURE 5-52

TO CUSTOMIZE MARKERS

STEP 1: Press the ESC key to remove the graph from the screen. Change the graph to a markers graph. (If you tried all the graph types in the previous section, you already have a markers graph.)

STEP 2: Choose Series|MarkersAndFills and then change the marker symbols to the ones shown in Figure 5-53.

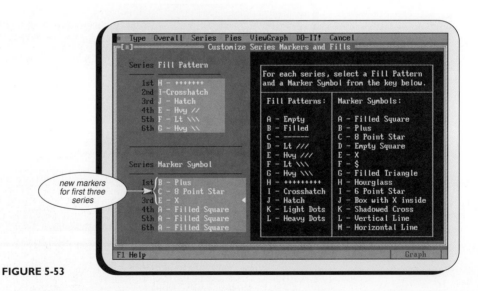

FIGURE 5-53

STEP 3: Choose ViewGraph|Screen.

The graph displays (Figure 5-54). The difference in markers is now more noticeable.

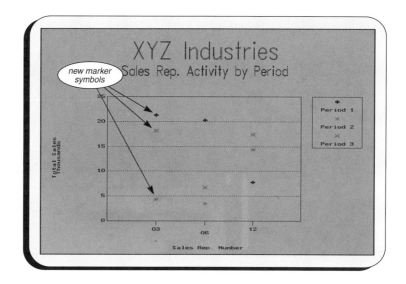

FIGURE 5-54

STEP 4:   Press the ESC key to remove the graph from the screen.

Customizing Pie Graphs

With pie graphs, Paradox allows you to make some special changes. In particular, you can change the patterns in each of the slices. You can also choose to **explode** one of the slices, that is, to have it stand out from the rest of the pie. The following steps customize a pie graph.

TO CUSTOMIZE A PIE GRAPH

STEP 1:   Choose Type and then change the type of the graph to Pie. Choose the Pies command.

The Customize Pie Graph form displays (Figure 5-55).

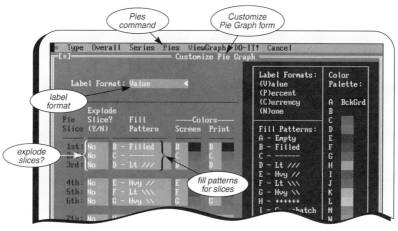

FIGURE 5-55

STEP 2:   Change the Label Format to Currency by typing the letter C̲. Use the TAB key
to move the cursor to the Explode Slice? (Y/N) entry for the 2nd slice and
change the No to Yes by typing the letter Y. Move the cursor to the Fill Pattern
entry for the third slice and change the pattern to Crosshatch by typing the
letter I.

The changes are made (Figure 5-56).

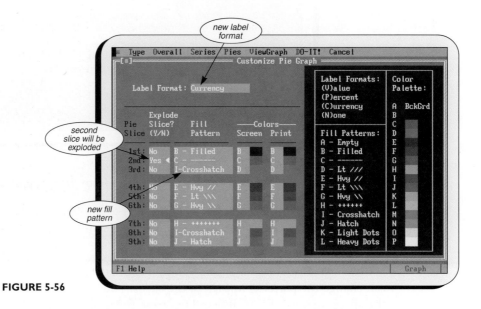

FIGURE 5-56

STEP 3:   Choose ViewGraph|Screen.

*The graph displays (Figure 5-57). The labels display in currency format, the second
slice is exploded, and the third slice has a crosshatch fill pattern.*

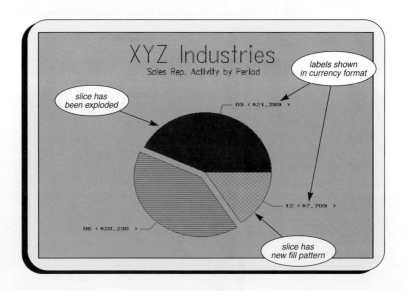

FIGURE 5-57

STEP 4:   Press the ESC key to remove the graph from the screen.

STEP 5:   Choose Cancel|Yes to return to the Crosstab table.

Saving the Graph Settings

Once you have customized a graph, you often want to save the **graph settings**, that is, the particular options you have selected, for future use. To save the settings, use the Image|Graph|Save command and then assign a name to the file that will contain these settings. The following steps save the graph settings in a file called slsrper (for sales rep by period).

TO SAVE THE GRAPH SETTINGS

STEP 1: Choose Image|Graph|Save and then type `slsrper` as the name of the file containing the current graph settings (Figure 5-58).

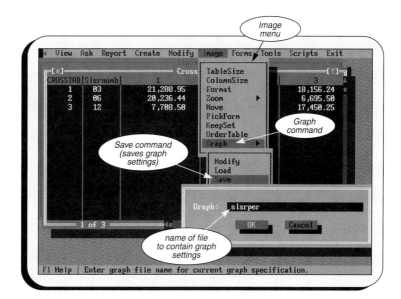

FIGURE 5-58

STEP 2: Press the ENTER key to save the settings.

STEP 3: Press ALT+F8 to close all windows.

Resetting Graph Settings

After you have changed graph settings, they remain in effect until you exit Paradox or reset them. This can produce unexpected results when you want to begin a new graph and don't realize that some special settings are in place. The easiest way to avoid any problems is to reset the settings before beginning a new graph by using the Reset command. The following step resets the graph settings.

TO RESET THE GRAPH SETTINGS

STEP 1: Choose Image|Graph|Reset|OK.

Creating a Script to Use the Graph

To use the graph settings in the future, you first create the appropriate Crosstab table. Choosing Image|Graph|Load and selecting slsrper, you can then view or print the graph and the graph will reflect the settings you just created in the previous section.

You can create a script to automate the whole process of creating the Crosstab table, loading the graph settings, and displaying the graph. The following steps create the script.

TO CREATE A SCRIPT TO DISPLAY THE GRAPH

STEP 1:   **Choose Scripts|BeginRecord and then type** `slsrper` **(Figure 5-59).**

FIGURE 5-59

STEP 2:   **Choose View and select the Slsinfo table.**

The Slsinfo table displays (Figure 5-60).

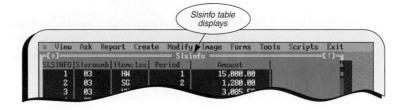

FIGURE 5-60

STEP 3:   **Choose the Image|Graph|CrossTab command.**

The menu of possible operations for the Crosstab table displays (Figure 5-61).

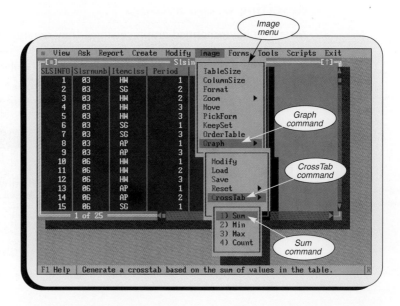

FIGURE 5-61

STEP 4: Press the ENTER key to choose Sum, select the Slsrnumb field for row labels, the Period field for column labels, and the Amount field for values.

The Crosstab displays (Figure 5-62).

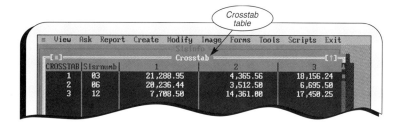

FIGURE 5-62

STEP 5: Choose the Image|Graph command and move the cursor to Load (Figure 5-63).

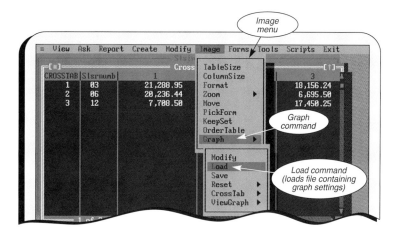

FIGURE 5-63

STEP 6: Choose the Load command, select the Slsrper file, and then choose the Image|Graph|ViewGraph command.

The file containing the graph settings is loaded, although the screen does not show any evidence of this fact. The Image|Graph|ViewGraph command is selected, and the cursor is on the Screen command (Figure 5-64).

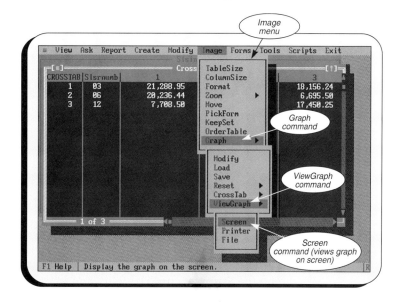

FIGURE 5-64

STEP 7: **Choose the Screen command.**

The graph displays (Figure 5-65).

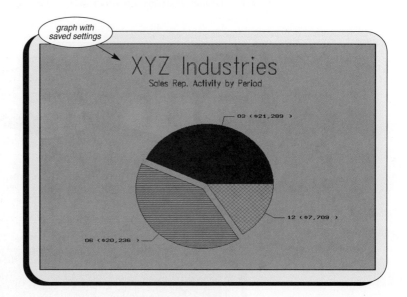

FIGURE 5-65

STEP 8: **Press the ESC key to remove the graph, then choose Scripts and move the cursor to End-Record (Figure 5-66).**

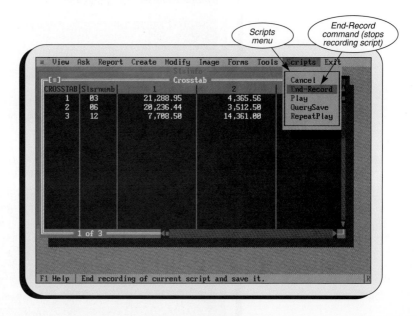

FIGURE 5-66

STEP 9: **Choose the End-Record command and then press ALT+F8 to remove the Slsinfo and Crosstab tables from the screen.**

The script is saved and the tables no longer display.

Using the Script

Once you have created a script, you can use it in the future by choosing the Play command on the Scripts menu. The following steps use the script just created.

TO USE THE SCRIPT

STEP 1:   Choose the Scripts|Play command and move the cursor to Slsrper (Figure 5-67).

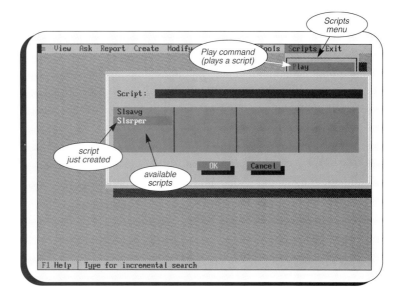

FIGURE 5-67

STEP 2:   Press the ENTER key to select Slsrper.

The graph displays (Figure 5-68).

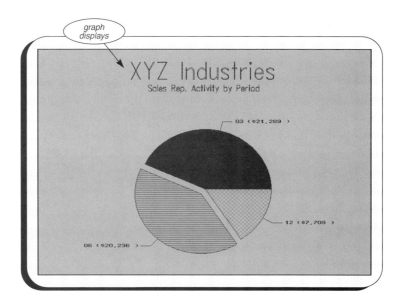

FIGURE 5-68

STEP 3:   Press the ESC key to remove the graph and then press ALT+F8 to remove the windows containing the Slsinfo and Crosstab tables.

The graph and the tables no longer display.

▼ **PROJECT SUMMARY**

Project 5 introduced you to graphing the contents of a table using Paradox. The project presented steps and techniques showing you how to create and modify graphs, how to create Crosstabs to summarize data in a variety of ways, and how to graph the contents of a Crosstab. Using the capabilities of Paradox, you learned how to save the settings for a graph you created and also to create a script that would use the graph settings that you previously saved.

▼ **KEY TERMS**

3D bar graph *(P246)*
Axes command *(P241)*
bar graph *(P236)*
BeginRecord command *(P252)*
chart *(P219)*
Colors command *(P240)*
Crosstab *(P227)*
Crosstab column label *(P231)*
CrossTab command *(P229)*
Crosstab row label *(P229)*
Device command *(P242)*
End-Record command *(P254)*
explode slice *(P249)*
fill pattern *(P244)*
font *(P239)*

graph *(P219)*
Graph command *(P222)*
graph settings *(P251)*
Grids command *(P242)*
label *(P242)*
legend *(P237)*
LegendsAndLabels command *(P242)*
line graph *(P247)*
Load command *(P252)*
markers *(P247)*
MarkersAndFills command *(P244)*
markers graph *(P247)*
Modify command *(P225)*
Overall menu *(P237)*

Pie graph *(P225)*
Pies command *(P249)*
Reset command *(P251)*
rotated bar graph *(P247)*
Save command *(P251)*
Screen command *(P223)*
Series menu *(P242)*
stacked bar graph *(P246)*
title *(P237)*
Titles command *(P237)*
Type menu *(P246)*
ViewGraph menu *(P223)*
x-axis *(P222)*
y-axis *(P222)*

▼ **QUICK REFERENCE**

In Paradox, you can accomplish a task in a number of different ways. The following table provides a quick reference to each task presented in this project with its available options. The commands listed in the Menu column can be executed using either the keyboard or the mouse.

Task	Mouse	Menu	Keyboard Shortucts
Change Colors on a Graph		From Overall menu, choose Colors	
Change Fill Patterns and/or Markers		From Series menu, choose MarkersAndFills	
Change a Graph Type		From Image menu, choose Graph|Modify	
Change Legends and/or Labels		From Series menu, choose LegendsAndLabels	
Change Title on a Graph		From Overall menu, choose Titles	
Create a Crosstab		From Image menu, choose Graph|Crosstab	Press ALT+X
Create a Graph		From Image menu, choose Graph|ViewGraph	Press CTRL+F7

Task	Mouse	Menu	Keyboard Shortucts
Create a Script		From Scripts menu, choose BeginRecord, enter key-strokes for script; from Scripts	
Explode a Slice of a Pie Graph		Choose Customize Pie Graph menu, choose Pies	
Play a Script		From Scripts menu, choose play	
Print a Graph		From Image menu, choose Graph|ViewGraph|Printer	
Rotate Columns in a			Press CTRL+R
Save Graph Settings		From Image menu, choose Graph|Save	
Use a Saved Graph		From Image menu, choose Graph|Load	
View a Graph from the Customize Graph Type Form		From ViewGraph menu, choose Screen	

SHORT ANSWER ASSIGNMENTS

SHORT ANSWER ASSIGNMENT 1
True/False

Instructions: Circle T if the statement is true or F if the statement is false.

T F   1. To create, modify, display, or print a graph, use the Graph command on the Forms menu.

T F   2. For values on the x-axis, Paradox uses the values in the first column of a table.

T F   3. When you create a graph, only numeric type values can be used for the x-axis.

T F   4. To create and view a graph, use the Graph|View command on the Image menu.

T F   5. To change the characteristics of a graph, use the Graph|Modify command on the Image menu.

T F   6. To view a graph on the screen from the Customize Graph Type form, choose ViewGraph.

T F   7. To remove a graph from the screen, press F10.

T F   8. To create a Crosstab, use the CrossTab command of the Tools menu.

T F   9. When you create a Crosstab, Paradox requires you to specify the column to use for row labels, the column to use for column labels, and the column containing the actual data values.

T F 10. The results of creating a Crosstab are placed in a permanent table called Crosstab.

SHORT ANSWER ASSIGNMENT 1 (continued)

T F 11. To change the order of columns in a table, use CTRL+R.

T F 12. To change the title of a graph, use the Titles command on the Overall menu.

T F 13. You can enter up to three lines of titles for a graph.

T F 14. To change the legends on a graph, use the Legends command on the Series menu.

T F 15. To change the patterns that Paradox uses for series on a graph, use the MarkersAndFills command on the Series menu.

T F 16. Graph settings are automatically saved when you press the F2 (DO-IT) key.

T F 17. To record a script, choose the Begin command on the Scripts menu.

T F 18. After entering the keystrokes for a script, choose the End-Record command on the Scripts menu.

T F 19. Once you have created a script, you can use it in the future by choosing the Play command on the Scripts menu.

T F 20. To use graph settings that have been previously saved, choose Image, choose Graph, and then choose Load.

SHORT ANSWER ASSIGNMENT 2
Multiple Choice

Instructions: Circle the correct response.

1. To create, modify, display, or print a graph, use the Graph command on the _____ menu.
   a. Forms
   b. View
   c. Image
   d. Create

2. To view a graph on the screen from the Customize Graph Type form, choose _____ .
   a. View
   b. Graph
   c. ViewGraph
   d. Image

3. To create a Crosstab, use the CrossTab command on the _____ menu.
   a. Tools
   b. Image
   c. Create
   d. Forms

4. To change the order of columns in a table, use _____ .
   a. CTRL+C
   b. CTRL+O
   c. CTRL+R
   d. CTRL+T

5. To change the legend on a graph, use the LegendsAndLabels command of the _____ menu.
   a. Type
   b. Series
   c. Overall
   d. Modify

6. To change the patterns that Paradox uses for series on a graph, use the _____ command on the Series menu.

    a. Patterns
    b. Fills
    c. PatternsAndFills
    d. MarkersAndFills

7. To record a script, choose the _____ command on the Scripts menu.

    a. Begin
    b. BeginRecord
    c. Start
    d. StartRecord

8. After entering the keystrokes for a script, choose the _____ command on the Scripts menu.

    a. End
    b. Stop
    c. End-Record
    d. Stop-Record

9. To use graph settings that have been previously saved, choose Image, choose Graph, and then choose _____.

    a. Open
    b. Use
    c. Load
    d. Retrieve

10. To create a Crosstab, choose Graph|CrossTab from the Image menu or press _____ .

    a. ALT+Z
    b. ALT+Y
    c. ALT+X
    d. ALT+R

SHORT ANSWER ASSIGNMENT 3
Understanding Graph Elements

Instructions: In Figure SA5-3, arrows point to various elements of the graph. Identify these elements in the space provided. Use Figure SA5-3 to answer the questions on the next page.

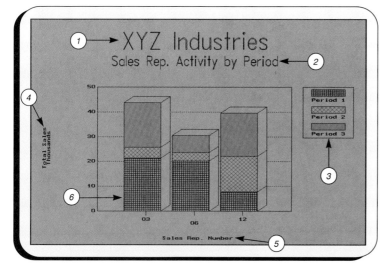

1. _____

2. _____

3. _____

4. _____

5. _____

6. _____

FIGURE SA5-3

SHORT ANSWER ASSIGNMENT 3 (continued)

1. What type of graph is displayed?

   _____

   _____

2. How do you remove a graph from the screen?

   _____

   _____

3. Which sales rep has the largest total sales amount for any one period? In which period did these sales occur?

   _____

   _____

4. Which sales rep has the smallest total sales amount for any one period? In which period did these sales occur?

   _____

   _____

5. In which period did sales rep 12 have the most sales?

   _____

   _____

SHORT ANSWER ASSIGNMENT 4
Understanding Graphs

Instructions: In this assignment, you are to answer questions about a graph to be created for the Customer table. To assist you, the table below lists the column headings (fields) for the Customer table.

CUSTOMER	Customer Number	Name	Address	City	State	Zip Code	Cust Type	Balance	Credit Limit	Sales Rep Number

1. What field would be used for the x-axis?

   _____

   _____

2. The cursor is in the Balance field when the graph is created. What field(s) would be used for the y-axis? Why?

   _____

   _____

3. What would be the title for the x-axis? The y-axis?

   _____

   _____

4. What would be the title of the graph?

   _____

   _____

5. How could you make the Name field the x-axis?

   _____

   _____

SHORT ANSWER ASSIGNMENT 5

Customizing Graphs

Instructions: Figure SA5-5 shows the initial graph created for a Crosstab table. The x-axis represents sales rep numbers and the y-axis represents total sales in a specific item class. Use Figure SA5-5 to answer the questions below the figure.

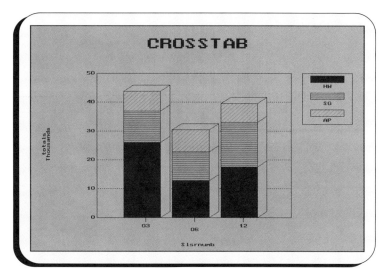

FIGURE SA 5-5

1. List the steps to change the graph type to rotated bar.

Steps: _____

_____

2. List the steps to change the title to Sales Rep Activity by Item Class; the x-axis to Sales Rep Number; and the y-axis to Total Sales.

Steps: _____

_____

3. List the steps to change the HW legend to Housewares; the SG legend to Sporting Goods; and the AP legend to Appliances.

Steps: _____

_____

SHORT ANSWER ASSIGNMENT 6

Understanding Crosstabs

Instructions: In this assignment, you are to answer questions on how to create a Crosstab for the Customer table. The Crosstab has Sales Rep Numbers as row labels, Cust Type as column labels, and the Balance field is summed to provide the actual values. To assist you, the table below lists the column headings (fields) for the Customer table.

CUSTOMER	Customer Number	Name	Address	City	State	Zip Code	Cust Type	Balance	Credit Limit	Sales Rep Number

SHORT ANSWER ASSIGNMENT 6 (continued)

1. What must you do to ensure that only Sales Rep Numbers are used as row labels?

_____

_____

2. What menu commands do you need to create the Crosstab?

_____

_____

3. Suppose that instead of summing the Balance field, you want to display the largest balance in the Crosstab. What menu commands would you use?

_____

_____

HANDS-ON
EXERCISES

HANDS-ON EXERCISE I
Using the Help Menu

Instructions: Perform the following tasks:

1. Start Paradox

2. Enter the Help system and search the topic, Crosstab. Press ENTER to display the Paradox Crosstab Command screen.

3. Choose Key from the menu.

4. Read the information on the Crosstab Key screen and answer the following questions.

   a. What keystroke combination can you use as a shortcut to create a Crosstab?

   _____

   _____

   b. What restriction is placed on the value field when you use this shortcut?

   _____

   _____

5. Exit the Help system.

6. Open the Customer table.

7. Choose Image|Graph.

8. Press the F1 key.

9. Read the information on the Graph Command screen and answer the following question.

a. What does the Reset command do?

_____

_____

10. Exit the Help system.

11. Close the Customer table.

12. Exit Paradox

HANDS-ON EXERCISE 2

Creating Crosstabs and Graphs

Instructions: Perform the following tasks:

1. Start Paradox.

2. Open the Slsinfo table from the PDOX45 subdirectory on the Student Diskette. Create the Crosstab shown in Figure HOE5-2.

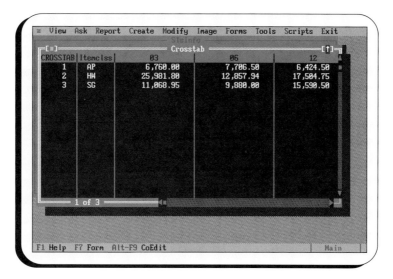

FIGURE HOE 5-2

3. Print the Crosstab table.

4. Create an initial bar graph for the Crosstab.

5. Customize the graph as follows:

a. Change the title to ABC Incorporated. Change the size to medium and the font to Sans Serif.
b. Add the subtitle, Item Class Activity By Sales Rep. Change the size to small.
c. Change the x-axis title to Item Class and the y-axis title to Total Sales.
d. Change the graph type to 3D bar.

6. Print the graph. (Check with your instructor before printing graphs.)

7. Save the graph settings as Slsritem.

8. Close all windows.

9. Exit Paradox.

HANDS-ON EXERCISE 3
Creating Scripts

Instructions: Perform the following tasks:

1. Start Paradox.

2. Create a script to display the graph created in Hands-On Exercise 2. Name the script Slsritem. Record the steps to create the script.

Steps: _____

_____

3. Play the Slsritem script.

4. Change the graph type to rotated bar.

5. Print the graph. (Check with your instructor before printing graphs.)

6. Close all windows.

7. Exit Paradox.

LABORATORY ASSIGNMENT I
Graphing the Part Database

Purpose: To provide practice in creating and using Crosstabs and graphs.

Problem: The organization needs the data in the database summarized in a variety of different ways. It also needs the data to be presented graphically.

Instructions: Use the database created in Laboratory Assignment 1 of Project 1 for this assignment. Execute each task on the computer and print the results.

1. Start Paradox and open the Part table.

2. Create a Crosstab that will display by item class the number of parts in each warehouse. (Hint: Use Count as the Crosstab operation.)

3. Answer the following questions about the Crosstab.

   a. How many sporting goods items are stored in warehouse 3?

_____

_____

b. How many houseware items are stored in warehouse 2? In warehouse 3?

4. Print the Crosstab table and then close all windows.

5. Create a query for the Part table. The query should restrict records to only items in the HW item class. Calculate the on-hand value (units on hand * price) for these parts.

6. Print the Answer table.

7. Graph the Answer table. Use part numbers for the x-axis and the on-hand values for the y-axis.

8. Change the title to PJP Wholesalers. Add the subtitle, Housewares Inventory. Change the title size to medium and the subtitle size to small. Use the Euro Style font for title and subtitle.

9. Change the graph type to Pie. Display the values as currency.

10. Explode the piece of pie containing the largest on-hand value.

11. Print the graph. (Check with your instructor before printing graphs.)

12. Close all windows.

13. Exit Paradox.

LABORATORY ASSIGNMENT 2
Graphing the Employee Database

Purpose: To provide practice in creating and using Crosstabs and graphs.

Problem: The employees in the Marketing department are paid a monthly commission on telephone sales. The department maintains an Empinfo table for each employee in the department that includes employee number, the week (1, 2, 3, 4) a sale was made, and the amount of the sale. A copy of this table is shown in Figure LA5-2. The department needs to calculate, by employee number, the total sales for each week.

```
10/04/94                        Standard Report              Page   1


Employee Number  Week   Sales
---------------  ----   ----------------
     1022          1         412.00
     1022          2         128.00
     1022          2         308.56
     1022          3         589.24
     1022          3         200.00
     1022          1         418.95
     1022          3         560.00
     1022          1         210.00
     1022          3         465.00
     1022          2         350.00
     1022          4         650.00
     1041          1         895.44
     1041          4         200.00
     1041          2         140.00
     1041          3         249.50
     1041          1         560.00
     1041          2         210.00
     1041          1         568.00
     1041          2       1,295.00
     1041          3         420.00
     1056          4         550.00
     1056          1         350.00
     1056          2         650.00
     1056          3         750.00
     1056          1         540.00
     1056          3         600.00
     1056          1         720.00
     1056          2         840.00
     1056          3         120.00
```

FIGURE LA5-2

LABORATORY ASSIGNMENT 2 (continued)

Instructions: Use the database created in Laboratory Assignment 2 of Project 1 for this assignment. Execute each task on the computer and print the results.

1. Start Paradox and open the Empinfo table from the PDOX45 subdirectory on the Student Diskette.

2. Create a Crosstab for the Empinfo table. The Crosstab should have employee numbers as row categories, weeks as column labels, and the sum of sales amount as values.

3. Print the Crosstab table.

4. Graph the Crosstab table.

5. Change the graph title to MARKETING DEPARTMENT. Use large size type and Simplex font.

6. Add the graph subtitle, Sales By Week. Use medium size type.

7. Change the y-axis title to Total Sales.

8. Change the legend so the word Week appears before each number in the series.

9. Print the graph. (Check with your instructor before printing graphs.)

10. Save the graph settings as Empweek.

11. Create a script that will create the Crosstab for the Empinfo table and display the graph with the Empweek settings. Name the script Empweek.

12. Play the script and change the graph type to 3D bar.

13. Print the graph. (Check with your instructor before printing graphs.)

14. Close all windows.

15. Create a query for the Employee table to display the average pay rate by department name. (Hint: You will need to join the Employee and Dept tables.)

16. Print the Answer table.

17. Use the Image|Graph|Reset command to reset any previous graph settings.

18. Graph the Answer table.

19. Change the graph type to combined lines and markers. Change the title to PERSONNEL STATISTICS. Use a large size type and Script font. Change the y-axis to Average Pay Rate. Remove the legend.

20. Print the graph. (Check with your instructor before printing graphs.)

21. Close all windows.

22. Exit Paradox

LABORATORY ASSIGNMENT 3
Graphing the Movie Database

Purpose: To provide practice in creating and using Crosstabs and graphs.

Problem: The family who collects these videotapes has never placed a value on its collection. As a start, the family members have been gathering data on five of their favorite movies. They have surveyed stores and catalogs to find the quoted price for each of these movies. The Movinfo table includes data on the movie number, the source of the price (STR = store, CAT = catalog), and the price being charged for the movie. A copy of the table is shown in Figure LA5-3.

```
10/04/94                 Standard Report           Page   1


Movie Number   Source   Price
------------   ------   ----------------
001            STR         20.00
001            STR         35.00
001            CAT         40.00
001            CAT         37.00
004            CAT         29.99
004            CAT         25.99
004            STR         20.00
004            STR         15.00
011            CAT         15.00
011            CAT         19.99
011            STR         33.00
011            STR         25.99
012            CAT         32.00
012            STR         37.00
012            STR         30.50
012            CAT         29.99
022            CAT         15.99
022            CAT         20.80
022            STR         33.99
022            STR         37.00
```

FIGURE LA5-3

Instructions: Use the database created in Laboratory Assignment 3 of Project 1 for this assignment. Execute each task on the computer and print the results.

1. Start Paradox and open the Movinfo table from the PDOX45 subdirectory on the Student Diskette.

2. Create a Crosstab that shows movie numbers as row categories, source as the column labels, and the highest price as the value. (Hint: You will need to use the Maximum Crosstab operation.)

3. Print the Crosstab table.

4. Graph the Crosstab table.

5. Change the title to MOVIE SURVEY. Use medium size type and a font of Complex.

6. Add the subtitle, Price By Location. Use small size type.

7. Change the graph type to Line.

8. Change the legends to Store and Catalog.

9. Print the graph. (Check with your instructor before printing graphs.)

10. Save the graph settings as Movprice.

11. Create a script to create the Crosstab and display the graph. Name the script Movprice.

12. Play the Movprice script.

13. Change the graph type to rotated bar.

14. Print the graph. (Check with your instructor before printing graphs.)

15. Close all windows.

16. Open the Movie table and create a query that finds the maximum movie length for each director code.

17. Print the Answer table

18. Use the Image|Graph|Reset command to reset any previous graph settings.

19. Graph the Answer table.

20. Change the graph type to line.

21. Change the title to Movie Length Comparison. Use large type and Complex font. Change the y-axis to Maximum Movie Length. Remove the legend.

LABORATORY ASSIGNMENT 3 (continued)

22. Print the graph. (Check with your instructor before printing graphs.)

23. Close all windows.

24. Exit Paradox.

LABORATORY ASSIGNMENT 4
Graphing the Book Database

Purpose: To provide practice in creating and using Crosstabs and graphs.

Problem: The bookstore owner has an opportunity to expand her business. Another bookstore owner with three branches is looking for a buyer. She has some data on the publishers, branch number, and books on hand at the three stores. The data is in the table, Publinfo, shown in Figure LA5-4. She would like for you to generate summary statistics from the data and create some graphs. She also needs some graphs created from data in the Book table.

```
10/04/94                    Standard Report                  Page    1


Pubcode  Brnumb  Oh
-------  ------  ------
BB          1      1
BB          1      2
BB          1      3
BB          2      1
BB          2      2
BB          2      3
BB          3      2
BB          3      1
BF          1      1
BF          2      2
BF          3      2
PB          1      2
PB          2      1
PB          2      2
PB          2      4
PB          3      2
PB          3      3
PB          1      3
SI          1      1
SI          2      4
SI          3      1
SI          3      2
SI          2      1
SS          3      3
VI          2      1
SS          3      2
SS          2      3
SS          3      1
VI          3      1
VI          1      2
VI          2      3
```

FIGURE LA5-4

Instruction: Use the database created in Laboratory Assignment 3 of Project 1 for this assignment. Provide the following:

1. Create a Crosstab that summarizes the data in the Publinfo table. (The Publinfo table is found in the PDOX45 subdirectory on the Student Diskette.)

2. Create a graph of the Crosstab. Add meaningful titles and legends.

3. Create a graph that shows the average price of books by book type. (Hint: You will need to create a query.) Add meaningful titles and legends. The owner expects to use this graph again.

4. Create a graph showing the on-hand value (price * units on hand) for all books with a publisher code of BB. (Hint: You will need to create a query.) Add meaningful titles and legends.

INDEX